ROUTLEDGE LIBRARY EDITIONS: STUDY OF SHAKESPEARE

Volume 7

"FANNED AND WINNOWED OPINIONS"

"FANNED AND WINNOWED OPINIONS"

Shakespearean Essays Presented to Harold Jenkins

Edited by
JOHN W. MAHON AND THOMAS A. PENDLETON

LONDON AND NEW YORK

First published in 1987 by Methuen & Co. Ltd

This edition first published in 2021
by Routledge
2 Park Square, Milton Park, Abingdon, Oxon OX14 4RN

and by Routledge
52 Vanderbilt Avenue, New York, NY 10017

Routledge is an imprint of the Taylor & Francis Group, an informa business

The collection as a whole © 1987 Methuen & Co. Ltd;
The individual contributions © 1987 the contributors

All rights reserved. No part of this book may be reprinted or reproduced or utilised in any form or by any electronic, mechanical, or other means, now known or hereafter invented, including photocopying and recording, or in any information storage or retrieval system, without permission in writing from the publishers.

Trademark notice: Product or corporate names may be trademarks or registered trademarks, and are used only for identification and explanation without intent to infringe.

British Library Cataloguing in Publication Data
A catalogue record for this book is available from the British Library

ISBN: 978-0-367-67310-9 (Set)
ISBN: 978-1-00-314862-3 (Set) (ebk)
ISBN: 978-0-367-68216-3 (Volume 7) (hbk)
ISBN: 978-0-367-68227-9 (Volume 7) (pbk)
ISBN: 978-1-00-313478-7 (Volume 7) (ebk)

Publisher's Note
The publisher has gone to great lengths to ensure the quality of this reprint but points out that some imperfections in the original copies may be apparent.

Disclaimer
The publisher has made every effort to trace copyright holders and would welcome correspondence from those they have been unable to trace.

"Fanned and Winnowed Opinions"

"Fanned and Winnowed Opinions"

SHAKESPEAREAN ESSAYS
PRESENTED TO
HAROLD JENKINS

EDITED BY
John W. Mahon
AND
Thomas A. Pendleton

METHUEN
LONDON AND NEW YORK

First published in 1987 by
Methuen & Co. Ltd
11 New Fetter Lane, London EC4P 4EE

Published in the USA by
Methuen & Co.
in association with Methuen, Inc.
29 West 35th Street, New York NY 10001

The collection as a whole © 1987 Methuen & Co. Ltd;
the individual contributions © 1987 the contributors

Printed in Great Britain
at the University Press, Cambridge

All rights reserved. No part of this book may be reprinted or reproduced or utilized in any form or by any electronic, mechanical or other means, now known or hereafter invented, including photocopying and recording, or in any information storage or retrieval system, without permission in writing from the publishers.

British Library Cataloguing in Publication Data
"Fanned and winnowed opinions": Shakespearean
essays presented to Harold Jenkins.
1. Shakespeare, William – Criticism and
interpretation
I. Mahon, John W. II. Pendleton, Thomas A.
822'.3'3 PR2976

ISBN 0 416 00422 9

Library of Congress Cataloging in Publication Data
Fanned and winnowed opinions.
Bibliography: p.
Includes index.
1. Shakespeare, William, 1564–1616 – Criticism and
interpretation. 2. Jenkins, Harold. I. Jenkins,
Harold. II. Mahon, John W. III. Pendleton, Thomas A.
PR2976.F27 1987 822.3'3 87–11335

ISBN 0 416 00422 9

CONTENTS

PREFACE
ix

INTRODUCTION
1

1
Troilus and Cressida: its dramatic unity and genre
HAROLD BROOKS
6

2
Motive and meaning in *All's Well That Ends Well*
RUTH NEVO
26

3
Amorous fictions and *As You Like It*
BRIAN GIBBONS
52

4
Shakespeare's disguised duke play:
Middleton, Marston, and the sources of
Measure for Measure
THOMAS A. PENDLETON
79

5
Shakespeare and history: from antithesis to synthesis
ARTHUR HUMPHREYS
99

"Fanned and Winnowed Opinions"

6
Sir John Oldcastle: Shakespeare's martyr
E. A. J. HONIGMANN
118

7
"It must be your imagination then":
the prologue and the plural text in
Henry V and elsewhere
ANTONY HAMMOND
133

8
"With a little shuffling"
GEORGE WALTON WILLIAMS
151

9
"The play's the thing":
Hamlet and the conscience of the Queen
RICHARD PROUDFOOT
160

10
The plays within the play of *Hamlet*
ALASTAIR FOWLER
166

11
Iago's questionable shapes
KENNETH PALMER
184

12
On the copy for *Antony and Cleopatra*
MARVIN SPEVACK
202

Contents vii

13
A world of figures: enargeiac speech in Shakespeare
S.K. HENINGER, Jr
216

14
"For now we sit to chat as well as eat":
conviviality and conflict in Shakespeare's meals
JOHN W. MAHON
231

15
"Wives may be merry and yet honest too":
women and wit in *The Merry Wives of Windsor*
and some other plays
SANDRA CLARK
249

16
Shakespeare and Massinger: resemblances and contrasts
KENNETH MUIR
268

HAROLD JENKINS:
LIST OF PUBLICATIONS
282

NOTES ON CONTRIBUTORS
288

INDEX
291

Preface

For the publication of this book we are indebted, first, to Harold Jenkins. His scholarship inspired our work, even in selecting a title, since 'fanned and winnowed opinions' is his reading of V.ii.189 in *Hamlet*. To demonstrate that the phrase is approbative, the reader is directed – as with everything concerning *Hamlet* – to the Arden edition.

We are grateful to all of our contributors not only for the excellence of their work but for their ready cooperation with deadlines and other demands and for their many helpful suggestions. Harold Brooks, through his wise counsel and extensive reminiscences, has served as virtual co-editor of this volume and deserves special thanks. Janice Price, our publisher, encouraged the venture from the start, and Sarah Pearsall, our editor, guided us to completion.

There are many colleagues and friends at Iona, especially Br Richard DeMaria and Professor Cedric Winslow, who have helped us to produce this Festschrift: we thank most particularly Florence Kaeser, who carefully read all of the essays and offered helpful comments and corrections. The Secretarial Services Center produced a typescript of superior quality; our thanks to all at the Center for their patience and professionalism over many tedious months: Mary Bruno, Nancy Girardi, Terry Martin, Adrianna DiLello, Marie Mariani, Patti Besen, and Antonia Piria.

Ellen Macleod Mahon, herself a Professor of English Literature, is the 'valiant woman' of Proverbs 31:10: 'The heart of her husband trusteth in her.' Carol Pendleton has been patient and encouraging.

Iona College, New Rochelle, NY John W. Mahon
February, 1987 Thomas A. Pendleton

Introduction

The idea of a Festschrift for Harold Jenkins developed in April, 1985 when he revisited Iona College to conduct a seminar on his study of *Henry IV*. He had first visited Iona in October of 1983 to receive an honorary doctorate of letters and to address our Honors Convocation. By the time of his second visit, the present editors' acquaintance with and admiration for Professor Jenkins had deepened into friendship, and accordingly we proposed this volume, managing to defeat his customary modesty and to win his acquiescence to the project. This collection of essays by some dozen or sixteen of his legion of colleagues, students, and friends is our joint tribute of regard and affection.

Harold Jenkins was born in Shenley, Buckinghamshire, on July 19, 1909 and was educated at Wolverton Grammar School and University College London. He spent a year as William Noble Fellow at the University of Liverpool before becoming Lecturer in English at the University of the Witwatersrand, South Africa, where he taught from 1936 to 1945. In 1939 he married Gladys Puddifoot, whom he had first met as a student in London. She travelled alone by ship to Cape Town to join him; the wedding party consisted of the groom and two friends, and the bride and a married couple she had befriended on shipboard. In his Preface to the Arden *Hamlet*, Harold writes: 'In daily conversation I have had available to me her intimate and wide-ranging knowledge of things Elizabethan and her wise, and sometimes sceptical, comments.' This daily conversation was the basis of a marriage which all who knew them can testify was exceptionally successful. They continued to travel remarkable distances. During his later career Harold's teaching would take them to Duke University and to the University of Oslo. They travelled together to New York in 1983 and in the following spring realized their dream of visiting China. Tragically, Gladys died in a traffic accident in 1984.

2   "Fanned and Winnowed Opinions"

After his years at Witwatersrand, Harold returned to England to begin twenty-two years of service in various posts at the University of London, culminating in his appointment in 1954 as Professor of English at Westfield College, the occasion of his much-admired lecture on 'the structural problem in *Henry IV*'. In 1967 he became Regius Professor of Rhetoric and English at the University of Edinburgh, which post he held until his retirement. Given his achievements as critic and editor, it is easy to overlook Harold Jenkins' many years as a devoted and inspiring teacher, but his former students treasure the memory of his classroom performances. Ruth Nevo was his student in South Africa:

> I would like to think that my debt to Harold's teaching is still perceptible. I certainly feel it to have been the most formative and valuable of influences. It was his sensitive and vigorous close reading, his masterly sense of controlling dramatic form and of the intermesh of form and theme, and his sane, tactful humanism, as much as his brilliance and eloquence as a teacher that enchanted us, his students.

Kenneth Palmer remembers that Harold could provide, off the cuff, information on almost any period about which one asked while disclaiming all knowledge of the matter: all who know him would agree that such a disclaimer is exactly Harold Jenkins in both style and substance. Sandra Clark, his student at Westfield, recalls simply, 'There was no teacher in the college to touch him.'

During the earlier part of his career, Harold produced a number of significant scholarly works, including studies of Henry Chettle and Edward Benlowes, an edition of *Sir Thomas More*, and essays on *Henry IV* and *As You Like It*. Brian Gibbons calls the last 'one of the very best essays produced on Shakespeare's comedies' because it displays Harold's 'sensitivity to tone, wit and sure sense of how not to say too much'. But his most celebrated scholarly attainments derive from his dual connection with the New Arden Shakespeare. In 1954, he was assigned to edit *Hamlet* for the series, and in 1958 he was appointed Joint General Editor of the Arden Shakespeare with Harold F. Brooks.

Dr Brooks, Harold Jenkins' friend for forty years and his partner for more than twenty, has shared a wealth of perceptive reminiscence. He recalls that Una Ellis-Fermor, the first

Introduction 3

General Editor of the New Arden series, had initially presumed that *Hamlet* was so formidable as to demand two editors, 'a first-class appreciative critic, and a first-class textual scholar'. Harold Brooks' response was, 'I know one man who is both – Harold Jenkins'. (Among the many things to which the Arden *Hamlet* is a monument is Harold Brooks' good judgement.) Four years later, when Methuen advised Dr Brooks that Harold Jenkins had been chosen to be his colleague as General Editor, his response was equally prescient, 'You couldn't have given me anyone I would rather have.'

The collaboration was long, congenial, and immensely successful. The Arden edition, which now includes all of the plays, is quite simply the best multi-volume Shakespeare ever done, a distinction it should retain for quite some time. The list of editors who had the benefit of Harold Jenkins' advice is exceptional: J.P. Brockbank, H.F. Brooks, A.S. Cairncross, T.W. Craik, R.A. Foakes, Brian Gibbons, Antony Hammond, F.D. Hoeniger, A.R. Humphreys, Agnes Latham, Clifford Leech, J.W. Lever, Brian Morris, H.J. Oliver, J.H.P. Pafford, Kenneth Palmer, and F.T. Prince.

Arthur Humphreys attests to Professor Jenkins' editorial talents and dedication: 'He brought a wonderful range of knowledge and textual expertise, and patient, scrupulous pertinacity, to bear on the textual details of my new Arden editions. I wouldn't have believed that so much care and attention could be devoted to another scholar's work, and he must have bestowed hundreds of hours of close attention to the work of the various Arden editors.' Brian Gibbons, whose *Romeo and Juliet* is one of the most recent editions, testifies that the editorial expertise persisted for more than twenty years. He calls Harold Jenkins 'the ideal General Editor'. Harold Brooks notes Harold Jenkins' constant concern for the quality of the writing in Introductions and Notes. Striving for exactitude and consistency of practice, he insisted on the need for economy in expression and presentation, as well as the need to distinguish clearly between what is possible, probable, and certain.

There can be no doubt that but for his labours as General Editor, his own *Hamlet* would have appeared sooner (though it could hardly have been better), but it would have done so at the cost of twenty-one other Ardens being the weaker for want of his editing. During the long years in which he worked

4 "Fanned and Winnowed Opinions"

on *Hamlet*, his studies of the play produced at least eight articles or major lectures, two of the most notable being his British Academy lecture in 1963 entitled *Hamlet and Ophelia*, and his 1967 inaugural lecture at Edinburgh, *The Catastrophe in Shakespearean Tragedy*. The undertaking, however, was enormous and must at times have seemed daunting. The indispensable Harold Brooks provides another anecdote: of receiving from his co-editor a copy of his 1960 article on the text of *Hamlet*, with a covering note, 'Since there is no sign that I shall have anything else to show, you had better have a copy of this.' We can both empathize and smile, for we know that like a Shakespearean comedy the story has a happy ending.

To say that his edition of *Hamlet*, which appeared in 1982, is the *chef d'oeuvre* of the Arden series might involve us in comparisons that Dogberry would think odorous, but it is certainly much the best edition of the most famous work of literature ever written, and even this might be faint praise. Harold Brooks calls it the best edition that can be done, and Philip Howard's review in *The Times* calls it 'the most majestical work of scholarship published this year, and if you fancy a spot of journalistic hyperbole, this century'. The FVS Foundation of Hamburg, in awarding Harold (the first scholar-editor ever so honoured) its 1986 Shakespeare prize, praised his 'exemplary' edition as the 'keystone' of the Arden series. There is hardly room here to praise adequately all the aspects of Harold Jenkins' *Hamlet* that one might admire, but the present editors find especially praiseworthy his gift for concise expression, demonstrated in his Introduction's consideration of battalions of fiendishly complicated matters, carried out with grace, precision, and magisterial judgement.

The qualities so extensively demonstrated in his *Hamlet* are in fact shared in all of his critical publications, a complete bibliography of which is appended to this volume. We have included a listing of the dozens of book reviews he has produced over the years, many of which are quite considerable critical essays, and none of which fails to illustrate something of the quality of Harold Jenkins' thinking. His learning, judgement, humane sympathy, wit, humour, and – presiding over all – his immense critical sanity make anything written by Harold Jenkins worth the reading.

The character and the dimensions of his talents have been

Introduction

recognized by many, and often in strikingly similar terms. Harold Brooks compares him to Shaw's Bohun in *You Never Can Tell*, whose specialty is 'being right, when other people are wrong', and Kathleen Tillotson epitomizes his gift as 'the trick of stating what thereupon seemed obvious, though nobody had seen it before'. And this recognition is perhaps not so surprising, since so many of our correspondents have likened the qualities of the criticism to the qualities of the man – generous, entertaining, kindly, perceptive, courteous, witty, scrupulously dedicated to his profession and the values which inform it.

Toward the end of the Preface to his *Hamlet*, Harold Jenkins writes, 'I have been fortunate in my friends.' We, the present editors, have also been fortunate in his friends, for one of the joys of compiling this volume has been the opportunity to work with and to meet so many distinguished scholars, who so enthusiastically united with us in our mutual friendship for Harold. Although many are friends of far longer standing than we, we will take the liberty of speaking on behalf of all the participants in this volume: we have been fortunate in our friend – Harold Jenkins.

NOTE

It is perhaps needless to state that, unless otherwise indicated, the copy texts used in all the essays in this volume are the Arden editions.

1

Troilus and Cressida: its dramatic unity and genre

HAROLD BROOKS

Few, I imagine, would challenge the assertion that '*Hamlet* is the most problematic play ever written by Shakespeare or any other playwright.'

So my colleague and friend of forty years' standing, Harold Jenkins, begins the critical introduction of his great edition. That assertion is not challenged when *Troilus and Cressida* is recognized as likewise one of Shakespeare's problem plays. Of its numerous problems, the one which has interested me most is the question of its genre; the more because too rigid conceptions of that genre seem to have led more than one reputable critic astray (an error not shared, however, by Kenneth Muir or Kenneth Palmer). A conclusion about the genre of *Troilus* might be approached by more than one route. A study of the themes and their dramatization would have been an alternative or a supplement to the one I have taken,[1] which, to suit the limited scope of an essay, is a consideration of its dramatic unity. I begin with some very familiar observations indeed.

The drama of *Troilus* is twofold, combining the martial action of the Trojan War with Hector at the centre of it, and the amorous action of the Troilus and Cressida story. Shakespeare unites them in more than one way. He introduces them together at the start. The 'Prologue arm'd', so as to be 'suited in like conditions as our argument', not only looks every inch a warrior, but directs to 'cruel war' the greater part of his speech. But he tells why the Greeks have vowed to sack Troy:

> The ravish'd Helen, Menelaus' queen,
> With wanton Paris sleeps – and that's the quarrel.
>
> (9–10)

Troilus and Cressida

The war itself springs from an amorous motive. Troilus begins the play in armour like the Prologue, but with the resolve to 'unarm again'. He finds his yet unrewarded love at odds with the call to war; and describes its effect upon him in terms of war, a 'cruel battle here within'. His dialogue with Pandarus is all about his frustrated love of Cressida and Pandarus's part as go-between; it establishes the present stage of relationships between the three well-known characters of the love story. On Pandarus's exit, the war story returns with the off-stage 'alarum', and Troilus's soliloquy relating the war again to its amorous cause, with his deflating comment

> Fools on both sides, Helen must needs be fair
> When with your blood you daily paint her thus.
> I cannot fight upon this argument.   (I.i.90–2)

With another alarum sounded, there enters a resolute warrior, Aeneas, who has already been in the battle: his war news, however, is about the rivals for Helen; Paris has been wounded by Menelaus. Finally, Troilus, having acknowledged that to stay aloof is 'womanish', goes off with Aeneas to the fight, comparing the sport of war, outside Troy, with the sport of love which is denied him within its walls. His siege of Cressida (we reflect) is like the Greek siege of Troy, vain so far. The volte-face here, with Troilus going off to battle after all, prepares for others of great importance in both actions, the martial and the amorous. They are the reversals of the split man or woman, such as Troilus shows himself in this scene, pulled in opposite directions by love and war.

The entire role of Troilus in the play is one of the main means by which the two actions are united. He is the protagonist of the love story; while in the war story, among the Trojans he is second only to Hector. He is chiefly responsible for the war being continued, when in the Trojan Council (II.ii) he withstands Hector's proposal for making peace – and to such effect that Hector, against his own better judgement, concludes by concurring in Troilus's view. Finally, Troilus takes over the war leadership of the Trojans after Hector's death.

Hector's martial challenge to the Greeks is in the name of love-chivalry, and is so accepted by Agamemnon (and Nestor):

> And may that soldier a mere recreant prove
> That means not, hath not, or is not in love.
>   (I.iii.286–7)

Hector, who among the Trojan warriors has the lover Troilus as his second, among the Greeks has his fatal antagonist, Achilles; and Achilles is a lover as well as a warrior. While he stays out of the fighting it is partly because he is in love with a Trojan princess, Polyxena, sister of Hector, Paris, and Troilus. This passion makes him a traitor to the Greek cause; and as warrior too he stoops to treachery against Hector. In the martial action, Achilles the unchivalrous is a foil to the too-chivalrous Hector; in the amorous action, he is a foil to Troilus. When they each have a mistress in the stronghold of their foes, through Polyxena Achilles commits disloyalty; through Cressida Troilus suffers it. Thus Achilles helps to unite the two actions, by being in war a foil to one of the two chief Trojans, and in amorous passion, a foil to the other.

Helen, also, helps to unite the two actions. She is the object of the war, a prize to be kept or regained, an object made an idol in the Trojan warriors' cult of honour. But she is a sex-object, as the hard-boiled Diomed sees her:

> For every false drop in her bawdy veins
> A Grecian's life hath sunk; for every scruple
> Of her contaminated carrion weight
> A Trojan hath been slain.   (IV.i.70–3)

As a sex-object, depicted in her scene with Paris and Pandarus, her shallowness matches and mirrors the shallowness which makes Cressida's nature, in the main love story, unreliable and meretricious. As in all versions of that story (including Chaucer's), it is from the war story – from the capture of Antenor and the successful plea of the Trojan deserter, Calchas, Cressida's father, to have him exchanged for her – that her separation from Troilus, and then her betrayal of him with Diomed, come about.

Pandarus belongs almost exclusively to the amorous action, yet he is the commentator on the spectacle of the leading Trojan warriors, as they pass one by one returning from battle. He is full of enthusiasm for their prowess, dancing up and down in his exclamations of admiration for Hector and Troilus, though of course his chief object is to commend Troilus to Cressida: a move in the love game. The other choric commentator in the play, Thersites, couples the two actions in his refrain: 'Still wars and lechery.'

Further, the two actions are united at a deep level in the

Troilus and Cressida

themes they are made to embody: themes common to both. Pre-eminent are those of evaluation – the criteria and processes which should or do determine it; time, in its bearing upon values, and its verdicts; identity – What am I? What is he? – in the light of time and of valuation; man's nature: his errors in valuation, his appetites, his propensity to see the better but follow the worse.[2] In the audience's invited judgements upon these themes, *their* valuations are challenged; not least by the tone in which each of the actions, and the thematic strands interwoven in both, are presented for their response.

In the martial action, the critical eye which (since medieval times) it was traditional to turn on the Greeks, is turned also on the Trojans. Both are infected with false pride, with false conceptions of dignity and honour. The true foundations of dignity and honour must be the universally valid principles of order and justice. Upon one form of these, degree, Ulysses speaks to the Greek Council (I.iii); upon another, the law of nature and of nations, Hector speaks to the Trojan one (II.ii). In the Greek army, the authority of the chief commander Agamemnon, and the support in united action it should receive, are undermined by the pride – the overweening sense of what is due to him, and to his reputation, his narrow personal honour – on the part of Achilles, the greatest Greek warrior. Moreover, Ajax, the second to him in prowess, has caught the infection from him; and the like pride and insubordination is spreading through the army. Achilles and Ajax overvalue what they pride themselves on, what has brought them honour: their prowess. Accordingly they despise the councillors' policy, 'Count wisdom as no member of the war, /... and esteem no act /But that of hand' (I.iii.198–200). Such is the damage that misplaced pride and misdirected notions of honourable reputation are doing among the besiegers. The damage to the besieged, in making them resolve to continue the war which will eventually destroy them, is done by something less ignoble than the mere thirst for individual honour among the factious Greeks, but by something just as misguided, a false national pride, a false conception of national honour, in conflict with the true order and justice embodied in the law of nature and of nations. These require that the price of peace should be paid by the surrender of Helen. But Troilus argues that the Trojans must stand by the value they set on Helen from the time Paris carried her off: they cannot 'blench from this and ... stand firm by honour' (II.ii.69). Hector, though he rejects Troilus's argument, adopts the same decision, on the same principle; that honour is the overriding consideration. It is a sense of honour falsely bound up with the keeping of Helen, unjust though that is: it is a 'cause', he declares, belonging to 'our joint and several dignities' (194).

Thus in the Council scene the Trojan sense of honour falls below the standard reality requires. In the martial conflict with the Greeks it loses touch with reality in the opposite direction, soaring beyond the stark realities of war into realms of chivalry. Aeneas, in the opening scene, hears in an alarum testimony of 'good sport'. When he brings Hector's challenge to the Greeks, he speaks in such high-flown terms of compliment that Agamemnon is uncertain whether they are not ironical. The whole episode of Hector's challenge, in honour of his lady, and the formal combat between him and Ajax, is a display of knighthood. It features two knights in the lists, with proper marshals, Aeneas and Diomed, who give the cue Hector wants, to curtail the fight and stop its being pursued to the utterance, so that, with honour satisfied and without effusion of blood, the champions may embrace, as their knighthood and kinship warrant. All is punctilious courtesy and chivalry, a game in contrast with the war, which will be decided by the death of this same Hector, basely contrived by the unchivalrous Achilles. Hector inappropriately carries his chivalry into the war itself. Even 'in his blaze of wrath' he 'subscribes to tender objects'. For this Troilus rebukes him, 'Brother, you have a vice of mercy in you', bidding fallen Grecians 'rise, and live' (V.iii.37, 42). 'O, 'tis fair play', is Hector's reply, prompted by his sense of personal honour, which is misplaced in a different way from his sense of national honour. It has genuine nobility, but, as Troilus insists, it is out of keeping with the demands of war. 'Fair play', says Hector; 'Fool's play', retorts Troilus: once in arms, let 'venom'd vengeance ride upon our swords'. To Hector's 'Fie, savage, fie', he answers, 'Hector, then 'tis wars' (47-9).

In his last battle, true to his code, Hector spares Thersites (who, we agree, is no fit antagonist). But when he encounters Achilles, he has perhaps his second chance to save Troy, not as in the Council scene, by peacemaking, but by a decisive victory. As with the former, he sacrifices the opportunity to his sense of honour: this time to the chivalrous mercy Troilus warned him against. With Achilles worsted, he spares him: 'Pause, if thou wilt' – a magnanimity, wasted on Achilles, who replies predictably 'I do disdain thy courtesy' (V.vi.15). The lesson Achilles learns from the combat is that he cannot avenge Patroclus in fair fight: fair means failing, he resorts to foul, and so (in cynically realistic terms, "tis wars') settles the outcome of the siege, sealing Troy's fate.

Further back, this fatal outcome results from Hector's rejection of all persuasions not to fight that day. In that scene we are made to think of the earlier decision not to make peace, since it is on these two occasions that Cassandra, with her supernatural knowledge of the reality, of the consequences which must ensue, breaks in with her prophetic warnings. Like the decision to continue the war, and like the sparing of Achillles, Hector's determination to fight on this day turns on his sense of honour:

> the gods have heard me swear. . . .
> And I do stand engag'd to many Greeks,
> Even in the faith of valour, to appear
> This morning to them. . . .
> I must not break my faith.   (V.iii.15, 68–71)

He has put into so many words the principle which governs him and to which he remains obstinately committed:

> Mine honour keeps the weather of my fate:
> Life every man holds dear, but the dear man
> Holds honour far more precious-dear than life. (26–8)

He sacrifices to his notions of honour, some valid, some invalid, his three great opportunities of saving Troy, or at least (if he had not fought that day) of not precipitating her ruin. Troilus, when he rebuked Hector for chivalrous mercy on the battlefield, was burning with the spirit of vengeance, kindled by Diomed's seduction of Cressida; but we have Ulysses' word for it that in contrast with Hector's romantic chivalry, as a warrior he was always a realist, 'Manly as Hector, but more dangerous; /. . . in heat of action /. . . more vindicative than jealous love' (IV.v.104, 106, 107). The comparison yet again brings war and love together.

In the amorous action there appears the same contrast of

romance and realism which in the martial action is so central. Set against Troilus's realism as a warrior is his romantic idealism in love, though in turn that resembles his unrealistic view of the honour at stake in keeping Helen. He knows that Helen's worth, as he estimates it, is not her own, but that imputed to her. He imputes to Cressid and her love a worth which she has it not in her nature to justify: but he does not know she has not; nor indeed, while she is in Troy, does she. Just as Hector's chivalry in the war meets its nemesis at the hands of the extreme opposite in Achilles, so the chivalrous love of Troilus meets its nemesis at the hands of its extreme opposite in Diomed. The nature of war gives scope for the cynical behaviour of Achilles; the nature of Cressid gives scope for the cynical behaviour of Diomed. Troilus's courtship of her was patient and adoring, while she has, and up to a point acts upon, the instincts of a coquette. She was 'Hard to seem won': reluctant to risk losing the power enjoyed by the girl while she is courted but has not committed herself in response. When she has surrendered it (for she has come to love Troilus as much as she has it in her), she half-regrets the loss: 'O foolish Cressid, I might have still held off, /And then you would have tarried' (IV.ii.17–18). The first time we see into her mind, she shows in soliloquy that she is aware of that power and sets store by it: 'This maxim out of love I teach': for the man, '"Achievement is command; ungain'd beseech"' (I.ii.297–8).

> That she belov'd knows naught that knows not this:
> Men prize the thing ungain'd more than it is.   (293–4)

Cressida is not a 'she' who 'knows naught': witness her share in bawdy dialogue with Pandarus (I.ii), which we may contrast with Ophelia's defensive replies to Hamlet in the play-scene. To that extent she is well up in the love game. What despite her knowingness she does not know is the comparative shallowness of her own nature, which will make her the 'false Cressid' proverbial in time to come. Her vow not to earn that title is sincere, and though like the Player-Queen in *Hamlet* 'the lady doth protest too much', she is unaware of doing so. Yet in performance there must appear in her love passages with Troilus sufficient of what Ulysses notes in her when she flirts with the Greek leaders on her arrival at the camp.

Troilus and Cressida

> There's language in her eye, her cheek, her lip –
> Nay, her foot speaks; her wanton spirits look out
> At every joint and motive of her body.   (IV.v.55–7)

This is not to offend us while it answers Troilus's true love, though it fails to warn him that the Cressid of his imagination is not the real Cressid, whose kind of passion is different from his. It is a kind of which Diomed – who has summed up Helen and her relation with the cuckold Menelaus and lecher-like Paris in brutal fashion – can take advantage in short order. Not for him the long romantic worshipping courtship Troilus bestowed upon her; Diomed recognizes her real nature and its desires: he knows she wants him. When she tries to 'hold off', either coquettishly as she did with Troilus, or out of some remains of remorse at betraying him, Diomed abruptly turns the tables on her and threatens to throw her over. He has the whip-hand and cracks the whip: so much for Cressid's knowingness about power in sex and love.

This cynical seducer, cashing in on the worser side of Cressid, is Troilus's opposite. As a lover, Troilus is so much the romantic idealist that he fears even requited love and its consummation with his adored mistress cannot match what imaginative love aspires to: 'the will is infinite, and the execution confined ... the desire is boundless, and the act a slave to limit' (III.ii.80–2). The realities of love, at their very best, are not adequate to the ideal of it. He is so much the romantic idealist that when he sees the real Cressid divide, as Diomed's Cressid, from his idealized image of her, not only does he exclaim 'This is, and is not Cressid' (V.ii.145); not only, like Hamlet in disgust at Gertrude, does he extend his sense of her falsehood and pollution to the whole of womanhood, and the part sex has played in engendering him and all men – 'Think, we had mothers!' (V.ii.129) – he even feels that such a breach between the two Cressids could only exist in an incoherent universe; what we should call an absurdist universe: 'If there be rule in unity itself, /This is not she' (140–1). Ulysses stands beside him, as if to remind us of the total opposition between Troilus's universe at this moment, and the one Ulysses invoked, the embodiment of Order. The crisis Troilus is enduring is the subject of one of the most memorable passages Charles Williams ever wrote: I quote a part of it:

14   "Fanned and Winnowed Opinions"

The crisis is ... that in which every nerve of the body, every consciousness of the mind, shrieks that something cannot be. Only it is.

Cressida *cannot* be playing with Diomed. But she is. The Queen *cannot* have married Claudius. But she has. [For Wordsworth] the British Government cannot have declared war on the Revolution. But it has. The whole being of the victim denies the fact. The fact outrages his whole being.

Troilus sways between two worlds. ... There is a world where our mothers are unsoiled and Cressida is his; there is a world where our mothers are soiled, and Cressida is given to Diomed. What connexion have those two worlds? 'Nothing at all, unless that this were she.'[3]

There are other reasons, besides the reminder of the world of 'unity itself', of order and degree, why Ulysses is the necessary companion of Troilus here, and watcher with him of Cressida and Diomed. It is he who sees the amorous relationship in perspective, inclining neither to Troilus's nor to Diomed's extreme. He dissents from Troilus's projection of Cressid's guilt upon all women (like Hamlet's projection of Gertrude's), answering his 'Think, we had mothers' with 'What hath she done, Prince, that can soil our mothers?' (V.ii.133). It is Troilus's former romantic idealization of Cressid that makes the revelation of her real nature so shatter his whole philosophy of love and sex. Ulysses never had any illusions about Cressida: he perceived her sexual nature at once, recognizing in her one of the 'daughters of the game'. On the other hand, her ripeness for the game, the attraction for Diomed, has none for him. Even in the merely flirtatious game of kissing between her and the Greek leaders, he takes his turn in such a way as to mark the distinction between the kiss of courteous greeting (normal in Shakespeare's society) and a kiss sexually charged, and makes clear his rejection of the amorous kind. He begins, in good manners, 'May I, sweet lady, beg a kiss of you?' 'You may', she answers; so he does, with a coolly polite, 'I do desire it': which is not what Cressid looks for as a tribute to her power over a man: she invites a larger 'beseech'; 'Why, beg two.' Recognizing the erotic tone given to the kissing, Ulysses replies: 'Why then, for Venus' sake, give me a kiss' – but when? 'When Helen is a maid again, and his', restored, a virgin bride, to Menelaus. The impossible condition converts what promised to be a half-acquiescent request into a snubbing refusal.[4] Such a kiss as Cressid desires he will claim only when that impossible condition is fulfilled: to kiss her 'for Venus' sake', 'Never's my day' (IV.v.52).

In the betrayal scene there is another onlooker besides Ulysses. Without Ulysses, the comments of Thersites would lack all counterpoise. Thersites underlines all that is base in Cressid's betrayal, both in her nature – 'any man may sing her, if he can take her clef; she's noted' (V.ii.10–11) – and in what he takes for her tactics. When, in a half-hearted impulse of remorse, she bids Diomed 'visit me no more', Thersites sees in that nothing but calculated provocation: 'Now she sharpens. Well said, whetstone' (75). What agonizes Troilus, Thersites gloats over; the evidence of sordid sex, which he sees as prevalent everywhere: 'Lechery, lechery, still wars and lechery! Nothing else holds fashion' (193–4). That generalization, identical in content with Troilus's though so opposite in tone, requires, no less than his, Ulysses' sane reminder, brief but convincing, that to generalize from Cressid is wrong.

As in the martial action, and the commentary upon it, we have the extremes of Hector's idealism and the cynicism of Achilles and Thersites, so in the amatory action we have Troilus's idealism, and the cynicism of Diomed and Thersites. The two actions are further united by the part Thersites, as well as Ulysses, plays in both. In the realm of sex he is the cynical commentator among the Greeks – upon Achilles, Menelaus, and Diomed as well as upon Cressida and Troilus. Troilus is for him 'the young Trojan ass, that loves the whore'; Diomed, the 'whoremasterly villain', a 'false-hearted rogue', that 'keeps a Trojan drab': one among the crew, 'all incontinent varlets'. As for Achilles, it is Thersites who makes the only remark on his homosexual partnership with Patroclus, his 'male varlet', his 'masculine whore'. Menelaus is contemptible as a cuckold: he is both ass, and ox with the cuckold's horns, so low in the scale of living creatures that Thersites would be willing to change places with any but him: a scorn of Menelaus which accords with the contemptuous treatment of him at Cressid's arrival, not only when she twits him, but when Patroclus intercepts the kiss due to him. His grievance against Paris and Troy is a fine cause for a war! In Thersites' opinion: 'All the argument is a whore and a cuckold: a good quarrel to draw emulous factions, and bleed to death upon' (II.iii.74–6). His malice makes him, however, a ready tool in the 'emulous factions' so that in the war story he is not only a commentator, but an active though minor contributor to the 'stomaching' (as Drake would have called it) which delays the Greek victory.

Nestor takes his bad influence seriously: 'Ajax ... sets Thersites ... to weaken and discredit' (I.iii.188–95), by his vile comparisons, the leaders and what they do. In his splenetic way, he rails at what he tells Ajax and Achilles is their stupid subordination to Agamemnon and his chief councillors, Ulysses and Nestor. It is all in the vein of a privileged bitter clown, a known railer, much discounted by the hearers, whom it entertains as comic satire; but it is 'sick' entertainment and prompts always in the wrong direction. He exacerbates the hostility between Ajax and Achilles when he deserts the one for the other. On Nestor enquiring why Ajax should 'bay at' Achilles, Ulysses explains 'Achilles hath inveigled his fool from him' (II.iii.94). Thersites is contemptuous of both: Ajax (who strikes him) is 'a valiant ass': Achilles much the same. As Kenneth Muir says,[5] some of his mud sticks; yet even when well-deserved, Thersites' satire is wholly destructive, spattering in all directions, to no particular purpose. He takes nothing but satisfaction in the failure of the plan to get Achilles back to the battlefield, which has only resulted in Ajax truanting too:

> the policy of those crafty swearing rascals – that stale old mouse-eaten dry cheese Nestor, and that same dog-fox Ulysses – is not proved worth a blackberry. They set me up in policy that mongrel cur, Ajax, against that dog of as bad a kind Achilles; and now is the cur Ajax prouder than the cur Achilles, and will not arm today; whereupon ... policy grows into an ill opinion. (V.iv.9–17)

This plan, of which the preparation and execution occupy so large a share of the camp scenes, is Ulysses' effort to turn the war in favour of the Greeks by bringing Achilles back into the fighting. His part in the amatory concerns of the play we have seen; this is his part in the martial concerns. With little less glee than Thersites, critics point out that his plan fails. It goes wrong, one must admit, with Ajax; and it does not bring Achilles from his tent. So much, some critics conclude, for Ulysses' politic shrewdness: Shakespeare has exposed it as futile and foolish. Yet in fact Ulysses is not mistaken about the effect of his tactics upon Achilles: they do result in Achilles resolving to fight next day. The plan, as regards Achilles, its target, would have succeeded, but for the unforeseen arrival of Polyxena's letter, which makes him relapse, so that only Patroclus's death finally rouses him to action. Yet though Polyxena's letter was something Ulysses could not have been expected to foresee, he had been able to tell Achilles that the distracting influence from that quarter was no secret.

There is, then, no need to question Ulysses' politic shrewdness in his dealings with Achilles; still less the political wisdom (which most of us take for Shakespeare's as well as his) in his great speech on order and degree. Some critics, hating perhaps to think that Shakespeare's view of society was so firmly hierarchical, note that the speech is spoken by a character who does not subsequently keep to the high ground of principle taken in it; and they make that a justification for subtracting from the authority of the speech itself. Spoken by Ulysses, they argue, who then shows himself at best a politic manipulator, one whose manipulations fail, how can it be intended by Shakespeare, and within the play accepted by us, as an utterance of profound and noble wisdom? Actually, Shakespeare has made its authority plain by creating, for the two chief spokesmen of his two Council scenes, the Greek and the Trojan, a significant parallel. He has given to Ulysses on order and degree, and to Hector on the *ius naturale* and *ius gentium*, utterances of unchallengeable validity, for Elizabethan hearers, on the plane of universal truth; and then shown each speaker lapsing to lower ground: Hector to his cult of honour; Ulysses, to the politic arts of the clever manipulator of men. That decline does not undercut what they have previously enounced. On the contrary, order and degree, and the *ius naturale* and the *ius gentium*, remain the touchstones of political right and wrong, and it is by comparison with the way the Greek and the Trojan hero spoke about them that we measure the decline.[6] Political arts and the cult of honour, after all, are not to be despised; but they are inferior and untrustworthy by comparison. In Ulysses, the descent is manifest when we compare with his Council speech on order the speeches to Achilles when he takes his text from the book he is reading. Those, too, are eloquent, and each begins with general truths about the estimation of human worth. Their themes are a man's self-esteem, its dependence on recognition by others, and the vulnerability of that recognition to the passing of time. To the understanding of the audience, Ulysses is elaborating the philosophy they heard from Troilus: 'What's aught but as 'tis valued?'; and what Ulysses says is not mere sophistry, it is true and penetrating; but as Hector's reply to Troilus showed, it is not the whole truth – value also 'holds his estimate and dignity /As well wherein 'tis precious of itself /As in the prizer' (II.ii.55–7).

On degree, what Ulysses says, irrespective of the application made of it, is the whole truth (for Shakespeare and his audience) about a principle governing the cosmos, and essential for men's life in communities: the speeches to Achilles are worldly wisdom, and arguments *ad hominem*; Ulysses chooses to present this partial view of value and esteem in order to work on Achilles. The argument, though it begins from a true appreciation of our need to employ our gifts, not have them fust in us unused, and embodies shrewd observation of human failings, is pointed at Achilles from start to finish, and potently conditioned by Ulysses' design of convincing him he must, by fresh deeds, refurbish his repute.

This Ulysses is the politic man, with even something about him of the 'dog-fox' Thersites calls him. In his decline from the philosopher-statesman we are bound to see a parallel with Hector's lapse from the champion of international justice into the man of chivalry, devotee of what he shortsightedly takes for national and personal honour.[7]

This and other flaws detract from Hector's impressiveness. The first we hear of him is of his inability to control his sense of humiliation at being worsted in combat; he vents it upon his dependents: 'He chid Andromache and struck his armourer' (I.ii.6) – a type of injustice which is always a bad sign in Shakespeare. His last deed in battle is symbolic of a weakness for the glitter of appearance. He pursues and (offstage) slays a Greek for his sumptuous armour. Ulysses' wisdom loses some impressiveness when it turns foxy, and when the foxy manoeuvring in the end fails of its object. Yet both he and Hector remain impressive. In the war story, each is the best of his compatriots; and the parallel between them is one of the features which draw into unity the Trojan and the Greek components of the drama.

Another link is supplied by Thersites and Pandarus who,

though they never meet, are obviously, in the play's pattern, opposite numbers.[8] They are the two comics – Greek and Trojan – of the play: both grotesques. They may have been planned to contrast in appearance. Traditionally (following Homer) Thersites is deformed in body as in mind; while it has been found effective in modern productions to make the fleshly laugher, Pandarus, flabbily, shapelessly fat. Certainly they are contrasted types. Thersites carries the type of the bitter fool (distinguished from that of the sweet fool by Leslie Hotson in *Shakespeare's Motley*) as far as it can go. As Achilles says, he 'is a privileged man' (II.iii.60). He 'doth nothing but rail', as (Olivia says) 'an allowed fool' may, though we cannot apply to him the rest of her defence, that in such a fool 'there is no slander'. Probably he was played by Robert Armin (though Armin was also a singer, and it is Pandarus who has a song); Armin enacts a more typical bitter fool in Lavatch (of *All's Well*) and brings some of the bitter traits to Lear's fool.

Pandarus, in view of his 'tetchy' first scene, his prurience, and the address to the audience with which he ends the play, bequeathing to the bawds among them his diseases, cannot be seen as the sweet fool. But whereas Thersites, in a spirit of envy and malice, rails at everyone to a slanderous degree, Pandarus, the complacent bawd or pander, is full of praises, for the wit (sense and judgement) of Cassandra and Antenor, the beauty of Cressida, Helen, Paris and Troilus, the valour of Troilus, Hector, Aeneas. Even geese are swans with him. Helenus will 'fight indifferent well', Paris is 'a gallant man' in the war, and Troilus's cuckoldy jest about him will bear retelling as an uproariously laughable climax to a delightfully funny episode. The anecdote is much inflated in his telling of it; it 'has been', says Cressida, 'a great while going by' (I.ii.170–1). This reported scene, with Hecuba laughing her head off, Hector laughing, and even Cassandra laughing, though more soberly, prepares for the on-stage scene of Pandarus with Helen and Paris. The two together indicate a trivial frivolity like that which Pepys was indignantly to record at the court of Charles II: 'the night the Dutch burned our ships, the King did sup with my Lady Castlemaine, and they were all mad with hunting a poor moth.' The trivial frivolity of this reported and this enacted scene in Troy matches the factious frivolity of the reported scene in the Greek camp, where Patroclus takes off Agamemnon, Nestor and the rest

(I.iii.142–84), and the enacted scene where Thersites takes off Ajax (III.iii.270–97).

Pandarus and Thersites are again a pair, alike, with characteristic difference, in both having the temperament of the *voyeur*, who relishes looking on at sexual behaviour. Pandarus has some genuine sympathy with Troilus and Cressida in their desires: he takes pleasure in bringing them together. But above all in gratifying them he is gratifying himself: he is partaking, through them as his proxies, in the sexual enjoyment. Thersites also has the taste for being an onlooker at a sexual situation: he would 'rather leave to see Hector than not to dog' Diomed to where 'they say he keeps a Trojan drab' (V.i.94–6). But while Pandarus, gloating, participates in the pleasure of sex, encouraging the lovers as they move towards it, imagining the fulfilment, and bantering Cressid about it afterward, what Thersites gloats over is Cressid's sexual treachery to love, and her lover Troilus's discomfiture. Pandarus is the witness of passion's consummation and the lovers' happiness; Thersites, of passion's catastrophe, the misery of Troilus, and Cressid's faint and futile remorse, which he slanders in supposing it a mere gambit.

The imaginations of both Thersites and Pandarus are contaminated. Pandarus's imagination runs to bawdy: Thersites is obsessed with the flesh afflicted with diseases or parasites. His first words gratuitously postulate Agamemnon covered in suppurating boils, just as an amusing supposition. After bringing Achilles the letter from Polyxena, he treats Patroclus to a whole catalogue of diseases. His vituperations abound with references to 'itch', 'the loathsomest scab', 'the dry serpigo' and the like, not to mention 'the louse of a lazar' and 'a tick in a sheep'; 'the Neapolitan bone-ache' – VD at its worst – is of course included. Pandarus in his speech ending the play like an epilogue, confesses the same bone-ache in himself. Thus he gives his taste for bawdy a turn which brings it into line with Thersites' obsession. His speech is delivered out into the audience; but it is not correct to say that he bequeathes 'the audience' (the whole of it) his diseases. He assumes that some of them are infected, and will complain, taking the allusion personally, if the bequest is made immediate: 'some galled goose of Winchester would hiss' (V.x.55). But the diseases are the nemesis specifically of bawds like himself: 'As many as be of Pandar's hall', 'Good traders in the flesh',

'Brethren and sisters of the hold-door trade', are those he addresses and apostrophizes. The bequest will be made definitive 'some two months hence'. Pandarus's diseases are terminal; his fate, in this a grotesque parody to Troy's, is postponed but certain.

This unsavoury speech – unsavoury but not unethical – is one conclusion to a play which is to be regarded as having two. The other is the free march of the Trojans to Troy, led by a Troilus, vengeful indeed, but undismayed by the sure destruction he sees ensuing on the death of Hector:

> I do not speak of flight, of fear, of death,
> But dare all imminence that gods and men
> Address their dangers in.   (V.x.12–14)

The tone of the two conclusions, in themselves and as appropriate to all that has led up to them, bears decisively upon the question I promised to end with: what is the genre of *Troilus and Cressida*?[9]

That from one point of view the play is comedy of a peculiar kind, the peculiarity earning it the title of dark or black comedy, it is impossible to deny. The tone is dark and the comedy reductive. The most famous martial epic, and even the most famous love story in the Matter of Rome the Great, are dramatized seamy-side out. Traditional epic heroes are often stripped of our respect. Agamemnon, and perhaps Priam, want royal authority; Ajax is a boor, stupidly proud; Achilles unscrupulous, factious, proud, and disloyal; even Nestor is somewhat long-winded, and as a challenger of Hector and champion against the hypothetical claims of Hector's grandame not a little ridiculous. Menelaus, the despised cuckold, is usher to a gallery of delinquent sex. Paris and Helen are adulterers whose 'love, love, nothing but love' will indeed 'undo us all' (III.i.108), both Trojans and Greeks, in the slaughter whose argument Thersites characterizes as 'a whore and a cuckold'. Patroclus is Achilles' 'masculine whore'; Achilles, the bisexual, who when he loves a woman loves an enemy, and as a result loses in the war his homosexual partner, the man he loves, nor can he avenge him except by a treacherous murder, which he delegates to his retinue. Diomed is the no-nonsense seducer of Cressida; she, proverbial (the play reminds us) as the everlasting type of faithless mistresses 'as false as Cressid'. Pandarus, finally, is coupled with her as the everlasting type of 'all pitiful goers-between' (III.ii.198–9), with his and their occupational diseases.

Troy is disfigured by irresponsibility, in the want of a sense of things as they are, and in frivolity. It is worth remark that Trojan Cressida enters the Greek camp with a game of kissing; and Aeneas, bearing Hector's challenge to a game of knighthood. The ceremonious combat for which in turn Hector arrives, though not without its dignity, is that game itself. The Greeks are more pragmatic; but this realism of theirs is ignoble, and they have their own brand of irresponsibility in their want of mutual loyalty and trust. That is reflected in the malicious mimicry of which Ajax, Achilles' rival, and his commanders, Agamemnon and Nestor, are made the butts by Patroclus and Thersites; and on a graver level by the performance, insincerely starring Ajax, which Ulysses stages to mortify Achilles. Such are the games which these people, Greeks and Trojans, play.

Thersites especially, but also Pandarus, by their outlook, diction, and imagery release into the air of the play a polluting miasma. Yet though they have their choric functions, they are not, as critics have sometimes made them, Shakespeare's spokesmen to the point of pronouncing his verdict. He has entrusted that, as always, only to the whole play.

It is a play 'Unpleasant', but in its darkness and unpleasantness qualities of goodness, truth, even nobility are seen to shine. Troilus's love has much more of idealistic passion than of infatuation in it. Misplaced no doubt it is, but not on a woman who never loved him. Cressida did love him after her fashion; she was facile, not originally dishonest. She was sincere in her emotions of love when they came together, and of grief when they parted; sincere also in her protestations then, of fidelity, and in her faint remorse even while succumbing to Diomed. Her emotions are really felt, facile though they are; and that allows us to pity as well as censure her when by her infidelity she brings about the ruin of Troilus's love.

Wonderfully rendered by the dramatist, his disoriented vision of an incoherent universe goes beyond anything that comedy, of whatever sort, can contain: it is tragic in its depth and intensity. The ruin of his love conveys a genuine sense of tragic catastrophe: of the tragic waste, and the high value of what is wasted. Hector, too, stirs the tragic response, both as we watch him sacrifice misguidedly to his cult of honour the opportunities he has of averting the sure destruction of Troy; and at his death, with the tragic waste of his great though blemished nobility when he leaves himself open to the treacherous attack. Even concerning Achilles, it is at least sad that he goes back on the resolve Ulysses' gambit has brought him to. Had he returned to the war then, he and Patroclus would have fought side by side; as it is, only Patroclus's death is motive enough to recall him to the battlefield: it is part of the heavy price he pays for his success in making certain the eventual victory of the Greeks. But much the worst of the price he pays is his self-degradation. He does seek his revenge and Hector's life at first in comparatively fair fight,[10] but when, foiled there, he resorts to virtual murder and without remorse insults the body, our indignation eclipses any pity for his fall such as lingers with us for Cressida's. But at all events, his base plan and its execution are not 'comicall satyre' or comedy even of a black kind. Like Aufidius's assassination of Coriolanus, they are instrumental in a tragic catastrophe: here, the catastrophe of Hector's death.

As is to be expected of a tragic hero, Hector has made tragic errors which have helped to bring his catastrophe about, the first being his abandonment of true justice in favour of supposed honour. As I have insisted, it is, however, by the touchstone of this justice that we recognize honour and chivalry as inferior ideals, just as it is by the touchstone of Ulysses' statesmanlike principle of degree that we recognize his adroitness in politic intrigue as a lower kind of wiseness. Both cosmic order and the principle of degree in society, and international justice, founded on the law of nature and of nations, have been movingly, convincingly and conclusively affirmed by the greatest Trojan and the best among the Greeks. Despite all that is reductive in the play, these affirmations remain irreducible. Once they have been made, what follows cannot challenge them; it is they that challenge what follows. The audience enters into them with full and strong approval; sympathizes with Troilus in his love; has some pity for Cressida mingled with its blame of her; but above all, feels the tragic catastrophe her falsehood is for him, and the final tragic catastrophe of Hector's death. It admires the resolute spirit in which Troilus, who had found Cressida's desertion almost impossible to accept as reality, at length faces that reality when he tears her letter. It feels the tragic exaltation when with like clarity and courage he faces the reality of Hector's death, with the inevitable doom it means for his city, and leads off the warriors in 'a free march to Troy'. The second conclusion, Pandarus's demeaning speech, is saying nothing about this one: it cannot: 'Hector is dead', about that 'there is no more to say' (V.x.22), except how heroes are to take it.

The audience has been given more than enough (and that conclusion is in keeping with those antecedents) to prevent their finding the play a sardonic comedy of bitter disillusion and nothing else. Yet all this, including the tragedies of Troilus and Hector, is interwoven with the black comedy in a way which makes it impossible to take the play as a tragedy. Each of the two conclusions rounds off one of the two strands: each conclusion complements but cannot obliterate the other. What is true of the conclusions is true of the play as a whole. Shakespeare is a dramatist; and drama, perhaps even more readily than other arts, allows its creator, if he chooses, to leave opposites unreconciled, yet build from them a unified though complex work. The tone and genre of *Troilus and Cressida* resist simplification. Tragedy and bitterly sardonic comedy both exist in it: each is indestructible by the other; yet neither can be endorsed at the expense of the other: neither makes the identical impression it would if the other were not there. Interpreters whose critical categories are too simple for the facts of *Troilus*[11] betray their kinship with a character I am fond of quoting, a booking-clerk in *Punch*. For ticket purposes, he exclaimed, 'cats is dogs, and rabbits is dogs'. Despairingly, he concluded: 'but this 'ere tortoise is a bloomin' hinseck.' *Troilus* is not a 'hinseck'; its analogy is with Antony's crocodile: 'It is shap'd ... like itself', and is 'Of it own colour too'.

NOTES

1 I have an unpublished study of the themes of values and valuation, time, and identity, and especially of their interrelation (identity, like value, is tested by time), in *Troilus and Cressida*.
2 Cp. Kenneth Palmer, New Arden edn (London, 1982), pp. 63–77, 91.
3 *The English Poetic Mind* (London, 1932), pp. 59f.
4 I venture this interpretation of Ulysses' somewhat puzzling line. One might have expected it to be Cressida who proposed the kiss 'for Venus sake', pointing the erotic implication. But of course the terms of Ulysses' proposal turn it immediately into a refusal.

5 'Troilus and Cressida', Shakespeare Survey, 8 (1955), 35.

6 By 'Ulysses' speech on degree ... and by Hector's appeal to the "laws of nature and of nations", the audience is meant to judge the action of the play' − Palmer, p. 321: cf. p. 47, n.2. While his comment, concluding the note on I.iii.75–137, that Ulysses' speech 'is not a text to which the play is a sermon' does sound a needed warning, it might discourage recognition of the truth it qualifies.

7 Shakespeare gives Othello and Macbeth, like Hector, each an insight, which, if he could have been faithful to it, would have prevented the catastrophe. Othello's doubt of Desdemona makes fatal headway because he doubts himself: is he the man whom she could be expected to go on loving? He gives himself the right answer: 'she had eyes, and chose me' (III.iii.193); but he lapses from it, as Macbeth lapses from 'I dare do all that may become a man; /Who dares do more, is none' (I.vii.46–7).

8 Cf. Palmer, p. 92: 'Pandarus is a romantic gone rotten. Thersites is a romantic gone sour.'

9 For Palmer on the genre, see p. 83f.; for Muir, Shakespeare Survey, 8, p. 37. See also Muir's Shakespeare's Comic Sequence (London, 1979), pp. 103f., 121–3.

10 Comparatively, because Hector has every right to complain (as he does, though not to his adversary) 'I would have been much more a fresher man, /Had I expected thee' (V.vi.20–1). Achilles, it is true, has not plotted this advantage; though resolved to fight no one else, he has not held off, but attacks Hector the moment he can find him: and with Patroclus to avenge, he could hardly be expected to behave otherwise. Yet it is an advantage the mirror of knighthood, Launcelot, would have foregone, though the more pragmatic Arthur would not (cf. *The Works of Sir Thomas Malory*, ed. Eugène Vinaver, 2nd edn [Oxford, 1967], II.735; also I.348f., II.526, 529; Tristram's reluctant and Palomides' obstinate unchivalry, and Lamorak's grievances, I.428f., II.600f., 661).

11 Cf. Muir on critical interpretations, by Oscar J. Campbell, Una Ellis-Fermor, Winifred Nowottny, John Palmer, E.M.W. Tillyard, Alice Walker, G. Wilson Knight and others; *Shakespeare Survey*, 8, pp. 35f.; *Shakespeare's Comic Sequence*, pp. 108f., 121–3.

2

Motive and meaning in *All's Well That Ends Well*

RUTH NEVO

All's Well That Ends Well has been classified among the problem comedies, perhaps mainly because Bertram has failed to captivate; he has been found even more devoid of charm than Angelo in *Measure for Measure*, the companion 'problem' comedy. Bertram is, as my students invariably inform me, a creep. And in this they have the critics on their side: that he is 'a thoroughly disagreeable, peevish and vicious person' (Lawrence, 61) seems to be the consensus. One is hard put to it, indeed, to think of a fictional character less popular than the young Count of Rossillion. Yet Helena has come in for her share of criticism too. She is forward, obstinate, manipulative, opportunistic. She does not heal the king out of patriotic fervour but because she has an eye for the main chance. And so on. To rebellious, feminist Katherine Mansfield,

> Helena is a terrifying female. Her virtue, her persistence, her pegging away after the odious Bertram (and disguised as a pilgrim – so typical!) and then telling the whole story to that good widow-woman! And that tame fish Diana. As to lying in Diana's bed and enjoying the embraces meant for Diana – well, I know nothing more sickening. It would take a respectable woman to do such a thing. The worst of it is I can so well imagine ... acting in precisely that way, and giving Diana a present afterwards. ... But to forgive such a woman! Yet Bertram would. There's an espece of mothers-boyisme in him which makes him stupid enough for anything. (*Journal*, 274)

Critics who, on the other hand, fall in love with Helena – Coleridge, it will be recalled, found her 'Shakespeare's loveliest character' (Raysor, II, 113) – attempt desperately, for her

Motive and meaning in *All's Well That Ends Well*

sake, to exculpate Bertram of at least the worst of his lies and infidelities. Those who scold her for being a shameless hussy forcing herself (twice!) upon an unwilling partner feel that a thoroughly unattractive couple, evidently conceived by Shakespeare 'in a time of illness or mental disturbance' (Nicoll, 116) get, in each other, no more than they deserve.

On the face of it, and considered in terms of the modular properties it shares with the festive comedies and their New Comedy paradigms, *All's Well* would not seem to be in line for presenting a problem at all. It possesses, conspicuously, many of the features of its distinguished predecessors. It has a resourceful heroine, an autocratic father-figure to be eluded or outwitted, true love which doesn't run smooth, a comic device involving mistaken identities which through its deception reveals a truth, a wonderful fop who is resoundingly exposed, and a fool whose ribaldries provide a low-life counterpoint to the concerns of his betters. And there is a final match-making which puts the recalcitrant young man firmly in his place in the scheme of things by making an honest father of him. To make of it a problem because its male protagonist is a callow youth and its female protagonist determinedly in pursuit of her man (which of the comic heroines, save Beatrice, is not?) is surely nonsense as criticism, reducing our expectation of a Shakespearean play to the level of a tabloid magazine.

Yet generic uneasiness, a sense of generic impropriety, remains. The paradigm ground-plan outlines as many problems as it sets out to skirt. For the play seems to break as many rules as it keeps. It starts, not with young men and women in search of a mate but with the death of a father, two fathers indeed, and with mourning. A foster-father is at once provided, but instead of constituting the obstacle to a match desired by the young he positively forces a marriage upon his resistant foster-son. Instead of the canonical *senex* of the Terentian New Comedy formula, whose law or writ or interference with young lovers must be overcome or evaded, we have a blocking son. This too is a clash between a father, or father-figure, and a son, but upside down, as it were. Similarly topsy-turvy, the young woman, enterprising and triumphant trickster-heroine of the earlier comedies, is a victim-bride (like her single precursor, Hero) who must be done to death before resolutions can be found, and she plays the role of therapeutic, even thaumaturgic, quasi-daughter to the King which becomes canonical for daughters only in the later romances.

Then again, though it looks like a courtship comedy, it is one which is constrained to get along without courtship, since the young man takes flight to the Italian wars, and the young woman follows him to Italy, but not, as previous comedies might have led one to anticipate, in page disguise. One has only to imagine Helena in pursuit of her Bertram in page disguise, with the opportunities thus offered for masked witty courtship, for a playful battle of the sexes in which a balance, for both sexes, between pursuit and defence, winning and losing, is articulated, to see that this device might well have transformed *All's Well* into the supreme successor to *Two Gentlemen of Verona*, *As You Like It*, and *Twelfth Night*. I make the point not because one would expect or wish a dramatist simply to go on repeating his inventions, but to throw into prominence the peculiar distribution of differences with which we are presented in *All's Well*. For what we have instead of the page disguise is the pilgrim disguise and the bed trick, a mock death and a trick consummation. And the bed trick notoriously pleases no one. On the contrary, it crystallizes the general sense of impropriety, and throws into relief the split in critical opinion concerning Helena: saint or strumpet, and the near-unanimous critical repudiation of Bertram, tricker tricked, but not, it is felt, thereby improved.

For all these reasons the festive end is felt to be a flop, or a merely mechanical or superficial closure. And it lacks the grand harmonic completion the festive comedies have accustomed us to. The King, cured of his wasting disease in Act I, and 'of as able body as when he number'd thirty' (IV.v.77–8), remains unmatched, though the widowed Countess, it would seem, is an available and ideally suitable partner for him. 'You shall find of the king a husband', says Lafew, incorrigible matchmaker, already in line 6 of Act I, but that carefully planted option is not taken up. Nor is a mate found for the virtuous and good-hearted Diana. There is even another unmarried young woman, possibly jilted, in the wings at the play's end. The play provides all the constituents for a grand celebratory wedding closure in which 'individual fulfillment, marital intimacy and communal renewal are celebrated' (Wheeler, 3), but it is felt to be a question whether there are

Motive and meaning in *All's Well That Ends Well*

any truly festive marriages at all, or rather quite the contrary: a disillusioned rendering (for good or ill – some will praise the absence of illusion) of a cynical and sterile world. *All's Well*, it is generally agreed, has no commanding centre, does not integrate its realism (which is usually admitted to be of a power and veracity equal to Shakespeare's peak period) either with its folk-lore motifs – the Healing of the King, the Clever Wench, the Fulfilment of the Tasks[1] – or with conventional expectations, and produces an effect of unease and confusion.[2] *All's Well* is unable, it seems, to make up its generic mind. It is neither fish, flesh nor good red herring; neither comedy, tragedy nor romance.

I would like to submit that *All's Well*, so far from having to be apologized for, can be seen as a particularly interesting successor to the festive or, as it might be better to call them, the maturation comedies; that the critics' problems are often reflections of their own unaware masculine or feminine identifications, embodying defences and resistances which themselves repeat the conflicts dramatized in the play; and that therefore, the better to understand both critics and play, we must attempt to read, as we say, between the lines, and to hear with a third ear. The space between the lines is the psychic space of evocation and resonance shared by both audience and *dramatis personae*. It is the space of precipitation by the text into consciousness of the normally unconscious. It is there that we can find what Peter Brooks calls the 'complex history of unconscious desire, unavailable to the conscious subject but at work in the text' (516). This, 'the self's other story', is what we must set out to discover if we wish to do justice to the drama enacted in *All's Well* and to see as significant the anomalies mentioned above. The complaint, for example, of the Arden editor that the play lacks a 'central, acceptable, and unified viewpoint' to define its values, and to integrate its incompatibilities (xxxv), acquires a different kind of truth when we perceive that *All's Well* places itself at a node where three dreams cross: the dream of the elders, reliving their lives through their children, the dream of the young man escaping parental domination, and the dream of the young woman desiring a child and a father. And these dreams neither coincide nor harmonize.

In *All's Well*, still in outline and plan a courtship comedy, parents have become, if not central as in the romances, at least not completely instrumental. The point of view is predominantly of the young, but since the parents, with their own problems of ageing, of holding on and letting go, are not mere obstacle figures, their point of view is operative too. They exist within the play both in their own right, and as their wills, desires, fantasies and memories intermesh with those of the younger generation. This intermesh is a feature neither of the festive comedies nor of the romances, and it is what gives to *All's Well* its peculiar richness and density.

If there is a problem in this text, it is to be found in the unfinished business – unresolved tensions or repressed fears and desires which every play, every text, leaves in its wake to motivate the writing of the works to follow. But so far as its comic project is concerned, it quite triumphantly contains, while it also reveals, its potentially explosive and painful material.

*

Comedy, Chaplin once said, 'is at its best when it flirts with death, plays with it, mocks it, pokes its nose into it'. If there is validity in the view that comedy is the mode of drama which defers, denies, evades or overcomes death, then one can see the play's opening not as an abrogation of comic conditions, but as a foregrounding of them. The deaths of the two fathers are undone by the adoption of Bertram and of Helena by the King and Countess respectively. The initial mourning, already past as the play begins, suggests precisely such a denial, renewal or overcoming. But if death is thus vigorously defended against at the very start, its shadow remains to haunt the play. If we listen, as perhaps we always should, with half-closed eyes to the verbal texture of the opening scenes, we become aware of major themes which are the older generation's: nostalgia, the vulnerable body, the dereliction of time, impotence. 'In delivering my son from me', says the Countess, 'I bury a second husband' (I.i.1). The King's disease – that mysterious fistula – is immediately introduced, together with the wishful fantasy of his restoration to youthful fitness. A strangely skeletal image – 'virtue's steely bones /Looks bleak i' th' cold wind' (I.i.101–2) – appears in Helena's defence of Parolles; the consequences she envisages should her gamble for Bertram fail are vividly imagined: 'Let the white death sit on thy cheek for ever' (II.iii.71). Parolles' adjurations on the

Motive and meaning in *All's Well That Ends Well*

subject of virginity not unexpectedly turn the age-old *carpe diem* theme into a very explicit *memento mori*: 'Your date is better in your pie and your porridge than in your cheek; and your viriginity, your old virginity, is like one of our French wither'd pears: it looks ill, it eats drily; marry, 'tis a wither'd pear' (I.i.154–9).

The peculiar anxiety the play's body-language expresses lies in a vacillation between images of desire and of decrepitude. The passionate Helena, who has loved (though it was 'a plague' to do so) 'To see him every hour; to sit and draw /His arched brows, his hawking eye, his curls' (I.i.91–2), who longs to 'feed [her] eye ... /To join like likes, and kiss like native things' (I.i.217, 219) grieves that 'wishing well had not a body in't /Which might be felt' (I.i.177–8). This vehemence is curiously echoed by Bertram, newly wed and in flight, as he parts from one of his new companions: 'I grow to you, and our parting is a tortur'd body' (II.i.36). We have the unvarnished plain speaking of Lavatch (of Touchstone's ilk) to drive the point home, as he seeks permission to marry his Isbel: 'My poor body, madam, requires it; I am driven on by the flesh, and he must needs go that the devil drives'; 'Service is no heritage, and I think I shall never have the blessing of God till I have issue a' my body; for they say barnes are blessings' (I.iii.26–8, 21–4). 'Issue of the body' is the leitmotif of the King's elegy for his own, and his old friend's, youth:

> But on us both did haggish age steal on,
> And wore us out of act ...   (I.ii.29–30)

> Would I were with him! ...
>   "Let me not live", quoth he,
> "After my flame lacks oil, to be the snuff
> Of younger spirits, whose apprehensive senses
> All but new things disdain; whose judgments are
> Mere fathers of their garments ..."
>   This he wish'd.
> I, after him, do after him wish too,
> Since I nor wax nor honey can bring home.
>   (I.ii.52, 58–65)

'Oil' for his flame, 'wax' or 'honey' for the hive, suggest that the loss of sexual potency underlies the melancholy of this Fisher King. We note his resigned reply to the courtier's

'You're loved, sir': 'I fill a place, I know't' (I.ii.67, 69). The lewd Lafew leaves no room for doubt about the nature of the King's disease, or at least of its symptomatic manifestation. He himself refers to his task – the bringing of the physician's daughter to her royal patient – as a pandar's role: 'I am Cressid's uncle /That dare leave two together' (II.i.96–7); describes what 'Doctor she' will achieve in language which barely cloaks its sexuality; and takes a salacious pleasure in persuading the melancholy King to attempt the cure:

> O, will you eat
> No grapes, my royal fox? Yes, but you will
> My noble grapes, and if my royal fox
> Could reach them. I have seen a medicine
> That's able to breathe life into a stone,
> Quicken a rock, and make you dance canary
> With spritely fire and motion; whose simple touch
> Is powerful to araise King Pippen, nay,
> To give great Charlemain a pen in's hand
> And write to her a love-line. (II.i.68–77)[3]

It is precisely the King's virility that Helena restores. After his recovery, he is 'lustique' enough to lead his 'preserver' in a coranto (II.iii.41). 'Your dolphin is not lustier', Lafew informs us (II.iii.26). This restoration by the daughter of his old friend is the magic fulfilment of a wishful fantasy; but it also provides the King with – what? a surrogate daughter as well as a surrogate son? An Avishag for his declining years? A greater warmth, perhaps, than one would feel for one's physician is to be caught in the King's resolve to become her patient: 'more to know could not be more to trust' (II.i.205). His violent repudiation of the recalcitrant Bertram, the transformation of 'My son's no dearer' (I.ii.76) into

> Check thy contempt;
> Obey our will ...
> Or I will throw thee from my care for ever
> Into the staggers and the careless lapse
> Of youth and ignorance; both my revenge and hate
> Loosing upon thee in the name of justice,
> Without all terms of pity (II.iii.157–66)

is the provision of the tyrannical *senex* of New Comedy with a vengeance. But if he is, as we intuit, more than half in love, not any longer with easeful death, but with a young woman who promises rejuvenation, it is not difficult to understand the intensity, and the ambivalence, of his emotional investment in this match.

By the same token we recall the words of the widowed Countess, as the play opens with the dispatching of Bertram to Paris: 'In delivering my son from me', says the Countess, 'I bury a second husband.' On the face of it, this is the patrician gesture of a dignified and courtly lady distancing with art a double sorrow. This second 'birth' is a second death, she says. But in the rhetorical condensation may we not descry a telltale parapraxis? The Countess is in mourning for her husband; she is also, we perceive, rather more than half in love with her son.[4]

The Countess's second exchange with her fool, which follows Helena's confession and her departure for Paris, is similarly revealing. She is sending him off in Helena's wake to the King's court and is prepared, with good-natured irony, to indulge his scapegrace effrontery. On the whole she treats his scurrilities with much the same matronly indulgence as Olivia does Feste's, but the open sexuality of his bawdry this time, it seems, is provocative of more than cool irony. His 'answer', he says, fits all questions 'like a barber's chair that fits all buttocks' (II.ii.16); is as fit

> as ten groats is for the hand of an attorney, as your French crown for your taffety punk, as Tib's rush for Tom's forefinger, as a pancake for Shrove Tuesday, a morris for Mayday, as the nail to his hole, the cuckold to his horn, as a scolding quean to a wrangling knave, as the nun's lip to the friar's mouth; nay, as the pudding to his skin. ... From below your duke to beneath your constable, it will fit any question. (II.ii.20–30)

'It must be an answer of most monstrous size that must fit all demands', is the Countess's reply; and then suddenly, in the midst of the thrust of parry and repartee, comes a striking *non sequitur*: 'To be young again, if we could' (37).

They are mourning their youth, this autumnal pair, it seems. And in consequence they are projecting upon their children (or their adopted children) their longing to relive their lives. It is no wonder that crossed currents of ambivalence will traverse this inverted family romance.

Read in this light the testing scene between the Countess and Helena becomes as iridescent as Helena's tears. The Countess receives the steward's confirmation of Helena's love for Bertram with an immediate, motherly empathy, shadowed, however, in its reference to 'faults', by the hint of a jealous reservation:

> Even so it was with me when I was young;
> ... this thorn
> Doth to our rose of youth rightly belong. ...
> Such were our faults, or then we thought them none.
> (I.iii.123–5, 130)

The scene which follows is masterly in its representation of ambivalence, of simulation and dissimulation, between the two women, both contenders for Bertram's love. 'You know, Helen, /I am a mother to you' (I.iii.132–3) is the Countess's opening ploy, and it serves her purpose of eliciting response and testing intention excellently when Helena replies, with modestly disavowing emphasis, 'Mine honourable *mistress*' (my italics):

> Nay, a mother.
> Why not a mother? When I said "a mother",
> Methought you saw a serpent. What's in "mother"
> That you start at it? I say I am your mother,
> And put you in a catalogue of those
> That were enwombed mine. ...
> You ne'er oppress'd me with a mother's groan,
> Yet I express to you a mother's care.
> God's mercy, maiden! does it curd thy blood
> To say I am thy mother? what's the matter,
> That this distempered messenger of wet,
> The many colour'd Iris, rounds thine eye?
> – Why, that you are my daughter? (I.iii.134–48)

The Countess exploits Helena's embarrassed feint – 'The Count Rossillion cannot be my brother. ... must not be my brother' (I.iii.150, 155) to point out that Helena as her daughter-in-law would solve the semantic problem, and she drives home her advantage:

> God shield you mean it not! daughter and mother
> So strive upon your pulse. What! pale again?

My fear hath catch'd your fondness; now I see
The myst'ry of your loneliness, and find
Your salt tears' head. . . .
                    Speak, is't so?
If it be so, you have wound a goodly clew.
                            (I.iii.163–7, 176–7)

She is playing the role of indignant matron that she has set herself. But in doing so, she is playing it out. The ambiguous irony of 'you have wound a goodly clew' allows us to register simultaneously the angry resentment she is professing, and the compensatory acceptance she is working her way towards. Since she cannot have a husband in her son, she will identify with the girl who would be his wife, and so transform her love for Bertram into a double maternal solicitude. This is an admirable solution: it is indeed the way of women in Shakespearean comedy to resolve their inner conflicts more successfully, more benignly, than do the men.

At the end of the scene, Helena has the Countess's leave and love and approval for her project. But in order to understand Helena in the testing scene we must retrace our steps.

The predicament that is developed in Act I of *All's Well* offers a powerful exemplification of Freud's observation upon family quadrangles. 'I am accustoming myself', he wrote in a letter to Fliess in 1899, 'to regarding every sexual act as an event between four individuals'. 'Every sexual thought' perhaps he should have said. Much of interest emerges when we turn our attention to the Countess's foster-daughter, also, like Bertram, in mourning for a father: 'The remembrance of her father never approaches her heart but the tyranny of her sorrows takes all livelihood from her cheek' (I.i.45–7), we are told. We are immediately riveted by a scene curiously reminiscent of the opening scenes of *Hamlet* but with the sexes reversed. 'I do affect a sorrow indeed, but I have it too' (50) is Helena's reply to the Countess's chiding: 'No more of this, Helena; go to, no more; lest it be rather thought you affect a sorrow than to have —' (47–9). Helena, it seems, like Hamlet, has something to hide, something that presses for utterance and chafes at the need for dissimulation. Helena, like Hamlet, as we speedily learn, is 'too much in the *son*':

    I think not on my father,
And these great tears grace his remembrance more

> Than those I shed for him. What was he like?
> I have forgot him; my imagination
> Carries no favour in't but Bertram's.   (I.i.77–81)

The lines are obscure, but possibly uncannily shrewd. To make sense of the antithesis we must read 'remembrance' as a metonymy for 'remains' – all that remains of her father is her memory of him. So: the great tears grace his memory more than those she shed at his funeral, tears shed 'for *him*', still, so to speak, present in the flesh. This is very condensed, more particularly since 'grace' carries with it its subliminal contrary – 'disgrace'. Surely a considerable tinge of guilt colours Helena's acknowledgement of the displacement, in her passionate affection, of father by beloved. The denials, like most denials, are self-betraying. What the speech tells us is that she is very far from having forgotten her father; but that her love for Bertram has, quite literally, and not without guilt, taken the place of her love for her father, the one image overlaying the other. If so, it is no wonder that her love is perceived by her as unattainable, out of reach, never to be consummated. Yes, he is socially above her, and this provides the ostensible reason for her despair. But since nothing, we are told, is fortuitous in the world of the mind, Helena's choice of the object of her affections could be in accordance with a deeply ambivalent inner need. If it is her father she loves, and therefore a father that she seeks in the mate she chooses, the latter will be, for that very reason, impossible, untouchable, a forbidden *prince lointain*: ''twere all one /That I should love a bright particular star /And think to wed it' (I.i.83–5).

We are offered a great deal more data for the fathoming of Helena's complex motivation in the dialogue with Bertram's friend, Parolles, whom she loves 'for his sake' though she knows him for the liar, fool and coward that he is. With Parolles she enjoys a relationship of ironic equality despite her lowly birth and his complacent patronizing. 'Save you, fair queen' is his greeting, and her reply, 'And you, monarch!' (I.i.104–5), shows, as does the flyting that concludes their conversation (187–200), that she can give as good as she gets in this power game. Helena is shrewd and self-reliant as the scene makes very clear: it ends with her bold resolve to seek the remedies that 'in ourselves do lie' (212):

> Who ever strove
> To show her merit that did miss her love?

The king's disease – my project may deceive me,
But my intents are fix'd, and will not leave me.
(I.i.222–5)

She is also preoccupied, as the scene makes clear, with the very subject Parolles, with preternaturally cunning complicity, has chosen for their conversation.

Parolles is a mine of information on the subject of virginity, which is the topic he first provocatively launches. Helena parries his provocations to good effect, but in the process of enquiring of Parolles, who should know, how one may 'barricado it' against man the enemy, Helena also enquires, 'How might one do, sir, to lose it to her own liking?' (I.i.147). Parolles' diatribe against withered pears concludes with the challenge 'Will you anything with it?' (I.i.159–60), and is followed by an elliptical speech from Helena, perhaps half to herself, which has proved no less a challenge to interpreters:

Not my virginity; yet ...[5]
There shall your master have a thousand loves,
A mother, and a mistress, and a friend,
A phoenix, captain, and an enemy,
A guide, a goddess, and a sovereign,
A counsellor, a traitress, and a dear. (I.i.161–6)

The ellipsis, a characteristic of Helena's which suggests a reflective inwardness, is open to a number of interpretations. Are we to hear an emphasis upon 'my' virginity? Is the implied other virginity, if any is implied, Bertram's? Is 'yet' temporal or concessive? Whatever is unspoken crystallizes finally upon what is evidently the dominant preoccupation – 'your master': 'There shall your master have a thousand loves.' But where shall this take place? In Paris? Or in 'my virginity', the immediate antecedent for the anaphoric 'there'? However we read what follows, whether as an envious and ironic catalogue of sonneteering epithets (a denigration of the loves Bertram will find in Paris) or as an ardent outdoing even of the chivalric passions of the sonneteers (and so a valorization of the love that she can offer), immediately after 'a thousand loves' there occurs an oddity which we can surely only interpret as another astonishing slip of the text. What follows is 'a mother, and a mistress, and a friend'. For while one has encountered fantastic, hyperbolic, even outrageous, epithets in High Renaissance sonnets, even the most assiduous reader of these confections will be hard put to it to recall a mother among them. No occurrence, the Arden editor assures us, is on record.

Why has this 'mother' entered Helena's mind? Has she perceived the bond between the Countess and Bertram? And, seeking herself a father surrogate in her love, does her wise unconscious fear a contrary quest in Bertram? Or, on the contrary, is it her wish too to 'mother' Bertram? These are the questions which resonate further in the testing scene between the Countess and Helena, which we will consider now from Helena's point of view.

The Countess's outburst:

> does it curd they blood
> To say I am thy mother? what's the matter,
> That this distempered messenger of wet,
> The many-colour'd Iris, rounds thine eye?
> – Why, that you are my daughter? (I.iii.144–8)

receives the opaque reply, 'That I am not'. Helena, elliptical as ever, may mean by this 'I am not *that*', by way of emphatic disavowal, or 'Because I am not' by way of concession. How are we to read the elliptical Helena? Does she inadvertently reveal her true feelings, or cannily mask her feelings with a declarative equivocation? The reason she gives for her continued insistence is disingenuous: 'Pardon, madam; /The Count Rossillion cannot be my brother':

> My master, my dear lord he is; and I
> His servant live, and will his vassal die.
> He must not be my brother. (I.iii.153–5)

Embarrassed, Helena falls into confusion as she struggles between the Scylla of impoliteness or ingratitude and the hypothetical Charybdis of brother/sister incest:

> You are my mother, madam; would you were –
> So that my lord your son were not my brother –
> Indeed my mother! or were you both our mothers
> I care no more for than I do for heaven,
> So I were not his sister. (I.iii.156–60)

It can surely escape no one that Helena's double bind here is factitious. The Countess can be her mother only metaphorically. Certainly the semantic absurdity does not escape the

Motive and meaning in *All's Well That Ends Well* 39

Countess, who, as we have seen, uses it to drive home her advantage.

Helena's agitation serves the Countess's testing purposes, and she is trapped into the confession the Countess wants to hear. But we must seek a deeper reason for her extreme discomposure. Her ostensible reason – the desire not to be Bertram's sister since she wishes to be his wife – since it is absurd, can only be a screen upon which we can read an inner conflict. That she is made so nervous by the idea of being Bertram's forbidden sister could well be symptomatic of the deeper taboo. Daughter and mother so strive upon her pulse in a sense truer than the Countess knows: shall she continue to be her father's docile daughter, submissive and self-effacing, or become her lover's active pursuer, challenger and replacer of his mother? That it is the father's daughter which at this point dominates her mind is to be inferred from the posture of helpless, hapless adoration from afar that she expresses, in excess, one feels, of what is required to pacify the Countess, but in keeping with the masochistic note we have already heard ('The hind that would be mated by the lion /Must die for love', I.i.89–90):

> I know I love in vain, strive against hope;
> Yet in this captious and inteemable sieve
> I still pour in the waters of my love
> And lack not to lose still. Thus, Indian-like,
> Religious in mine error, I adore
> The sun that looks upon his worshipper
> But knows of him no more....
>   O then, give pity
> To her whose state is such that cannot choose
> But lend and give where she is sure to lose;
> That seeks not to find that her search implies,
> But riddle-like lives sweetly where she dies!
>   (I.iii.196–202, 208–12)

Richard Wheeler says that Helena's main task is to overcome a difficulty 'that originates in Bertram's revulsion from her' (15). But this is surely not so. Helena's main task is to overcome a difficulty that originates in the Oedipal taboo. She is as passionate a woman as she is an affectionate daughter, but not yet able to break the father's spell. The phoenix image fantasizes a sublime self-immolation, but pursuit of Bertram to Paris is seductive too. The will to pursue Bertram to Paris under the guise of healing the King, since it is also the will to heal the King under the guise of pursuing Bertram, is for her a wonderfully composite and legitimizing wish-fulfilment. Using the craft of her own father, she will restore a proxy father-figure to health, and receive, at his grateful hand, a husband.

Helena consciously conceives her problem as a conflict between boldness and self-effacement, presumption and modesty, in terms both of the social hierarchies and the maidenly proprieties, but also in terms of chastity and sensuality. 'Loving dearly', for Helena, is no matter for platonic abstractions and Diana, her much invoked goddess, was, it will be recalled, the goddess of childbirth as well as of virginity. But it is Diana, not of the Ephesians but of virgins, whom she invokes in order to formulate her plight at this point:

> My dearest madam, ...
> if yourself,
> Whose aged honour cites a virtuous youth,
> Did ever, in so true a flame of liking,
> Wish chastely and love dearly, that your Dian
> Was both herself and love— (I.iii.202–8)

Only later, and, typically, when she steels herself for possible humiliation in the self-exposure of the choosing scene, does she see herself as deserting Diana for 'imperial Love, that god most high' (II.iii.75).

Helena's fantasied plot of success, in which she will choose her man and the King-father will sanction her choice, fails. It is at the French court, following the triumph of her cure of the King, that humiliation – the 'Tax of impudence, /A strumpet's boldness, a divulged shame' (II.i.169–70) which, she told the King, she was ready to venture, in other words, had deeply feared, as the consequence instinctively associated for her with sexual love – becomes indeed her lot. In a way she has tempted Providence, for her replies to the reluctant courtiers are self-abasing: 'Love make your fortunes twenty times above /Her that so wishes'; 'I'll never do you wrong, for your own sake. /... in your bed /Find fairer fortune if you ever wed!'; 'You are too young, too happy, and too good, /To make yourself a son out of my blood' (II.iii.82–97). We conceive the drama that she has conceived, empowered by her father's power: the response she hoped for from Bertram would have reversed the situation, dignified her humility by triumphantly vindicating her intrinsic worth. But at her grand moment of choice, she is despised and rejected, punished, if you will, by a chauvinist text. The choice-of-a-suitor scene has understandably troubled critics, both on her behalf and on Bertram's. The latter indeed has troubles of his own, to which I now turn.

They interestingly mirror Helena's. For where Helena seeks, and struggles with, a father in her love, Bertram fears, and flees, a mother in his. Understanding this, we will understand the pathos of the crossed vectors of desire, the knot of conflicting needs which this comedy of maturation must untie.

Critics scold Bertram for being so unchivalrous about Helena, but we should surely register the authenticity of his resistance to a marriage forced upon him by a foster-father, to the socially inferior, and domestically familiar, receiver of his mother's patronage. Even to a kind of sister – Helena's anxiety on this score can alert us to his. That he chafes is hardly to be wondered at. Bertram has emerged from beneath the maternal wing only to fall under the sway of a new paternal authority. It is surely incumbent upon us to see the matter from his point of view when he bursts out with

> My wife, my liege! I shall beseech your highness,
> In such a business give me leave to use
> The help of mine own eyes.   (II.iii.106–8)

And seeing it thus we may perceive the bind in which he is placed. It would hardly make things better for Helena if his repulsion were so great as to make him defy the King's threatened 'revenge and hate'. His surrender has been construed as abjectly, cynically opportunistic. But it could also be read as a bitter acceptance of *force majeure*:

> Pardon, my gracious lord; for I submit
> My fancy to your eyes. When I consider
> What great creation and what dole of honour
> Flies where you bid it, I find that she, which late
> Was in my nobler thoughts most base, is now
> The praised of the king; who, so ennobled,
> Is as 'twere born so.   (II.iii.167–73)

It depends where we locate the irony, whether we monopolize that commodity as a critical prerogative, or allow the dramatized persona access to the sarcasm which is the defence of the powerless. And Bertram *is* powerless. That he is 'not yet old enough for a man, nor young enough for a boy' (as Malvolio says of Cesario in *Twelfth Night*, I.v.158–9) is the play's generational starting point.

Already in Act II Bertram's plight is presented as one of extreme frustration. He is

>   commanded here, and kept a coil with
> "Too young", and "The next year" and "'Tis too early"....
> I shall stay here the forehorse to a smock,
> Creaking my shoes on the plain masonry,
> Till honour be bought up, and no sword worn
> But one to dance with.   (II.i.27–33)

Seeking honour in battle, action, manhood, he is kept childishly at home by a King who is as patronizing as he is paternal. And this situation reaches a crisis when even freedom of marital choice is denied him.

But more is at stake for Bertram than freedom of marital choice. Lafew's comments throughout the scene of Helena's choice brand all the reluctant courtiers as beardless boys, objects of his macho contempt before their lacklustre performance. 'Do all they deny her? And they were sons of mine I'd have them whipp'd, or I would send them to th' Turk to make eunuchs of' (II.iii.86–8). They are 'boys of ice. ... bastards to the English; the French ne'er got 'em' (93–5). In particular he despises Bertram, and in terms which suggest the condescending arrogance of the grown man for the sexually immature youth. 'There's one grape yet. I am sure thy father drunk wine; but if thou be'st not an ass, I am a youth of fourteen; I have known thee already' (99–101).

In the scene which follows, the mutual hostility between Lafew and Parolles also hinges specifically upon the question of manliness: Lafew excoriates Parolles for his effeminate clothes – he is a 'good window of lattice' (II.iii.212) – and for his foppish airs and affectations – 'I must tell thee, sirrah, I write man; to which title age cannot bring thee' (197–8). And his insinuations go further than aspersions cast merely upon Parolles' sartorial foppishness: 'Why dost thou garter up thy arms a' this fashion? Dost make hose of thy sleeves? ...

Thou wert best set thy lower part where thy nose stands' (245–8). To Lafew, aggressively male, Parolles is 'a hen'. As far as Lafew is concerned, it seems, Parolles is nothing but a male punk and he cannot stand him. Parolles for his part throws Lafew's 'antiquity' in his face, and, once Lafew is safely absent, swears 'Well, thou hast a son shall take this disgrace off me; scurvy, old, filthy, scurvy lord! ... I'll beat him, by my life, if I can meet him with any convenience' (231–5). It is to this braggart 'sweetheart' that Bertram turns for sympathy when he enters, 'Undone and forfeited to cares for ever!' (263). Parolles' bravado, characteristic defence of the sexually and personally insecure, presents the refuge of a homosexual attachment as a valorization of the male cameraderie of warfare:

> To th' wars, my boy, to th' wars!
> He wears his honour in a box unseen
> That hugs his kicky-wicky here at home,
> Spending his manly marrow in her arms,
> Which should sustain the bound and high curvet
> Of Mars's fiery steed.   (II.iii.274–9)

And off to the wars go the bachelor companions in perfect agreement that 'A young man married is a man that's marr'd' (II.iii.294).

For Bertram, frustrated by his forced marriage, Mars is a welcome substitute for Venus. But that a fear of impotence lies just beneath the surface of his martial posture is suggested not only by the Parolles connection but by his own tell-tale envoi:

> I have writ my letters, casketed my treasure,
> Given order for our horses; and tonight,
> When I should take possession of the bride,
> End ere I do begin.   (II.v.23–6)

Effeminate Parolles, 'jackanapes with scarfs' (III.v.85), is Bertram's refuge from 'the dark house [a displaced image of female enclosure?] and the detested wife' (II.iii.288). The danger, bawdy Lavatch informs us, is in 'standing to 't': in battle, 'that's the loss of men'; elsewhere, 'the getting of children' (III.ii.40–1). Bertram, who runs away, the clown's irony seems to suggest, has double indemnity. Lavatch's caustic comment is important because it links the two masculine prerogatives, and puts them both in question *vis-a-vis* Bertram. But we must ask our own questions of the text that represents Bertram.

First of all, we note, the nearly universal critical prejudice against him leads to a cardinal misjudgement. Bertram does in fact exhibit prowess in battle. And he does not, at this stage at least, lie to Helena. He does not declare to her a love he does not feel. He will not kiss her even when they part, and she pleads for at least a formal embrace.

Moreover the riddle with which he sets Helena her impossible task: '*When thou canst get the ring upon my finger, which never shall come off, and show me a child begotten of thy body that I am father to, then call me husband*' (III.ii.56–8) is double-tongued, like all riddles. It states an apparent impossibility but represents an unacknowledged desire. To see this, one has only to suppose the conditional *form* changed, not the primary substance; to read instead of 'When thou canst ...', 'If only thou couldst ...'.[6]

And when he dispatches her to his mother, it is with almost a plea on his part for her understanding:

> And rather muse than ask why I entreat you;
> For my respects are better than they seem,
> And my appointments have in them a need
> Greater than shows itself at the first view
> To you that know them not.   (II.v.65–9)

The need 'Greater than shows itself', as Richard Wheeler persuasively demonstrates, stems from the fact that Helena is ineluctably bound up in his mind with his mother: 'A son's affection for a mother is directed by Bertram toward the countess; a son's fears of female domination and of his own oedipal wishes are aroused in Bertram by Helena' (42). Hence 'I cannot love her nor will strive to do't' (II.iii.145). Wheeler concludes, however, that the play's 'comic purpose, to free Bertram from anxieties that originate in family ties', is not achieved. 'The action of *All's Well*', he says, 'dramatizes neither a liberation from nor a transformation of obstacles that obstruct the marriage to Helena' (80).

It is at this point that my own reading of *All's Well* diverges from Wheeler's. He reads into the play the problems of the Sonnets, with Helena as a screen figure for the humiliated and self-humiliating lover and Bertram as the Sonnets' young

Motive and meaning in *All's Well That Ends Well*

man, presented now with a savage mockery the self-excoriating author of the Sonnets could not permit himself. My own reading is dramatically opposed. I see these two as chiastic doubles, mirrors of each other. Where Helena seeks a (forbidden) father in her love, Bertram fears a (forbidden) mother; but the text also inscribes their shared desire for sexual enfranchisement, for fatherhood and motherhood, and provides the means for its attainment.

The reversals, which will make possible the happy ending, occur in the play's middle Act. Helena's great speech of renunciation is worth quoting at length for the subtlety with which it articulates a momentous transformation.

> Nothing in France, until he has no wife!
> Thou shalt have none, Rossillion, none in France;
> Then hast thou all again. Poor lord, is't I
> That chase thee from thy country, and expose
> Those tender limbs of thine to the event
> Of the none-sparing war? And is it I
> That drive thee from the sportive court, where thou
> Wast shot at with fair eyes, to be the mark
> Of smoky muskets? O you leaden messengers,
>   ... do not touch my lord.
> Whoever shoots at him, I set him there;
>   ... I am the cause
>   ... No; come thou home, Rossillion,
>   ... I will be gone;
> My being here it is that holds thee hence.
> Shall I stay here to do't? No, no, although
> The air of paradise did fan the house
> And angels offic'd all. I will be gone,
>   ... Come, night; end, day;
> For with the dark, poor thief, I'll steal away.
>   (III.ii.100–29)

In the parting scene Helena begged for her kiss 'like a timorous thief, [who] most fain would steal' (II.v.81) what is legally hers. Now she will herself steal away, so only she be no obstacle to Bertram's return. It is to be noted, too, that in thus renouncing him she refers to him in his own patronymic right, as Rossillion. It is a turnabout for the determined young woman who has outfaced a king and a court to gain her end, and gained it. But what the accents of the speech tell us is that this self-abrogation, which springs no doubt from the masochism of infantile taboo, has undergone a transformation. Her guilt here is reality-tested, objective, since she really is the cause of Bertram's escape into soldiering. The tenderly maternal solicitude that we hear in this speech is a transference wonderfully, and movingly, caught. Helena has broken the spell of the father in this fantasy of herself as a mothering, protective figure to the man she desires.

It is for this reason, I suggest, that there is no page disguise in *All's Well*. Helena's problem has not been the sorting out, balancing and harmonizing of masculine and feminine components in her own personality as it was for her hermaphrodite sisters of the earlier comedies. They had to reconcile themselves to a woman's role without loss, if possible, of the adventurous, maverick male attributes they also possessed, and cherished. She has had to free her sexuality from the archaic bond of infancy, to undertake a pilgrimage into mature sexuality. It is beautifully in keeping with this trajectory of 'the other plot' that we are following that disguise as a girl called Diana, women's camaraderie, and the bed-trick mark her achievement of the passage from virgin chastity to marital sexuality. The bed-trick represents enabling fantasy for both partners. For Helena it offers camouflage – anonymity, invisibility – under cover of which she can transcend the inhibitions of a threatening sexuality. For men, conversely, bed-trick fantasies represent fears of being tricked in bed. But for Bertram the bed-trick is his sexual conquest of the woman he believes to be Diana and so fulfils an analogous liberation. Helena is dead. We do not know the nature of the change that came over Bertram when he received the news of Helena's death, but 'on the reading it he chang'd almost into another man' (IV.iii.3–4). Already in his wooing of Diana, he was liberated enough to be able to contemplate, and to exorcise by invoking, a primal scene: 'now you should be as your mother was', he says, 'When your sweet self was got' (IV.ii.9–10). Now, in bed with a light o'love – Fontybell! – and therefore unhampered by any honourable intentions whatsoever, 'he fleshes his will' (IV.iii.15), confirming his potency. Thus Bertram outgrows Parolles. Or rather, he is in a position to outgrow Parolles. His repudiation of his erstwhile 'sweetheart', however, is still to be brought about.

*

Motive and meaning in *All's Well That Ends Well* 47

Parolles, often seen as a quasi-vice figure in a morality play contest with virtuous Helena, and about whom Wheeler, oddly, has very little to say, is perhaps the most brilliant dramatic invention in *All's Well*. Bertram's virtual sibling, brother-at-arms, alter ego, he is our essential vehicle for an understanding of Bertram's rake's progress as an authentic reflection of masculine adolescence. Perhaps too much so for the comfort of spectators, male and female, who cannot free themselves from masculine idealizations of romantic protagonists.[7] But let us examine the exposure of the inimitable Parolles.

The exposure of Parolles in Act IV marks, together with the bed-trick, the remedial phase of the Shakespearean comic plot. Characteristically, folly, become hyperbolically excessive, extrudes itself, exposes itself, or is exposed, exhausts and so eliminates itself.[8] The lords have a double remedial project in hand in the gulling scene. Parolles, 'most notable coward, an infinite and endless liar, an hourly promise-breaker' (III.vi.9–10), is to be openly and palpably disgraced, but Bertram too is due for chastisement for the brazen callousness with which he has received the news of Helena's death and for his seduction of 'a young gentlewoman ... of a most chaste renown' (IV.iii.13–14). The French lords will 'gladly have him see his company anatomiz'd, that he might take a measure of his own judgments wherein so curiously he had set this counterfeit', and they economically set their trap so that each will be 'the whip of the other' (IV.iii.30–5). The first stage of the trap exposes Parolles, in sham pursuit of his lost drum, as the fraud and coxcomb, the 'counterfeit module' (IV.iii.96) and craven informer that he is. The second stage turns the tables upon the now indignant, and betrayed, Bertram. The latter appears, in extremely high spirits after his rendezvous with Diana, and that he deserves what he gets is underlined by his airy account of the 'sixteen businesses' he has dispatched (IV.iii.82–9) since the news of Helena's death.

Parolles, having surrendered unconditionally at the first syllable of the Lords' 'terrible language', is now beyond shame – 'If ye pinch me like a pasty' (IV.iii.119–20), he says, he can betray no more military intelligence than he possesses, which, when it comes to a run-down on the French commanders, he is determined to embellish with details that will, he is confident, endear him to his interlocutors. Thus it comes about that the trickster Lords, including Bertram – 'a foolish idle boy, but for all that very ruttish' (207) – hear no good of themselves. The blindfold removed, face to face with the objects of his 'pestiferous' slanders, Parolles' exposure is complete.

The 'cure' proves wonderfully effective; more so than Malvolio's even, perhaps because Parolles has had a measure of self-knowledge all along concerning at least his 'foolhardy tongue': 'Tongue, I must put you into a butter-woman's mouth, and buy myself another of Bajazeth's mule if you prattle me into these perils' (IV.i.41–3). But he goes on paroling himself into perils, and that it is by the Lords' gobbledegook – 'choughs' language' (IV.i.19) – that a mean-spirited braggart is undone is no more than poetic justice. Or homeopathy. Self-knowledge, self-acceptance can hardly go further than that of Parolles, shamed beyond words, disgraced, despised, but alive:

> Yet am I thankful. If my heart were great
> 'Twould burst at this. Captain I'll be no more,
> But I will eat and drink and sleep as soft
> As captain shall. Simply the thing I am
> Shall make me live. . . .
> Rust, sword; cool, blushes; and Parolles live
> Safest in shame. . . .
> There's place and means for every man alive.
>
> (IV.iii.319–28)

But what of Bertram *vis-a-vis* his ex-alter ego? He repudiates him, of course. He is now, 'A pox upon him! ... a cat' (IV.iii.254–5) whom he detests. But does he see anything of himself in this unmasking? 'What a past-saving slave is this!' 'Damnable both-sides rogue!' (IV.iii.135, 214), he says, failing to recall that the only after-thought he had about Diana was a fear of ever hearing of her again. We might adapt the courtier's rhetorical question regarding Parolles: 'Is it possible he should know what he is, and be that he is?' (IV.i.44–5). Is it possible that Bertram knows what Parolles is, and be as *he* is?

Bertram's own exposure, indeed, is still to come. At present he still 'thinks himself made' (IV.iii.16–17) by his battle honours and bed victories. If the gulling of Parolles dramatizes the demise in Bertram of Parolles the effeminate tongue-man, Parolles the feather-man remains to be demolished. Parolles himself, though he smells, is still very much alive – on handouts from the contemptuous Lafew. He must still run the gauntlet of Lavatch's olfactory insults, just as Bertram will run the gauntlet of the women's unmasking. The foppish kinship between them is neatly brought out by Bertram's affectation of a velvet patch (we have not heard that he was wounded) upon which Lavatch lavishes his scurrilous witticisms.

The final scene has the curious effect of a replay, only this time with the young women firmly in charge of the act. The elders are once more engaged in match-making, Lafew's daughter and Bertram this time, an opportune circumstance Bertram seizes with alacrity. Once more paternal benevolence turns into ferocity when Diana's possession of Helena's ring, given her, we recall, by the King as a pledge of his gratitude, makes the King suspect foul play, even murder, on Bertram's part.

And Bertram, trapped between rings, the inherited, patrilinear ring that he gave, the virginal, betrothal ring that he took? Yes, he lies, and wriggles and prevaricates. His snobbery is distasteful; chivalry was never his strong point. Like Parolles, in his recognition scene, he is disgraced, left with no face to save, his 'champion Honour' exposed for the broken reed it is.

But what, after all, do his critics expect? He is trapped, as he was at the beginning; he has a face, a life, to try to save.

He too is restored by Helena, who, like Mariana in *Measure for Measure*, wants no other, nor no better, man. Her 'O my good lord, when I was like this maid /I found you wondrous kind' (V.iii.303–4)[9] is, for his wounded ego, the one most restorative thing she could say. The bed-trick, it turns out, served his fantasy of virile masculinity, and trumped it. For he finds in the woman he seduced, the woman he fled – a nurturing, saving presence, a sexually compatible bride and the mother of his child. He is still bewildered when he says to the King, 'If she, my liege, can make me know this clearly /I'll love her dearly, ever, ever dearly' (V.iii.309–10). But I myself do not find his 'Both, both. O pardon!' (V.iii.302) necessarily perfunctory. Certainly an actor need not make it so.

Are they a mismatch? More, or less, than anyone else in life or in literature?

Is *All's Well* a 'problem' play, and as such deserving of relegation to second-class status? It has been my claim that no such special category is required for the elucidation of *All's Well*. It exhibits a firm structural family resemblance to the earlier maturation comedies. If it anticipates in certain aspects a late romance like *Cymbeline*, it is no more problematic for that reason than any other play in the Shakespearean opus (or any other), each play being manifestly transitional between its precursors and its successors.

Certainly the vicissitudes of motive and meaning caught and displayed in the web of its text engage our closest attention. If we allow its complexities, its psychological depth and finesse, their due, we might well admit it once more into the canon of Shakespeare's most admired plays. Where, to adapt once more Parolles' famous self-summation: simply the thing it is shall make it live.

The King, by the way, is still, at the end of *All's Well*, indefatigably in search of a marriage partner – this time for Diana Capilet.

NOTES

1 See W.W. Lawrence, *Shakespeare's Problem Comedies*.
2 See e.g. Richard A. Levin, '*All's Well* and All Seems Well', *Shakespeare Studies*, 13 (1980), 131–42.
3 Richard Wheeler, p. 75, quotes Eric Partridge, *Shakespeare's Bawdy* (New York, 1955) on the sexual suggestiveness of 'stone', 'fire', 'motion', 'touch', '[a]raise', and 'pen'.
4 Otto Rank noted the Oedipal motif in the very first lines of the play as early as 1912, and found 'the tabooed relationship of mother and son underlying a good deal of the play'. See Norman Holland, 154. Literary critics, on the other hand, have made surprisingly little of suggested unconscious motivations. Significantly, however, Bernard Shaw, in whose 'deeper affections' the play was 'rooted', found the Countess 'the most beautiful old woman's part ever written': *Shaw on Shakespeare*, ed. Edwin Wilson (London, 1961), p. 10.
5 G.K. Hunter provides an account of the textual problem in his commentary on the lines in the New Arden edition.
6 Cf. Helena's 'riddle' in I.iii.212: 'But riddle-like lives sweetly where she dies', in which the wit masks a wish by way of the Elizabethan *double entendre* in 'dies'. Phyllis Gorfain, 'Puzzle and artifice: the riddle as metapoetry in *Pericles*', *Shakespeare Survey*, 29 (1976), makes the interesting suggestion that the paradoxes and contradictions out of which riddles are contrived constitute a 'schema of marriage' – children being born of male and female, and mediating between past and future. See also Freud's account of the *aliquis* 'riddle' in *The Psychopathology of Everyday Life* (PFL 5, 46–9).

Motive and meaning in *All's Well That Ends Well*

7 G.K. Hunter admits Parolles' stage success as a humour character but finds no way to 'fit him into this play', or 'to balance him against the different kind of reality' of Helena (xlviii). But see Robert Rogers, *A Psychoanalytic Study of the Double in Literature*, ch. 8 and passim, for a very useful account of character 'doubling', especially the latent, 'secret sharer' kind, as 'a fundamental mechanism' for the representation of psychic conflict.

8 I have attempted to develop a theory of exorcist Shakespearean comic form in *Comic Transformations in Shakespeare* (London, 1980).

9 'Sexually responsive' was one of the many nuances of the word in Elizabethan English, which included the archaic 'natural' and the modern 'well-intentioned' or 'good-natured'.

REFERENCES

Brooks, Peter, 'Repetition, repression and return: *Great Expectations* and the study of plot', *NLH* (1980).

Frye, Northrop, *Anatomy of Criticism* (Princeton, NJ: Princeton University Press, 1957).

Holland, Norman, *Psychoanalysis and Shakespeare* (New York: Farrar, Straus, 1979).

Lawrence, W.W., *Shakespeare's Problem Comedies* (New York: Macmillan, 1931).

Mansfield, Katherine, *Journal*, ed. John Middleton Murry (London: Constable, 1927; repr. 1954).

Nicoll, Allardyce, *Shakespeare* (London, 1952).

Raysor, T.M., ed., *Coleridge's Shakespeare Criticism* (London: Dent, 1960).

Rogers, Robert, *A Psychoanalytic Study of the Double in Literature* (Detroit: Wayne State University Press, 1970).

Ure, Peter, *Shakespeare: The Problem Plays* (London: Longman, 1961).

Wheeler, Richard P., *Shakespeare's Development and the Problem Comedies* (Berkeley and Los Angeles: University of California Press, 1981).

3
Amorous fictions and *As You Like It*
BRIAN GIBBONS

The date of *As You Like It* is usually accepted as 1599, although the play's direct source, Thomas Lodge's *Rosalynde*, had been first published as long ago as 1590 and so too had the finest pastoral romance of all in English, Philip Sidney's *Arcadia*. Such was their popularity that *Rosalynde* was reprinted in 1592 and 1596, and *Arcadia* in 1593, before both of them were again reprinted in 1598. According to some scholars it was a revival of Lyly's pastoral comedies by the children's companies that gave an immediate incentive to Shakespeare and his company, with their new Globe Theatre, to respond to the revived fashion for pastoral comedy.[1] It is my contention that what we know of the circumstances of Shakespeare's company in 1599, and of Shakespeare's work of the time, makes his decision to turn to pastoral more than opportunist.

As You Like It is a self-consciously stylish play, and in this essay I seek to explore its style as a work of theatre, not simply of literature. I do so by comparing and contrasting it with the non-dramatic works of Lodge and Sidney in the hope of identifying Shakespeare's particular use of pastoral on this occasion and of showing the ways he found to translate into the language of theatre, effects achieved in non-dramatic pastoral literature. I take it that the new pressure of intelligence to which Shakespeare subjects the pastoral mode in *As You Like It* (which represents an advance on his earlier limited use of pastoral elements in his plays) owes more to the example of Sidney than Lodge. I certainly find that to return to *The Arcadia* with *As You Like It* in mind sharpens response to Sidney's art.

As You Like It, which was almost certainly completed in 1599, the year after the works of Lodge and Sidney were reprinted, contains like *Henry V* allusions to the new Globe Theatre. *Henry V* is also probably of 1599, and although the differences between the two plays are obvious, they have one important thing in common: *Henry V*, like *As You Like It*, is strikingly preoccupied with highlighting questions of narrative technique and dramatic and literary form, with theatre's unique expressive resources and, conversely, with its stark limits. It is reasonable to attribute this marked emphasis to the fact of the newly acquired playhouse, but it may also be significant that 1599 is the year of Ben Jonson's first revolutionary experiment with metatheatrical comedy, *Every Man Out of His Humour*. In this context, Shakespeare's choice of pastoral as one of the modes to translate into theatre at this time seems to me to be an inevitable one.

In the space of two or three years from 1598 Shakespeare produced, in addition to the epic history, *Henry V*, and the pastoral comedy, *As You Like It*, two romantic tragi-comedies, *Much Ado About Nothing* and *Twelfth Night*, a satiric history, *Troilus and Cressida*, a farce, *The Merry Wives of Windsor* (though this yet awaits satisfactory classification), and *Hamlet*. In a burst of such extraordinary creative activity, in which he seems as a matter of deliberate decision to have chosen sharply contrasting kinds of play and several new modes (something which the old designation 'middle period' scarcely emphasizes) – in a phase when, in short, Shakespeare's interest in the expressive resources and limitations of different kinds of theatre seems clearly to have been intense – it is entirely appropriate that he should decide to turn to pastoral, given that mode's particular reputation and particular traditions, its oblique treatment of its narrative subject, its invitation to the artist to reflect on his art, its prompting an audience to recognize his artistry.

So when, in *As You Like It*, Orlando interrupts a conversation between Jaques and Ganymede by making an exuberant entrance, exclaiming 'Good day and happiness, dear Rosalind' (IV.i.28), Jaques reacts immediately to this as an unwelcome tone, lyric, and with it an alien mode, romance, to say nothing of the intolerable sense, simple well-being! He turns on his heel with the retort, 'Nay then God buy you, and you talk in blank verse!' In this collision between satire and romance the elaborate prose of the melancholy man is shown up as symptomatic of his vanity, while at the same time the open eager style of the lover, as we are amused to note, finds expression in less than artless metrical form. Here Shakespeare gets excellent comic effect by joining together what Ben Jonson held all men should keep asunder.

At first sight Shakespeare's title for the play, *As You Like It*, emphasizes style only to disarm critics as they enter the theatre. Here, it seems to say, shall you see only pleasure of a familiar kind in a well-tried style – and the seemingly simple art of the opening scenes may confirm such an impression. Yet pastoral is often mischievous in its manipulation of the audience, and *As You Like It* is almost studious in its adherence to the conventions of pastoral. We may well, on second thoughts, suspect ambiguity in the play's title, recognizing it to be glancing outwards at the restrictions imposed by audience taste (what *you* like) and simultaneously glancing inwards at the author's attentiveness to decorum, pastoral being too dominant a genre, and too complete a system of construction, to permit more than variations on old themes. Shakespeare in the event takes the opportunity with both hands, finding in the theory and style of pastoral itself a fertile comic subject, and transforming its themes into dramatic poetry of a kind that honours the shade of Sidney.

If we accept that the Epilogue is an integral element in the play we must find it acting to reinforce this critical view of the audience's taste for mere fiction and false appearances. The boy-actor of Rosalind-Ganymede, still in costume as a woman, steps forward for the Epilogue, half out of (yet still half in) the fictional frame, and asks the audience what they have earlier heard Ganymede ask Oliver in the play: was not this well counterfeited? This is just as piquant the second time, since we still do not have a real girl or real boy but yet another created dramatic part, this time of boy-actor half-impersonating the play's heroine. This no-man's-land, so to speak, the obverse of a Jonsonian induction, this fictional representation of half-created fiction, corresponds to that other no-man's-land where pastoral is situated, between the present representation and the ideal world it strives to recover, to translate.

The play begins by wilfully underlining the fact of its fictionality as Le Beau gives his news: 'There comes an old man, and his three sons –' (I.ii.109) and Celia at once reacts to his style: 'I could match this beginning with an old tale.' In fact

Shakespeare has done exactly that, matching the number of the old man's sons to those of Sir Rowland de Boys, as his source, Lodge, had not. So here *As You Like It* is even more like an old tale than is the prose narrative of *Rosalynde* on which it is based. But this is to anticipate. For the moment let it be enough to observe how Shakespeare's teasing Epilogue makes an audience recognize how readily, even at this moment after the play has ended, they would surrender to the counterfeit of art, even when its deceptions are half-exposed.

And this too is consistent with the treatment of pastoral as we find it in the non-dramatic writing of Shakespeare's contemporaries, who felt expected to include threads of reflective commentary in the fabric of their narratives, often teasingly playful in drawing the reader's attention to the artifice. Thus Sidney in his *Old Arcadia* writes out for the reader a song which he says Cleophila sang, and then he remarks, 'I might entertain you, fair ladies, a great while, if I should make as many interruptions in the repeating as she did in the singing' (29). Sidney then gives a description of how much her sighing did interrupt the song, and this actually takes twice as long to read as the song itself did. Again, in Bk III, ch. 39 of *The Countess of Pembroke's Arcadia*, he begins: 'But Zelmane, whom I left in the cave hardly bestead ... makes me lend her my pen awhile to see with what dexterity she could put by her dangers' (654). Sidney pretends whimsically to have no control at all over his narrative: he would have us imagine it unfolding in various strands simultaneously in separate places, only one of which can be recorded at any one time. More startling still for its playful and absurd disturbance of the reader who may have succumbed to the charm of the fiction is Sidney's description of one of the disguised princes taking his lady's hand, 'and with burning kisses setting it close to her lips (as if it should stand there like a hand in the margin of a book to note some saying worthy to be marked) began to speak these words' (176).

Sidney's humorous but also carefully self-conscious reference to his own act of writing paradoxically serves to win the centre of the stage for the events narrated. The lover's hand is given immediacy by contrast with the mere sign for a hand printed in a book's margin, and this immediacy of the narrated event over the act of describing is stressed when we read on: for as the lover begins poetically to lament love's power to change men's states and torture them, he is interrupted by a rather more urgent instance of inconstant fortune in the form of a real lion and a she-bear, ready to tear him (and his lady) limb from limb on the spot.

Such emphasis on the act of writing serves not only to foreground the events narrated but, more basically, to stress the gap between the verbal process of narration – the narrator's and the reader's time – and the time and place in which the narrated events occur. This is consistent with pastoral exactly because its whole cast is reflective, expressive of a longing for simplicity of life and of art, for simplicity of language to describe forms of life remote from a present preceived as more complex, confused or colourless. Pastoral laments the gap between representation and its imagined subject, and in a sense its subject is this gap. Situated between a fallen present and an imaginary place and time, persistently endeavouring and persistently failing to translate that remote subject into the here and now, pastoral creates its own provisional condition: its presence involves simultaneous awareness of the absent imagined subject, and its nature is hence reflective, its status paradoxical.

This is apparent, for instance, in the song of the young prince Musidorus in Arcadia who, disguised as a shepherd, sings to the chaste princess Pamela 'to show what kind of shepherd I was'. The kind of shepherd he was, as we see from the song, is a shepherd only in metaphor; he remains a prince, his shepherd's weeds a discardable disguise. In his song, the pastoral metaphors are only that. They can be simply removed to leave the decoded statement. The prince in his own condition is a complex figure, only one aspect of whom is apparent in shepherd's costume. His language here, if shorn of its sheep's clothing, suddenly acquires the complexity of court poetry. The shapely closure of pastoral's decorum offers only illusory containment, as the adjectives 'fruitless' and 'endless', and the verb 'upholds' indicate:

> My sheep are thoughts which I both guide and serve,
> Their pasture is fair hills of fruitless love:
> On barren sweets they feed, and feeding starve:
> I wail their lot, but will not other prove.
> My sheephook is wanhope, which all upholds:
> My weeds, desire, cut out in endless folds.

Amorous fictions and *As You Like It*

> What wool my sheep shall bear, while thus they live,
> In you it is, you must the judgement give. (232)

To speak of Shakespeare 'translating' pastoral romance into a play, as I do, may serve to emphasize the nature and scale of the process, 'removing from one person, place or condition to another' and 'changing into another language while retaining the sense'.[2] Looking more closely at the idea of translation one sees that there is a qualification to be made to this sort of definition, since there is something ineffaceable in a work of art which will alter the native character of the language into which it is translated, thereby creating something new: there inheres in a translation the shadow of the absent original which makes it a different thing from an independent work of art in either language. In fact Shakespeare seems to have wanted actually to stress the derivative literary model which he translated in *As You Like It*, and I hope to examine some of the ways in which he makes us aware of it. It is not only *As You Like It*, but also the preceding non-dramatic narratives *Arcadia* and *Rosalynde*, which stress their status as imitations, which call attention to the gap between themselves and antecedents with stronger claims to authenticity, being less veiled by repeated translations. Such purer narratives take the form of romance, an extended action whose configurations correspond to deep emotional patterns and whose process irresistibly absorbs the solitary reader, who finds his secret hopes, desires, and dreams represented there in forms his conscious mind permits him to feed on uninhibitedly.

Sidney's *Arcadia* is a great work of literary imagination, whose power and wit must have influenced Shakespeare at levels deeper than most of the materials from which he borrowed his plots. To Sidney Shakespeare could look for subtle observation of the play of motive and counter-motive, for openness to the surprising mixtures of elements in intimate relationships developing – this above all – in time. The striking features of Shakespeare's romantic comedies are their depiction of major personal development in the chief protagonists, presented in a context of busy, diverse, humorous contrasts. I would not rule out the notion that *The Arcadia* was used as a source (in the orthodox sense) in more places than Shakespeare-source-hunters have so far suggested, but here I am concerned with influence at a much more profound level. Sidney sets an example in depicting processes of change, of growth, and capacity for love, without protecting his characters from painful as well as ridiculous revelations about their personal inadequacy, and the mingled yarn from which experience is made; and Sidney continuously alters the degree of sympathy with which the narrative engages the reader, and the angle of vision from which it is recorded, so that his style enacts rather than simply conveys this incessantly dialectical record.

Sidney's narrator, and his characters in *The Arcadia*, always speak, sing and write within a decorum. In this sense there are no truly internal voices of self-communion. In place of a hesitant, erratic inner voice, Sidney presents one aspect of a character using oratorical means to address himself or herself.

Sidney makes distinct his frequent shifts from one style to another, and this sometimes has an abruptly dramatic effect. The reader, made conscious of the art of a particular style, becomes aware also of what its decorum excludes (this is comically evident in the speech of Miso, for instance). In style, and in the narrative itself also, Sidney makes outlines emphatic, but the eye is consequently drawn also to what lies beyond (or behind) the present subject, implied or as yet unseen or unsaid. This awareness of gap, of vacant space, is a characteristic feature of the pastoral mode: in defining the frame so consciously, Sidney ensures that we think also about what is precisely not said, so keeping us critically alert. In isolating and outlining an attitude or a group of figures, a detachable and summarizable meaning may be indicated, emblemizing the speaking picture, yet this emblemizing process is also resisted by the fluid current of dramatic action and the contrast and comparison of styles involved in it, making our assent to such emblems, when they seem too restricted or static, more than reluctant.

To approach Shakespeare by way of some detailed episodes from Sidney's *Arcadia* may serve to identify in the non-dramatic, written mode, techniques and effects which Shakespeare translates into pastoral drama in *As You Like It*; for the process is much more thorough and complex than might be suggested by Duke Senior's speeches, which well merit the implied ironic criticism of his courtier, Amiens, that style alone is not enough:

> Happy is your Grace,
> That can translate the stubbornness of fortune
> Into so quiet and so sweet a style.   (II.i.18–20)

Amorous fictions and *As You Like It* 59

In *As You Like It* Shakespeare employs the circumstances of stage performance to set the written in contrast to the spoken word. Episodes in verse are juxtaposed to prose; the revelation of character through realistic conversation is contrasted to formal emblematic descriptions of people (Jaques and the stricken deer, II.i.25–66; or Ganymede's mock-portrait of the typical lover's 'careless desolation', III.ii.359–71). Written poems are brought on stage and pinned up, or read aloud to other characters and to the theatre audience in a critical spirit. Faultless songs are sung to musical accompaniment, creating emotion no mere words, spoken or written, can equal.

In terms of theatre spectacle, the physical charm of Ganymede, the strength and grace of Orlando, the mimic skill of Touchstone, the foulness of Audrey, make a direct impact on the audience's eyes and senses; but surprising emphasis is also placed on what is withheld from the audience's view, though described with literary art and having tantalizingly visual interest: the natural landscape; the weather; Orlando found sleeping under a tree, 'stretched along like a wounded knight' (III.ii.236); Oliver asleep and menaced by a green and gold serpent and a lioness; Orlando, bleeding, falling in a faint (only a shadow of this is seen on stage, when Ganymede faints on hearing of his wound).

Shakespeare not only reproduces the ingredients of non-dramatic pastoral as readers like it, he ensures also that the variety of ways of representing experience, which the contrasting styles afford, will constitute an implicit critical debate, to which nonsense and parody make telling contributions. While this is possible in non-dramatic narrative like Sidney's, it is stressed in the extra dimension of theatre in *As You Like It*, where Shakespeare's necessary concern with movement, and with time, sets against the writer's or painter's belief in the value of pattern the theatrical truth that a tableau is no sooner achieved than it must dissolve.

Sidney's account of the princess Philoclea falling in love with a graceful Amazon (whom she fails to detect as a prince, Pyrocles, in disguise) begins apparently by chance; the narrator has been describing a day's hunting when he suddenly remembers the princess: 'And alas, sweet Philoclea', he cries, 'how hath my pen till now forgot thy passions' (237). As he turns to tell her story, the day's hunting nevertheless lingers in his mind, yielding the brooding simile, 'she was like a young fawn who, coming in wind of the hunters, doth not know whether it be a thing or no to be eschewed' (238). We are told that Philoclea falls for the Amazon at first sight. She behaves exactly like a character in a stage play, miming the conventional signs of infatuation. Sidney presents this as a scene to be acted, and in a style visually reminiscent of the Commedia dell'Arte:

> And if Zelmane sighed, she should sigh also; when Zelmane was sad, she deemed it wisdom and therefore she would be sad too. Zelmane's languishing countenance, with crossed arms and sometimes cast up eyes, she thought to have an excellent grace, and therefore she also willingly put on the same countenance, till at the last, poor soul, ere she were aware, she accepted not only the badge but the service, not only the sign but the passion signified. (239)

Sidney maintains a distance between tenor and vehicle in his own prose even if Philoclea cannot in reality. His own metaphors depict her susceptibility to signs and images; but though Sidney is not unsympathetic to the girl's tender pictorial fancies he makes clinically clear their graduated increase in sexual feeling, as he tells us how she progressed from emblematic frame to emblematic frame: 'First she would wish that they two might live all their lives together, like two of Diana's nymphs. ... Then would she wish that she were her sister. ... Then grown bolder, she would wish either herself or Zelmane a man, that there might succeed a blessed marriage betwixt them' (239). These brittle images disintegrate under pressure from below, where in her dreams Philoclea encounters self-begotten images that frighten her. Her whole personal development is presented in terms of her relation to images. Those of her secure childhood identity are reflected in her mother and sister. They become painfully defamiliarized as she acquires a separate selfhood through love for the Amazon, who at first seems an ideal female image, but very soon becomes disturbingly ambivalent.

Her sister Pamela, who reflects her childish self, repeats her own transformation into melancholy lovesickness. Her mother, who also falls for the Amazon, suddenly appears in the hostile role of sexual rival, presenting an image, distressingly close to Philoclea, of lust and jealousy: adult sexuality at

Amorous fictions and *As You Like It* 61

its most rank. So, torn by alienation, burned by desire for she knows not what, she feels as if, while acting a part (as we see she did when imitating the Amazon), the part has taken possession of her, and an alien person acts out a role through her own body: 'For now indeed love pulled off his mask and showed his face unto her, and told her plainly that she was his prisoner. Then needed she no more paint her face with passions, for passions shone through her face' (240).

We recognize that, viewed externally, this looks farcical, yet we sympathize with her inner dilemma. Sidney deploys metaphors drawn from the theatre – masks, costumes, disguises, expressive gestures and signs – and these we can see to be psychologically valid (as well as being appropriate to an intrigue plot, in which she finds herself). Philoclea's development proceeds from one imprinting (in the ornithological sense) to another, more appropriate to her maturation: she passes from a state of narcissism to the brink of love for the opposite sex, in the process discovering jealousy at her own mother; and Sidney even intensifies the image of adolescent crisis by making her father also lust for the Amazon, so producing a situation claustrophobic and perverse as much as farcical. Philoclea is not willingly perverse; rather we recognize that she is undergoing a reorientation of the personality which is serious rather than ridiculous. Sidney's use of the analogy of stage comedy achieves, then, a double perspective, making the reader recognize two separate, opposed codes in the narrative: one detached, one sympathetic.

To depict the full onset of sexual love in Philoclea, Sidney creates a set of episodes, constructed in a subtly modified version of exemplary drama, in which setting, action and gesture are endowed with symbolic and emblematic visual meaning. Philoclea, suffering isolation 'by the smoke of those flames wherewith else she was not only burned but smothered', seeks comfort in a wood which was a favourite haunt in happier times; now, that familiar tuft of trees 'with the shade the moon gave through it, it might breed a fearful kind of devotion to look upon it' (240). In this place is 'a goodly white marble stone that should seem had been dedicated in ancient time to the Sylvan gods'. Sidney explains that only a short time before she first met the Amazon, Philoclea had taken her pen and written a poem on the white and smooth marble, praying that she might remain chaste. In the poem (which Sidney records for us to read) she makes the marble an emblem of her pure mind.

Though Philoclea does not know, apparently, what Sidney tells the reader about the place's dedication to the Sylvan gods, she does half-notice that the trees resemble a little chapel and that the place is half-concealed from Phoebus and Diana. Her poem may be addressed to chastity, but her attempt to dedicate the marble cannot succeed, cannot efface its more ancient consecration to powers of which her immaturity makes her dangerously ignorant:

> Thou purest stone, whose pureness doth present
>   My purest mind; whose temper hard doth show
> My tempered heart; by thee my promise sent
>   Unto myself let after-livers know. (241)

Now, returning to the marble stone at night in a state of emotional torment, she finds the moonlight will not allow her to read the words, and in any case the ink is now 'forworn and in many places blotted'. Although Philoclea sees at once how aptly the blotted lines reflect her present shame, she will not see her previous condition as other than pure. She composes new verses lamenting her shame, but this time she has no pen. These 'words unseen' thus represent her new discovery of mutability. Though she does not write them down, Sidney does do so. Though for Philoclea the words are ephemeral, as expressing a sense of futility, for Sidney they are to have a durable place in the larger frame of his narrative. Not for him, one sees, is a poetic truth ephemeral. We witness Philoclea's dilemma as tender rather than ridiculous, as the pictorial view by itself might suggest.

As readers, our perspective is via Sidney's text, in which everything is expected to yield to interpretation, rather than having the contingent tendency to randomness of real life, with which Philoclea is shown struggling. For her the clear marble's meaning has changed like the moon, and the sense of obscurity will never quite evaporate. To the reader, that poem written in ink on the marble perfectly defines a state of mind both deluded and ephemeral. In Sidney's text it is preserved, in Arcadia effaced.

When she returns to the lodge she finds her sister Pamela also solitary and distraught, and reads in her appearance 'the badges of sorrow'. Pamela is discovered silent and motionless, not writing but reading: 'looking upon a wax candle which burnt before her; in one hand holding a letter, in the other her handkerchief which had lately drunk up the tears of her eyes' (244). Sidney presents a double image which refracts and clarifies, by subtle contrasts, the differences between two women so close, so very alike in all sorts of ways. We may well think of how often Shakespeare uses pairs of lovers (Hermia/ Helena and Rosalind/Celia, for example) in his comedies to present comparable effects. The sisters, lovelorn, console one another in a shared bed 'with dear though chaste embracements, with sweet though cold kisses' (245). Sidney makes the reader see in this the pictorial suggestion of Narcissus, but the dramatization gives immediacy to the characters' emotion: for each sister longs for another mate in the phantom embrace here: and in the psychological sense, narcissism is waning. Philoclea's development, though repeatedly depicted in fixed emblematic images which suggest it is frozen, can yet be glimpsed and felt *in motion* in the underlying narrative current, which draws the reader expectantly beyond the frame of such tableaux. Sidney prompts the thought that the Narcissus story only *begins* with a mirror-image.

There is tension between the narrative's weaving process and the moments of stillness in which a framed scene is displayed. Sidney's characters are often composed in a scene which for a moment metamorphoses into a set-piece out of Ovid, making them mythological. This is clear in the episode where Philoclea, wandering alone, comes upon the Amazon, whose face is bent over a stream, weeping: 'one might have thought', Sidney says, that he 'began meltingly to be metamorphosed to the under-running river'. The Amazon composes poetry, writing with a willow stick in the sand of the river bank (one degree even more ephemeral than ink on marble) verses which emblemize the stream as mirror of his tearful eyes:

In watery glass my watery eyes I see;
Sorrows ill eas'd, where sorrows painted be.   (326)

The Amazon unknowingly echoes Philoclea's second set of verses about the blotted marble, which (we recall) she did not write down at all. The Amazon's poem declares that the place has an echo, and as the poem ends Philoclea materializes in response to it by stepping into view (so neatly reversing the fate of Echo in Ovid).³ As the lovers begin to talk and the princess Philoclea learns that her Amazon is really a prince, Sidney, with another neat reversal of Ovid, compares her to Pygmalion finding his beloved statue coming to life as a real woman. Sidney then dissolves the mythological tableau in order to foreground the Arcadian narrative once more, taking up a string of recapitulatory metaphors: Philoclea is like a 'fearful deer', though now a deer coming to the 'best feed' (329); she cannot resist revealing her heart to the prince, yet fears such boldness will provoke him 'to pull off the visor'; but for her part, she exclaims, 'Shall I labour to lay marble colours over my ruinous thoughts?' (330).

It is as if we are observing the aboriginal emergence of fables in the simple archetypal world of pastoral which precedes the codifying of Ovid — and so it is only natural that Ovidian translation of pastoral should fleetingly intervene between the simple story of Arcadia and the reader. In *As You Like It* the direct physicality of performance gives present tense to the pastoral action, sometimes stilled so that Ovidian allusion may be foregrounded. We see how in Sidney such shifts in narrative register create drama: so, in the episode between Philoclea and the Amazon, the Ovidian configuration is more restricted (as well as more faintly outlined) than the Arcadian frame in which the princesses are described, and the reader is made aware of the ceaseless movement between the text's surface and its remoter vales.

Sidney's writing has a limpid clarity and exactness, his descriptions are focused, and the typically sharply etched outlines make figures and signs stand out distinct and separate from one another. We are aware of margins literally and figuratively. Ultimately indeed it is a fastidious subtlety of mind rather than eye to which his writing appeals, its system of contrasts appealing to our judgement as spectators in a vivid theatre of the mind. Yet, grounded as it is in scenic form, it must give any dramatist reading it food for thought.

By contrast, Thomas Lodge in *Rosalynde* requires caution. In his opening pages (160–1) he almost falls over his own metatextual conceits. After a formula from oral tradition, disarmingly simple – 'There dwelled adjoyning to the citie of *Bourdeaux* a Knight of most honorable parentage' – there intervenes a rhetorical pattern: 'Whom Fortune had graced with manie favours, and Nature honored with sundrie exquisite qualities, so beautified with the excellence of both, as it was question whether Fortune or Nature were more prodigal in deciphering the riches of their bounties.' These personifications prepare the reader for ever more bookish elements. The knight is rapidly given attributes fitting a writer's hero in an Elizabethan prose fiction, 'the stroake of his Launce no less forcible, than the sweetnesse of his tongue was perswasive'. Lodge insists on the overwhelming importance of eloquence, as against simple oral narration, because his work invokes the shade of John Lyly in its preface; but this hardly excuses the ridiculous lengths to which the narrative is pushed. The old knight Sir John senses that he has not long to live and resolves to deliver a speech, as well as his written Will, to his three sons. Lodge says that the old man is conscious of, and uses, the possibilities of his aged face as a source of persuasion, since 'the map of age was figured on his forehead: Honour sat in the furrowes of his face, and many yeares were pourtraied in his wrinkled liniaments, that all men perceive that his glasse was runne.'

Nevertheless, to take such a view of one's own features, as adjuncts to one's rhetorical performance (old age as a visual aid, so to speak), though it may possibly be allowable in a narrator, appears ludicrous if not grotesque in a dramatic character himself. The old man, however, Euphuist to the last, 'Having therefore death in his lookes to moove them to pitie, and teares in his eyes to paint out the depth of his passions', begins his oration to his three sons. Lodge sets the speech out on the page as an important textual event in its own right, with an upper-case title imitating the layout of a legal document or public proclamation:

SIR JOHN OF BORDEAUX LEGACIE HE
GAVE TO HIS SONNES

We notice, however, that it is supposed to be delivered spontaneously. Generally in *Rosalynde* stereotyped character and motive are baldly, explicitly accounted for in the authorial narrative. Scenes are staged in emblematic expository style. Action is held up while characters make formal orations for and against the alternative courses of action facing them, and their rhetoric is tediously elaborate, as when Rosader, coming upon his sleeping brother who lies in mortal danger from a lion, analyses the situation with all the restraint of a designer of mazes:

> Now Rosader, Fortune that long hath whipt thee with nettles, meanes to salve thee with roses; and having crost thee with manie frownes: now she presents thee with the brightnesse of her favours. Thou that didst count thy self the most distressed of all men, maist accompt thy selfe now the most fortunate amongst men; if fortune can make men happie, or sweete revenge be wrapt in a pleasing content. (216)

This effusion is prefaced, according to Lodge's custom, with the upper-case, centred title ROSADERS MEDITATION, and it is set out as an oration of (detachable) general interest.

*

It is interesting, in terms of Lodge's formal rhetorical mode, to examine *As You Like It* II.vii, where Orlando makes a heroic intrusion upon the courtly exiles as they are about to banquet. He draws his sword, and utters a suitably lofty command in keeping with his role: 'Forbear, and eat no more.' To his audience on stage, his pose and style are all too familiar, but stagey, quite disjunct from this occasion. His melodramatic claim 'I almost die for food, and let me have it' is answered with the relaxed and polite 'Sit down and feed, and welcome to our table', even perhaps with an air of faintly amused condescension. This sophisticated and subtle reaction to Orlando's speech becomes unmistakable in the Duke's mock-solemn repetition, with slight stylistic improvement, of Orlando's formal oration:

> If ever you have look'd on better days;
> If ever been where bells have knoll'd to church;
> If ever sat at any good man's feast;
> If ever from your eyelids wip'd a tear.... (II.vii.113–16)

This, to someone who has recently been reading Lodge, if not Sidney, parodies the typical procedure (and unintended absurdity) of romance, where formal rhetoric is utterly dissynchronized from the situation, time and place of the narrative action. Lodge does not provide Shakespeare with any central informing poetic idea; that of Fortune, which some critics have canvassed, is clumsily superimposed in Lodge and in *As*

Amorous fictions and *As You Like It* 67

You Like It serves as a butt of ridicule, parody and subversion from all sides, particularly from the dramatist himself. But Lodge does give Shakespeare one excellent thing, not to be found in Sidney: a heroine with gaiety and sprightliness.

Critics sometimes describe the mode of *As You Like It* as if it were anticipatory Chekhov. It may be worth recalling how different it is. Here is an intelligent comment on Chekhov's dramatic style in *The Cherry Orchard*:

> the call of the business to be done behind the scenes is almost more insistent than the call of what is to be enacted by the footlights; the stage is not so much a point or a focus as a passage over which his personages drift or scurry, a chance meeting place where we hear only fragments of their talk and see less important moments of their action.[4]

The same critical view sees much of the dialogue as elliptical, more important for its subtextual content than its overt function as exchange between characters. Compared to this, it is obvious that the structure of *As You Like It* foregrounds positively competitive encounters between contrasting characters, making dialogue often exciting as debate, in a manner Shaw himself, but for his determined obtuseness towards *As You Like It*, would have had to find congenial.

Viewed analytically, this play's style is indeed so far from Chekhov that it shows significant affinities with the technique of Shakespeare's last romances, where Shakespeare exploits sudden changes in style and even mode as part of an overall dramatic strategy, awaking surprise, shock and wonder in the audience. In these plays certain episodes are presented with a realism of social and psychological observation which would be congenial to a George Eliot; then suddenly a medieval rhyming Chorus-figure will take over, insisting on the simple primitive folk-tale level of the narrative, or highly self-conscious and mannered allusions to acting, to the technique of spectacular staging, or to the openly acknowledged presence of the audience, will insist that the entrances and exits and dialogue are recognized as artifice. Then, without warning, an irresistibly powerful dramatic illusion will be restored to seize the audience's full imaginative concentration.

In *As You Like It* many passages of dialogue present an illusion of lifelike spontaneous conversation, even in characters given to oratorical flights or witty repartee; particularly naturalistic are the conversations which, so far from being lively, animated and competitive, reveal one or both speakers to be dull in mood and halting in speech, as when Rosalind confesses she has not one word to throw at a dog (I.iii.3), or Jaques says to Orlando 'Let's meet as little as we can' (III.ii.253). Yet such episodes of naturalism are embedded in a plot whose overall shape is determined by the inexplicable and astonishing: at the beginning the sudden and violent malevolence of Duke Frederick; at the very last moment, the sensational news delivered by a messenger who is in himself surprising: he is Jaques de Boys:

> Let me have audience for a word or two.
> I am the second son of old Sir Rowland
> That bring these tidings to this fair assembly.
> Duke Frederick hearing how that every day
> Men of great worth resorted to this forest,
> Address'd a mighty power, which were on foot
> In his own conduct, purposely to take
> His brother here, and put him to the sword.
> And to the skirts of this wild wood he came,
> Where, meeting with an old religious man,
> After some question with him, was converted
> Both from his enterprise and from the world.
>
> (V.iv.150–61)

This announcement generates wonder; there is wonder too for this third de Boys brother, discovering he is just in time for the weddings of both his brothers as well as two other couples; the sending in of this forgotten third brother at the last moment seems deliberately to exaggerate the plot's artifice and the contrived tying up of all loose ends. Its chief effect is comic wonder and explicitly theatrical delight, but it reminds an audience of sensational moments elsewhere in the play: Frederick's anger, Orlando demanding food for his dying old servant at sword point, not to mention the heroine's dead faint, and the epiphany of Hymen, elements which seem clearly to anticipate *Cymbeline* and *The Tempest*.

What is most alien to the theatre of Chekhov here is the use of the style which states nothing obliquely, leaves nothing to be inferred, which employs expository soliloquies or asides, clearly announces entrances and exits, makes spectators expressly aware of the reasons for stage action, formally pat-

Amorous fictions and *As You Like It*

terms language so that its structures are brought to the surface, supporting other patterned codes.

In *As You Like It* strong emphasis is made on this open expository style right at the beginning, when a vigorous, well-spoken young man enters with an old man whose name, repeated for emphasis, is Adam. Adam's name helps suggest Biblical as well as folk-tale resonances. Orlando stresses his plight in physical terms, born gentle but stalled like an ox (I.i.10), denied education while even the horses of his brother are 'bred better; for besides that they are fair with their feeding, they are taught their manage' (I.i.11–12); nourishment for the mind we take for granted as essential to a hero of literary romance, but it is striking that equal stress is here placed on nourishment for the body. Adam, though aged and virtually worn out in body, is sustained by spiritual vigour. We recognize in this pair youth and age, and an emblem of the interplay of body and spirit. Shakespeare then adds to the group the lonely saturnine figure, Oliver, of whom Orlando has been speaking. Oliver's perfectly stereotyped cold villainy awakes instantly the hot resentment of his younger brother, who seizes him and proves the better wrestler. The tableau which results is a speaking picture: Adam, fatherly spectator, intervenes to prevent the potential fratricide.

From the play's outset, then, such archetypes, directly shown or formally described, secure for the play a deep structure in fable and keep the audience subliminally in touch with the primitive sources of the narrative's power. The basic dramatic structure maintains a naive expository attitude against which the varied display of fashionable literary manners, of wit and nonsense, is set in contrast.[5] In his consistent change of emphasis from his source, Lodge's *Rosalynde*, Shakespeare can be seen emphasizing a central theme of transformation through love which is very reminiscent of Sidney, while at the same time calling persistent attention to the effect upon pastoral themes and styles of their translation into dramatic form.

The extensive space and emphasis Lodge gives to the description of fights, roistering and general violence on a larger scale, is reduced in narrative terms and focused in the two violent wrestling bouts performed before the audience's eyes, making a shocking physical impact extremely early in the play. The first bout, between Orlando and Oliver (I.i.52–4) is violent, however short and inconclusive; the second (I.ii.200–3) is violent, complete and very conclusive indeed: Charles the professional having to be carried away speechless.

Once the impact of the violent wrestling bout is made, and the literal meaning of 'a fall' in wrestling is demonstrated, the word can become metamorphosed in the dialogue as a term for falling in love, and verbal wrestling, wit combats, many of which are vigorously competitive, can become the prevailing sport for everyone in Arden.

The repercussive shock-waves from the initial physical violence persist throughout the play, mainly below the surface of explicit action but glimpsed in the verbal account of the stricken deer, and again in the entry of the deer-slayers, before making one more direct impact when Rosalind falls unconscious on hearing of Orlando's wound as she looks at the bloody napkin.

The emotional malevolence of the wicked brothers Oliver and Duke Frederick is an indirect expression of violence and persists through the action. It propels the lovers into exile: their journeys are identified with the body and physical hardship, but the 'desert inaccessible' (II.vii.110) is soon reached, and is a place full of civilized people, whose hunting, before being a brute necessity for physical survival, is first of all a cultural rite, inspiring poetry and music. In the play hunting has a double value, as reality and as metaphor: in pastoral Arden, hunting is as much an embodiment of literary love imagery and a metaphor for political tyranny as it is the real thing from which metaphors are created. In the same way physical exile is a fact of the narrative but also a metaphor for spiritual freedom. The equal status of thing signified and sign is a feature of pastoral writing; so Shakespeare insists on recognition of the imperatives of the body as an essential precondition for true wit, and insists, remarkably, that the body's irrationality is essential as an informing substance for true style. In translating pastoral he gives pronounced emphasis through the language of the theatre to this literary and dramatic judgement. Self-consciousness in the writer of Elizabethan pastoral is, as we have seen, a constituent feature of the mode; in *As You Like It* Shakespeare begins to draw the audience's attention to style, in a spririt of playfulness, extremely early on.

In I.i.85–7, Shakespeare gives the villainous Oliver a moment alone on stage so that he can tell the audience directly

Amorous fictions and *As You Like It* 71

and simply of his feelings and plots. He calls for Charles the wrestler, to whom he puts a series of abrupt questions, making no comment whatever on the long and rather surprising answers. The overall dramatic style seems to be expository: the questions are not revelatory of Oliver's character or state of mind, they are merely a dramatist's device: 'What's the new news at the new court? ... Can you tell if Rosalind the Duke's daughter be banished with her father? ... Where will the old Duke live?' On the other hand, considering the muscle-bound masculinity presumably to be ascribed to a wrestler, the answers are so unexpectedly polished in their eloquence, and so romantically idealistic in feeling, that the incongruity must surely be deliberate and the audience is invited to savour the effect. Even though Charles, it could be argued, may be supposed to be partly protected by the obvious expository form, his effusions on the tenderness of feminine affection, or on the merry men who flock to Arden where they fleet time carelessly as they did in the golden world, seem altogether too improbable to explain away, and furthermore invite us to make an ironic reassessment of Orlando himself, who speaks uncommonly well for one who has been, as he claims to have been, starved of education. A moment or two later the two young ladies offer some excellently witty word-play, and show a quick sensitivity to other people's styles, so reinforcing the impression that Shakespeare wishes to alert his audience to the absurdities in pastoral and romance convention.

Soon after, in staging which has a hint of allegorical stiffness, young Orlando enters in exile accompanied by the faithful servant Adam, and the two young ladies take as their companion Folly, in the shape of Touchstone. They are all received by a Duke in exile presiding over a no-Court in which everybody habitually translates their surroundings, Nature and the elements, into consciously elaborated metaphor and allegory. (For the audience this is more complex, since the natural world they inhabit can also be recognized as having pastoral, literary-fictional status). The 'moralizing' of the natural world produces a bizarre reversal: courtiers in Arden, supposedly a 'desert', read it as allegory of civilization, finding 'books in the running brooks' (II.i.16) exactly like characters in *The Arcadia*.

Such details amount cumulatively to a thorough-going stylistic subversion which Shakespeare seems wilfully to encourage, and later this has become quite explicit, when in an exchange which is Shakespeare's invention, Orlando tells Ganymede that he finds it surprising Ganymede should speak so well: 'Your accent is something finer than you could purchase in so removed a dwelling' (III.ii.333–4). To the audience (including Celia, an on-stage spectator) who are here enjoying Rosalind's first moments in the riskily improvised part of 'saucy lackey', Ganymede's momentary embarrassment at this question is comic, but so also is Orlando for asking it, in a pastoral. Such a matter-of-fact attitude looks even more ridiculous, too, when he swallows Ganymede's explanation, which is as highly improbable as the purest traditions of pastoral fiction allow.

When the ladies begin their first scene Rosalind idly proposes, as a sport, falling in love. Given the self-conscious dramatic style Shakespeare creates here, the prompt appearance of the Fool is partly a comment on her flippancy. A moment or two later there is another interruption, this time the sophisticated courtier Le Beau (presumably he is supposed to live up to his name in dress and manner). This event the ladies treat as a frankly artificial bit of theatre, and Le Beau is to be put out of his part with mockery. Indeed the ladies' attitude does invite us to question such stagecraft, sending in this courtier, so conventional a stage type, in this perfunctory way, in order to get the story going.

Le Beau begins his tale with a sentence startlingly incongruous for a sophisticate: 'There comes an old man, and his three sons' (I.ii.109). Is this conscious parody? Celia is amused by its predictable and childish quality and mocks it (purely from the point of view of style) with flippant indecency: 'I could match this beginning with an old tale.' All the same, Le Beau's words might well serve to begin a non-dramatic version of *As You Like It* itself, and a moment later the ladies, despite themselves, do in fact become gripped by the tale when they realize that while they have been exchanging melancholy and silly remarks three young men have fallen to Charles the wrestler and now lie with little hope of life. The words Le Beau uses give way to the physical reality they describe: in confronting that, Rosalind can say no more than 'Alas'. Words fail her on the first of three memorable occasions in the play.[6] Presumably the number is not a coincidence.

For the climax of physical action Shakespeare shows tension

Amorous fictions and *As You Like It*

building up for Rosalind (IV.iii), although he does not build it up in the same degree for the audience. Rosalind notes Orlando's lateness with evidently real impatience. When someone enters it is not he but only Silvius. Then, when the next person enters, it is his brother Oliver, whom neither lady has ever before seen. Oliver, taking his time, delivers his fabulous report of having just been saved from two mortal dangers, a golden-and-green serpent as well as a nursing lioness (Lodge could only manage a lion). This speech, climaxing in the announcement that the bloody napkin which he brandishes is 'Dy'd' in Orlando's blood, has two simultaneous effects: it makes Celia fall in love, and Rosalind fall in a dead faint. In telling his tale Oliver demonstrates with his own body the physical wound Orlando suffered, to positively gruesome effect:

> and here upon his arm
> The lioness had torn some flesh away,
> Which all this while had bled; and now he fainted.
> (IV.iii.146–8)

This whole on-stage episode is Shakespeare's invention; Lodge offers no parallel to the meeting, the direct report, the falling in love at first sight of Celia, or the dead faint of Rosalind/Ganymede. Shakespeare gives pronounced visual and physical emphasis to this reception on stage of off-stage events, the romantic nature of which Shakespeare makes even more fantastic as he takes them over from Lodge. The pronounced extravagance of Oliver's tale is made evident to the audience by the sharp contrast of the matter-of-fact style in which it is delivered, by the very unexpected absence of witty raillery by the ladies, and by their completely unquestioning acceptance of it: indeed Rosalind's anxious impatience to hear what the bloody napkin has to do with Orlando makes her oblivious to everything except that one thing. The existential fact of the bloody cloth before her eyes blinds her to the tale's blatant romantic incredibility. Certainly, we can say that Love triumphs literally in her fall, but the literalness is not without absurdity, as she half-acknowledges when she revives: the cloth, a sign for passion, has exposed the actual passion she was concealing under the sign of a boy. To put it another way, Oliver's role as messenger is obvious to the audience, and the highly artificial tale he tells endows the napkin with a degree of unreality, as a stock stage property, to be recognized as a literary motif in the same breath as the literary lion and literary serpent, whose actual presentation on stage would be an absurdity too heavily distracting from Shakespeare's chief purpose here. The normally witty Rosalind's reaction exposes the gap between the pastoral fiction in which Ganymede figures and the dramatic present of *As You Like It* where Rosalind is to be found.

Our response to her faint is sympathetic, but also amused. Her reaction of fainting betrays intense emotion, acute vulnerability, and gives the lie to Ganymede's mockery of love's ideals, thereby honouring the shades of Ovid and of Marlowe, the 'dead shepherd'. Anticipating Orlando Rosalind here finds she 'can live no longer by thinking' (V.ii.50), cannot suppress or disguise her serious emotion. Yet at the same time the self-conscious theatricality of the episode's style is given almost as much prominence, for the audience: Oliver's matter-of-fact tone contrasts with the extraordinary story he relates in a manner so extreme as to appear absurd. The audience finds comedy in his assumption, when he addresses Ganymede, that he is talking to a fellow male and so perhaps should emphasize his stiff-upper-lip attitude. His brisk thrusting forward of the bloody napkin is, again, as the audience see, bound to give Ganymede an unintended violent shock.

All these details help to give comic momentum to his speech and to his splendidly unimpressed (and wonderfully incurious) comment on Ganymede's dead faint: 'Many will swoon when they do look on blood' (IV.iii.158). The further reflection an audience may make, that the attractive presence of Celia acts as a stimulus to Oliver's boastfully manly attitude, adds an even more Sidneian complexity to a complex comedy of mistaken identity, already reminiscent of Sidney in the sense that it is precisely *through this mode* that Shakespeare expresses the profounder theme, of self-discovery in love for another.

The pleasures and perils of eloquence are given pronounced critical attention in this play, as they are in *Much Ado* and *Twelfth Night*, but unhesitating eloquence as a value in itself appears suspect. Many forms of utterance, copious, curt, artless, elaborate, fantastic, curmudgeonly, formally oratorical or nonsensical, are displayed for their delightfulness and variety, but each is subjected to the process of contrast and comparison which informs Shakespeare's whole idea of theatre in *As You Like It*.

Sidney, it will be remembered, juxtaposes, as stuff for low comedy and caricature, the unselfconscious human animal in Miso, Mopsa and Dametas, against those who have the breeding and education to set their erected wit against their infected will. In III.iii.14–15, Audrey's remark to Touchstone, 'I do not know what "poetical" is. Is it honest in deed and word? Is it a true thing?' summons unwittingly the shade of Sidney in *An Apologie of Poetrie*, where the relation between decorum of behaviour and decorum of speech is affirmed, and their status as arts is basic to the discussion. That Touchstone, doughty defender of the claims of the body, should be provoked to some of his greatest exertions of wit by the basic Audrey and the plain Corin, is characteristic of the play's faux-naive working; indeed Corin's simplicities – for example 'I know the more one sickens the worse at ease he is; and that he that wants money, means, and content is without three good friends' (III.ii.23–5)—are so accurate as criticism of Touchstone's situation as to seem like urbane irony, or even flat parody of one of the Fool's habits of wit, as when he responds to Rosalind's 'O Jupiter, how weary are my spirits!' with the remark, 'I care not for my spirits, if my legs were not weary' (II.iv.1–2).

It is true that in Rosalind/Ganymede Shakespeare presents speech which might be thought to approach an ideal of artifice fused with spontaneity, but this is rather a reader's than a playgoer's judgement. It is certainly true that Rosalind's key qualities of nerve, of risk-taking and vitality, springing from acute, quick response to the moment, live in her eloquent speech; but in a performance of the play it is when she shows herself ready in her double self to immerse in nonsense, self-contradiction, parody, incoherence, and, climactically, speechlessness, that the play's and her most important moments come.

So Shakespeare stresses the practical physical hardship, the physical risk, and the physical pleasures which a real journey, real countryside, and real sexual feeling, must involve, and he has of course real physical actors to perform the play. Nevertheless, and wholly consistent with pastoral's ambiguity, he keeps this sense of practical experience in tension with artifice and reflection. His basic style in *As You Like It* is by no means to be described as realism.

*

At the centre of *As You Like It* Rosalind, in the guise of Ganymede, watched by a usually silent Celia, performs a translation of herself as she projects for Orlando a delicious dream-courtship, controlled and devised according to the rules of romance. Neither Orlando nor Ganymede makes love in his own person, exactly; that is deferred by the rules of the game. In the contemplation of this 'fiction' Celia too is silently transformed in unconscious preparation for meeting the transformed Oliver, Orlando's brother. The persona of Ganymede is an uncertain entity, insisting that all things are provisional, including the fiction in which he himself exists, a pretty youth in a *paysage moralisé* which is realized only by the play's language and which, on the Elizabethan stage, can only be distinguished (if at all) from the Court, or from nowhere (an unlocalized playing space) by at most a few token property trees.

Rosalind appears 'in her own person' again at the end of the play, but here she is translated anew, being no longer the Rosalind of the beginning of the play but now a Rosalind in whom the shadow of the absent Ganymede remains, making her now different from either the one or the other. She introduces a classical deity: Hymen is a mythological, if not a magical, figure, and in his actual appearance on stage a new kind of theatre supervenes. In Lodge there is a real priest who conducts a real marriage service. Elizabethan law forbade the presentation of a marriage service in a play, thus posing an obvious technical problem for the Globe playwright. Shakespeare's solution is to bring on stage this mythological deity to stand beside the play's familiar human characters, effecting a transformation of the dramatic decorum. The theatrical artifice of the episode is qualified by the highly ritualized staging and music, which translate initial disbelief among the characters on stage into wonder, while leaving the audience still partly conscious of an element of trickery.

Hymen has several simultaneous meanings. He is pure theatrical surprise, a 'happening' inducing wonder. He is an evident metaphor for Christian marriage, devised to evade Elizabethan censorship. He is a fashionable Renaissance theatre figure, from the Court Masque. Finally, he is literally

Amorous fictions and *As You Like It* 77

and simply the ancient god of marriage, truly at home in Arden and the remote world of pastoral. Through Rosalind the equivocal relation of trickery to magic, of theatrical to spiritual wonder, is evoked, and through Jaques, with his disenchanted realistic voice and presence, a double view of this ending is indicated, bringing an audience to a new sense of ending and unending. Hymen exists in the true dimension of pastoral, between here and there, dialectically: a place of the mind, and of the theatre, in Shakespeare's translation.

NOTES

1 Agnes Latham, ed., *As You Like It* (London, 1975), p. xxvi. Quotations from Lodge's *Rosalynde* are from Geoffrey Bullough, ed., *Narrative and Dramatic Sources of Shakespeare*, vol.2 (London and New York, 1968). Quotations from Sidney are from: (a) Jean Robertson, ed., *The Old Arcadia* (Oxford, 1973). This work was not published in Shakespeare's lifetime; (b) the version known as *The Countess of Pembroke's Arcadia*, ed. Maurice Evans (London, 1977). The episodes discussed in the present essay appeared in the 1590 edition and subsequent editions. The 1590 edition consisted of Sidney's revised version of *The Old Arcadia*: Bks I, II and part of III, ending in mid-fight and mid-sentence.

2 These definitions of 'translate' are from the *Oxford English Dictionary* (I,i and II,2). For a searching discussion of the idea of translation see Hans-Jost Frey's article in *Colloquium Helveticum*, no. 3, Bern, 1986.

3 *Metamorphoses*, Bk III; Echo, a nymph vainly in love with Narcissus, pines away for grief to nothing but her voice.

4 George Calderon, writing in 1911, quoted by Jan McDonald, 'Productions of Chekhov's plays in Britain before 1914', *Theatre Notebook*, 44 (1980), 33.

5 By changing Lodge's story so that the usurper Duke becomes brother of the exiled Duke, and by excluding the third de Boys brother, Shakespeare contrives a highly symmetrical pattern whose function is expository, in which the characters are paired, bound either by close kinship or by love. Shakespeare adds a bond of love between the exiled Duke and Orlando's dead father, which completes the pattern of strong ties between all the main characters. In reducing the vague supporting cast of *Rosalynde*, he gives each Duke one leading courtier: Le Beau is discreetly disloyal to Frederick, Amiens is discreetly ironic in flattering Senior's stylish pose of literary stoicism. If these courtiers are instances of equivocal service, then Shakespeare's important new characters Touchstone and Jaques present, as marginal figures, more detached questioning of the pastoral and social ties between human beings. Even the wrestler Charles is shown to be honourable (accepting no bribes as in Lodge), despising Orlando only after being made to believe him 'a secret and villainous contriver' against his elder brother. Shakespeare drastically abbreviates, reduces and concentrates Lodge's story to give central emphasis to love's power, and he juxtaposes clearly contrasted groups, in highly symmetrical patterns of twos and threes, to generate a visual, and then

a more general, dialectic of contrast and comparison. The prolonged bad relations between the brothers in Lodge are telescoped by Shakespeare and simplified, so that Orlando goes directly into exile, with Rosalind fresh in his mind. When she arrives in Arden, with a Celia who has come with her out of pure love (not as in Lodge banished like Rosalind), the poems they find on trees and shrubs are by Orlando himself, not, as in Lodge, by a minor character, Montanus. Arriving in Arden, Orlando interrupts the Ducal banquet with sword drawn and heroic martial challenge, although in Lodge Rosader shows only polite civility.

6   I.ii.123; I.iii.1–3; IV.iii.156.

4

Shakespeare's disguised duke play: Middleton, Marston, and the sources of *Measure for Measure*

THOMAS A. PENDLETON

Reference to 'the sources of *Measure for Measure*' inevitably summons up those versions of the 'monstrous ransom' story – especially Whetstone's and Cinthio's – with which Shakespeare was familiar and which have been exhaustively studied by previous investigators. Yet there has been something incomplete in the investigation, for *Measure for Measure* is a monstrous ransom play only in a unique and limited sense. Shakespeare's Isabella, apparently alone among all the comparable ladies in all the comparable versions, refuses to pay the ransom. Indeed, it hardly seems that the traditional moral dilemma the ransom imposes is for Isabella a dilemma at all. She is, of course, extremely regretful that Claudio must die, but he must. 'More than our brother is our chastity' (II.iv.184) she announces, and at no point in the play does she appear to feel that the moral priorities are open to debate.

Isabella's refusal is so sharp a divergence from the traditional story that it is clear that Shakespeare created her specifically to refuse and that he located her in the convent as a first step in making her refusal plausible and to some degree sympathetic. Yet neither horn of the ransom dilemma was to be allowed to pierce. Both Isabella's virginity and Claudio's life were to be preserved, and by plot devices that previous source study has surely derived accurately: the substitute bride from Boccaccio by way of *All's Well*, and the substitute head from Whetstone's *Promos* and perhaps Cinthio's *Epitia*. But these devices are no more than means utilized by the superintending agency of Duke Vincentio, whose role and its assurance of a fortunate outcome is Shakespeare's second, and more important, divergence from the usual monstrous-ransom plot. The wronged woman in that plot does of course obtain justice from an authority figure superior to the corrupt magistrate who has coerced her, but, as is often noted, in no version but *Measure for Measure* is the authority figure so prominent. Only Duke Vincentio oversees the action, prevents the crimes and assures the outcome, as well as distributing the final rewards and punishments in the role of the traditional authority figure.

Shakespeare has so increased the Duke's operation and importance that (as the title of this article suggests), *Measure for Measure* can be seen as far more Vincentio's play than Isabella's or Angelo's or Claudio's. Surprisingly, he speaks more lines than all three of the ostensible principals combined; and in fact, his role is the sixth longest in the Shakespeare canon.

An account of the 'sources' of *Measure for Measure*, therefore, ought to explain where so prominent and significant an addition comes from. Previous investigators have suggested the general frequency of disguised monarchs in many literatures, the popularity of the Alexander Severus legend, the disguised duke of Barnabe Riche's *Brusanus*, and the figure of King James himself – all of which may have had some influence, direct or indirect. There has also been some comment in passing about Middleton's *The Phoenix* and Marston's *The Malcontent*. Bullough, for example, allows that 'Very probably Shakespeare was influenced by Marston and Middleton', but proceeds to no further detail, whereas his materials on the monstrous ransom occupy 140 pages. Eccles seems to allow a comparable influence, at least bearing on the date of *Measure for Measure*, but he says nothing further on the matter, although he gives the monstrous ransom ninety-two pages. Lever seems interested in *The Phoenix* and *The Malcontent* only as examples of the flexibility of the disguised duke motif, and clearly thinks *Brusanus* a more defensible source. Muir cites *The Phoenix* as a recent theatrical use of the device, but makes no mention of *The Malcontent*.[1]

Yet it is by means of the disguised duke structure that Shakespeare transformed the monstrous-ransom plot into the play we have, and both external circumstance and internal detail provide extremely strong evidence that Shakespeare's disguised duke derives immediately from Middleton's and

Marston's practice. The indebtedness is salient enough and wide enough, I submit, to speak of these contemporary plays as 'sources' of *Measure for Measure*.

To engage this indebtedness, one must first address the frequent proposition that the disguised duke was merely a theatrical convention. W. W. Lawrence's characterization of Vincentio as 'a stage Duke'[2] has often been disputed critically, but it seems equally faulty as literary history. For there is no play earlier than the three discussed here that I know of, or that any previous investigator has adduced, which is structurally dominated by a disguised monarch who observes, exposes, thwarts, and judges the vices and follies of his realm. That is, there is no earlier play that utilizes the device of the disguised duke as it is utilized in common by *The Phoenix*, *The Malcontent*, and *Measure for Measure*.

There are, of course, numerous examples of monarchs in disguise in earlier Elizabethan drama. But, as is noted by Rosalind Miles, who has done the most extensive survey of this material,[3] there are two crucial distinctions to be drawn. First, these monarchs almost never disguise for the purpose of observation, or moral correction, or some comparable motive. Typically, they disguise as wooers – like the Gallian King in *Leir* (1590), or William the Conqueror in *Fair Em* (1590) – or they disguise for a whim or a prank, that often leads to misadventure – like Heywood's *Edward IV* (1599), Henry V in *The First Part of Sir John Oldcastle* (1599), or King Edward and King James in *George-a-Green* (1590). Lever (xlvii) aptly characterizes such incidents as 'light entertainment in an English setting', and Shakespeare's having Hal and Poins play at being highwaymen and then tapsters falls into the same category.[4]

Perhaps even more important, these earlier instances are, almost without exception, mere episodes, not structural devices. Occasionally, one finds a single scene in which a monarch disguises for some serious purpose: King Edgar in the semi-allegorical *A Knack to Know a Knave* (1592) disguises to observe corruption in his kingdom; and, of course, the 'little touch of Harry in the night' leads to Henry V's reflection on kingship, if not to moral correction. But for an earlier play dominated by such a disguise, one finds only such barely relevant instances as the quasi-Arcadian world of *Mucedorus* (1590) or just possibly the puzzling welter of identities of

Chapman's Irus, *The Blind Beggar of Alexandria* (1596). One can even perceive some sense of how unusual the disguised duke's operation is in Vincentio's finding it necessary to assure Friar Thomas that it is not 'the dribbling dart of love', but 'a purpose /More grave and wrinkled' (I.iii.2, 4–5) that animates him.

The distinctions drawn here concerning the reformative purposes of the disguised monarch and the use of such a monarch to structure the drama are not simply arbitrary and retrospective critical propositions; they are on the basis of the evidence we have descriptive of the actual practice of the dramatists of the time. For although there were literally or virtually no such plays before 1602 or 1603, from that time on disguised duke plays become suddenly popular for five or six years. Beyond *The Phoenix*, *The Malcontent*, and *Measure for Measure*, there is John Day's *Law Tricks* in 1604; Marston's own *The Fawn*, probably also in 1604;[5] and Edward Sharpham's *The Fleire* in 1606. Samuel Rowley's *When You See Me You Know Me* (1604) belongs to the older, episodic tradition, but may well have been produced in response to the popularity of this newer kind of play. And, according to Ms Miles, the vogue may be traced two further stages: to its slackening in two 1608 plays – Day's *Humour Out of Breath*, and *The Dumb Knight* by Gervase Markham and Lewis Machin; and finally to parody, with Justice Overdo's disguising as a fool in Jonson's *Bartholomew Fair* (1614).

Quite why this theatrical vogue occurred cannot, of course, be answered with certainty. Presumably significant was the accession of James with his self-pronounced concern for wise kingship; and certainly, the technically superior position of the disguised duke can translate easily – as in *The Phoenix* – into a textbook figure of sagacious majesty. Contemporary interest in tragicomedy also may well have been influential: Guarini's *Il pastor fido* first appeared in English in 1602, and Marston quoted from this translation repeatedly in *The Malcontent*, which was in fact entered in the Stationers Register as a '*Tragicomedia*'. The superintendence of the disguised duke offers an easy tactic – as in all three plays – to secure the plot from tragedy, or to ensure, in Fletcher's formulation, that 'it wants deaths ... yet brings some near it' (*The Faithful Shepherdess*, 'To the Reader'). Finally, as many critics have noted, the basis for Malevole's duality as both secret revenger

Shakespeare's disguised duke play 83

and social critic is already present in Marston's early work. For example, the Antonio of *Antonio's Revenge* is specifically invited to pursue vengeance in the guise of 'some trans-shaped cavalier, /Some habit of a spitting critic'.[6]

But why the theatrical vogue occurred is less significant than that in fact it did occur. And the very term 'theatrical vogue' immediately suggests that the success of the earlier versions begot the imitations of the later, as is quite evidently the case with Marston's reworking the disguised duke motif of *The Malcontent* with *The Fawn*, or with Sharpham's imitating *The Fawn* with *The Fleire*. Surely it is reasonable to suppose that what was true for Marston and Sharpham was also true for Shakespeare, and thus, if *Measure for Measure* was not the earliest of the disguised duke plays, one should expect it was influenced by its predecessors. In fact, the evidence is quite strong that it was later than both *The Phoenix* and *The Malcontent*.

The single piece of external evidence for dating *Measure for Measure* is its performance before King James at Whitehall on December 26, 1604. Yet there has been virtual unanimity, from Chambers on, that 1604 was the year of its composition and premiere. The agreement derives from a general sense of where the play belongs in Shakespeare's development, supported by the likelihood that it was a new play when the King's Men did it at court, but one that had been tested in public performance. There is some substantiation in a number of plausible topicalities that Lever has claimed: most significantly perhaps, the allusions (I.i.67–72; II.iv.20–30) to James's visiting the Exchange on March 15, 1604, with the King's Men in attendance. More broadly, it is hard to deny weight to the proposition that elements in *Measure for Measure* were designed to appeal to the new king, if not indeed to reflect the attitudes of his *Basilicon Doron* (1603). Finally, the fact that theatres were closed, virtually continuously, from March 19, 1603, shortly before Queen Elizabeth's death, to April 9, 1604, seems to offer only the winter of 1602–3, an implausibly early date, as an alternative to the generally accepted location of the premiere of Shakespeare's comedy in the spring or summer of 1604.

If such is the case, *The Phoenix* is in all probability earlier. Although it was not published until 1607 (SR, May 9, 1607), there has been unanimous agreement that it was one of Middleton's earliest plays. R. C. Bald, consciously pioneering in the problems of Middleton's chronology, 'on the grounds of style' favoured 'as early a date as possible', and chose 1602. All subsequent investigators have agreed with the stylistic judgement, but have more frequently put *The Phoenix* in 1603 or 1604.[7]

Within this time frame, there seems to be only one further bit of evidence; but it is, I think, significant and persuasive. E. K. Chambers, noting the 1607 quarto's claim that *The Phoenix* had been 'presented before His Maiestie' by the Children of Paul's, deduced that the only occasion on which such a performance could have been given was February 20, 1604 – about ten months before the King saw *Measure for Measure*.[8] It is of course possible that the quarto's claim was fallacious or that there was some unrecorded court performance by the Paul's boys; but there is no particular reason to suspect either. There were seven other Paul's plays printed in 1607, and two more in 1608, as the company went out of existence; the title pages of all but two of these quartos claim their plays had been acted 'lately' or 'sundry times' or 'divers times' at Paul's, but only *The Phoenix* is said to have been played at court.[9] Chambers' date suits well with the consensus about where the play belongs in Middleton's career, and – conveniently for my thesis here – a court performance by a boys' company would very likely have caught Shakespeare's attention.

Evidence for dating both *The Phoenix* and *Measure for Measure* is scanty, though not surprisingly so for plays of this period; for *The Malcontent*, it is firm and plentiful. The termini are unarguable: the play is earlier than its registration on July 5, 1604, and later than the 1602 translation of *Il pastor fido* (SR, September 16, 1601), from which it borrows heavily. Within these limits, a great deal of evidence points to an early date. Registry less than three months after the theatres reopened suggests a premiere before they closed in March of 1603. Negatively, the lack of influence of Florio's 1603 translation of Montaigne, which saturates Marston's next two plays, *The Fawn* and *The Dutch Courtesan*, argues strongly that he wrote *The Malcontent* before he discovered Florio – seemingly in late 1603 or early 1604. Further, there are a great many indications in the prefatory materials to the three 1604 quartos of *The Malcontent* that it had been in existence for some time before its publication. For example, 'To the Reader' complains that the play has been maliciously criti-

Shakespeare's disguised duke play

cized and speaks of this slander as having been abroad long enough to redound to the discredit of its initiators. 'To the Reader' also pleads 'that the unhandsome shape which this trifle in reading presents may be pardoned for the pleasure it once afforded you, when it was presented with the soul of lively action'.[10]

Some time in 1604, the King's Men staged *The Malcontent*, and for their performance (as Hunter's edition has made virtually certain), Marston expanded the comic sequences by about 450 lines, and John Webster provided an induction. In the induction, the play to come is discussed by members of the company: on the one hand, Sly and Sinklo as two gallants who usually patronize the private theatres; on the other, Burbage, Condell, and Lowin *in propriae personae*. The script for this performance became the text of the 'augmented' third quarto of *The Malcontent*, and Webster's induction validates the impression of a premiere considerably earlier than 1604. For instance, it clearly establishes that *The Malcontent* had originally been played by the Children of Blackfriars, and relatively frequently. Sly claims, 'I am one that hath seen this play often. ... I have most of the jests here in my table-book' (15–17); he also reports, 'This play hath beaten all your gallants out of the feathers; Blackfriars hath almost spoiled Blackfriars for feathers' (40–2); Sinklo wagers that 'the play is not so well acted as it hath been' (88–9); and Condell explains how the King's Men obtained it, 'Faith, sir, the book was lost ... we found it and play it' (75–6).

It is not clear exactly what Condell means; his speech cannot be literally true, and the frequent suggestion of a reciprocal theft for an adult's play seems unlikely with Marston supplying a new copy for the King's Men. But whatever it means, the play's having been 'lost' and then 'found' undeniably points to an initial performance significantly earlier than its appearance at the Globe in 1604. The very fact of the Globe performance points the same way; for it is difficult to imagine the Blackfriars company allowing performance, or losing control, of a play that had premiered only after the reopening of the theatres, or of the King's Men incurring the expense of an induction and substantial additions for a play that had not proved itself over some time in repertory.

To summarize then, unless one can find reason to set aside the traditional dating of *Measure for Measure* in 1604, it is probable than Middleton's *Phoenix* is an earlier play; and if it was indeed played before the King's Men's new patron on February 20, 1604, it is extremely likely to have engaged Shakespeare's attention. The case with Marston's *Malcontent* is similiar, but far stronger: the evidence that it premiered in 1602 or 1603 is all but pre-emptive; and the Globe performance is, in effect, documentation that Shakespeare came to know it in detail – a situation, incidentally, that obtains for none of the traditionally adduced sources of his play. In terms of external likelihood, then, it is completely to be expected that both of these earlier disguised duke plays would have influenced *Measure for Measure*; in terms of direct evidence, each shares likenesses with Shakespeare's play that coincidence can hardly explain.

The most striking resemblances between *The Phoenix* and *Measure for Measure* occur in the expositions. To begin with, the abuses in Middleton's Ferrara have been provoked, like those in Shakespeare's Vienna, by the undue leniency of the ruler – here Phoenix's father. He confesses in his first speech,

> Forty-five years I've gently rul'd this dukedom,
> Pray heaven it be no fault!
> For there's as much disease, though not to th' eye,
> In too much pity as in tyranny.[11]

Comparably, Vincentio acknowledges,

> Sith 'twas my fault to give the people scope,
> 'Twould be my tyranny to strike and gall them.
> (I.iii.35–6)

Further, in Middleton, complaints against the resultant corruption have been neglected 'seven, nay seventeen years' (I.i.106), as in Shakespeare the laws have been unenforced for either nineteen (I.ii.157) or fourteen years (I.iii.21).

Most significant, however, is the fact that Prince Phoenix, very much like Vincentio, utilizes the false report that he is travelling abroad 'to look into the heart and bowels of this dukedom, and, in disguise, mark all abuses ready for reformation or punishment' (I.i.100–2). Middleton could hardly have emphasized the travel device more. By my count, the word *travel* and its cognates occur twenty times in the text – ten in the opening scene; and at least seven times before the final scene some character mentions Phoenix's supposed travelling to another. The idea of travel enters the play in the villain Proditor's mock solicitude that Prince Phoenix is 'untravell'd', for 'travel confirms the man' (I.i.22, 27), a theme the Duke then expatiates upon for seventeen lines (32–48). Phoenix, however, appropriates and reverses the theme – 'I'll stay at home, and travel' (88) – and it becomes indicative of his corrective purpose. Predictably, it is most strongly reasserted as the final judgement arrives: Phoenix closes Act IV, scene ii, by soliloquizing, 'I'm sick of all professions; my thoughts burn; /He travels best that knows when to return' (101–2); and after undisguising in the last scene, he announces,

> I thought it a more natural course of travel,
> And answering future expectation,
> To leave far countries, and inquire my own.
> (V.i.174–6)

Lever (xlvi) has suggested that Shakespeare may have derived the travel device from Riche's *Brusanus*, but if he did indeed know *The Phoenix*, it is pointless to seek another source. No reader or viewer could have missed Middleton's emphasis.

There is also some strong similarity in the conduct of the judgement scenes; for, like Vincentio, Phoenix plays the varied roles of accuser, culprit, and – after removing his disguise – judge. He begins the scene in disguise as accomplice to the arch-villain, Proditor; then as a letter from the supposedly absent Prince Phoenix indicts the various malefactors, Phoenix in disguise as Proditor's henchman turns state's evidence to convict them; and finally, as the undisguised prince, he assumes the judgement seat to dispense the final rewards and punishments. There are, of course, differences from *Measure for Measure*, but clearly this is the same general pattern that Shakespeare utilizes of prolonging the scene by presenting the ultimate judge first as witness-accuser and then in apparent jeopardy before his undisguising.

There are even some smaller thematic likenesses in the immediate reactions of the prime culprits to the undisguising of the hero: Angelo, realizing that the Duke 'like power divine, /Hath looked upon my passes' (V.i.367–8), and Proditor, literally grovelling before a comparably divine power – so the Biblical allusion implies: 'Tread me to dust, thou in whom wonder keeps! /Behold the serpent on his belly creeps' (V.i.165–6). Even more interesting is the analogue in *The*

Phoenix to the ultimate moral test imposed on Isabella – that she plead for mercy for Angelo (V.i.441–52). In Middleton's play, the Jeweller's Wife, one of the lesser malefactors, is denied mercy by Phoenix, and obtains it only after the Niece, a virtuous character, intercedes for her. There is even the possibility of a more fascinating analogue: Phoenix grants the Niece not just the pardon she beseeches, but rewards her with a husband – her lover Fidelio. He does so with the words, 'Fidelio, hand her' (V.i.263). After Isabella's plea, the pardon is delayed until Claudio is brought on stage and unmasked; but pardon and marriage offer are then linked:

> If he be like your brother, for his sake
> Is he pardon'd; and for your lovely sake
> Give me your hand and say you will be mine.
> (V.i.488–90)

As with the travel impostures at the beginning, so the judgement scenes at the end of *The Phoenix* and *Measure for Measure* are too significantly alike to be explained as coincidence; if indeed Shakespeare had Middleton's example, he must have borrowed from it the basic framing of the plot with the device of the disguised duke.

The final judgement on Proditor – 'Thy life is such it is too bad to end' (V.i.199) – may be remembered in Vincentio's characterizations of Barnadine as 'Unfit to live or die' and 'A creature unprepar'd, unmeet for death' (IV.iii.63,66). Beyond this, the middle acts of the two plays provide few likenesses worth noting. There is a curious concern in *The Phoenix* with 'bribes' (I.i.119; I.iv.213, 218; I.v.56; III.i.193) – repeated often enough that it may have influenced Isabella's striking 'Hark, how I'll bribe you' and Angelo's angry response (II.ii.146–7). There is also the similar fondness of Phoenix and Vincentio for choric soliloquies of moral analysis. In Middleton's play, the Prince delivers long apostrophes to law (I.iv.197–227) and matrimony (II.ii.162–96), evoked by the perversions of these ideals by Justice Falso and the Captain. In Shakespeare, the Duke's rhymed octosyllabics at the close of Act III are the most significant example of this kind of speech. They contrast so sharply not just in form but in content from such material as Angelo's tortured self-examinations that they too seem much distanced from merely personal expression, although they remain closer to the

Shakespeare's disguised duke play 89

specific narrative problem than Phoenix's apostrophes do. Perhaps comparable soliloquies are in effect corollary to the conception of the disguised duke implied in the commonly shared travel device and final judgement. Both Middleton and Shakespeare occasionally move their observers outside the action to express the value-judgements of their dramas; but the disguised-duke device implies some such judgemental functon, and soliloquy is a natural theatrical means to express it.

Since the dating of *The Phoenix* and its priority to *Measure for Measure* depends so heavily on the presumed court performance in February, 1604, one might wish to argue that the influence between the two plays flowed in a direction opposite to what I have claimed, and that Middleton in fact was the debtor. It might, however, be replied that the nature of the likenesses between the plays accords far better with the idea of Shakespeare's borrowing. In both the opening and closing of the disguised duke frame, what is simple in Middleton generally is complicated in Shakespeare. Phoenix undertakes the travel deception in response to the villain's suggestion, and the leniency that has fostered the abuses he will observe is his father's, not his own. In *Measure for Measure*, the travel deception is Vincentio's *ab ovo*, his purpose seems to be the double intention to 'mark all abuses' and to mark Angelo's correction of the abuses as well, and as is emphasized rather heavily towards the beginning of the play, it is his own laxity that has promoted the evils of Vienna. Comparably, Vincentio's role in the final judgement is also considerably more involved: Phoenix begins the judgement scene as an accomplice turning state's evidence, but Vincentio's roles as witness and possible culprit are two distinct phases; and, of course, Vincentio as duke has already presided over the developing judgement for the first 258 lines of the scene, prior to exiting and returning in disguise. It will also be noted that much of Shakespeare's greater complication results from his interiorizing within Vincentio elements that exist in Middleton as relatively neutral narrative fact. It is far more difficult to imagine that Middleton filtered out Vincentio's greater responsibility, complexity, and ambiguity to attain the comparatively simple figure of Prince Phoenix than that Shakespeare adapted that simple figure for his own more intricate purposes.

The likenesses between *Measure for Measure* and *The*

Malcontent – neatly enough for this argument – pertain far more to the middle acts of the plays, rather than to the setting-up and closing of the disguised duke imposture. In Marston, there is no travel device, no undue leniency of the previous reign, and no protracted judgement scene. Malevole is already in disguise as the play begins; indeed, we do not learn that the Malcontent is really the deposed duke Altofronto until the fourth scene. And the play's finale is shorter and differently structured: Malevole and his allies enter as masquers, dance and converse with the ladies, unmask, 'environ Mendoza, bending their pistols on him' (V.vi.113 SD), and the turn-about is achieved. The masque device obviously derives from Marston's own practice in *Antonio's Revenge* (and more remotely from revenge-tragedy tradition), and the judgement that follows is comparatively quite brief, only some fifty lines.

The most significant likeness between Malevole and Vincentio occurs in the middle acts of their plays, as each utilizes his disguise to control the plot as a counter-intriguer thwarting the villains' nefarious and even murderous intents. Angelo tries to deflower Isabella, to kill Claudio, and to desert (or continue to desert) Mariana; Mendoza to kill Ferneze, Pietro, Malevole himself, and the Hermit of the Rock (Pietro in disguise), to banish Aurelia, and to force Maria into marriage. These supply the basic motive power of the plays, but the disguised duke in each case foils all the intended villainies and preserves all the intended victims.

There is, however, another dimension to this operation which, I believe, establishes a unique similarity between Shakespeare's and Marston's dukes. Both Vincentio and Malevole conceal from other characters the fact that the murderous plots have failed, and no less than Angelo and Isabella in *Measure for Measure*, Pietro and Aurelia in *The Malcontent* are compelled to work out their moral destinies under the misapprehension that irrevocable evils have occurred. It is often noted that Shakespeare's duke, after seeming initially to commit himself to general civic reform, actually devotes his energies to individual spiritual rehabilitations. To some degree, the same is true of Marston's Malevole; his general purpose is to regain his dukedom, but in doing so, he reclaims Pietro, Aurelia, and Ferneze to virtue. And there are even some meaningful likenesses in the techniques of moral

Shakespeare's disguised duke play 91

reclamation. As Vincentio's function as moral mentor reaches its high point with the famous 'Be absolute for death' speech to Claudio, so Malevole also operates as preacher in the *de contemptu mundi* tradition (as Hunter, lxix, notes), most significantly with his speech against lust to Ferneze (II.v.146–61), and his devaluation to Pietro of this world as 'the only grave and Golgotha wherein all things that live must rot' (IV.v.110–11). The moral counselling goes a step further when the usurper Pietro – now deposed, converted to virtue, and functioning as yet another disguised duke – plays spiritual advisor to his unfaithful wife, Aurelia; and most significantly for the relation between these plays, Pietro does so while disguised in 'a hermit's gown' (III.v.25 SD), which on stage would probably have been identical to Vincentio's friar's robes.

There is sufficient similarity between the general operation of the two disguised dukes to make it more than probable that Shakespeare derived the providential and reformative aspect of Vincentio from Marston's example. It is well to recall here that it is exactly by this operation that Shakespeare transformed the traditional authority figure of the monstrous-ransom story, and that the other disguised dukes of the early seventeenth century – including Prince Phoenix – do not devote themselves to comparable personal rehabilitations.[12]

Finally, there are between *The Malcontent* and *Measure for Measure*, sufficient random likenesses in small matters of language, theme, and situation to put out of doubt the question of Shakespeare's borrowing. For example, the verb 'touse' (V.i.309) makes its only appearance in Shakespeare; Marston uses it in three different forms in *The Malcontent* ('touses', III.iii.62; 'toused', III.v.19; 'touseth', IV.v.145). The First Gentleman replies to Lucio's gibe with 'Well, there went but a pair of shears between us' (I.ii.27), and Malevole claims, 'there goes but a pair of shears betwixt an emperor and the son of a bagpiper' (IV.v.116–18) – a proverbial expression, to be sure, but one that appears nowhere else in Shakespeare. Lucio's self-characterization – 'I am a kind of burr, I shall stick' (IV.iii.177) – has some parallels in Shakespeare's earlier work (*A Midsummer Night's Dream*, III.ii.260; *Troilus and Cressida*, III.ii.119; *As You Like It*, I.iii.13–14) – but none is as close in situation as Malevole's insulting the parasite Bilioso as 'thou burr that only stickest to nappy fortunes' (II.iii.30–1) – a repeated and characteristic image in Marston (cf. Hunter, xlix). Malevole's next words are to wish Bilioso 'The serpigo', a disease also mentioned in the Duke's 'Be absolute for death' speech to Claudio (III.i.31).

As Lever (98) notes, Isabella's 'Upon the heavy middle of the night' (IV.i.35), and Mendoza's "Tis now about the immodest waist of night' (II.v.88), both bear the same association with pregnancy. *Measure for Measure* twice specifies 'the suburbs' as the brothel district of Vienna (I.ii.89, 93; II.i.64); and a proclamation dated September 16, 1603, called for the pulling down of bawdy houses in the suburbs of London (see Lever, xxxii–xxxiii). Shakespeare's attention may well have been directed, or re-enforced, by Marston, for Malevole dismisses the court bawd Maquerelle 'unto the suburbs' (V.vi.161) and facetiously claims that there are no brothels in England (V.iv.31). There also seems to be some connection between Escalus' joking about Pompey's name – 'in the beastliest sense, you are Pompey the Great' (II.i.215–16) – and Malevole's reference to 'Pompey the Huge' (I.iii.62). It seems that the point of both – and of 'Pompey the Huge' in *Love's Labour's Lost* (V.ii.676) – is some sort of bawdy joke using the name to signify the buttocks.

Vincentio tells Isabella, 'The hand that hath made you fair hath made you good' (III.i.179–80), and Mendoza tells Maria, 'Be wise as you are fair' (V.vi.6). There are also a pair of summary speeches by the disguised dukes that are remarkably alike in structure: Vincentio speaks of having been 'looker-on' in Vienna,

> Where I have seen corruption boil and bubble
> Till it o'errun the stew: laws for all faults,
> But faults so countenanc'd that the strong statutes
> Stand like the forfeits in a barber's shop,
> As much in mock as mark   (V.i.316–20)

and Malevole exclaims,

> O, I have seen strange accidents of state:
> The flatterer, like the ivy, clip the oak,
> And waste it to the heart; lust so confirmed
> That the black act of sin itself not shamed
> To be termed courtship.   (IV.vi.136–41)

There is even a curious likeness between Escalus's much worried 'Some run from brakes of ice and answer none, /And

Shakespeare's disguised duke play 93

some condemned for a fault alone' (II.i.39–40), and some lines from the Epilogue to *The Malcontent*:

> Then let too severe an eye peruse
> The slighter breaks of our reformèd Muse,
> Who could herself herself of faults detect,
> But that she knows 'tis easy to correct. (7–10)

The two supposed allusions in *Measure for Measure* to King James's aversion to public acclaim (I.i.67–72; II.iv.20–30) are paralleled by Malevole's

> Let them remember that th' inconstant people
> Love many princes merely for their faces
> And outward shows; and they do covet more
> To have a sight of these than of their virtues.
> (V.vi.143–6)

Angelo's self-reproach, 'Having waste ground enough, /Shall we desire to raze the sanctuary /And pitch our evils there?' (II.ii.170–2), posits a very Marstonian image, which appears (as in a number of his plays) in *The Malcontent*: 'Nay, monstrous, I ha' seen a sumptuous steeple turned to a stinking privy' (II.v.128–9).

The rhetorical scheme in the title and in Vincentio's '"An Angelo for Claudio; death for death. /Haste still pays haste, and leisure answers leisure; /Like doth quit like, and Measure still for Measure"' (V.i.407–9) is duplicated a number of times in *The Malcontent*: e.g. *'One stick burns t'other, steel cuts steel alone. /'Tis good trust few; but, O, 'tis best trust none'* (IV.iii.143–4; see also IV.iii.95; IV.iv.14–15; V.v.114). The repentant Angelo twice seeks death rather than mercy (V.i.371–2, 474–5), as the repentant Aurelia does three times (IV.iv.3–8; V.vi.45–6, 80–1). The loyal Provost of *Measure for Measure* (see especially IV.ii. 181–94) is paralleled by the Captain of the Citadel, who serves as Maria's jailer and who, amazingly in view of the political situation, is still loyal to the banished Altofronto (V.ii.77–9). As Escalus and the Provost are paired in Vincentio's final speech (V.i.525–8), so the good counsellor Celso and the Captain are paired in Malevole's last speech (V.vi.164). There is even perhaps in *The Malcontent* a hint of Isabella's response to Angelo's coercion in Maria's response to Mendoza's attempt to force her into marriage under the threat of death: 'I'll mourn no more; come, girt my brows with flowers; /Revel and dance, soul, now thy wish thou hast; /Die like a bride, poor heart, thou shalt die chaste' (V.vi.42–4). Compare Isabella's 'Then, Isabel live chaste, and brother, die' (II.iv.183) and Claudio's 'If I must die, /I will encounter darkness as a bride /And hug it in mine arms' (III.i.82–4).

As with any compilation of parallels, some may seem insignificant, some coincidental, some perhaps deriving from a common source. There may even be a couple of cases – the 'burr' and the idea of dying like a bride – in which Marston's example simply suggested or re-enforced images Shakespeare had already used. But it should be noted that there are some indications in *Measure for Measure* of Shakespeare's having been aware of Marston when he wrote. For example, Isabella has a famous speech which portrays the man of borrowed authority who misuses the thunder which properly 'Splits the unwedgeable and gnarled oak,' and who thus conducts himself like 'an angry ape' (II.ii.117,121); the two images were also collocated in Marston's *Certain Satires*: 'Why thus it is, when Mimic Apes will striue /with Iron wedge the trunks of Oakes to riue.'[15] Somewhat more remotely, Lever (22, n.) suggests a likeness between Vincentio's purpose to see 'what our seemers be' (I.iii.54), and the title of Marston's satire against 'Precisians' – *Quaedam sunt, et non videntur* (*Certain Satires*, 2). And it is of course in this play that Lucio refers to 'Pygmalion's images' (III.ii.44) – *The Metamorphosis of Pygmalion's Image* being Marston's first and perhaps most notorious work.

The Malcontent, on the basis of the evidences we have, was a quite popular and influential play, as *Measure for Measure* itself seems not to have been. Marston's play went through three quartos in 1604, Webster's Induction continually speaks of it as a stage success, it was known well enough for John Davies of Hereford in 1610 to mock the author's supposed malcontentedness, and it was strongly influential not just on later disguised duke plays, but also on revenge plays, notably *The Revenger's Tragedy*. And within this general context of *The Malcontent*'s popularity, which suggests Shakespeare would have known the play, we have the 1604 King's Men's performance, which all but documents its influence on him. It should also be remembered that for that performance Shakespeare's partner and leading tragedian, Richard Burbage, played Malevole, and although there is no specific proof he also created Vincentio, it is extremely difficult to suppose that some other member of the company undertook so lengthy and dominant a role.[14] The example of Burbage as the disguised duke in *The Malcontent*, assuring the resolution of the tragicomic problems, would, I suggest, have been an enormous impetus to create a similar role for him in *Measure for Measure*, especially since in his most recent comedy, *All's Well*, Shakespeare had presumed on the power of romantic love to assure the outcome, up to and perhaps beyond credible limits.

And it should further be remembered that Marston provided about 450 lines of new material for the King's Men's performance, which in all probability means that he provided it for Shakespeare's personal scrutiny. By 1604, Shakespeare had been a sharer in the company for about ten years, and, more important, he was self-evidently the foremost authority on what would succeed on the public stage. That Marston's additions would have been presented for his approval is overwhelmingly likely. Thus, when we find in one of these additions 'thou burr that only stickest to nappy fortunes. The serpigo ... seize thee!' (II.iii.31–3), we are probably looking at text submitted to Shakespeare, who shortly after reproduced the 'burr' and 'the serpigo' in *Measure for Measure*. His borrowing from Marston's play is, I would submit, closer to certainty than probability.

That Shakespeare borrowed substantially from Middleton and Marston to transform the narrative kernel of the monstrous ransom to the disguised duke play he actually produced is the basic contention of this paper, and there is little space here for a critical evaluation of how successful the amalgam was.

Very briefly, *Measure for Measure* seems to me, as Lever (xcvii) characterized it, 'a flawed masterpiece', and largely because of Vincentio – who is the ultimate issue all evaluators of the play must engage. That character is derived – I hope I have shown – from very contemporary practice; it is too early to speak of a recognized sub-genre, or perhaps even of a fully realized theatrical vogue. Like Prince Phoenix, Vincentio in his power and benevolence guarantees that vice will be detected and virtue will triumph. In fact, as reigning duke, his power is even greater than Phoenix's, and even in disguise he is usually accorded a deference not much less than he commands *in propria persona*. And in this regard, although he also operates in the style of Malevole as counter-intriguer and even moral regenerator, he is quite different from Marston's protagonist. For Malevole, intriguing is a tense and dangerous business, for he has only his disguise and his wits against the superior power of his adversary. It is always evident in *Measure for Measure* that Vincentio (like Phoenix) can at any time assert his ducal power and solve the plot problems; indeed, he comes close to doing so with the Provost in Act IV, scene ii, and affects to apologize to Isabella (V.i.386–97) for not having done so to save Claudio.

The disguised duke frame Shakespeare took from Middleton – the travel imposture and the final undisguising and judgement – works coherently enough for satiric social observation and correction, and for these tasks an overseer as woodenly impersonal in his virtue and power as Prince Phoenix is sufficient if unexciting. But, in narrative terms at least, Vincentio is even less personalized than Phoenix, who, after all, has a father, a confidant, and a name. Shakespeare's duke, called Vincentio only in the Folio *dramatis personae*, not in the text, has only his function: neither he nor any other character speaks of or apparently thinks of him as other than as the Duke.

The counter-intriguing and spiritual regenerations Shakespeare observed in Marston's play provided an entrée into questions of ethical depth and complexity, although the vituperative language and personality of the Malcontent himself could have presented little attraction. To engage these deeper and more complex questions with a dramatic structure designed for the simpler satiric purposes of Middleton leads directly, I would suggest, to the traditional shortcomings charged to *Measure for Measure*. To submit the anguishes of Angelo, Isabella, and Claudio to the superintendence of an overseer in the style of Phoenix is to lessen their force, to trivialize them. And to allow the readjustment and rehabilitation of such natures to become the substance of the plot is to reduce the social observation and correction – for which the disguised duke frame ostensibly exists – to virtual inconsequentiality.

Vincentio's 'inefficiency' as civic reformer is ordinarily explained by those who insist on the achievement of the play by his education, his moral growth, the readjustment of his focus from social corruption to 'the inner economy of individuals caught in a corrupt world' (Hunter, lix). If such is claimed as

Shakespeare's intention, it can be answered only that the closing of the disguised duke envelope seems a strange means to express such concerns, and the extremely powerful and extremely unpersonalized character of Vincentio seems far better calculated to emphasize his public reformative role, not the shape and significance of his own interiority.

The examples of Marston's Malevole and Middleton's Phoenix provide no solution to the problems and difficulties of Vincentio's characterization; rather they suggest he is not so much a stage duke as a failed stage duke.

NOTES

1 Geoffrey Bullough, *Narrative and Dramatic Sources of Shakespeare, vol. 2: Comedies, 1597–1603* (London: Routledge & Kegan Paul, 1958), p. 411; Mark Eccles, ed., *Measure for Measure, A New Variorum Edition of Shakespeare* (New York: Modern Language Association, 1980), pp. 300–1; J. W. Lever, ed., *Measure for Measure*, Arden edn (London: Methuen, 1965), p. xlviii; Kenneth Muir, *The Sources of Shakespeare's Plays* (New York: Yale University Press, 1978), p. 178.

2 *Shakespeare's Problem Comedies*, 2nd edn (1958; repr. Baltimore: Penguin, 1969), p. 104.

3 *The Problem of 'Measure for Measure'* (New York: Barnes & Noble, 1976), especially pp. 134–60.

4 Unless otherwise indicated, dates are from Alfred Harbage's *Annals of English Drama 957–1700*, rev. S. Schoenbaum (London: Methuen, 1964).

5 For a cogent argument on dating *The Fawn*, see Anthony Caputi, *John Marston, Satirist* (Ithaca: Cornell University Press, 1961), pp. 266–8.

6 IV.i.3–4; W. Reavley Gair, ed., The Revels Plays (Manchester: Manchester University Press, 1978).

7 'The chronology of Middleton's plays', *Modern Language Review*, 32 (1937), 36; later judgements are conveniently tabulated in Anthony Corvatta, *Thomas Middleton's City Comedies* (Lewisburg: Bucknell University Press, 1973), pp. 171–2.

8 *The Elizabethan Stage* (Oxford: Clarendon, 1923), vol. 3, p. 439.

9 The plays are Beaumont's *The Woman Hater*, Chapman's *Bussy D'Ambois*, Marston's *What You Will*, W. S.'s *The Puritan*, Dekker and Webster's *Westward Ho* and *Northward Ho*, and Middleton's *Michaelmas Term*, *A Mad World My Masters*, and *A Trick to Catch the Old One*; the last two published in 1608. Only *What You Will* and *The Puritan* do not claim recent or frequent performance; see Chambers, 2, p. 22; 4, pp. 390–1.

10 Quotations are from G. K. Hunter's Revels edition (London: Methuen, 1973).

11 Quotations are from A. H. Bullen's *The Works of Thomas Middleton* (1885; repr. New York: AMS Press, 1964), vol. 1, pp. 99–210.

12 The only such rehabilitation in *Phoenix* is Quieto's restoration of Tangle's sanity, which, according to Ms Miles (pp. 155–7), totally undermines Phoenix's function.

13 IV.107–8; *The Poems of John Marston*, ed. Arnold Davenport (Liverpool: University Press of Liverpool, 1961).

14 The roles are quite similar in scope: Vincentio (by Miles's figures, 294) has 853 lines, or 31.5 per cent of the play; Malevole (by my count) has 728, or 32.2 per cent, including 156 (34.9 per cent) of the Globe additions. Phoenix's role is much smaller – 517 lines, or 21.5 per cent (my figures).

5

Shakespeare and history: from antithesis to synthesis

ARTHUR HUMPHREYS

Shakespeare's later historical sequence, from *Richard II* to *Henry IV*, is marked by what C. L. Barber calls 'an astonishing development of drama in the direction of inclusiveness ... realised only because Shakespeare's genius for construction matched his receptivity'.[1] E. M. W. Tillyard argued for an epic breadth of treatment in the *Henry IV* plays, distinguishing them from the mood of tragedy by their wealth of panorama and their complex 'vision of contemporary England':

> Now as the stylistic mark of tragedy is intensity, that of the epic, though tragic intensity may occur, is breadth or variety. And in *Henry IV* there is a variety of style, fully mastered, which is new in Shakespeare and which can hardly be matched even in his later work.[2]

The development from dominant tragic intensity towards symphonic complexity is the theme of the present discussion of the history plays.

In *3 Henry VI* Shakespeare allows himself a sleight-of-hand trick which doubles the stage 'reality' of historical events with the genuine reality of actual life. The great 'King-maker', Warwick, whose support is crucial to whichever side he favours, learns that his brother has been killed by the stormy Lancastrian, Clifford. He explodes passionately:

> Why stand we like soft-hearted women here,
> Wailing our losses, whiles the foe doth rage;
> And look upon, as if the tragedy
> Were play'd in jest by counterfeiting actors? (II.iii.25–8)

Well, played by counterfeiting actors it is, though not in jest; that is the sleight-of-hand trick, like others which jolt the audience by rejigging the world/stage analogy. This is done delightfully in *1 Henry IV* when the Hostess enthuses over Falstaff's parody of the King – 'O Jesu, he doth it as like one of these harlotry players as ever I see!' (II.iv.390). It is done with formidable irony in *Julius Caesar* when Cassius imagines the reputation the conspirators will have earned for themselves:

> How many ages hence
> Shall this our lofty scene be acted over,
> In states unborn, and accents yet unknown!
> (III.i.111–13)

And it is done satirically in *Troilus and Cressida* when Ulysses likens the posturing Patroclus to 'a strutting player, whose conceit /Lies in his hamstring' (I.iii.153). At such moments far-off historical past and immediate theatrical present click together, like images superimposed on each other for depth of impact. In *1 Henry VI*, Warwick stabs home the message that what the stage presents symbolizes no imaginary fiction but the shocking force of historical reality: we must look through the stage to the actuality of violence.

In *Shakespeare, Ariosto, and Corneille*, Benedetto Croce described Shakespeare's historical figures thus: 'The personages of these plays arise like three-dimensional statues, that is to say, they are treated with full reality, and thus form a perfect antithesis to the figures of the romantic plays.'[3] Nearly fifty years ago, before the main revaluation of the histories took place, R. W. Chambers's essay, 'The Elizabethan and Jacobean Shakespeare' (in *Man's Unconquerable Mind*, 1939), stressed the histories' dramatic-tragic power, notably in the first tetralogy, as counterbalancing the lyrical wealth and romantic glamour which many critics had seen as Shakespeare's preferred mode in the 1590s. The great historical (particularly the early historical) characters are certainly, as Croce observed, 'three-dimensional', but they are anything but 'statues', and when in 1951–3 the Birmingham Repertory, followed in 1953 by the Old Vic Company and ten years later the Royal Shakespeare Company, revived the early plays, these burst upon audiences with electrifying force and tragic relevance.[4] In a programme note Sir Peter Hall, the RSC's director, insisted that these were no plays of a remote era:

Shakespeare and history

The new men – the Warwicks, the Yorks, ... the Suffolks – are ruthless and hypocritical. They justify their behaviour by invoking the great sanctions – God, the King, Parliament, the People ... or any of those alibis that unscrupulous statesmen, activated by the desire to be on top, have used over the ages.

This impression of moral rigour, however, should be qualified by the insight of one reviewer (J. C. Trewin) who saw Shakespeare presenting these strenuous power-seekers not for censure but for compassion:

> As one leaves the theatre after six hours' unforeseen experience, one's mood is neither of judgment nor condemnation of these unscrupulous, unhappy characters; but rather of sympathy, even of affection, for people we have come to know so long, who have been tried so hard, and have failed so bitterly.

The word 'antithesis' appears for these early plays in my title, as against 'synthesis' for the later, because Shakespeare centres his dramatic interests less in rounded character and its social context, such as so enriches the *Henry IV* plays, than in assertive, often acerbic, confrontations, crackling with vitality and captivatingly exciting, polarized in ideas and passions. This is true not only of external relationships (in quarrels and challenges) but of inward ruminations and self-searchings where the protagonist's mind oscillates furiously among the dilemmas it faces.

Conflict, controversy, the dialectics of extreme positions, are the means by which the contestants define the contours of their predicaments. This is how, as Warwick lies dying on Barnet Field (*3 Henry VI*, V.ii.5–28), he rages in pride, exasperation, and anguish at Fate's constrictions, exploring his situation by lurching fiercely within its antitheses – past/present, pride/despair, glory/shame, grandeur/abasement, life/death:

> Ah, who is nigh? Come to me, friend or foe,
> And tell me who is victor, York or Warwick?
> Why ask I that my mangled body shows? –
> My blood, my want of strength, my sick heart shows? –
> That I must yield my body to the earth,
> And, by my fall, the conquest to my foe.

> Thus yields the cedar to the axe's edge
> Whose arms gave shelter to the princely eagle,
> Under whose shade the ramping lion slept,
> Whose top branch over-peer'd Jove's spreading tree
> And kept low shrubs from winter's powerful wind.
> These eyes, that now are dimm'd with death's black veil,
> Have been as piercing as the mid-day sun
> To search the secret treasons of the world;
> The wrinkles in my brows, now fill'd with blood,
> Were liken'd oft to kingly sepulchres;
> For who liv'd King but I could dig his grave?
> And who durst smile when Warwick bent his brow?
> Lo now my glory smear'd in dust and blood!
> My parks, my walks, my manors that I had,
> Even now forsake me; and of all my lands
> Is nothing left me but my body's length.
> Why, what is pomp, rule, reign, but earth and dust?
> And live we how we can, yet die we must.

This could come only from one in high place drastically brought low, the great tree felled which sheltered once those symbols of supreme power – the eagle and lion, the sun-strong eyes now darkening in death, the brow which, by extraordinary hyperbole, dug in the depth of its frowns the graves of kings. Its force comes from its vehemently picturesque images setting up the strongest profiles of contrasting fates. The rhetoric of strenuous extremism is, of course, common in early Elizabethan tragedy, owing much to Senecan imitation. In other writers it runs readily to Ercles' vein, out-Heroding Herod. Shakespeare can, for apt reasons, certainly bombast the verse if he wishes; but intense imagination and concentrated diction seizing the sharp edges and hard core of emotional violence – these are the very different means he draws on for the stormy figures circling around Henry VI. And the effect is a wonderful enlargement; as John Arthos sensitively remarks, were such speech vigour merely sensational we should feel depleted and depressed, but its energies are so inspiriting that we are 'sustained, even elevated, [by] the conviction of dignity and greatness'.[5]

What keeps these plays at high pitch is the fascination of hostilities. In *2 Henry VI* (I.iii.42–64) Queen Margaret, that outrageous embodiment of power-seeking individualism, married to King Henry by a court intrigue worked by William Pole, Earl of Suffolk, voices her fury at the frustrations English court life imposes on her, her voice hitting the words like hammers clashing on steel:

> My Lord of Suffolk, say, is this the guise,
> Is this the fashions in the court of England?
> Is this the government of Britain's isle,
> And this the royalty of Albion's king?
> What! shall King Henry be a pupil still
> Under the surly Gloucester's governance?
> Am I a queen in title and in style,
> And must be made a subject to a duke?
> I tell thee, Pole, when in the city Tours
> Thou ran'st a tilt in honour of my love,
> And stol'st away the ladies' hearts of France,
> I thought King Henry had resembled thee
> In courage, courtship, and proportion:
> But all his mind is bent to holiness,
> To number Ave-Maries on his beads;
> His champions are the prophets and apostles,
> His weapons holy saws of sacred writ,
> His study is his tilt-yard, and his loves
> Are brazen images of canoniz'd saints.
> I would the college of the Cardinals
> Would choose him Pope, and carry him to Rome,
> And set the triple crown upon his head:
> That were a state fit for his Holiness.

Finally the Queen comes to the climax of her rage, the mutual jealousy between her and the Duchess of Gloucester:

> Not all these lords do vex me half so much
> As that proud dame, the Lord Protector's wife:
> She sweeps it through the court with troops of ladies,
> More like an empress than Duke Humphrey's wife.
> Strangers in court do take her for the queen:
> She bears a duke's revenues on her back,
> And in her heart she scorns our poverty.
> Shall I not live to be aveng'd on her? (I.iii.75–82)

This passionate prejudice is typical of the ways in which the dominant figures project a heroic and ferocious energy, urging their positions and self-justifications. When the Royal

Shakespeare Company mounted the early trilogy in 1977 it held a public discussion of what it was doing, and the actors made the point that in these plays nothing can be small; this extraordinary expression of personality absolutely demands energy and volume. There are some exceptions, it is true. The plays' moral landscape poignantly and tragically contrasts ruthless secular power and the heaven-allied humanities which that power outrages. Duke Humphrey's parting from his condemned wife (*2 Henry VI*, II.iv), King Henry's sad reflections on his isolation and helplessness, and his encounter with the son who has killed his father and the father who has killed his son (*3 Henry VI*, II.v) – these and other brief respites from the onrush of violence speak for values alien to this explosive world. And indeed a fundamental antithesis opens between the intimacies of Henry's soul-searching and the self-centred worldliness of his entourage. Michael Billington, reviewing for *The Guardian* (15 November 1977) the RSC production of Part 2, made the point tellingly:

> The theme that runs through the play [is] that heavenly justice has been replaced by earthly intrigue. When Alan Howard's Henry (a king gifted with insight but no flair for action) comes to the couplet
> And poise the cause in Justice' equal scales,
> Whose beam stands sure, whose rightful cause prevails,
> [II.i.196–7]
> his voice falters as though he knows he is speaking an untruth. And I shall not easily forget Howard's blank-eyed despair as he sees the Duke of Gloucester impeached, and realises at last that he is surrounded by a nest of vipers. This is no milksop monarch but a man who understands that England is crumbling under his feet. When, after the death of the toad-like self-seeking Bishop of Winchester, he cries 'Forbear to judge!' it is in the racked tones of one who knows that justice is dead.

Each history centres on the ruler and his entourage, and status invests the participants with a prominence which their intense rhetorics maintain. Their rise is formidable, their fall resounds with the crash of eminence. John Arthos has expressed this feelingly:

> What we ... become aware of is ... that multitudes of persons of the greatest stature and energy give their full

strength to manage fortune, and that for all their greatness
and even splendour they are like those other great ones
who ebb and flow by the moon.[6]

Still, they seek to manage fortune with superlative energy,
and when fortune resists they rage magnificently. Queen
Margaret's remonstrance crackles with malevolence against
the antitheses which restrict her. She spurns her humiliated
position; Henry's submission to the Duke of Gloucester burns
in her with a fierce sense of discrepancy; her lost illusion of
Henry as knightly hero clashes with her present knowledge of
his humility; the King's rivals rouse her to paroxysms of envy;
and she turns her final fury on Gloucester's wife whose power
outranges hers. The only later play comparable for acri-
monious discrepancies is *Coriolanus*, where the goading sense
of 'violentest contrariety' makes harsh dialectics crackle across
unbridgeable gulfs.

As a last example of this special quality of the *Henry VI*
plays, consider Richard of Gloucester's monologue which
ends Act 3, Scene 2, of Part 3. The action stands still while
Richard vents his frenetic energy, yet the stillness is charged
with the extremest potential for the future. What imposes
itself, as in Margaret's tirade, is the mental horizon of opposing landmarks, bafflements, mazes – those violentest con-
trarieties defying him to cleave his way through them. Many
lives stand between him and the crown, and his deformity
seems to bar him from sexual love:

> Why then I do but dream on sovereignty;
> Like one that stands upon a promontory
> And spies a far-off shore where he would tread,
> Wishing his foot were equal with his eye;
> And chides the sea, that sunders him from thence,
> Saying he'll lade it dry to have his way:
> So do I wish the crown, being so far off;
> And so I chide the means that keeps me from it;
> And so I say I'll cut the causes off,
> Flattering me with impossibilities.
> My eye's too quick, my heart o'erweens too much,
> Unless my hand and strength could equal them.
> Well, say there is no kingdom then for Richard;
> What other pleasure can the world afford?
> I'll make my heaven in a lady's lap,

> And deck my body in gay ornaments,
> And 'witch sweet ladies with my words and looks.
> O miserable thought! and more unlikely,
> Than to accomplish twenty golden crowns.
> Why, Love forswore me in my mother's womb:
> And, for I should not deal in her soft laws,
> She did corrupt frail Nature with some bribe,
> To shrink mine arm up like a wither'd shrub;
> To make an envious mountain on my back,
> Where sits Deformity to mock my body;
> To shape my legs of an unequal size;
> To disproportion me in every part,
> Like to a chaos, or an unlick'd bear-whelp
> That carries no impression like the dam.
> And am I then a man to be belov'd?
> O monstrous fault to harbour such a thought!
> Then, since this earth affords no joy to me
> But to command, to check, to o'erbear such
> As are of better person than myself,
> I'll make my heaven to dream upon the crown;
> And, whiles I live, t'account this world but hell,
> Until my misshap'd trunk that bears this head
> Be round impaled with a glorious crown.
> And yet I know not how to get the crown,
> For many lives stand between me and home:
> And I, – like one lost in a thorny wood,
> That rents the thorns and is rent with the thorns,
> Seeking a way, and straying from the way;
> Not knowing how to find the open air,
> But toiling desperately to find it out –
> Torment myself to catch the English crown.
>
> (III.ii.134–79)

Hunched back, club foot, shrunk arm, Richard is immensely *there*, frenetic in embittered frustration. But his is only the supreme example of the prevalent dramatic mood of these plays, that of explosive ambition constrained, and seeking any weak spot through which to burst to self-realization. What comes over, as L.C. Knights has observed of *King Lear*, is the lesson 'of the self-mutilation inherent in egotism and isolation, of the inevitable denaturing effect of an attitude that wilfully blinds itself to the fact that personal life has its being in relationship'.[7]

Shakespeare and history

The dialectics of violence are of four kinds: political and personal clashes; concepts and arguments acrimoniously reflecting these clashes; introspections fiercely contending within individuals; and power motives set against spiritual welfare. There are few nuances such as turn the violences of *Macbeth* into so haunting a nightmare, no Yeatsian 'shadowy waters': instead, cataracts turbulent with ambitions, reversals, quarrels, hurtling together English and French, Lancastrian and Yorkist, Earth and Heaven, harrying the attention this way and that with the cacophony of contradictory forces. As *1 Henry VI* opens, on the funeral of heroic Henry V, uniter of a divided land, there bursts the quarrel of Gloucester and Winchester. Reminders of the adored King alternate with disruption; the loyal lords briefly concur in patriotic grief; the disloyal Winchester provokes a quarrel; successive messengers herald danger; the loyalists close ranks; and, left alone at the end, Winchester delivers a threatening monologue on his greed for power. The *Henry VI* plays throughout, as Arthos observes, 'make almost everything that can be made of the idea of kingship and of the ferocity and intricacy of ambition'.[8]

Drama, of course, must work in some such way, by contention and drive. The special note of the first tetralogy is the vehemence with which this is expressed, and the vitality of its sense of life. For Geoffrey Bullough, Part 3 is 'an astonishing *tour de force* in its handling of sprawling, recalcitrant material'; for Tillyard, the great barons are 'all positive characters ... at the centre of living'; for James Winny, Shakespeare's concern is not political doctrine but 'the driving energies impelling growth and change'.[9] Surely these are the right comments on what earlier critics viewed as tedious brawling. In *Troilus and Cressida* Agamemnon heartens the Greeks by proclaiming that what brings manhood out is 'the protractive trials of great Jove /To find persistive constancy in men' (I.iii.20–1), and Nestor follows his lead – 'In the reproof of chance /Lies the true proof of men' (33–4); 'The strong-ribb'd bark' (40) will show its worth in storm, not in calm. This is the primary-epic world of heroic conflict and assertion, of the *Iliad* and *Beowulf*. The first tetralogy traverses half a century to express the struggle of order and catastrophe, as, in *Paradise Lost* (ii.894–7), Satan, fallen from Heaven, surveys a scene

> where eldest Night
> And Chaos, Ancestors of Nature, hold

> Eternal Anarchie, amidst the noise
> Of endless warre, and by confusion stand.

But to leave it there would be to ignore the plays' ultimate though nebulous antithesis. Behind the worldly dimensions lie the other-worldly ones. In Part 2 the good Duke Humphrey believes in heaven's power but still is murdered. Yet justice, we yearn to think, will catch his slayers – and Winchester dies in crazed horror; Suffolk is slain in ignominy after hearing a scathing indictment of his crimes. If the good die undeservedly, the bad die deservedly, and it is with the good that one would choose to be. Philip Brockbank comments on divine dimensions lying behind the secular ones:

> In its last phase ... Part 3 finds new sources of authority in Henry's despised virtues ... and the king-slaying becomes the play's most significant act. ... It is Shakespeare's first essay in the direction of *Macbeth*: kingship owes its sanctity to the vulnerable and innocent qualities that sustain it.[10]

No positive affirmation is possible by the end of Part 3; that must await the end of *Richard III*. Yet for all his weakness Henry VI is a haunting presence, with a poignant goodness in him which wrings the heart and speaks with such validity that one murmurs, as *Richard II*'s Northumberland would do in quite different circumstances:

> even through the hollow eyes of death
> I spy life peering; but I dare not say
> How near the tidings of our comfort is.   (II.i.270–2)

Henry's good intentions pave the way to England's hell. But his plays, while in no way seeing him as a bonus in her political life, leave no doubt that his instincts derive from heaven. Human purposes negotiate with spiritual mysteries, wittingly or unwittingly; even the spiritually blind live under unrecognized, dilatory, but inevitable retribution. Martyred virtue is always meaningful. If in their political collisions the great individualists of these plays show every kind of worldly – and violentest – contrariety, nevertheless in the polarities of their dialectics of worldliness and unworldliness Shakespeare locates them in a sphere where each spectator may judge of values. And no one, surely, will think the values of Queen Margaret, or Winchester, or Suffolk, or Richard of York, preferable to those of Duke Humphrey and King Henry.

In quality of execution, and in conceptual power, certainly *Richard III*, arguably *King John*, and beyond question *Richard II* surpass the *Henry VI* plays. In respect of this essay's theme none marks a major evolution towards a fuller synoptic sense of England's identity. Yet in some ways Shakespeare amplifies his implied perspectives on the nation's life. Richard III, Falconbridge, and Richard II outrange in dramatic personality any earlier historic figure, and do so in manners appropriate to this discussion. Each focuses, and magnifies, history's conceptual world, not indeed as all-embracingly as the great characters of the *Henry IV* plays, but certainly as symbolizing in their individual centres characteristic worlds of the national temper. In *Richard III* and *King John* this temper figures as one of self-seeking duplicities, hailed by Richard himself with relish, by Falconbridge (and Pandulph too) with sophisticated cynicism. In *Richard II*, beyond the manoeuvres of policy, it figures as a vision of 'This royal throne of kings, this sceptred isle', an ideal of ceremony and patriotic well-being.

A total sense of 'England', only passingly glimpsed in *Henry VI*, begins uncertainly to emerge. In *Richard III* it is projected by the very fact that Richard's kingdom is the diabolical opposite of what England truly should be. Like the spider to which Queen Margaret compares him, Richard, until destroyed, extends his grasp over his world, and under his macabre policies the whole land (as in *Macbeth*) shudders more centrally than in *Henry VI*. This result of his dominance is not lessened by the fact that his is a populous play. His virtuosity, in his crowded world of competitive selfishnesses, is that of a soloist in a concerto, a virtuosity at once individual and symphonic. With whatever variations of separate or collective thrust, the national ravage under unscrupulous power, while not more comprehensive than in *Henry VI*, emerges less episodically and with more consolidated impact.

In *King John*, through the diplomatic chicane and the commentaries of Falconbridge and Pandulph, Shakespeare draws a world with unscrupulousness as its guiding principle, in – as my friend Roger Warren writes to me – 'a clear-sighted revelation of exactly what abstract terms like "honour", "conscience", "zeal and charity", actually mean in political terms'. Shakespeare deflates the hypocrisies at first with satirical relish by 'a highly-developed *humorous* treatment of public issues', and later by unqualified exposure. Through panoramas of Commodity, Falconbridge, man of the world, creates a shrewd, unblinking 'vision of England', partly in wry acceptance of it, partly to project the opposing vision of what England should be. And this suggests a Shakespeare moving, as Geoffrey Bullough has observed, 'to free himself from the conception of the History play as tragic or rhetorical drama',[11] and reaching out for a comprehensive view of his country, briefly voiced in Falconbridge's final lines.

Far more evidently *Richard II*, though so much a court play, offers an imaginative concept of England, not by exhibiting her but by so richly indicating what kingship should mean. The Richard who so wilfully flouts the true nature of his office nevertheless by poetic idealization projects the opposite case, that of good kingship fostering a cherished land. The play's beauty of style and sense of ceremony evoke the haunting idealism of England so marvellously explicit in Gaunt's dying eulogy. Shakespeare does not yet synthesize his country's nature from a wide spectrum of her social life, but nothing in any of the histories approaches Gaunt's celebration of what she should in her true self be, and the play haunts the mind with its yearning for that true self and the royal tradition.

Why, turning to the later plays, do we salute them as plays of historical synthesis? It is because Shakespeare now presents the constituents of national life as a symphony of varieties rather than a cacophony of exclusivenesses. Characters and policies of course are still often in conflict: that is the essence of historical drama, and only in the late, collaborative *Henry VIII* are sharp confrontations changed to rising and falling destinies in resigned alternations. The difference between the acrimonies of the earlier and the interrelatednesses of the later histories is a difference in the sense of life, a sense now of the nation as an organic whole to be ruled, not a mere territorial prize to be gained. This totality of living persons is psychologically complex and extensively demanding. As Nevill Coghill notes:

> In all the stories he chose to dramatise, the corporate structure of a whole society is always indicated. ... The Histories, crowded as they are with high personages and affairs of state, make time for their Bullcalfs, their Warts, their drawers, gardeners, porters, grooms, and citizens, and can find place for the consciences of common soldiers, and even of common murderers.[12]

Shakespeare and history

Yet the early tetralogy discloses this 'corporate structure' only incidentally, in brief glimpses of non-baronial life amidst which the great power-seekers thrust forward, neither complex in their sense of the world nor sympathetic with the worlds of others, while Henry VI sits baffled amidst the conflicting lines of force, presiding not over a society but over a coexistence of competitors. If the *Henry VI* trio is epic in the primitive-heroic sense, the *Henry IV-Henry V* trio is epic in Tillyard's sense of breadth and variety rather than tragic intensity. As Dryden remarked when he praised Chaucer in the Preface to his *Fables*,

> There is such a variety of game springing up before me that I am distracted in my choice, and know not which to follow. 'Tis sufficient to say, according to the proverb, that here is God's plenty.

Having in *Richard II* movingly contrasted the glamour of kingship with the urgencies of rule, Shakespeare went on in the *Henry IV* pair to a historical vision incomparably rich, varied, vivid, lucid yet complex, massive in thrust yet alive in every particular, full of the many-levelled and wide-ranging activities of the land, the whole great story conducted with masterly assurance and steeped in a wisdom astonishing in a man in his early thirties. Polonius might have offered them in the category of tragedy (Henry's fate), comedy (Falstaff), history (which they certainly are), pastoral (Justice Shallow and Gloucestershire), and all combinations of these in scene individable or poem unlimited. They offer a synthesis immeasurably fuller than anything earlier and, as Tillyard observed, hardly to be matched even later. The verse itself ranges widely in effect. At one end there is the grandiloquence of high policy, high-charged as in the earlier histories with the vehemence of challenge but with a vehemence now modulated a formidable music which makes the earlier angers sound merely harsh. Its compulsive euphony sounds in such characteristic lines as Henry IV's reproof:

> Worcester, get thee gone, for I do see
> Danger and disobedience in thine eye:
> O sir, your presence is too bold and peremptory,
> And majesty might never yet endure
> The moody frontier of a servant brow.
>
> (*1 Henry IV*, I.iii.14–18)

At this level the verse moves, in Tillyard's phrase, 'with a gait at once ceremonial and consummately athletic',[13] but its varieties include also Glendower's enchanting lyrical eloquence and the comic–violent ejaculations of Hotspur:

> All studies here I solemnly defy,
> Save how to gall and pinch this Bolingbroke:
> And that same sword-and-buckler Prince of Wales,
> But that I think his father loves him not,
> And would be glad he met with some mischance –
> I would have him poison'd with a pot of ale!
> (*1 Henry IV*, I.iii.225–30)

In Part 2 the rebel Archbishop of York has a nobly sententious idiom, the ailing King an angry, despairing melancholy, Prince John a sharp decisiveness, the Lord Chief Justice a considered and courageous dignity, and the redeemed Prince a tempered majesty:

> The tide of blood in me
> Hath proudly flow'd in vanity till now.
> Now doth it turn, and ebb back to the sea,
> Where it shall mingle with the state of floods,
> And flow henceforth in formal majesty.
> Now call we our high court of parliament,
> And let us choose such limbs of noble counsel
> That the great body of our state may go
> In equal rank with the best-govern'd nation.
> (*2 Henry IV*, V.ii.129–37)

The prose is, if anything, even more expressively various, ranging from the sparkling felicities of Falstaff's phrasing, through the garrulities of Mistress Quickly and the wiseacre senilities of Justices Shallow and Silence, to the hearty violences of Doll Tearsheet and Pistol – if indeed Pistol's vociferations qualify as prose at all. They certainly confound the simple theory which in *Le Bourgeois Gentilhomme* (Act 2, scene 4) the *maître de philosophie* expounds to Monsieur Jourdain, that all that is not prose is verse, and all that is not verse is prose. Combining the most histrionic inflations of verse with the most swaggering banalities of prose, Pistol's Pegasus is given to spread-eagled belly-landings. The dramatic idiom throughout gives the England the plays are about 'a stylistic exhibition of most phases of the commonwealth'.[14]

Shakespeare and history

'What sort of drama', J.L. Styan asks in *The Dramatic Experience*, 'would one expect to see on the bare, but spacious and varied, stage of the Globe?' The answer, he suggests, is

> First, a drama which places a remarkable emphasis on the actor; both on his voice and his words, and on what meaning he can create with his body, its gesture and movement. Secondly, a drama which involves the spectator not only by his physical nearness to the stage, but also by what is demanded of him through an active imagination. A drama, finally, which offers the playwright an imaginative freedom in space and time, an unprecedented opportunity to juxtapose scene with scene in striking and incongruous arrangements of place and mood, and to create a rhythm in his action controlling the very life of the play.[15]

He could have been describing precisely the *Henry IV* pair. The spectator's imagination not only accepts what is seen and heard but surrounds all this with, embeds it all in, an extraordinary context of imaged life in space and time, a context of which what is seen and heard is the representative outcome. The England of these plays, and her history, are realized symphonically. By rich and copious imagery, and perpetual expansions beyond the immediate moment and the visible here-and-now, a rich and sustaining panorama of national life is created. In *The Frontiers of Drama* Una Ellis-Fermor asked how drama could compass the breadth of epic:

> How then can we account for the sense of vastness, of immense extent and complexity of factors which is part of our experience in reading the *Oresteia* or *Antony and Cleopatra*, or in recalling the sequence of Shakespeare's historical plays?[16]

We account for it, or partly account, by invoking Yeats's 'Emotion of Multitude' (from his essay of that name in *Ideas of Good and Evil*), 'Multitude' meaning the 'rich, far-wandering, many-imaged life of the half-seen world [beyond] the little limited life of the fable'. Shakespeare's subjects start with an advantage; their 'fables' already are charged with resonant meanings, to which the 'many-imaged life' gives a fully realized dimension. As for the 'unprecedented opportunity to juxtapose scene with scene', this is wonderfully seized as court, tavern, battlefield, and country household combine in the great curve which brings Henry IV from usurpation to deathbed, sees the rise and fall of Hotspur and the Archbishop, moves Hal from circumference to centre of the circle of power, spreads from Whitehall council chamber to Shrewsbury, Gloucestershire, and Gaultree, and acknowledges equally the vitality of youth, the assurance of maturity, and the experience of age.

As Part 1 opens, a wonderful new velocity of conception makes itself felt. The urgency of time, the impetus of events, the undertow of anguish, the dynamic geography of crucial places and impetuous travel, the spirit of dangerous challenge – these are all offered with superb assurance. Then, in Eastcheap, the manner totally changes. Instead of time and haste, there reign timeless indulgence and insouciance, a world where time and fact matter only as the occasions of wit, sensuality, and that 'boundless luxury of [Falstaff's] imagination' of which Hazlitt writes, in his essay on *Henry IV* in *Characters of Shakespeare's Plays*. Yet the wit of the Boar's Head is as active as the strategies of Westminster. All is expansive and volatile, pulsing with life. Occupations, expectations, attitudes, crowd in compulsively at all levels. The ample material of the plot goes along with an inexhaustible play of attitudes, attitudes incompatible politically (the political world cannot accommodate Henry and Hotspur, or Hotspur and Hal, or – ultimately – Hal and Falstaff) yet each so richly valid in its own terms (Henry's sense of authority, Hotspur's of honour, Falstaff's of hedonism, Hal's of self-direction towards rule) as to create a world of coexistent visions.

Part 2, though the plot must play a waiting game until time brings Henry's death and Hal's accession, employs its unusual length in an unusual way, covering its broad canvas far less with its ostensible historical subject than with an unparalleled abundance of social particulars. If I may repeat some lines from my introduction to the New Arden edition,

> No play gives a richer sense of [life's] reality. War and government with their plans, tavern-life with its humours, age with its ailments, local affairs run by such as Masters Tisick, Shallow, and Silence – trades, sports, songs, and dissipations, all form the variety of the action. Play-tags, military terms, ballad-snatches, Biblical fragments, and Homily echoes jostle references to shopkeepers' satins, pewterers' hammers, brewers' buckets, the tilling of land, the skills of archery, and caliver-management. Slang and

Shakespeare and history 115

colloquialisms abound, the language of swaggerers, catchpoles, and whores. And what is seen and heard on the stage affects us as the mere observable portion of an inexhaustible circumambient life.[17]

Every item in this many-coloured spectrum has its part to play in the plays' 'fair field full of folk' (to apply to them Langland's phrase for his vision in *Piers Plowman*).

As for *Henry V*, less richly complex though it is in exhibiting the constituents of England's life, its professed aim is to present a society under a king who (whatever the reservations of critical scrutiny) is, in Pistol's phrase, 'a bawcock and a heart of gold'. Dr Johnson, querying its use of the Chorus, observed that by it Shakespeare was annulling the line which should divide actors and spectators. To answer him is not difficult. Even though recognizing danger and suffering, the Chorus (and Henry in the St Crispin's Day oration) can celebrate a nation imbued with one courageous spirit; enthusiastically invited into the action, the audience, standing for Elizabeth's England, shares in the imagined exhilaration of Henry's. Throughout the play, as the last lines claim, 'most greatly lived /This star of England'. The reference is specifically to Henry himself. Yet identified as he is with his realm he shares his brilliance in joint splendour with it. The conspiracy against him having failed as early as Act 2, no internal dissension remains, and England's united aspirations release themselves against France, eagerly supported by symbolic representatives of Wales, Scotland, and Ireland. Gloucestershire has, alas, vanished below the horizon, and Eastcheap has dwindled to the grieving comedy of dead Falstaff plus a few battlefield ignominies. Yet we do not forget everyday England behind the glamour of court. Indeed, that remarkable eve-of-Agincourt debate between the incognito King and his indomitable but long-suffering soldiers is one of the outstanding scenes in all the histories. In effect, *Henry V*, if less comprehensive in social-dramatic synthesis than its precursors, offers the substantial reality of England's nature, with enough epic 'breadth and variety' to supplement its epic panache of heroic action.

Between the tetralogies, Shakespeare evolved from a fascination with men's drives to a fascination with their whole natures, and with the lives that circle round them. With the Talbots, Yorks, Margarets, Gloucesters, and Cades the dramatic thrill had been in their sheer force, in human urgencies fated to succeed or fail, a thrill climaxed in the nature and career of Richard III. Not surprisingly Jan Kott, viewing the histories through the dark glass of recent Europe, saw a 'Grand Mechanism' of power in the first tetralogy's 'cruel and tragic farce'.[18] By the time of *Richard II* success or failure had been (with Richard supremely, yet to an extent with Bolingbroke too, in the final scenes) less significant than the sense of personality and temperament on which politics impinges. In *Henry IV* this is enormously strengthened. Only in Prince John of Lancaster is there a survivor of the earlier limitations of range, and what we are to think of him Falstaff indicates in deriding 'this same young sober-blooded boy' impervious to love, laughter, and good sherris-sack (*2 Henry IV*, IV.iii.85). About the rest of his creation Shakespeare displays a fascinated sympathy with their natures, their lives past and present, their memories and aspirations, their relationships and neighbourhoods, their minds and concerns. As Maurice Morgann perceived two centuries ago, 'those characters ... which are seen only in part, are yet capable of being unfolded and understood in the whole, every part being in fact relative, and inferring all the rest'.[19] Henry IV reflecting on his realm past and future, Hotspur retelling Bolingbroke's usurpation or mocking the popinjay lord or garrulous Glendower, Falstaff lavishly commenting on all he touches, Lady Hotspur remembering her dead hero, Shallow evoking his neighbourhood's life or his wild youth, Mistress Quickly fussing over neighbours or sharing Falstaff's end with us, Henry V discussing with Bates, Court, and Williams a king's responsibilities or foreseeing for his followers the long perspectives of St Crispin's Day memories – these and scores of other excursions in experience enable us to unfold and understand 'in the whole' Shakespeare's 'gradually widening and deepening conception of patriotism and of that which constitutes a nation'.[20]

NOTES

1 *Shakespeare's Festive Comedy* (1959), p. 192.
2 *Shakespeare's History Plays* (1944), p. 295.
3 (1921), p. 211.
4 Between 1899 and 1906 Frank Benson at Stratford-upon-Avon staged the *Henry VI* trilogy to some critical applause but little general effect.

5 *Shakespeare: The Early Writings* (1972), p. 195.
6 ibid., p. 193.
7 *Further Explorations* (1965), p. 22.
8 *Shakespeare: The Early Writings*, p. 183.
9 *Narrative and Dramatic Sources of Shakespeare*, vol. 4 (1962), p. 167; *Shakespeare's History Plays*, p. 174; *The Player King* (1968), p. 17.
10 In Christopher Ricks, ed., *The History of Literature in the English Language*, vol. 3 (1971), p. 174.
11 *Narrative and Dramatic Sources of Shakespeare*, vol. 4, p. 24.
12 *Shakespeare's Professional Skills* (1964), p. 61.
13 *Shakespeare's History Plays*, p. 295.
14 ibid., p. 298.
15 (1965), pp. 24–5.
16 (1945; repr. 1964), p. 12.
17 (1966), p. liii.
18 *Shakespeare Our Contemporary* (1964), p. 34.
19 *The Dramatick Character of Sir John Falstaff* (1777), p. 61n.
20 Gareth Lloyd Evans, *Shakespeare II: 1587–1598* (1969), p. 40.

6

Sir John Oldcastle: Shakespeare's martyr

E.A.J. HONIGMANN

In Shakespeare's first show of Harry the Fifth, the person with which he undertook to play a buffoon was not Falstaff but Sir John Oldcastle, and ... offence being worthily taken by personages descended from his title (as peradventure by many others also who ought to have him in honourable memory) the poet was put to make an ignorant shift of abusing Sir John Falstaff, a man not inferior of virtue, though not so famous in piety.   (Richard James)

Sir John Mennis saw once his old father in his shop – a merry cheeked old man that said 'Will was a good honest fellow, but he durst have cracked a jest with him at any time.'   (Thomas Plume)[1]

What could have been Shakespeare's purpose in assigning so large a part in *Henry IV* to Sir John Oldcastle, and in changing the Protestant martyr into a buffoon? And what was lost when the name Falstaff was substituted for Oldcastle? These are questions that affect interpretation and, as I hope to show, they can be answered, but only when we learn to see Sir John through Elizabethan eyes.

First, though, let us consider the two most popular explanations of Sir John Oldcastle's unhistorical character and importance in *Henry IV*: either Shakespeare did not foresee that offence might be 'worthily taken by personages descended from his title', or he did anticipate such a possibility but didn't care – or, perhaps, even wished to offend. Geoffrey Bullough preferred the former: Shakespeare adopted the name Sir John Oldcastle 'from *Famous Victories* without *arrière pensée* and without linking his Sir John with the martyr'.[2] I find this

Sir John Oldcastle

very hard to believe. Even if Sir John Oldcastle appeared as a shadowy character in the play later reconstructed as *The Famous Victories of Henry V* (1598), and was not inserted in *Famous Victories* because of the notoriety of Sir John in *Henry IV*, Shakespeare could not have failed to be aware of Sir John Oldcastle, the Protestant martyr. As Francis Thynne said in his dedication of his manuscript *History of the House of Cobham*, dated 20 December 1598, Sir John Oldcastle is so well known that 'we need not to say anything, his life and doings being so largely set forth in all our chronicles'.[3] However meagre the dramatist's reading – and Bullough's useful volumes suggest that he read more widely than was once assumed – he must have known of 'Sir John Oldcastle, which by his wife was called Lord Cobham, a valiant captain and a hardy gentleman'. These are the words of Holinshed, near the beginning of his life of Henry V, a principal source for *Henry IV*. Here and elsewhere in Holinshed, and also in Stow's *Chronicles* (1580) and in Foxe's much longer entry in the *Acts and Monuments* (1563), it is made absolutely clear (i) that Sir John Oldcastle was also Lord Cobham of Kent, and therefore belonged to the same family as William and Henry Brooke, the Elizabethan Lords Cobham, Shakespeare's contemporaries, and (ii) that Sir John's character and standing in the world differed greatly from the dramatic Sir John's.

If it seems inconceivable that Shakespeare changed a minor character from an earlier play into his inimitable Sir John Oldcastle without connecting him with the celebrated Protestant martyr of the same name, it is just as hard to believe that he failed to notice that Sir John Oldcastle was also 'the Lord Cobham'. All families take pride in famous ancestors; even if Sir John Oldcastle was not a direct ancestor of the Elizabethan Lords Cobham, having been the fourth husband of the heiress from whom the title descended, he did use the title 'Lord Cobham' and he was a member of the family. Any misrepresentation of an earlier Lord Cobham would certainly displease his Elizabethan counterpart – hence the theory that Shakespeare's Sir John Oldcastle was meant to give offence.

The Cobhams were an important family in the 1590s; to offend them would be folly – unless one had the backing of powerful friends. William Brooke, a courtier, a close ally of the Cecils and a member of the Privy Council, rose to be Lord Chamberlain (from August 1596 until his death on 5 March

1597); as such he controlled all dramatic activities, and could censor or suppress plays, though his powers were ususally exercised by the Master of the Revels, who was responsible to him. Henry Brooke, on succeeding to the title in 1597, hoped to follow in his father's footsteps; a brother-in-law of Sir Robert Cecil, he intrigued for political advantage; his greatest triumph, perhaps, was that he helped to bring about the fall of Robert Devereux, the second Earl of Essex.

The enmity of Essex and the Cobhams cannot be ignored by students of the Oldcastle plays, even if it may also be overemphasized. It culminated in Essex's obsessive hatred of the Queen's 'evil counsellors' – Cobham, Raleigh, and Cecil – who, he asserted just before his 'rebellion' in 1601, plotted to take away his life.[4] But it had already festered for years. Essex disagreed with Lord Cobham in 1595–6 about the defence of Ostend and Calais, and 'he [Essex] was stung by the baron's refusal to acknowledge that a Spanish success at Ostend would imperil Calais. His bitterness increased when Calais did in fact fall to Spain in April 1596.'[5] This was a contributing factor, yet Essex's relations with Henry Brooke, Lord Cobham's son and heir, were more important. 'Essex and Cecil, even Essex and Raleigh ... knew periods of reconciliation, but never Essex and the younger Lord Cobham. The seeds of this mortal hatred were germinating fast by the time that the year 1596 ended.'[6] Henry Brooke had become an influential figure at court by 1594; Essex's secretary wrote in May and August 1596 that Brooke was spreading malicious rumours to discredit him, and Essex himself wrote in 1597 that 'I will protest unto the Queen against him [Brooke], and avow that I will think it is the reward of his slanders and practice against me, if the Queen should lay honour upon him'.[7]

By this time the Earl of Southampton, to whom Shakespeare had dedicated *The Rape of Lucrece* (1594) and 'love without end', had committed himself to Essex's political faction, and was one of his closer friends: he served under Essex in the expeditions to Cadiz (1596) and to the Azores (1597). And at the same time, in 1596 or 1597, William Shakespeare composed his first Oldcastle play, metamorphosing the most renowned member of the Cobham family, the Protestant martyr, into a penniless adventurer and buffoon.

Should we regard Sir John Oldcastle as a salvo fired off

by Shakespeare in the Essex-Cobham wars? No, thought Bullough:

> Little more plausible is the suggestion that the name Oldcastle was preserved as a hit at the Cobhams of Shakespeare's own time, who were hostile to Essex (whom the dramatist praises in *Henry V*, Act V, Chorus). But William Brooke, 7th Lord Cobham, was Lord Chamberlain from July [August, in fact], 1596 to March, 1597. Even if the actors had difficulty with him for some reason unknown, they would not be likely to insult him deliberately.[8]

The same conclusion was reached by D.M. McKeen in his study of the House of Cobham, which contains a detailed and careful account of the Oldcastle plays and their Elizabethan background. McKeen argued that 'no indubitable link between Southampton and Shakespeare other than the two dedications has been found. Without such proof of their association after 1594, it is futile to try to number the dramatist among the partisans whom Southampton brought to Essex.'[9] Here McKeen overlooked the praise of Essex in *Henry V*, another link, since Essex and Southampton were undoubtedly 'associated' by 1599. (When Essex prepared for the Irish campaign in 1599 as Lord Deputy, he nominated Southampton general of his horse; the Queen would not confirm the appointment, and Essex, after strenuously backing his friend, had to give way.) In the absence of evidence to the contrary we must conclude that Shakespeare saw himself as a member of the Southampton circle from 1593-4 until at least 1599: and the Oldcastle plays, as is generally agreed, date from these years.

But, said McKeen, in the 1590s Southampton and the Cobhams were 'on most civil terms with one another. The elder Cobham's proposal of marriage to Southampton's stepgrandmother indicates some degree of friendship', and Henry Lord Cobham's offer in 1598 to help Southampton to reinstate himself with the Queen seems to have been well-meant.[10] William Lord Cobham, however, lost his wife in 1592, and Lady Montague – whom he wished to marry – was widowed six weeks later, so it is most likely that he proposed marriage before the Essex-Cobham feud became politically important; and, since Lady Montague gave her suitor a very positive refusal (as will be seen), this argument really cuts both ways. As for Henry Lord Cobham's offer to help Southampton in 1598, 'the sycophant' (as Essex apparently nicknamed him)[11] was so devious and dangerous that I suspect that he wished to detach Southampton from Essex. To take the offer at face-value would be naive; yet even if it was an act of the purest friendship, it is one or two years too late to throw light on Southampton's relationship with the Cobhams at the time when Shakespeare wrote his first Oldcastle play, in 1596 or 1597. At this time Shakespeare must be considered a protégé of Southampton, who was close to Essex and, as far as we know, no friend of the Cobhams. Neither Southampton nor Shakespeare had any reason to love the Cobhams: all the surviving evidence suggests, on the contrary, that they were supporters of Essex.

We return, then, to Bullough's point that Shakespeare and his company would not want to insult the Lord Chamberlain, who could so easily make life unpleasant for them. Bullough made two assumptions: (i) that the dramatist did not connect 'Sir John Oldcastle' with the Lord Chamberlain's family, and (ii) that *1 Henry IV* was written while William Lord Cobham was Lord Chamberlain. In both cases we are asked to believe in a Shakespeare so dim-witted that he did not foresee what is obvious to us – the Cobhams would take offence, and the Lord Chamberlain could compel the players to back down. These difficulties disappear, however, if *Henry IV* was written – or at least begun – before Lord Cobham became Lord Chamberlain. Move back *1 Henry IV* a few months, to the first half of 1596, and a very different picture emerges. No one expected that the elderly Lord Cobham would be appointed Lord Chamberlain (he was born in 1527, therefore was close to 70 in 1596); on the other hand, Essex's instability of character did not yet disquiet his friends, and in the summer of 1596 his 'brilliant career reached its apex in the capture of Cadiz'.[12] Appointed joint commander of the English forces with the Lord Admiral in 1596, Essex was seen as the hero of the capture of Cadiz; a rising political star, the advocate of a more vigorous war-policy, the Earl was immensely popular. At this time many ambitious men courted Essex's favour – and why not William Shakespeare?

Is there any reason for not moving back *Henry IV* a few months, to the period before Lord Cobham became Lord Chamberlain (in August, 1596)? The play, said Bullough, 'contains allusions to conditions in 1596':

Sir John Oldcastle 123

Early in 1596 there were complaints about the maltreatment of impressed men by army officers, and Sir John Smithe was up before the Star Chamber on 19 June for inciting Essex recruits to mutiny. In September when a hundred men were to be levied in Northamptonshire for service in Ireland the Council's order insisted that they should be serviceable men, not the baser sort. . . . Falstaff's attitude to his soldiers (IV.2) would be topical in 1596/7. The price of corn rose very high in 1596, and the reference to Robin Ostler's death, 'Poor fellow! never joyed since the price of oats rose' (II.1.12), seems to allude to a fairly recent change.[13]

True, these were topical allusions in 1596. It should be remembered, though, that Privy Council orders and the like did not suddenly bring to public notice matters unheard of before, as sometimes happens today: the Privy Council was usually the end of the road, not the beginning, where public comment on abuses was concerned. There would be mutterings, semi-official complaints, delays: the malpractices referred to in *1 Henry IV*, in short, must have continued for a while, and cannot help us in assigning a precise date to the play. So, too, the price of corn – again, not a sudden, once and for all emergency, but a calamity that had already continued for three years in 1596. Bad weather, E.K. Chambers noted in another context, 'began in March, 1594, prevailed during the greater part of that year, and ushered in a long period of corn shortage'.[14]

Lacking exact indications of date, we have to fall back on more general pointers. 'The links with *Richard II* make it likely that the play was written soon after that tragedy', said Bullough, 'perhaps late in 1596 or early in 1597'. But where do we date *Richard II*? Bullough himself decided that '*Richard II* was probably written in 1595', without ruling out the possibility that it could have been 'written in 1594 or earlier'.[15] E.K. Chambers and Peter Ure also thought 1595 the likeliest date for *Richard II*; if *1 Henry IV* was begun 'soon after' *Richard II*, as Bullough quite plausibly suggested, Sir John Oldcastle could have 'fought a long hour by Shrewsbury clock' in the first months of 1596, or even in 1595.

It has been said that Richard James's statement ('offence being worthily taken by personages descended from his [Oldcastle's] title') is 'the only incontestable proof' that the

Cobhams took any notice of Shakespeare's play.[16] Yet the circumstantial evidence is considerable. In November 1599 the Admiral's Men produced Part I of *Sir John Oldcastle* and in their Prologue condemned Shakespeare's 'Oldcastle' as a fraud:

> It is no pamper'd glutton we present
> Nor aged counsellor to youthful sin,
> ... Let fair truth be graced,
> Since forg'd invention former time defac'd.

By 1599 the Lord Admiral was one of Essex's chief political opponents: Essex objected that the Lord Admiral was rewarded with the Earldom of Nottingham for exploits that he claimed as his own. Why did the Admiral's Men reply so belatedly to Shakespeare's Oldcastle plays? On 17 January 1599 John Chamberlain wrote to Dudley Carleton that 'there is a marriage spoken of twixt the Lord Cobham and the Countess of Kildare'.[17] The widowed Countess was the daughter of the Lord Admiral – who, partly because of his feud with Essex, was now (in 1599) a political ally of Henry Brooke, Lord Cobham. The staging of *Sir John Oldcastle* by the Admiral's Men is therefore another sign that the Oldcastle plays had political overtones. And John Weever also wrote *The Mirror of Martyrs* (sub-titled 'the life and death of that thrice valiant captain and most godly martyr, Sir John Oldcastle') as an exercise in rehabilitation; he had his reasons for courting the Cobham family[18] and, rightly or wrongly, asserted that his was the 'first true Oldcastle', having been 'made fit for the press' two years before its publication in 1601. We need not doubt, then, that Shakespeare's 'untrue' Oldcastle gave offence to 'personages descended from his title'. Equally, two letters from members of the Essex-Southampton circle, in which the writers gleefully refer to someone nicknamed 'Sir John Falstaff' – almost certainly Lord Cobham[19] – prove that the dramatic 'Oldcastle' delighted one political faction no less than he offended the other.

Whatever Shakespeare's original purpose, his Sir John Oldcastle was later seen as a significant factor in the complicated power-struggle that finally destroyed Essex and very nearly led to the execution of Southampton. But what did Shakespeare think he was doing, if he quite deliberately transformed Sir John Oldcastle into a buffoon in the early

Sir John Oldcastle

months of 1596? He could not anticipate that Lord Cobham would become Lord Chamberlain, and therefore felt he might take a liberty with Cobham's celebrated predecessor which would amuse Southampton and Essex. (Like Southampton, Essex was an enthusiastic supporter of the arts. One evening in 1598 he and his friends watched two plays at Essex House, 'which kept them up till one o'clock after midnight'.[20]) After the event, when Lord Cobham was unexpectedly placed in the key position of Lord Chamberlain, it was natural that the whole episode had to be explained away as a misunderstanding – 'Oldcastle died a martyr, and this is not the man' (*2 Henry IV*, Epilogue) – but, given the political circumstances of the 1590s, the enforced renaming of 'Oldcastle' and its after-vibrations, I cannot believe that Shakespeare proceeded 'without *arrière pensée*', in total innocence.

Accordingly we must now examine the other side of the coin. Could Shakespeare have created Sir John Oldcastle as a deliberate exercise in debunking – just as he devised dramatic portraits of Julius Caesar, Achilles, Ajax, and others that were also ironical reinterpretations of 'historical' worthies? Could it be that Sir John Oldcastle was meant to represent Sir John Oldcastle?

It is sometimes said that only some slight traces remain of Falstaff's origin as Sir John Oldcastle – in the words addressed to him, 'my old lad of the castle' (*1 Henry IV*, I.ii.41), the speech prefix '*Old.*' (for Falstaff) that survived accidentally (*2 Henry IV*, I.ii.119), and the substitution of 'Broom' for 'Brook' in *Merry Wives*. Once we accept that we need not swallow the apology that 'this is not the man', other traces of Oldcastle show through at many points.

Before I attempt to explain how, a brief account of the historical Sir John is necessary. The son of Sir Richard Oldcastle of Herefordshire, Sir John served in the Welsh campaign with Prince Henry (later Henry V), and won his friendship. In 1408 he married Joan, the heiress of Cobham (in Kent), was summoned to Parliament as Lord Cobham, and at about the same time adopted 'Lollard' views inspired by Wycliff. Just before the death of Henry IV, Cobham was accused of heresy, but was then protected by his friendship with the new king. He appeared before an ecclesiastical court, and, refusing to assent to some orthodox Catholic doctrines, was convicted of heresy. The king granted him forty days to change his mind; he escaped from captivity, headed a Lollard conspiracy, and was finally captured in 1417, hanged, and burned.

If Shakespeare did not completely rewrite the Oldcastle plays in response to Cobham complaints but merely substituted 'Falstaff' for 'Oldcastle', as is usually assumed, we would expect many obvious traces of Oldcastle to be still visible. On the other hand, if Shakespeare offended the Cobhams by exhibiting their famous predecessor, the Protestant hero and martyr, as a man totally devoid of conscience or principles – the very opposite of the popular image – almost all signs of 'Oldcastle' are bound to disappear once the character is renamed. To understand why the Cobhams were offended we must consequently reject the name 'Falstaff' and revert to 'Oldcastle'. For Shakespeare's wicked joke seems to have been to create a character unlike any martyr that ever lived, who, nevertheless, being given the name 'Sir John Oldcastle' and placed in Sir John's historical situation, claims to be the genuine article, more authentic than Foxe's martyr.

As others have seen,[21] there are concealed ironies in the dialogue when the name 'Oldcastle' is reinstated. 'Shall there be gallows standing in England when thou art king?' Sir John asks Hal. 'I doubt not but to die a fair death ... if I scape hanging', 'I hope I shall as soon be strangled with a halter as another': we know that Oldcastle died on the gallows. 'I'll be a traitor ... when thou art king' Sir John warns Hal, another example of unconscious anticipation. Informed that 'there are pilgrims going to Canterbury with rich offerings', he helps to waylay them (the historical Oldcastle disapproved of images and pilgrimages). And, of course, he campaigns with Hal in the wars, if not as strenuously as the historical Oldcastle; he is a friend of the youthful prince; he has his own little private army; and, when Hal succeeds his father, his relations with the new king change for the worse, though not for religious reasons. As an independent-minded critic of the powers that be, he fences with the representatives of the law (as did the historical Oldcastle), he is sent to prison, and, says the king:

> And, *as we hear you do reform yourselves,*
> We will, according to your strengths and qualities,
> Give you advancement.   (*2 Henry IV*, V.v.68–70)

It is surely significant that Sir John begins and ends in *Henry IV* on the same note – '*I must give over this life, and I will give it over*' (*1 Henry IV*, I.ii.92–3) – and refers so insistently, as do others, to the need to *reform* and *repent*. The improbable possibility therefore remains that, like the historical Oldcastle, he changed in his later years, in which case the popular image of the martyr could have been based upon some grains of truth! Shakespeare's Oldcastle, that is to say, was not a straight inversion of the traditional one (a martyr transformed into a rogue) but, rather, was Sir John seen through a distorting mirror, with certain recognizable features.

He is much given to religious phrases and allusions, which also point towards the martyr, or the man later thought to have been one. 'Grace thou wilt have none', 'trouble me no more with vanity', 'now am I ... little better than one of the wicked', 'if men were to be saved by merit', 'they are villains and the sons of darkness', 'watch to-night, pray to-morrow', 'I could sing psalms or anything', 'for my voice, I have lost it with hallooing and singing of anthems'. His 'religiousness' is a joke at this stage of his life, which must have displeased the Cobhams – a joke with a special edge to it, considering his later reputation as a Lollard – and one that has a double function in the final scene of *2 Henry IV*. For, as in other final scenes in the histories, Shakespeare gives advance notice of what is to come in the next play in the series. 'I know thee not, old man. *Fall to thy prayers*' (V.v.47). Sir John will only receive advancement if he *reforms*. How did he react elsewhere when faced with an ultimatum? 'Zounds, ye fat paunch, and ye call me coward by the Lord I'll stab thee.' 'I call thee coward? I'll see thee damned ere I call thee coward, but I would give a thousand pound I could run as fast as thou canst' (*1 Henry IV*, II.iv.141–5). Pretending to comply with the ultimatum, he goes on as before. It seems to have been Shakespeare's plan to repeat Sir John's characteristic manoeuvre in *Henry V* – that is, to bring back a 'reformed' buffoon, a pious fraud who pretends to be what the king commands, and who thus acquired his reputation as a Lollard.

As I see it, the dramatist who 'durst have cracked a jest' at any time (countless other stories about him confirm his father's statement, cited in the epigraph above) transformed the historical Sir John Oldcastle quite deliberately in *Henry IV*, and expected this to be noticed. He wanted to amuse Essex,

Southampton, and their friends, to annoy the Cobhams – a send-up that the Cobhams would dislike, and yet could choose to ignore. In *Henry V*, however, a different treatment would be almost inevitable, partly because 'Oldcastle' would now be firmly associated in everyone's mind with the Cobhams and partly because Sir John's character would have to continue to deteriorate (as already in *2 Henry IV*). It is certain that Shakespeare hoped, even after he was forced to change 'Oldcastle' to 'Falstaff', to 'continue our story, with Sir John in it'. He abandoned this plan, perhaps because it would have involved him in a less light-hearted jest at the very time when Essex and Southampton looked politically vulnerable and their opponents more dangerous; or, perhaps, because his original intention of next presenting Sir John as a religious hypocrite, who deserved his later reputation as a martyr no more than his military fame after Shrewsbury, lost its point when 'Oldcastle' became 'Falstaff'.

In *Henry IV* Shakespeare's treatment of Oldcastle seems to me more amusing than malicious. When Queen Elizabeth reacted so favourably to Falstaff (or could it have been Oldcastle?) and commanded Shakespeare to write 'one play more, and to show him in love', the result was a more topical entertainment and one in which greater risks were taken. Two contemporary documents by and about William Brooke, Lord Cobham, provide new clues; both were cited by D.B. McKeen but were not connected by him with *The Merry Wives of Windsor*.[22]

First, a letter from Lord Cobham to Henry Brooke, his eldest son, dated 1595:

> Son Harry. I pray tell Mr. Broome that his wife is come over and landed well at Dover. He shall do well to send his contrivance for her to come to London, and to provide her a place to remain there until he have been in Ireland. I send [here enclosed (?)] a letter to the commissioners of Dover to suffer her to come away with her necessaries. ... From the court at Richmond, the 9 of October. Your loving father W. Cobham. [P.S.] I send you my son's Cecil [i.e. his son-in-law Robert Cecil's] letter for the receipt of the 30 li. Let him [Broome] have some five pounds to send for his wife; the rest he shall have when he is ready to go into Ireland.[23]

Sir John Oldcastle 129

McKeen commented that 'nothing more is heard of Mr. Broom. His association with the Brookes would seem to have been an official one, having to do with his service to Cecil and the government rather than with any personal relations which existed between him and the Lords Cobham. Shakespeare's use of his name almost certainly would not have been construed as an allusion to anyone in the Brookes' circle.'[24] I have also failed to find out more about Mr Broome, but I am more curious about Mrs Broome. It was surely most unusual for a nobleman – or any other man – to tell a husband to provide a 'place' for his wife, presumably a room or rooms not used by the husband himself. Why should Lord Cobham be so interested? What business was it of his? And what of the intriguing advance of five pounds? Since the Broomes are not known to have been related to Lord Cobham, the answer suggests itself that we have here a 'Sir Walter Whorehound' triangle – a wealthy lover, his mistress, and her more or less complaisant husband. In the Elizabethan period Lord Cobham's grown-up son would not be too shocked by such an arrangement; the gentry and nobility cohabited even more openly with other men's wives than did Thackeray's wicked Lord Steyne.

And Mrs Broome, I suggest, throws new light on a famous crux in *Merry Wives*. In the Quarto the disguised Ford calls himself 'Brooke', whereas in the Folio he is consistently Broome; 'Brook' must have been his original alias, as is proved by one of Falstaff's quips. 'Brook is his name? ... Such Brooks are welcome to me, that o'erflows such liquor' (II.ii.143–6). E.K. Chambers thought that the change to 'Broome' looks like 'a bit of cautious censorship. Brooke was the family name of that Lord Cobham to whose intervention the extrusion of Oldcastle from *Henry IV* was probably due.'[25] Yet the very opposite could also be true – namely that, having been ordered to remove the name Brook from *Merry Wives*, Shakespeare or his colleagues added insult to injury by dragging in the Broomes. This would have been a clever counter-thrust; the Cobham–Mr Broome–Mrs Broome triangle is repeated in the play, with Cobham (i.e. Oldcastle, i.e. Falstaff) offering to cuckold 'Mr. Broome'. Such an impudent change would give even more offence, but could not have been objected to without exposing Lord Cobham's relationship with the Broomes to further ridicule.

The second document is also concerned with a lady.

William Brooke, Lord Cobham, was in his mid-6os when his second wife died in 1592:

> He had not, except during a few months in 1559, been without a wife since he was eighteen. He had perhaps become too accustomed to living with a woman of strong character to do without one, for at some time in the last four and a half years of his life he is said to have proposed marriage to a lady who rivalled the queen herself in individuality. She was Magdalen Browne, the widow of ... Viscount Montague.

Lady Montague was widowed six weeks after Lord Cobham's wife died. Her husband being dead, wrote Richard Smith in 1609,

> the Lord Cobham, a man of great estate, honour and authority in the realm, did most earnestly seek her in marriage and offered her a very fair dowry, but she gave him so resolute a denial, that thenceforward she was no more solicited by suitors. This example is not ordinary in England in this so corrupt an age.[26]

As the Elizabethan Cobhams were quickly identified with Sir John Oldcastle, the story about Lord Cobham's ill-fated wooing is close enough to Shakespeare's comedy to deserve some attention. Admittedly, Lord Cobham offered immediate marriage, and only to one lady, not two, whereas Falstaff's proposal was not quite so attractive. 'I would thy husband were dead; I'll speak it before the best lord, I would make thee my lady' (III.iii.43–5). Yet Falstaff 'is well-nigh worn to pieces with age' (II.i.21), and Mrs Page and Mrs Ford are no longer 'in the holiday-time ' of their beauty (II.i.1–2); Lord Cobham and Lady Montague (aged 53 when she was widowed) were also an elderly couple – and, if 'Sir John Oldcastle' was already identified in the public mind with Cobham's family, Lady Montague's 'resolute denial' could have suggested Mrs Ford's robust treatment of Falstaff. (According to Thynne's *History of the House of Cobham*, the historical Sir John Oldcastle died at the age of 35;[27] Shakespeare transformed Sir John into an older man.)

Lord Cobham's deceased wife had been a favourite attendant of Queen Elizabeth; his wooing of a third wife was evidently no secret, and an oblique allusion to his discomfi-

Sir John Oldcastle 131

ture would probably have appealed to the queen's earthy humour. Even though Lord Cobham's relations with Mrs Broome remain conjectural, it seems that he did not lose his interest in the ladies, and that may be why the queen asked for a play showing Falstaff (i.e. Cobham?) 'in love'. The logic of my argument drives me to the conclusion that *Merry Wives* was intended for the Garter Feast in April 1597, the date favoured by most recent commentators; if Lord Cobham's pursuit of the ladies served as the play's germinal idea, it will have been written by 5 March 1597 when he died.[28] The alternative date for *Merry Wives*, 1601, seems altogether less likely, for Shakespeare would not have sacrificed Falstaff in 1599 (by dropping him from *Henry V*) and then brought him back in 1601, the year of Essex's fall and of the new Lord Cobham's triumph.[29]

NOTES

1 For James and Plume see E.K. Chambers, *William Shakespeare* (Oxford, 1930), vol. 2, pp. 242, 247. Here and elsewhere I have modernized the spelling.
2 *Narrative and Dramatic Sources of Shakespeare* (London, 1962), vol. 4, p. 171.
3 British Library, Add. MS. 37, 666, fo.20b.
4 Thomas Birch, *Memoirs of the Reign of Queen Elizabeth*, 2 vols (1754), vol. 2, p. 465.
5 David B. McKeen, '"A Memory of Honour": A Study of the House of Cobham of Kent in the Reign of Elizabeth I', p. 615. This valuable dissertation (Birmingham, 1964) will soon be published. I quote from the typescript, and gratefully acknowledge that I am much indebted to it.
6 McKeen, p. 623.
7 See Birch, vol. 2, pp. 4f.; McKeen, p. 650; E.M. Tenison, *Elizabethan England*, 12 vols (privately published, Leamington Spa, 1933–), vol. 10, pp. 178f., 321.
8 Bullough, vol. 4, p. 171.
9 McKeen, p. 977.
10 ibid.
11 McKeen, p. 764.
12 O.J. Campbell and Edward Quinn, eds, *A Shakespeare Encyclopedia* (New York, 1966): 'Essex'.
13 Bullough, vol. 4, p. 155.
14 Chambers, vol. 1, p. 360.
15 Bullough, vol. 4, p. 156; vol. 3, p. 353.
16 McKeen, p. 992.
17 McKeen anticipated me in seeing that the Lord Admiral's Men's *Oldcastle* play, a surprisingly late rejoinder to Shakespeare, must be connected with the Lord Admiral's political (and his daughter's marital) alliance with Cobham.

18 See my biography of John Weever (Manchester, 1987).
19 Leslie Hotson, 'The Earl of Essex and "Falstaff"' in *Shakespeare's Sonnets Dated* (London, 1949), pp. 147f.
20 *Manuscripts of the Lord De L'Isle and Dudley at Penshurst Place* (London, 1934), vol. 2, p. 322.
21 See Alice-Lyle Scoufos, *Shakespeare's Typological Satire: A Study of the Falstaff–Oldcastle Problem* (Athens, Ohio, 1979), pp. 74f.; Gary Taylor, 'The fortunes of Oldcastle', *Shakespeare Survey*, 38 (1985), pp. 85f.
22 McKeen, pp. 999, 577f. For Queen Elizabeth's command, see Chambers, vol. 2, p. 266.
23 Spelling modernized. McKeen (and HMC, *Hatfield House*, vol. 5, p. 407) has 'find his contrivances'; the original has 'seeynde' (send).
24 McKeen, p. 999.
25 Chambers, vol. 1, p. 433.
26 McKeen, pp. 577f.
27 British Library, Add. MS. 37, 666, fo.21, margin.
28 See also Chambers, vol. 2, pp. 262–3.
29 I have not mentioned the theory that Shakespeare and the actors disliked Lord Cobham because of his supposed Puritanism and anti-theatrical bias: William Green disposed of this red herring in *Shakespeare's 'Merry Wives of Windsor'* (Princeton, NJ, 1962), pp. 113f. But that does not dispose of Lord Cobham. McKeen and Taylor went too far in arguing that there is 'no reason to believe that Shakespeare set out to insult or caricature Oldcastle's living descendants': though indebted to both, I disagree with them about Shakespeare's attitude to the Cobhams, the date of *1 Henry IV*, and much else.

7

"It must be your imagination then": the Prologue and the Plural Text in *Henry V* and Elsewhere

ANTONY HAMMOND

Among Shakespeare's plays only *Henry V* and *Pericles* employ the highly elaborated formal structure of prologue, choruses before each Act, and epilogue. Other plays employ some of these dramatic devices, but not even *Pericles* uses them as centrally and as structurally as does *Henry V*;[1] nor do the other plays which violate the unities as flagrantly as it. This fact has influenced interpretation of the play, often unconsciously. Everyone knows that *Henry V* is a play about war, and that Henry himself is a great warrior-hero. How do we know? Because the Chorus (that is, the character who speaks these metatextual speeches) tells us so. Honest critics, examining the play closely, have been somewhat puzzled by this, because, in fact, there are no battles, really, in the play, and because although Henry plays numerous roles in the course of the action (he is politician, outraged feudal lord, orator, anxious general, bumbling lover, and so on), warrior is not one of them. This is all very perplexing. If it is not a patriotic play about a warrior-king, why does the Chorus say it is?

The absence of choruses from Q1 of *Henry V* has led some writers[2] to speculate that they were not by Shakespeare, but were the creations of that celebrated author, Another Hand. This supposition is self-evidently absurd, and no one who could seriously believe that 'O, for a Muse of fire' could have been written by anyone other than Shakespeare need be listened to on any issue whatever. Nonetheless, the assumption that if the choruses were not authorial they could safely be disregarded saved the begetter of this notion from the intellectual difficulty posed by them, and by their relationship to the body of the play. In the same way, those who read the play as a paean of patriotic enthusiasm are apt to say that it must have been written in a hurry, to account for its episodic structure and the apparent plethora of contradictory concepts it incorporates. These intellectual difficulties are the subject of the present paper: they deserve to be encountered firmly, and I hope in the process to shed some light on some of the interpretative problems in the play which continue to elude satisfactory definition. Certainly, I hope to present a solution of these difficulties more constructive than that of Q1, whose compilers, evidently judging that the provincial audience for whom (as Gary Taylor has shown[3]) that text was prepared was less sophisticated than that of the Globe, omitted not only the choruses, but most of the rest of the controversial matter in the play, thus making it 'exactly the sort of simple patriotic play critics have often taken *Henry V* to be'.[4]

If taken whole, *Henry V* is not an easy text, and most certainly not a simple patriotic play. Only by cutting and/or special pleading can it be made, as Laurence Olivier made it, patriotic propaganda about one of England's greatest warrior-kings, a triumphant celebration of the fact that England occasionally won wars handsomely rather than just muddling through them. Even some quite recent writers have maintained this view. John Dover Wilson's Cambridge edition, which appeared in 1947, dedicated to Field-Marshall Wavell, really belongs like the film to the Second World War. But J.H. Walter, in the introduction to his 1954 Arden edition, was at pains to demonstrate how Henry fulfilled Renaissance writers' conceptions of the ideal hero-king. It never seemed to occur to him that Shakespeare could have included all this ideology in his play, only to leave us with a hero whose morality is persistently and pervasively equivocal: or, to put it another way, that Shakespeare just might have been able to see further than most, and in his play to reveal universal opinion to be mistaken or limited. Since Walter's edition appeared there has been Suez, the CND, the Cuban missile crisis, the Vietnam horror, the permanent catastrophe of the Middle East, Northern Ireland, Afghanistan and Cambodia, not to mention such lesser items of tragical-comical-historical-pastoral as the Falklands and Grenada: dear God knows how many other illustrations for our time that the military way is the worst possible way for the greatest number of people. One of the consequences of this newly-appalled perception of the horror and inefficiency of war is that *Henry V*'s condition has changed from that of honest history play to problem play. It is not, of course, the first time that this has happened; I believe that the first writer to express distrust of the military motive in the play was actually Hazlitt. 'And Hazlitt's convictions have become, for the most part, our own.'[5]

The essential clues to the contradictions built into the play are to be found in the choruses, and I would like to rehearse the issues in a little detail. The Chorus, in his prologue, adopts two tones of voice. First there is the heroic, which sustains some of Shakespeare's most thrilling rhetoric until line 8. In the middle of this line, the Chorus suddenly switches to an exculpatory mode:

> But pardon, gentles all,
> The flat unraised spirits that hath dar'd
> On this unworthy scaffold to bring forth
> So great an object....

He continues in this vein for the rest of the prologue, apologizing for the fewness of the actors' numbers,[6] and for the absence of what in our time have come to be called 'special effects': especially the lack of horses. For the remedy of these deficiencies, the Chorus urges the audience again and again to use its imagination: 'let us ... On your imaginary forces work'; 'Piece out our imperfections with your thoughts'; 'For 'tis your thoughts that now must deck our kings.' The Chorus to Act III is even more insistent: 'imagin'd', 'thought', 'Suppose', 'Play with your fancies ... behold ... Hear ... behold', 'do but think', 'Grapple your minds', 'Work, work your thoughts, and therein see', 'Suppose', 'eke out our performance with your mind'. Well, goodness, we get the point. The audience is required to work for its living in *Henry V* along with the author and the actors.

One can scarcely refrain from recalling Theseus's defence of the mechanicals' play in *A Midsummer Night's Dream*: 'The best in this kind are but shadows, and the wost are no worse, if imagination amend them' (V.i.208–9). Theseus has been blamed for his seeming inability to distinguish between a play by Shakespeare and one by Peter Quince – but the plain fact is that people *are* moved, often to tears, by the most awful tripe: I cite, with due deference, the people that cry their eyes out at *Madama Butterfly* (or the children who bawl at *Bambi*), or the folks whose lives revolve around the polystyrene characters of soap operas. As Hippolyta acidly responds, 'It must be your imagination then, and not theirs', and she is undoubtedly right. To be greatly moved by art that is so inferior as scarcely to deserve the name at all requires a great imaginative faculty on the part of the spectator, reader, listener, or viewer. Theseus and his court decline, in fact, to exercise this faculty during the playing of *Pyramus and Thisbe* – 'This is the silliest stuff that ever I heard' – and so does the audience at the pageant of the Nine Worthies in *Love's Labour's Lost*. The royal audience of 'The Mousetrap', however, finds his imagination suddenly working overtime, and experiences what used to be called character-identification.

All these plays-within-plays are silly stuff, but *Henry V* is clearly not: it may be perplexing, but it is certainly not stupid. Why, then, does the Chorus insist with such iteration on the importance of the audience's imagination and the inadequacies of the company? Obviously not because he seriously means nothing more than that the author and the company are unqualified for their subject.[7] On the whole recent critics have recognized the irony in the Chorus's apologies – Robert Ornstein remarks on 'the artfulness that wears so naive a guise' in them,[8] and Taylor recognizes that they are not 'reflections of a real sense of artistic dissatisfaction: rather the reverse' (1982 edn, 56). Indeed: there is something of a covert Jonsonian appeal to the understanding heads in the auditory in this process of apologizing for things that need no apology.

The Act II chorus follows the pattern of the prologue:

> Now all the youth of England are on fire,
> And silken dalliance in the wardrobe lies: ...
>
> Linger your patience on; and we'll digest
> Th' abuse of distance ...
>
> There is the playhouse now, there must you sit. ...

The Chorus gets himself into a terrible tangle worrying about the unity of the place: 'the scene /Is now transported, gentles, to Southampton', he announces confidently, and goes on to promise safe passage across the Channel to France, only to recollect himself in the last two lines, when he remembers he has not got to Southampton yet. The lines are curious:

> But, till the king come forth and not till then,
> Unto Southampton do we shift our scene.

Walter complains that these lines 'hardly agree' with lines 35–6 (which asserted roundly that the playhouse is now in Southampton), and discusses the apparent inconsistency in his Introduction,[9] seizing upon a complex theory of revision to account for them. He seems unaware that the Chorus is saying something that on the literal level anyway is absurd and obviously untrue: the Globe is still firmly on the Bankside. Taylor in his edition provides a much more sophisticated explanation than Walter's, dismissing the idea that the concluding couplet is an afterthought, and remarking helpfully, 'Tonally, the last 12 lines of the speech lead very naturally into the comedy of 2.1.' He develops this insight further:

> That the Chorus does nothing to prepare us for the scene which immediately follows is hardly surprising: the prologue does nothing to prepare us for 1.1. either. In both cases, Shakespeare arouses an expectation and then (temporarily) frustrates it, using the expectation not only as a contrast to the foreground scene, but as a means of sustaining our interest, assuring us of the main line of development, during an intermediate and subordinate action.
> (Appendix B.I, 291)

This explanation actually describes Shakespeare's practice better in other plays than in *Henry V*: it suits very well the chorus and first scene of *Romeo and Juliet*, for instance. Here, the Chorus announces in a portentous sonnet the 'misadventur'd piteous overthrows' the 'star-cross'd lovers' will encounter; the speech's solemnity is thrown into extreme contrast by the coarse comedy of sex and violence of the opening dialogue. Shakespeare seems to have enjoyed *beginning* his plays with a peripeteia, and this is an easy way of achieving one. It does indeed establish a tonality for the entire play which survives the less-than-heroic first few scenes, and its language is instantly recognizable when Romeo and Juliet meet in a sonnet at the Capulets' ball. Of course, there are many ways of confounding audience expectation in the opening scenes: but the prologue is clearly one of them.

Among its functions is to serve as a signal for peripeteia in the opening scene. The effect is not unlike that of, say, Mozart's Thirty-Ninth Symphony, whose grave introduction with its dissonant harmonies contrasts powerfully (yet satisfyingly) with the main subject of the allegro.

This description alone, however, will not do for the Chorus in *Henry V*, nor, for that matter, for the prologue to *Troilus and Cressida*. In this, the Prologue's stately language ('princes orgulous', 'strong immures', 'warlike fraughtage', 'massy staples /And co-responsive and fulfilling bolts') suddenly modulates, as the 'prologue arm'd, but not in confidence /Of author's pen or actor's voice' advises his audience that the play begins *in medias res*, 'starting thence away /To what may be digested in a play'. This mild concession to the limitations of the drama is not as apologetic as the Chorus's lines in *Henry V*, but is, as it were, cousin-german to them.

The chief objection to Taylor's explanation of the *Henry V* choruses is that the expectation aroused by them is not temporarily frustrated: it is *never* satisfied by action on the stage. Ornstein's comment that the Chorus's 'apology is as sly as it is gratuitous because Shakespeare makes no attempt in the play to represent an epic confrontation of armies',[10] makes the point clear. The audience must at some point become aware that as a prophet the Chorus is a great deal less than reliable, inspiring though he may be (a common enough condition amongst prophets, come to think of it). Taylor's argument will simply not suffice for a Chorus who contrives to get, really, *everything* wrong.

The prologue promises military wonders: Act I comprises two of the prosiest scenes in Shakespeare, as the churchmen wonder whether the new king will tax their revenues, and subsequently defend Henry's proposed invasion of France at mind-numbing length. (I have yet to see a performance of the play in which the Archbishop's 'So that, clear as is the summer's sun ...' did not get a laugh.) This leisurely politicking lasts some 318 lines (nearly a tenth of the play) before the French ambassador is called in (I.ii.222), and Henry given a handy opportunity to make the quarrel formal, and the fault of the French. All very necessary stuff, no doubt, but not the inspirational things the prologue talked of. In the same way, the chorus to Act II promises us that 'all the youth of England are on fire': that the war is universally popular; and that 'honour's thought /Reigns solely in the breast of every man'. But instead of seeing the youth of England on fire, we meet those tired old rogues, Nym, Bardolph, and Pistol, grumbling collectively; instead of finding honour in every breast, we are confronted with the treacherous conspiracy against Henry headed by the Earl of Cambridge.

This contrast is emphasized rather than contradicted by the chorus and first scene of Act III: the Chorus again lays stress on the bravery and gallantry of the expeditionary force, asking rhetorically

> For who is he, whose chin is but enrich'd
> With one appearing hair, that will not follow
> These cull'd and choice-drawn cavaliers to France?

The chorus is followed by Henry's famous aria before the walls of Harfleur; but the dramatic point is that it *is* an aria, not an ensemble: while one presumes the stage to be as full of supers as the company's roster allows, the citizens are mum, say not a word. What actually *does* happen is that our friends Nym, Bardolph, and Pistol come on again, and Nym, for one, is not sufficiently impressed by the oratory actually to do anything until Fluellen appears and beats him off to action (and all the action must be presumed to be taking place off-stage). There promptly follows what must be the great-grandfather of all the jokes that begin 'A Scotsman, an Irishman and a Welshman ...', the trio of Jamy, Macmorris, and Fluellen. There is no military action whatever.

Henry's oratory proves insufficient to rouse his troops to take the town; he needs another aria, this time directed at the citizens of Harfleur. In this, Henry's language modulates surprisingly from his former heroic-mindedness to threats that would not have sounded misplaced on Tamburlaine's lips;[11] in particular, as Jonathan Dollimore and Alan Sinfield remark,[12] his association of himself in imagery with the tyrant Herod is surely astonishing (explain it away as Walter tries) in a king from whom th' offending Adam had, so the Church declared, been whipped. Threats against women, children, and the aged are simply not attractive. Nor is it possible to evade the fact that Henry says he cannot control his army (III.iii.22–9), whose soldiers are characterized as 'rough and hard of heart', 'enrag'd', 'blind and bloody' – a far cry from the gentlemen-adventurers described by the Chorus. The scene has a desperate quality about it: the war has ground to a halt before Harfleur, and Henry must take the city if his campaign is to continue. The war he threatens is not pretty war; it is not heroic war, or idealized war such as the Chorus urges upon us: it rather foreshadows the total war of the twentieth century. Yet hard on Harfleur's surrender comes perhaps the most abrupt peripeteia Shakespeare ever wrote, as we find ourselves transported, gentles, to Princess Katharine's boudoir, for a scene of light comedy spiced with naughty double-entendres. The tonal lurch is almost impossible to exaggerate: it would be no more extreme to break into the middle of the last Act of *Tristan und Isolde* with a Gilbert and Sullivan patter song (an apt enough comparison, as even the play's language changes from English to French). Some productions choose to locate the interval between the two scenes, but such a division goes flatly against what seems to me a clearly purposeful juxtaposition of the two.

The chorus to Act IV follows the scene in which the French nobles await the Battle of Agincourt with careless impatience, and the Chorus prepares the audience's mind for the great event to come with some fine military metaphor suggesting the collective activity and anxiety that must pervade armies on the eve of battle. Shakespeare had done a good awaiting-for-battle scene before, in the fifth Act of *Richard III*, and it is instructive to compare the two, the most extended military sequences in the canon. That in *Richard III* occupies V.iii–V.v inclusive, or about 406 lines of dialogue; in *Henry V*, if we include the scene of the French anticipation and the chorus, Agincourt occupies III.vii –IV.viii, or no less than 1,175 lines, a third of the play and nearly three times as long as Bosworth (whose shadow, however, is cast over much of Act IV). Those of us who have seen (as who has not?) Olivier's famous film of the play will not be surprised by this figure, for he made of Agincourt one of the most memorable battle-scenes that the screen has ever achieved. But not very many of those 1,175 lines actually were spoken in the film. If we count again, and even if we exclude the scene of the French at the end of Act III, we find the extraordinary fact that 355 lines of the total are comedy, involving either Pistol and Le Fer or Fluellen and Williams. A third of the battle-scene is a joke, then, which makes us wonder again about the last lines of the chorus to Act IV: 'Yet sit and see; /Minding true things by what their mock'ries be'. Neither Walter nor Taylor glosses 'mock'ries', and indeed the principal meaning, of imitation in the dramatic sense,[13] is clear. But the other meaning, 'a subject or occasion of ridicule, a person, thing or action that deserves or occasions ridicule' (*OED* sb 1.b), was well-established. The same Chorus that makes puns about wooden Os and guilt/gilt is certainly not to be automatically exempt from suspicion of a pun here.

III.vii is itself at least partly comic, as the French nobles play languid word-games with each other. The ensuing chorus to Act IV first speaks of the armies' mutual preparation, then describes the alarming weakness and fatigue of the English troops. But Henry is reported to have the situation well in hand:

> For forth he goes and visits all his host,
> Bids them good-morrow with a modest smile,
> And calls them brothers, friends, and countrymen.
> Upon his royal face there is no note
> How dread an army hath enrounded him....

And the Chorus tells us that he cheers up everyone with the famous 'little touch of Harry in the night'. But once again the Chorus is mistaken: what Henry actually does is to borrow a disguise and go about the army in careful incognito. This entire episode is invented by Shakespeare: it does not occur in Hall or Holinshed.[14] But he was not without a model for it: I at least am reminded that, before Bosworth, Richard orders Ratcliffe,

> come, go with me:
> Under our tents I'll play the eavesdropper,
> To see if any mean to shrink from me. (V.iii.201–3)

Shakespeare does not have Henry play the eavesdropper, exactly; but he makes him retain his incognito even when, on any reasonable grounds, we might have expected him to drop it to encourage his sensible and yet anxious troops. His own anxiety of mind is stressed by his soliloquy (IV.i.236f.) – his only serious soliloquy in the play.

We may therefore presume Shakespeare invented the scene as he wanted it, and that the apparent contradiction between the Chorus's account and what happens on stage subsequently is deliberate and purposeful. Even Taylor, who, as noted above, is more alert to the ambivalent functions of the Chorus than most editors, fudges this issue. His note on the 'little touch of Harry' concludes: 'in performance it is hard to exclude the extra-syntactical suggestion that we too will see a little touch of Harry; but this need not imply we will witness a dramatization of the *same* activity described here' (IV.0.45n.). One may justifiably respond that the case is on a par with the Chorus's general tendency to describe events that are not performed, which is not the usual function of a Chorus. On the contrary, it seems to me that the contradictions are absolutely essential to the function of the Chorus in this play, and this, the most blatant refusal on the dramatist's part to satisfy the expectations his Chorus has aroused,[15] is the key to understanding the nature of the entire play.

This understanding is confirmed by the final Act, whose chorus begins with further apologies and appeals to imagination, and contains eulogies similar to the earlier ones. Once again, it is followed by a scene of clownage: Fluellen's revenge upon Pistol; succeeded by a scene of political manoeuvring, followed by a scene of light comedy as Henry and Katharine come to an understanding. The Chorus concludes with an epilogue in sonnet form, which once more strikes the note of apology:

> Thus far, with rough and all-unable pen,
>   Our bending author hath pursu'd the story;
> In little room confining mighty men,
>   Mangling by starts the full course of their glory.

It is difficult indeed to make a concord of this discord. The Chorus spends half of his time telling the audience of the glorious deeds that are the subject of the play, and the other half criticizing the company for their failure to achieve, in their art, the theatrical equivalent of those brave times. In the epilogue, quite clearly, he criticizes the author, in a vein that goes a good deal beyond the normally self-deprecating tone adopted for epilogues.[16] One thing he does not do is criticize the company for not performing what he said they were going to: I marvel that he left it out.

One way of dealing with the problem is to declare roundly that Shakespeare could not have written the choruses. We have dismissed that, but it affects a lot of critical thinking on the subliminal level. Consider, for instance, these remarks by John Wilders: 'The Chorus, who overlooks many of the subtleties in *Henry V*', and 'the piety of Holinshed's portrait has found its way into the play (in the attitude of the Chorus, for example)'.[17] These observations really sound as if Wilders was bemused into thinking that the Chorus was a creatively independent entity from the 'Shakespeare' who composed the rest of the play. Perhaps it was just his way of putting it; but a text which encourages such apparently confused description from such an intelligent critic needs special care.

As I see it, there are two problems in *Henry V* which need to be treated separately, but which are ultimately part of a single issue. The first problem is that the Chorus seems to be describing a play he has heard about, but which is not the one that actually takes place. The second is the problem of the morality of Henry's behaviour. I have already said something about both problems, and propose now to try to summarize them. Let us take the second first. Many modern critics would like Henry to show some awareness of the ambivalent moral dimensions of the actions he undertakes. Partly, the absence of any such awareness arises from deliberate choice on the dramatist's part: Shakespeare gives Henry no opportunity to react to Falstaff's death. But his general coldness is often remarked upon: for instance, he shows no signs of feeling when Bardolph must be executed. Wilders, among others, rightly rejects Walter's learned defence of Henry on the basis of the rules of warfare: 'Shakespeare makes us think of the virgins and infants of Harfleur, not of the rules of warfare. These vivid details are, incidentally, Shakespeare's; they do not appear in Holinshed.'[18] He might have added that the 'rules of warfare' are made to look pretty silly anyway by Fluellen's absurd devotion to them. All these criticisms, and many more, must be conceded by those who admire Henry.

But those who find him dislikable must also concede that Shakespeare gives him two of the finest battle orations ever written, must concede his humility, his piety, and his refusal of the opportunity for self-promotion that Agincourt provides, and finally must concede that the play stoutly resists any attempt to play it in any sense hostile to Henry: if the production works at all, it will work by making the play more like the one the Chorus describes than most sceptical readers would be prepared to believe or, perhaps, prefer. Taylor confirms this with his observation that those who hold that

Shakespeare himself disliked Henry, and tried to convey this to the audience, are faced with 'the fact that productions of the play apparently never succeed in communicating this message' (1982 edn, 1); indeed, most of us who have our reservations about Henry's morality will find these reservations at least temporarily silenced by the effect of a great, self-confident production.

The only intelligible conclusion is that the duality is built into the play: Henry is a great hero, and a cold, conniving bastard. Something similar can be said of Marlowe's Doctor Faustus, who is a great, poetic, imaginative spirit, and an absolute idiot as well. There are other examples, none perhaps as extreme as these two, in plays of the period which suggest that a *unified* character was not necessarily the dramatists' goal, and that contradictory feelings can not only be accommodated, but are even the *purpose* of some plays.[19] The ambivalences one feels towards other Shakespearian characters such as Shylock, Othello, Macbeth or, at a different level, Bertram or Claudio, are not the same thing: these are characters who reveal complex aspects of the single personality, some likable and admirable, some decidedly otherwise. But for Henry V we are holding two contradictory things in our minds: the Henry in the theatre who is a hero; the Henry whom we think about subsequently, or whom we read in the script, and whom we find objectionable. They cannot, as experience has shown, coexist on the stage, but they are both encoded into the text, and can be decoded on different occasions: their contradictions will jostle uncomfortably in our minds. That uncomfortable jostle is, perhaps, the true central experience of this particular play. The inconsistencies force us to *think*, not perhaps always comfortably, or comfortingly, about what it is that being a hero actually means. Ideology is challenged. And the Chorus forces us into awareness of the dichotomy by talking about only one of the Henries.

I find it useful here to draw upon Stanley Fish's concept of the disruptive text, that fails to fulfil the expectations it generates, thus challenging the reader to confront problems, difficulties, and questions which cannot readily be resolved into an easy and reassuring harmony. Fish calls this a 'dialectical' rather than a 'rhetorical' text, and comments further:

> A dialectical presentation ... is disturbing, for it requires of its readers a searching and rigorous scrutiny of everything

Prologue and plural text in *Henry V*

they believe and live by. It is didactic in a special sense; it does not preach the truth, but asks that its readers discover the truth for themselves, and this discovery is often made at the expense not only of a reader's opinions and values, but of his self-esteem.[20]

The 'rhetorical' text, by contrast, satisfies its readers or, to put it another way, endorses ideology. Another recent critical term can be helpful in understanding *Henry V*: Northrop Frye's elegant phrase, 'myth of concern' – the enunciation in imaginative writing of something that is held by the public to be believable.[21] In the 1590s there was a substantial ideology extant concerning Henry V, the last successful warrior-king in English annals. He was thought to have been one of the lads in his youth, but to have succeeded to the throne in gravity and then upon the field of battle to have become the 'star of England' the Chorus speaks of. This ideology became revitalized when the ageing Queen and the young Earl of Essex started playing out their dominance games. Few would deny that the compliment to Essex that is woven into the chorus to Act V is an expression of this ideology, and that the play as a whole is a myth of concern, in which the ideology surrounding Henry is in part transferred to the current young hero, in a mixture of hope, optimism, and unspoken but apparent anxiety. That Henry did not need to invade France, and that Elizabeth could perfectly well have left the Irish alone, are irrelevant either to the ideology or the myth of concern: indeed the two come close together in this, as in most discussions of military activities.

The Chorus proposes a 'rhetorical' play, in Fish's terms: a myth of concern which will give expression to ideology: a drama which will reiterate Henry's greatness, and urge the military motive and its ideology as an ideal. What we are given, however, is a 'dialectical' play, which incorporates the Chorus's ideology and intentions, to be sure, but much more besides; it indeed is disturbing (as any challenge to ideology must be), and requires its spectators/readers to discover the truth for themselves, at the expense of their opinions and values, and possibly their self-esteem too. So *Henry V*, by insisting upon being taken plurally, by resisting any attempt to incorporate these contradictions which are so vital to its structure into a single reading, interprets and challenges ideology at once. It is, and is not, patriotic; it is, and is not, an attack on militarism.

Although it is seldom possible to transfer neatly critical concepts evolved for one literary form to another, a distinction drawn by Tzvetan Todorov may be useful to elucidate further the role of the Chorus in this process: 'The individual who says *I* in a novel is not the *I* of the discourse. ... He is only a character. ... But there exists another *I* ... the "poetic personality" which we apprehend through the discourse.'[22] Critics of the drama will not be amazed at this revelation, since for them the problem of dissociating the 'implied author' (Wayne Booth's phrase) from the first-person statements of the dramatic characters has always been evident. Yet even such alert critics as John Wilders and Robert Ornstein have been misled by the *implied* special status of the Chorus into treating his pronouncements as if they were those of Todorov's 'poetic personality'.[23] In fact, they are the statements of a character in a play, a play which is a larger and more complex discourse than the play that the Chorus himself describes, or than *Henry V* without the Chorus would be. A three-dimensional sphere can look like a two-dimensional circle, but only if you restrict yourself to looking at it in two dimensions (as in a photograph). The range of discourses that exist in *Henry V* without the Chorus is indeed two-dimensional and, I suspect, inexplicable without further alteration of the text. With the Chorus, the 'poetic personality' in its plurality starts to make three-dimensional sense, a sense which is dependent on the seemingly contradictory meanings imposed upon it, as it were perpendicularly to all its other dimensions, by the Chorus. Thereby, the play transcends both ideology and the myth of concern, by making their contradictions apparent, and thus producing new meanings.

We have still to relate the Chorus's persistent concern with the limitations and deficiencies of theatrical representation to the play itself. To do so I would like to return briefly to *A Midsummer Night's Dream*, the wonderful scene in which Peter Quince's company invent, independently of Brecht, the *Verfremdungseffekt*. Precisely for the purpose of alienation, Bottom proposes that Quince

> Write me a prologue, and let the prologue seem to say we will do no harm with our swords, and that Pyramus is not killed indeed; and for the more better assurance, tell them that I, Pyramus, am not Pyramus, but Bottom the weaver.
> (III.i.15–20)

Epic theatre can seldom have been so concisely achieved. The terror of the lion is likewise deconstructed, and then the technical realistic difficulties of staging such perplexing features as the moonlight and a wall are pondered. In both cases the solution is the same: realistic, non-theatrical means are rejected: the idea of allowing the literal moonlight to shine into the chamber is canvassed, only to be dimissed in favour of a theatrical way of achieving the effect. Such effects as can be emblematized by the actors themselves are preferred.

The difficulties with the moon and the wall are very much those faced by the company in staging so great an object as Henry V's French wars. Even today, producers seem to puzzle themselves more about how to bring in the walls of Harfleur (as the fatally over-elaborate RSC production of 1984 demonstrated) than how to make the actors interpret their lines intelligently and intelligibly. In fact, it is very curious how companies flatly disregard the Chorus's apologies: as Taylor says, 'nineteenth-century theatres found the Chorus an embarrassment because they actually did their damnedest to cram within their wooden Os the exact number of casques that did affright the air at Agincourt' (1982 edn, 57). What the stage struggles to do, film achieves with ease,[24] and Olivier's *Henry V* was very much a play about the Battle of Agincourt, with enough horses for a thousand Westerns. Splendid and stirring though this was, and odd as it may seem to say so, it suggests that Sir Laurence had a lesser grasp of the essential nature of the theatre than did Bottom and Peter Quince.

Be that as it may, Bottom and Quince and the Chorus of *Henry V* are approaching the problem of theatrical verisimilitude with the same criteria in mind. Quince and Co. are afraid first that the effect of their play will be so lifelike that the audience will no longer be able to distinguish fiction from reality, and will fall into panic; and secondly that their resources do not admit of their staging their play adequately. On the first point, they are happily self-deluded, but this does not mean that they are mistaken in their belief that people *do* confound art and life, and the means Quince and his actors adopt to ensure that this does not happen are a delightful anticipation of Brecht's solution. More relevantly, their second concern leads them with equal sureness to purely theatrical solutions; in their innocence, they do not see the absurdity of their proposed devices. The Chorus to *Henry V*, however, is well aware of the limitations that restrict any theatrical action; far from fearing that the company's account of Henry's campaigns will generate panic in the audience, he is concerned that they will fail (in Coleridge's justly celebrated phrase) willingly to suspend their disbelief, and urges upon the audience the need for them to employ their own imaginations to help the enterprise out. But the Chorus's attitudes are not *ipso facto* the author's, the company's, or ours: in fact merely by introducing the question of the suspension of disbelief the Chorus ensures that an audience will be aware of the artifice of the theatre. He, too, of course, is a *Verfremdungseffekt*.

It does not always work: grumpy old Ben Jonson remained firmly unconvinced that an emblematic staging was worthwhile; and there are always those who rebel at anything other than realistic (that is, illusionistic) staging: Jonson wouldn't have liked Peter Brook's *Midsummer Night's Dream* either. The point is that both Quince and the Chorus are alert to the limitations of the theatre, and each, in their several ways, proposes to seek solutions within the theatrical frame, solutions which in the end are not so very different. The man who must say he is the man in the moon is not so very distant from the Chorus who asks us to 'Think, when we talk of horses, that you see them /Printing their proud hoofs i' th' receiving earth'; the difference is that it does not occur to Quince to think his solution problematic; the Chorus is only too aware that his is, and that all depends upon the willing imaginary powers of the audience. Not the willing suspension of disbelief, but the active employment of imagination.

Shakespeare seems to have been very actively interested in the theory of dramaturgy at this stage of his career: the early plays, with their showy demonstrations that he had mastered the techniques of rhetoric and the styles of earlier dramatists, give way to the more complex creations of the later 1590s, with their constant harping on what it is that drama does, and how it does it. Unlike John Dryden, Shakespeare never put into a non-imaginative, essay form his thoughts about artistic creation. Yet dull would he be of soul that would deny that these plays are centrally *about* the imagination and how it works. This is unmistakably crucial to the comedies *As You Like It*, *A Midsummer Night's Dream* and *Twelfth Night* at the least. In such a context, the appeals of the Chorus of *Henry V* for imagination are more than conventional apologetics, and must be read or heard intertextually for their true force to be perceived.

Some have thought that because the Chorus apologizes for the limitations of the stage Shakespeare was really embarrassed by them. On the contrary, as we have seen, the Chorus's apologies are clearly ironical; what they are saying is not how the theatre has failed, but how it has triumphed:[25] and so it has, provided that the production has the nerve to *accept* the limitations of its nature and realize that what the Chorus 'apologizes' for are precisely the parameters of its imaginative options. In the same way, the appeals for imagination from the audience are the verso of a leaf whose recto is the glorious imagination of the poet and his company. 'Such tricks hath strong imagination': what Shakespeare has given his audience in *Henry V* is a play where imagination functions and demands at all sorts of levels. First we are asked to watch a history play, which accepts in ways that the younger Shakespeare would have found·difficult that politics is a complex and often immoral business, whose choices play a bitter counterpoint to the brazen glory of military music. *Henry V* is an extended theatrical experience, which is not switched on at the rise of the curtain (as it were), and switched off at its fall, but something that continues to provoke and challenge its audience to grapple indefinitely with its plurality. The same, no doubt, can be said of all serious drama, but *Henry V* is somewhat different: its mimetic action attempts to end in closure, but the Chorus's epilogue denies the finality of that closure, and challenges the myth of concern by stressing the transitory nature of Henry's achievement. The only way this extended action will work is if we, the audience, indeed stretch our imaginations, not in the ways that the Chorus ironically fusses over, but to meet the challenges of the complexity of the moral action. It is, finally, not simply your imagination, or theirs, but both, which are the essence of the expression of this text.

NOTES

1 In any event, the question of the authorship of Gower's choruses in *Pericles* remains open. Throughout this paper I distinguish the Chorus, the character who speaks, from the chorus, the text spoken by that character.

2 For instance W.D. Smith, 'The *Henry V* choruses in the First Folio', *Journal of English and Germanic Philology*, 53 (1954), 38–57.

3 *Modernizing Shakespeare's Spelling* (by Stanley Wells) *with Three Studies in the Text of Henry V* (Oxford: Clarendon, 1979), pp. 72–123.
4 ibid., p. 103n.
5 Gary Taylor, ed., *Henry V* (Oxford: Clarendon, 1982), p. 3.
6 Not as few as played the Quarto version, which, as Taylor has shown, was intended for a total cast of no more than nine or ten adults and two boy actors: thrift, thrift, good Horatio.
7 I say 'obviously', yet heads as wise as those of Bullough and Whitaker have missed the point: see *Narrative and Dramatic Sources of Shakespeare*, vol. 3 (London: Routledge & Kegan Paul, 1962), p. 349, and *Shakespeare's Use of Learning* (San Marino: Huntington, 1964), p. 131.
8 *A Kingdom for a Stage: The Achievement of Shakespeare's History Plays* (Cambridge, Mass.: Harvard University Press, 1972), p. 176.
9 J.H. Walter, ed., *King Henry V* (London: Methuen, 1954), pp. xxxvi–xxxvii.
10 Ornstein, p. 176.
11 As John Dover Wilson noted, *King Henry V* (Cambridge: Cambridge University Press, 1947), p. xxvi.
12 'History and ideology: the instance of *Henry V*', in *Alternative Shakespeares*, ed. John Drakakis (London: Methuen, 1985), p. 226.
13 *OED* sb 2: 'mimicry, imitation' (not then pejorative), citing this line.
14 Kenneth Muir, *The Sources of Shakespeare's Plays* (London: Methuen, 1977), says the episode may have been suggested either by *The First English Life of Henry the Fifth* or by Tacitus's account of Germanicus (111).
15 See Anthony Brennan, 'That within which passes show: the function of the Chorus in *Henry V*', *Philological Quarterly*, 58 (Winter 1979), 40–52: 'the Chorus' version of Henry's tour among his soldiers is deliberate misdirection, a lack of preparation for the scene as Shakespeare writes it' (48).
16 There is, of course, no evidence whatever for Dover Wilson's romantic notion that Shakespeare himself played the Chorus.
17 *The Lost Garden: A View of Shakespeare's English and Roman History Plays* (London: Macmillan, 1978), pp. 52, 58.
18 ibid., p. 58.
19 It is not within my brief to go into this in detail in this paper. But the characters of Webster's *The White Devil*, especially Vittoria, Flamineo, Brachiano, Monticelso, and to a lesser extent Francisco, seem to have been evolved with some such dramatic purpose.
20 *Self-Consuming Artifacts: The Experience of Seventeenth-Century Literature* (Berkeley: University of California Press, 1972), pp. 1–2.
21 *The Myth of Deliverance: Reflections on Shakespeare's Problem Comedies* (Toronto: University of Toronto Press, 1983), pp. 8–9.
22 'Language and literature', in *The Structuralist Controversy*, ed. R. Macksey and E. Donato (Baltimore, Md: Johns Hopkins University Press, 1970), p. 132.
23 Ornstein says, 'in his Epilogue, Shakespeare meditates' (p. 202). Dover Wilson explicitly equates the two (xiii).
24 Brennan remarks, aptly enough, 'The only invention that would satisfy [the] literalist Chorus is the movie-camera' (41).
25 Brennan again remarks justly: 'When Shakespeare points our attention to the theatrical he does not weaken its hold over us, he strengthens it' (41).

8

"With a little shuffling"

GEORGE WALTON WILLIAMS

In this paper, I want to consider how Claudius came to be King of Denmark after the lamentable death of his brother. He was, of course, elected. But a political realist may yet ask: since Claudius did not have old Hamlet's dying voice or young Hamlet's living voice, how was it that the election lit on him? Professor Jenkins believes that 'the manner of Claudius's succession ... [is left] in some ambiguity'.[1] This paper seeks to enquire into that ambiguity, to pluck out the heart of Claudius's mystery.

While Hamlet was, evidently, yet at Wittenberg, Claudius participated in three events: the murder of old Hamlet, the marriage to Gertrude, the accession to the throne. These events, all closely related, are nevertheless separable. Though the nature of his participation differs from event to event, Claudius is, I think it is safe to say, the instigator of each one. The last two derive from the first and may even have been a single solemnity; but the events are separable. They do, however, have one quality in common: each has a public aspect and a private or secret aspect.

As I do not propose here to consider the two aspects – public and private – of the marriage, leaving to others the problems in that union that approach the theological, I merely state that Claudius publicly takes the position that he may and probably should marry his deceased brother's widow; Hamlet privately takes the position that he should not. (These two conflicting positions the Elizabethan audience would have found in Deuteronomy and in Leviticus; many would have recognized the dilemma.) Claudius's interpretation of the problem, highly favourable to himself and to his course of action, is the one supported 'freely' (I.ii.15) by the Privy Council; it is the one on which Danish polity is founded.

"Fanned and Winnowed Opinions"

Hamlet's interpretation is the one supported by the theatre audience. (It was even more clearly supported by the majority of Shakespeare's audience, for it was the one on which Elizabethan polity was founded.[2])

The two aspects of the murder, on the other hand, are very clear; we know them well. The public aspect is the official report distributed by Claudius's Bureau of Public Information that while old Hamlet was sleeping in the orchard, his custom always of the afternoon, a serpent stung him. We hear this report only from the Ghost, but it must certainly be truthful and accurate, for no alternative is suggested, and Gertrude's astonishment at the idea that old Hamlet was murdered (III.iv.30) reflects the fact that she and probably most of the court had never entertained the thought that murder might have been an explanation for the sudden death of the old King. This report is, to be sure, a 'forged process'; it abuses the whole ear of Denmark (I.v.37). The secret account of the murder – the poisoning – we have also only from the Ghost, but it must certainly be truthful and accurate, for it is the technique to which Claudius reacts, we are to suppose, when he sees and hears it played before him.

The two aspects of the accession are not so clearly put before us. The public knowledge is that Claudius was elected King by a process normal and legal. Hamlet, indeed, tells us that he once had had 'hopes' (V.ii.65) that he would succeed his father, but no one in the play, not even he, seems at all surprised at the way the election went. The electoral process has given every indication of legality and orderliness.[3] Though Claudius is a murderer and a villain, he is not a usurper.

Yet Claudius's unfitness for the high office as it becomes apparent through the play raises uncertainties; Professor Jenkins finds an 'unscrupulous opportunism' in him (III.iv.99n.), and Hamlet himself says that Claudius 'stole' the crown (III.iv.100). Since 'the manner of Claudius's succession ... [is left] in some ambiguity', is it possible that the electoral process was, like the official report, also a 'forged process'?

The only character in the play who can answer that question fully is Claudius, and Claudius only when he is telling the truth. That rare moment arrives in III.iii, the 'prayer scene'. Here we must suppose that Claudius, talking to his Maker and his Judge, is telling the truth. With a wonderful honesty he confesses the crime of murder; he accepts its rankness and acknowledges that it hath the primal eldest curse upon it.

He is somewhat less straightforward about his accession:

> In the corrupted currents of this world
> Offence's gilded hand may shove by justice,
> And oft 'tis seen the wicked prize itself
> Buys out the law. But 'tis not so above:
> There is no shuffling, there the action lies
> In his true nature, and we ourselves compell'd
> Even to the teeth and forehead of our faults
> To give in evidence.   (III.iii.57–64)

The pointed contrast is the essence of my argument. If *there*, there is no shuffling, then *here* there is. How does that bear on Claudius? What did he do? What does 'shuffling' involve?

The word 'shuffling' with its cognates appears eight times in the canon. As seven of those eight are in the period 1597–1601 (three in *Hamlet*), at that stage of his career the word had special significance for Shakespeare. All of the uses of the word from this period concern us in our enquiry into this passage in *Hamlet*. The earliest is Hotspur's rejection of 'mincing poetry' – 'the forc'd gait of a shuffling nag' (*1 Henry IV*, III.i.128–9); the second and third are from *The Merry Wives of Windsor*: in the confused darkness of the game at Herne's Oak, Dr Caius is to 'shuffle' Anne Page away (IV.vi.28), and in all his dealings Falstaff himself is obliged 'to shuffle, to hedge, and to lurch' (II.ii.23–4). The term suggests then something that is constrained from the natural; it is furtive and devious; it keeps company with 'hedge' and 'lurch', one of which means to turn aside 'from the direct forthright' (cf. *Troilus and Cressida*, III.iii.158) and the other to rob (cf. *Coriolanus*, II.ii.101). The fourth instance is crucial, for it is the direct opposite of Claudius's remark. In *Twelfth Night*, Sebastian regrets that he cannot properly reward his dear friend:

> My kind Antonio,
> I can no other answer make, but thanks,
> And thanks, and ever thanks; and oft good turns
> Are shuffled off with such uncurrent pay.
>   (III.iii.13–16)

The appearance of the same cluster of words in this passage and in *Hamlet* – oft, shuffled, 'current' – suggests that

Shakespeare is thinking of the same thing in both plays. If in *Twelfth Night* oft good turns are shuffled off with bad or uncurrent pay, then it must follow that in *Hamlet* bad turns in the corrupted currents of this world are – and oft 'tis seen – shuffled off with the good pay of the wicked prize itself.

In the corrupted currents of this fallen world, we expect the general principle of shuffling; we must therefore not be surprised to find it at play in any specific instance – here, in Denmark, for example. I believe for two reasons that Claudius shuffled for the crown, first, because, as we have just seen, in his prayer he very nearly tells us he did (the fifth instance of the word). In this moment of truth-telling he chances to allude to bribery; he does so with a conviction so deep and earnest that it suggests to me that he has himself used bribery and knows whereof he speaks. In proclaiming his marriage he reminds the Privy Council that they have 'freely gone /With this affair along' (I.ii.15–16). My reading of that adverb 'freely' makes me think that their going along was not free; they allowed themselves to be manipulated – and rewarded. The gentleman doth protest too much. The second reason is that when he embarks in Acts IV and V on further and particular moral irregularity through Laertes, his instrument, he uses the same word (the sixth instance) to describe the same technique:

> with ease –
> Or with a little shuffling – you may choose
> A sword unbated, and in a pass of practice
> Requite him for your father. (IV.vii.135–8)

Laertes's shuffling is perfectly obvious; Claudius's is covert. We may see Laertes's; we must infer Claudius's.

Hamlet's use of the word (the seventh instance) comments on Claudius's uses in an exaggerated manner, as we can well suppose, and gives it a metaphysical resonance. When the suicide has 'shuffled off this mortal coil' (III.i.67), he has done something more than turn aside from the forthright: he has violated God's canon "gainst self-slaughter' (I.ii.132). Hamlet's interpretation of the word is absolute: shuffling is a sin.[4]

I propose that Claudius used the technique of shuffling to

secure his election; the wicked prize itself bought out the law and shoved by justice. If Hamlet says that Claudius stole the precious diadem, he does not necessarily mean that he did so crassly; more likely it is that he purchased it deftly and politicly with 'such thanks /As fits a king's remembrance' (II.ii.25–6) or, to quote a recognized usurper, with 'good word [and] princely favour' (Bolingbroke in *Richard II*, V.vi.42).

I will speculate further. One of the minor ambiguities of the play is the lack of certainty as to the participation of Osric in Laertes's shuffling with the foils. It looks as though Osric might have been an accomplice, but the play does not admit a final decision on the matter. Similarly, there might have been an accomplice in Claudius's shuffling with the succession, but again the play does not admit a final decision.

As we have just noted, Claudius's honest prayer about the murder of his brother relates that event to its Biblical archetype – Cain's murder of his brother Abel. That Claudius thinks subconsciously of fratricide in archetypal terms and that he suppresses that thought only by will is shown by its unexpected appearance in his inaugural address. In his elaborate generalization on mortality, his guilty conscience lets slip another reference to the murder of Abel, 'the first corse' (I.ii.105). The two references link the prayer and the inaugural address.

I want to propose another link, perhaps not subconscious, between the prayer and the address. In the prayer, Claudius talks about shuffling. In the inaugural address, he talks about Polonius:

> What wouldst thou beg, Laertes,
> That shall not be my offer, not thy asking?
> The head is not more native to the heart,
> The hand more instrumental to the mouth,
> Than is the throne of Denmark to thy father.
>
> (I.ii.45–9)

Professor Jenkins has ably explicated these lines: the King sees himself as the 'head' of the body politic 'closely joined in nature' to the 'counsellor heart'; as the 'hand' of the body providing for the 'mouth' of his people; and as the throne relating to the individual Polonius (182). I would suggest that Claudius does not sustain the careful parallelism that a perfectly official speech requires. The first pair defines the government (king and council), the second pair defines the monarchy (king and subjects), the third pair defines the relationship between the throne and one man. In moving from the general to the particular, Claudius creates a unique situation. The royal throne, though it may be seen symbolically as instrumental to all the people, serving them as the hand serves and feeds the mouth, cannot be seen in any reasonable way as instrumental to a single individual. In fact, as we know and as Claudius knows, the reverse is true. The individual is intrumental to and serves the throne. No doubt it gratified Polonius to be told that the throne served him, but we know that the flattery in that line was as false as it was fulsome: Polonius served the throne. The falseness of Claudius's third pair, reversing the significance of throne to father, may be thought to reverse also the second pair – hand distributing to mouth – and to make it mouth distributing to hand. On the public level, the royal hand gives sustenance to the public mouth; but on the particular and private level, the reverse is true: the royal mouth gives words, direction, commands to the private hand. We may go so far as to understand the last two lines to carry this particular meaning:

> The hand is not more instrumental to the mouth,
> Than is thy father to the throne of Denmark.

Polonius's hand is, I suggest, the instrument of Claudius's mouth.[5] We know that like the old King, the people of Denmark have been poisoned or rankly abused by something poured into their ears – he by the 'juice of cursed hebenon' (I.v.62); they by a false report, 'a forged process'. That report, to be sure, issues from Claudius's mouth. I speculate that Polonius has been contaminated by poisoned speech poured into his ears from the same source. The people respond with acquiescence; Polonius responds with action.

With a little shuffling, a shrewd ruler can make of all of his court accomplices – witting or unwitting – to a purpose he hides from them by disguising it as the welfare of the nation. Osric, who 'takes the place of Polonius in the last act of the play',[6] was, as Dover Wilson thought, 'necessarily an accomplice' in the shuffling of the foils; and Wilson was certain that 'the chief agent in [Claudius's] usurpation, as the address to the Council (sc.2) shows, was Polonius'.[7] Both attendants become, wittingly or unwittingly, accomplices to the King's shuffling. They become so by the act of receiving poison from the royal mouth poured into their ears.[8]

Though there is no overt reference to the poisoning of Polonius's ear by false report or meretricious conniving, there is a clear parallel in the effect on his son's ear when Laertes returns from Paris:

> [Laertes] wants not buzzers to infect his ear
> With pestilent speeches of his father's death.
>
> (IV.v.90–1)

In a state founded upon rumour and forged process, poisoned words from mouth to ear, Laertes's ear, infected by rumour and false report, has produced in him an unwholesome response; like son, like father: Polonius's ear, poisoned by the King's words, has transformed his hand into an instrument of Claudius's commanding mouth.

The parallel, as I imagine it, goes farther. Laertes's ear, cured of that infection by Claudius's honest statement of the manner of Polonius's death, has become 'a knowing ear' (IV.vii.3), and into that ear, an ear too ready to receive it, Claudius pours the new poison of his plan to kill Hamlet. Laertes then makes himself the 'organ' (IV.vii.69) of Claudius's 'exploit, now ripe in [his] device' (IV.vii.63). In that capacity, as the instrumental hand of Claudius's mouth, he kills Hamlet by means of a 'treacherous instrument ... in [his] hand' (V.ii.322). As a treacherous instrument himself, Laertes dies. When Polonius after the Mousetrap places himself 'in the ear / Of all ... conference' (III.i.186–7) between Hamlet and his mother, he makes himself, a second time, a treacherous instrument of the King. It costs him his life. Woodcocks to their own springes both, Laertes and Polonius make love to the employment of instrumentality, doing the King's work by suggestions poisonously poured into their all-too-receptive ears. They find that 'to be too busy is some danger' (III.iv.33).

That Polonius is not an unwitting but a willing accomplice of Claudius's shuffling his own behaviour strongly suggests. When he wants to know the truth about Laertes in Paris, Polonius works through an instrument: he sends Rinaldo as his spy – or, rather, as his ear – to hear. And to know the truth, he resorts to falsehood, laying 'slight sullies' on his son, 'a little soil'd i'th' working' (II.i.40, 41); dealing thus in 'indirections' (II.i.66), he too shuffles. The system by which Polonius uses the instrument of Rinaldo to achieve his purpose with Laertes may well be thought to reproduce the system by which Claudius used the instrument of Polonius to achieve his purpose in attaining the crown.

But I will speculate still further: I would pluck out the heart of Polonius's mystery. If he has shuffled in the minor detail of manipulating Rinaldo, Polonius has, very likely, shuffled on a grander scale as well. Perhaps we may, also by indirections, find out the direction of Polonius's guilt.

Claudius confesses his sins bravely and openly in the prayer scene, but before then he has in an aside revealed his guilt: 'The harlot's cheek, . . . /Is not more ugly . . . /Than is my deed' (III.i.51–3). And in the speech just before that, Polonius has, disingenuously, confessed his guilt as well. After directing his daughter (in effect) to her own self to be false – instructions opposite to those he gave his son (I.iii.78) – Polonius discloses how often he has failed to his own self to be true: 'oft . . . / . . . with devotion's visage /And pious action we do sugar o'er / The devil himself' (III.i.46–9); Polonius confesses himself guilty of an action that has sugared o'er the devil.[9] Claudius's guilty conscience blurts out the reference to a brother's death (I.ii.105); Polonius's guilty conscience blurts out an acknowledgement of something devilish – perhaps his having aided Claudius to the crown. Gertrude's observation is apt and valid:

> So full of artless jealousy is guilt,
> It spills itself in fearing to be spilt.   (IV.v.19–20)

Shuffling, like the crime of murder, 'though it have no tongue, will speak /With most miraculous organ' (II.ii.589–90). It achieves its ends for a short term; but in this play, for the long term, its effects are fatal. Claudius and Laertes, the principal shufflers of the play, meet their deaths; like son, like father, Polonius joins them.

NOTES

1 Harold Jenkins, ed., *Hamlet* (London: Methuen, 1982), pp. 433–4.

2 For a full account of the Scriptural background of the marriage and its particular relevance to Elizabeth's subjects, see Jason P. Rosenblatt, 'Aspects of the incest problem in *Hamlet*', *Shakespeare Quarterly*, 29 (1978), 349–64.

3 Professor Roy Battenhouse, to whom I am much indebted for valuable suggestions in the preparation of this paper, calls attention to the political techniques Claudius has used to smooth his way to the crown: he has emphasized (1) the danger of foreign invasion, (2) the legitimacy of the electoral process giving Hamlet (after the fact) special status, (3) his reluctance to allow Hamlet to return to Wittenberg (implying thereby Hamlet's greater interest in study than in practical action), and (4) his intention to rule jointly with the Queen, thus assuring continuity.

4 The eighth use, later in time, is Imogen's 'your life ... /Must shuffle for itself' (*Cymbeline*, V.v.104–5). The word is cognate with 'shove': 'shuffling' 'may shove by justice' (III.iii.58). I am obliged to Dr John Cunningham for guidance here and elsewhere. Another meaning may underlie some of these uses. The word means 'to mix cards' and, from early on, to mix them deviously. Marlowe so uses it: 'shuffle the cards to deal yourself a king' (*Massacre at Paris* [1592]), as does Greene in *Selimus* (1593).

5 Though there are many differences between the two plays, in similar instrumentality Mark Antony becomes 'Caesar's arm' (*Julius Caesar*, II.i.188).

6 Lily B. Campbell, 'Polonius: the tyrant's ears' in *Joseph Quincy Adams Memorial Studies* (Washington: Folger Shakespeare Library, 1948), p. 311.

7 John Dover Wilson, *What Happens in Hamlet* (Cambridge: Cambridge University Press, 1951), pp. 281, 331. Coleridge thought that Hamlet thought Polonius was guilty: 'It was natural that Hamlet ... disliking Polonius for political reasons, as imagining that he had assisted his uncle in his usurpation, should express himself satirically' (T.M. Raysor, *Coleridge's Shakespeare Criticism* [New York: Dutton, 1960], vol.2, pp.266–7). Harley Granville-Barker's observation on Osric is true for both accomplices: 'If we had time to reason the matter out, there would be grounds for suspicion' ('Preface' to *Hamlet* in *Prefaces to Shakespeare* [Princeton, NJ: Princeton University Press, 1946], p. 149n.). For Mythili Kaul, Polonius 'becomes a personification of the degrading nature of courtly intrigue and its consequences. Of course, the councillor is agent rather than principal, a pasteboard mask, almost a caricature' ('Hamlet and Polonius', *Hamlet Studies*, 2:1 [Summer 1980], 13–24).

8 Campbell sees Polonius's 'ears' as collectors, gathering gossip and delivering it to Claudius, for whom Polonius is 'the steadfast reporter and spy and agent' (312); I see his ears (like old Hamlet's) as receptors, receiving instructions from the King. Thomas A. Pendleton, in 'Hamlet's ears', *Mid-Hudson Language Studies*, 1 (1978), 51–61, points out that 'ear' in *Hamlet* 'usually appears in a context of violence, injury, or even defilement and destruction of the hearer' (52). I see the primary cause of such offenses as Claudius's poison; but for a further account of poison in the ear, see John N. Wall, 'Shakespeare's aural art: the metaphor of the ear in *Othello*', *Shakespeare Quarterly*, 30 (1979), 358–66.

9 In heaven, Claudius tells us, 'the *action* lies /In his true nature' (III.iii.61–2, italics mine). We need no spirit come from the grave (or this footnote) to tell us that *Hamlet* is filled with instances of beauty covering ugliness, but we might note that Polonius uses the same word 'pious' to describe what he supposes to be the sugaring o'er of Hamlet's false vows to Ophelia (I.iii.130); and Hamlet tells us the devil can assume a pleasing shape (II.ii.596, and cf. III.iv.162).

9

"The play's the thing":
Hamlet and the conscience of the Queen

RICHARD PROUDFOOT

> About, my brains. Hum – I have heard
> That guilty creatures sitting at a play
> Have, by the very cunning of the scene,
> Been struck so to the soul that presently
> They have proclaim'd their malefactions.
> (Hamlet, II.ii.584–88)

Hamlet's soliloquy at the end of II.ii begins with his reaction to the first player's tears for Hecuba and ends with his plan to 'catch the conscience of the King' in a dramatic mousetrap. Though the grief of Hecuba for the death of Priam provides Hamlet with a picture to hold up beside that of his mother's infidelity, Gertrude is not named or alluded to in the speech. In III.ii, however, the conscience-catching play makes much of woman's frailty and insincerity before homing in on Claudius and murder, while in the closet scene Hamlet's first charge against his mother is that of regicide. I wish to suggest in what manner a few familiar stories of 'guilty creatures sitting at a play' might have led informed spectators to anticipate a play-scene which included bait for the conscience of the Queen and to expect the murder of old Hamlet to be among Hamlet's charges against her.

The stories are well known. The first is the famous anecdote alluded to by Sidney in his *Defence of Poetry* concerning the tyrant Alexander of Pherae, related in various forms by Plutarch and Aelian; the second is a fifteenth-century Dutch play; and the third a sensational murder story current in the 1590s.[1] The first and third could be seen as having a direct bearing on *Hamlet*: the second is of interest mainly as an analogue of the third.

Hamlet and the conscience of the Queen 161

Plutarch's story, in the version found in the 'Life of Pelopidas', was translated into English by Thomas North in his version of the *Lives* (1579) and, in the variant version from the *Morals*, by Philemon Holland (1603).

> And an other time being in a Theater, where the tragedy of *Troades* of *Euripides* was played, he went out of the Theater, and sent word to the players notwithstandinge, that they shoulde go on with their playe, as if he had bene still amonge them: saying, that he came not away for any misliking he had of them or of the play, but bicause he was ashamed his people shoulde see him weepe, to see the miseries of *Hecuba* and *Andromacha* played, and that they neuer saw him pity the death of any one man, of so many of his citizens as he had caused to be slaine.
> (*Lives of the Noble Grecians and Romans* [1579], pp. 324–5)

> *Alexander*, the tyrant of *Pherae*, (whom indeed I should call by this addition onely [tyrant] and not steine and contaminate so good a name as *Alexander*, by stiling therewith so wicked a wretch:) this tyrant I say, whiles he beheld one day an excellent plaier acting in a tragoedy, was so much moved with a certaine tickling delight comming upon him, that his heart began to relent even upon a tender commiseration and pitie: whereupon he suddenly left the theater, made haste away, & went faster than an ordinary pace untill he was out of sight, saying withall, that it were a great indignity for him to be seene for to weepe and shed teares, in compassion of the miseries and calamities of queene *Hecuba* or lady *Polyxena*, who every day caused so many citizens and subjects throats to be cut. This monstrous tyrant was so mischievously bent, that he went within a little of punishing that excellent actour most grievously, because he had mollified his hard heart and made it melt like a peece of iron in the furnace. ('Of the Fortune or Vertue of K. Alexander. *The second Oration*', *The Philosophy commonly called the Morals* [1603], p. 1273)

The inclusion of the grief of Hecuba in the player's speech, in conjunction with the tyranny of Pyrrhus; the player's compassionate tears; Hamlet's 'What's Hecuba to him, or he to her, /That he should weep for her?' (II.ii.553–4); and his self-accusation for unfeeling inactivity all gain in point by reference to this anecdote. Not only is Hecuba's grief a tragic *topos*: it is a passion whose dramatic rendering had power, in the verses of Euripides, to make milch the eyes of a hardened tyrant and mass-murderer. Alexander's sudden departure from the theatre for reasons understandably obscure to the players likewise contains the germ of the more complex effect created by Shakespeare when Claudius interrupts the play for reasons apparent only to himself, Hamlet, Horatio (in some measure), and the audience.

A further version of the anecdote, related by Aelian and translated by Abraham Fleming, speaks of a dramatization of 'the history of *Aerops*' [*sic*: for '*Merops*'] by '*Theodorus* ye tragediographer' and lays even heavier emphasis on Alexander's ambiguous departure.

> *Alexander* arose out of his seate, (the teares trickling downe his cheekes) and departed from the Theater, or Stage, where this tragedie was played with such liuely and effectuall representations: The soudaine goyng away of whom, ministred no small doubt to the mindes of many men, but cheefely to *Theodorus*: whereupon *Alexander*, excusing the Poet, saide in plaine wordes thus to *Theodorus*, I departed not ye place to this ende & purpose, therby to make the contemptible and despised, but rather, for that I was touched with a sodaine shame of mine owne person, whom the representations of things, moued to that compassion and pittie, which could not pearce my flinty harte, in the ponderous and waighty estate of my poore people and subiects. (*A Register of Histories* [1570], Bk 14, fo.175^v)

The Dutch play of *Mary of Nimmegen*, printed in Antwerp in 1518/19, probably dates from the 1470s. An English prose narrative, translated and adapted from it, also appeared at Antwerp at a date between 1519 and 1530. It tells of Mary's seven years of riotous and dissolute life as the mistress of a devil. Her eventual penitence is brought about by seeing a play performed 'on the pageant-wain'.[2] This play is represented as a debate between Maskeroon (Lucifer's advocate), God (in the figure of Christ) and Our Lady. Mary lives out her remaining years as a penitent in a nunnery. *Mary of Nimmegen* is overt in its advocacy of religious drama as an instrument of moral teaching. Mary's impulse to watch the play stems in part from memories of the opinion of her uncle,

Hamlet and the conscience of the Queen

a priest, 'that a play were better than a sermant to some folke'.[3]

It is unclear whether this story was current in Shakespeare's London. If so, it could have afforded the suggestion of a woman as the central figure – and a woman accessible to remorse and penitence, whose evil life had its origin in diabolic seduction at a moment of hardship and weakness.

The third story is closer to *Hamlet*, both in date and place. It is told both in the anonymous play, *A Warning for Fair Women* (1599), and Thomas Heywood's *Apology for Actors*, written about 1607, though printed only in 1612. What appears to be a remote analogue of it is found in a speech of Hamlet's in the derivative German text, *Der bestrafte Brudermord*.[4] Harold Jenkins, discussing the story in his edition of *Hamlet*, does not exclude the possibility that it might be deemed a minor source: 'A tale that is common knowledge is not incompatible with a particular reminiscence' (103). Two points which remain in dispute are whether the story is wholly fictional and what the relation may be between the two principal versions of it. The most recent editor of *A Warning for Fair Women* reaches these conclusions: 'Heywood may have taken the anecdote from *A Warning*, or both the author of *A Warning* and Heywood may have taken the anecdote from someone else.'[5] The two versions are as follows:

> M[aster] Ia [mes]. Ile tell you (sir) one more to
>   quite your tale,
> A woman that had made away her husband,
> And sitting to behold a tragedy
> At Linne a towne in Norffolke,
> Acted by Players trauelling that way,
> Wherein a woman that had murtherd hers
> Was euer haunted with her husbands ghost:
> The passion written by a feeling pen,
> And acted by a good Tragedian,
> She was so mooued with the sight thereof,
> As she cryed out, the Play was made by her,
> And openly confesst her husbands murder.
>   (*A Warning for Fair Women* [1599], H2)

Marginal note: A strange accident happening at a play.
... a domestike, and home-borne truth, which within these few yeares happened. At *Lin*, in *Norfolke*, the then Earle of

Sussex players acting the old History of Fryer *Francis*, & presenting a woman, who insatiately doting on a yong gentleman, had (the more securely to enioy his affection) mischieuously and secreetly murdered her husband, whose ghost haunted her, and at diuers times in her most solitary and priuate contemplations, in most horrid and fearfull shapes, appeared, and stood before her. As this was acted, a townes-woman (till then of good estimation and report) finding her conscience (at this presentment) extremely troubled, suddenly skritched and cryd out Oh my husband, my husband! I see the ghost of my husband fiercely threatning and menacing me. At which shrill and vn-expected out-cry, the people about her, moou'd to a strange amazement, inquired the reason of her clamour, when presently, vn-urged, she told them that seuen yeares ago, she, to be possesst of such a Gentleman (meaning him) had poysoned her husband, whose fearfull image personated it selfe in the shape of that ghost: whereupon the murdresse was apprehended, before the Iustices further examined, & by her voluntary confession after condemned. That this is true, as well by the report of the Actors as the records of the Towne, there are many eye-witnesses of this accident yet liuing, vocally to confirm it.   (*An Apology for Actors* [1612], G1^v–2)

Belief in the veracity of this tale may be slightly encouraged by the recent publication of fresh documentary evidence. The Congregation Book of King's Lynn (KL /C 7.8, fo. 35^v) records the following payment among records for the year 1592/93: 'bestowed vpon the Erle of Sussex players xx^s'.[6] In the light of this new information, it becomes impossible that Heywood's account should derive exclusively from *A Warning for Fair Women*, which fails to name a company of players. The remaining alternative explanations are that both versions derive from a common source – or from common knowledge – or (a remoter possibility) that Heywood was author or part-author of *A Warning*. At least, Heywood's story is thus far vindicated by 'the records of the Towne'. Unfortunately, the documents which might have told us more have not survived: no records of Sessions at King's Lynn now exist for dates before 1620. The play of *Friar Francis* also remains tantalizingly obscure, but we do know that it was in the repertoire at the Earl of Sussex's Men in January 1594, when they played it three

Hamlet and the conscience of the Queen

times at the Rose.⁷ That they may have played it some eighteen months earlier at King's Lynn seems wholly plausible.

The connection of this story with *Hamlet*, especially if it may have been not merely notorious but also true, is, I would suggest, less that of a minor source than of a revealing analogue. Hamlet's curious lack of reference to Gertrude in the 'player' soliloquy will appear less absolute if the story most likely to be conjured up by allusion to 'guilty creatures sitting at a play' was one of the remorseful confession of a remarried widow for the secret murder of her first husband, prompted by theatrical representation of such a murderess haunted by her victim's ghost. Further information about either the King's Lynn episode or the likely contents of the old history of *Friar Francis* might reinforce the likelihood of such allusion – or might dispel it. Provisionally, it seems worth suggesting. So oblique – not to say subliminal – a hint at Hamlet's suspicion of his mother's complicity in the murder of his father and at his unconfessed design to include her conscience among the targets of his play would at least be congruous with the general obliquity of his behaviour towards her in the central acts of *Hamlet*.

NOTES

1 See W.A. Ringler, Jr, 'Hamlet's defense of the Players', in R. Hosley, ed., *Essays on Shakespeare and Elizabethan Drama in Honour of Hardin Craig* (London, 1963); H. Jenkins, ed., *Hamlet* (London, 1982), pp. 482–3: long note on II.ii.585–8.

2 *A Marvelous History of Mary of Nimmegen*, trans. H.M. Ayres (The Hague/London/Copenhagen: Christiania, 1924), p. 48.

3 *Mary of Nemmegen*: a facsimile of the unique copy in the Huntington Library, ed. H.M. Ayres and A.J. Barnouw (Cambridge, Mass., 1932), fo. B5ᵛ.

4 See A. Cohn, *Shakespeare in Germany in the Sixteenth and Seventeenth Centuries* (London/Berlin, 1865), p. 268.

5 C.D. Cannon, ed., *A Warning for Fair Women* (The Hague, 1975), p. 37.

6 *Malone Society Collections XI*: Records of Plays and Players in Norfolk and Suffolk, 1330–1642, ed. D. Galloway and J. Wasson (Oxford, 1980/1), p. 65.

7 R.A. Foakes and R.T. Rickert, eds, *Henslowe's Diary* (Cambridge, 1961), p. 20.

10
The plays within the play of *Hamlet*

ALASTAIR FOWLER

Although Shakespeare's art was for all time, the structure of *Hamlet*, at least, is not without the characteristics of a particular age. All students of the visual arts are familiar with the elaborate frames and framing devices (whether external or partly assimilated to the work) that characterized mannerism and the baroque. And Jacobean drama had a closely comparable period style. This style shaped structural forms of at least three sorts: namely, inserted playlets; numerological symmetries; and the organic structures within the action of scenes that Marco Mincoff and Mark Rose have drawn attention to.[1] Rose insists that the centres of Shakespeare's symmetrical arrays are 'natural' emphases without iconographical content; and it is true that such abstract emphases occur. Nevertheless, the traditional sovereignty of the centre point often has a bearing on the very patterns Rose himself discusses – as with *Hamlet* I.i, where the central segment, flanked by appearances of the ghost, describes the encounter of two kings, the elder Hamlet and Fortinbras.[2] R.A. Foakes's review of Rose's *Shakespearean Design* (1972) objects that the symmetries would not be noticed by audiences. That may be true today. But for Renaissance audiences, habituated as they were to following complex oral literature and to participating in intricate ceremonies of many kinds, it was another matter.

The more numerological and iconographical approach that I sketched in *Triumphal Forms* (1970) was developed in regard to *Hamlet* by Keith Brown,[3] who brilliantly demonstrated that the contents of the scenes of the first two Acts, in conjunction with those of the last two Acts, form a symmetrical array, /abc ... / ... cba/. Thus, the armed elder Hamlet (I.i) corresponds to the armed Fortinbras (V.ii); the anomalous wedding

The plays within the play of *Hamlet*   167

ceremony (I.ii) corresponds to the anomalous funeral (V.i); Laertes' initial warning to Ophelia against involvement with Hamlet (I.iii) corresponds to Laertes' learning the outcome of that involvement (IV.vii); old Hamlet's return from death (I.iv) corresponds to young Hamlet's return from his intended death (IV.vi); and so on. Brown pursues these symmetries into the central Act III, and suggests that the play has a mannerist double centre. The 'strategic centre' is the play scene, III.ii, which is also the quantitative centre of the play's wordage; whereas the numerological centre, the centre scene, is the closet scene, III.iv, which contains 'the one truly sovereign figure, Old Hamlet'.[4] Brown's description has a subtlety I cannot suggest here; and his analysis seems to have met with acceptance. But, having admired it, I wish to add a little supplementation in two particular respects. First, although the correspondences he traces are striking and persuasive, they do not cover all the main contents of the scenes concerned. For example, what of the fencing match in V.ii? Second, there is that problematic double centre. Why should the centre be doubled? Consideration of these points may lead us to conclude that the placements are not mere scaffolding (as Brown momentarily retreats to suggest), but patterns meant for the pleasure and instruction of audiences or readers. For this, we need to explore the function of the inserted plays.

Shakespeare and his audiences certainly took delight in performances inset within the primary play, like the masques in *Love's Labour's Lost*, *Romeo and Juliet*, *Much Ado About Nothing*, and *Henry VIII*, or the inserted plays and shows in the comedies and romances – the Pageant of the Nine Worthies; the play of Pyramus and Thisbe; Prospero's revels; the unveiling of Hermione's statue; the heraldic procession in *Pericles*. Indeed, the Elizabethans could be described as connoisseurs of such framing. More than a hundred Renaissance plays have inserted playlets; and the count would be very much larger if it took in instances of framed action without a formal audience. An obvious example is the sonnet-reading scene in *Love's Labour's Lost* (IV.iii), with its sequence of observers concealed in their Chinese boxes.

Such 'performances', which positively clamour for Goffmanian frame analysis, also invite discussion in terms of a common period style; although it must be admitted that they have almost as many functions and values as there are dramatists and plays. Sometimes the framing allows an effect of different, widening perspectives. Or the inserted playlet may be in a distinct mode from the main play – perhaps more formal or more allegorical, or even in masque-antimasque relation to it (*The Maid's Tragedy*; *The Changeling*).[5] With the triumph of mannerism, the border between the inset fiction and the 'real' matrix increasingly came to be blurred. Indeed, this was generally the case with inserted masques, where the persons were not characters realized by actors but roles assumed without complete cancellation of 'real-life' identity. In plays of this period, characters will refer to the actors who act their parts, or seek to attend their own play; or actors under their own names will figure in the action. Such problematic framing may raise questions of the authenticity of the self, or even of the nature of reality. For Sarah Sutherland rejects too absolutely the 'metacritical' idea of inserted plays commenting on the relation of reality and illusion.[6] After all, Prospero himself compares the dissolution of his revels – 'this insubstantial pageant' – to the dissolution of its actors after life's dream (*The Tempest*, IV.i.148f.).

Certainly an inserted playlet with a stage audience can have the paradoxical effect of drawing the real-life audience further into the main fiction – reinforcing the theatrical illusion – while at the same time the insert itself is distanced, its iconic emphasis enhanced. The latter's redoubled impersonality can raise the magic of theatre, as it were, to a higher power. The insert may also have an oblique inwardness. Like the innermost chamber of a Renaissance suite, the inner stage can be a place at once of intimacy, status and power:

> Like Rosalind's play-acting with Orlando, the pretense of Guiderius and Arviragus in the cave that they are Imogen's brothers, or Perdita's performance first as Whitsun Queen and then as the daughter of Smalus, King of Lybia, it [the inserted play] is a way of uncovering the real nature of its participants.[7]

A more specific function characterized a type of inserted entertainment most often used as a structural device at the action's climactic point. Starting with Marston's *Antonio's Revenge* (?1600), a number of revenge plays have inserted

The plays within the play of *Hamlet*

revels which, by giving access to the great, offer opportunities for the execution of justice. The masques in *Antonio's Revenge* and *The Revenger's Tragedy* are used to avenge wrongs done by those they ostensibly honour; while that in *Women Beware Women* multiplies the device in such a way as to combine several revenge plots unexpectedly, ending them all at once. There may have been no more than ten fatal masques in Renaissance drama;[8] yet together with other inserted entertainments they came to form a distinct generic group. Modern views of the fatal insert have led to questions rather than answers. Does it distance the violence? Or does it tighten the tension screw by introducing the mechanical advantage of a formal instrument? When the less 'real' insert terminates in real violence that erupts into the main play, this eruption can carry out through another frame and involve the real audience. Yet Inga-Stina Ewbank is not wrong in speaking of a 'ritual of revenge';[9] for the impact of the fatal insert has to do with its inhuman impersonality as a preactivated murder machine. The insert in a revenge came to signal impending denouement and the execution of divine justice.

The group of revenge plays with fatal masques stands in a tradition initiated by the seminal work that dominated revenge tragedy for decades: *The Spanish Tragedy* (?1587). Despite its early date, Kyd's sophisticated work has a complex structure in the style of European mannerism.[10] The main play of Hieronimo is itself an insert, within the frame dialogue of the supernatural spectators Andrea and Revenge. And in the domain of natural reality which they preside over (and therefore doubly framed) are two playlets: the 'innocent' masque or mime presented by Hieronimo before the Portugese ambassador – whose friendly reception arouses Andrea's impatience – and the contrasting fatal performance of *Soliman and Perseda*.[11] Between these, moreover, after Act III, a third playlet is inserted in the frame. This mime, of a Hymen robed in sable and saffron, Revenge himself 'presents' as he sleeps – that is, during a delay in the execution of justice. It is obscure, as dumb-shows seem generally to have been, like the visual part of emblems; so that Andrea cries, 'Awake, Revenge, reveal this mystery' (III.xv.29). As explained by Revenge, the mime is a prophetic mystery, instancing the power of destiny.

Far more intricate, however, is the structure of framed inserts in *Hamlet*. For example, the dire insert of the Player's speech about Pyrrhus (II.ii.464–514), although from one point of view only a lead-in to 'The Mousetrap' play, is itself prefaced by Hamlet's rehearsal of its opening. Moreover, Polonius and Hamlet interrupt the insert, producing an effect of arrested action[12] that amplifies its content, since within the speech Pyrrhus is repeatedly described in the arrested act of killing King Priam – 'his sword ... seem'd i'th' air to stick ... Pyrrhus stood ... Did nothing'. The interdigitations relate insert with main play, Hamlet with Pyrrhus – who, as Harold Jenkins comments (478), is identified with the types of both violent murderer and heroic avenger.

The Murder of Gonzago, so far as its performance is allowed to proceed, consists of two scenes, introduced by a prologue which is itself introduced by an interpretative epitome in the form of a prophetic dumb-show. Each section is separated from the next by main-play dialogue; and the playlet itself is interrupted by Hamlet, and eventually cut short by the King's departure. This elaborate structure is matched by that of the individual sections. The dumb-show almost amounts to a complete playlet in itself: it may even be meant to appear divided into five 'acts' or scenes: *King, Queen: Queen's protestation / King, Poisoner: murder / Queen: 'passionate action' / Queen, Poisoner, others: removal of body / Queen, Poisoner: wooing*. Moreover, the subsequent speeches of Prologue, Player King, Player Queen and Lucianus have a formalized architecture of harmoniously proportioned line counts.

These set up yet another framing structure, which has the effect of emphasizing Player King's longest speech:[13]

Prologue	/	K	Q	K&Q	Q	K	Q	K&Q	/	Lucianus
3	/	6	12	8	4	30	8	4	/	6

The initial 3 lines of prologue, to whose length Hamlet draws attention, is in harmonious diapason ratio with Lucianus's 6-line speech at the end of the fragment. (This pattern, of a prologue and coda in 1:2 proportion, was extremely common in the period.[14]) The completed scene opens with 6- and 12-line speeches by Player King and Player Queen, again in 1:2 proportion with one another (and with the prologue). Player King's second speech ends with an incomplete line; so that he shares a line with Player Queen, and their exchange has for numerological purposes to be counted as an indivisible King-and-Queen exchange of 8 lines. It is in 2:1 proportion with the Queen's speech following, and with the corresponding

The plays within the play of *Hamlet* 171

exchange after the King's long speech. The symmetry may be clarified by simplification:

3 / 6 12 12 30 12 / 6

– which is in effect the lineation in Q2, since Hamlet's interjection at III.ii.176 ('That's wormwood') is there printed as a marginal aside, and does not set off Player Queen's solitary speech. The array is typically mannerist in its asymmetrical axiality – except for two things, which stand out as its emphases or 'statements': the repeated proportions of harmony, and Player King's 30-line speech. The latter is framed by 12s and 6s (or 8s and 4s and 6s) in such a way that 24 lines come before and 12 after – again the 2:1 proportion. As for the line-count of the framed speech – 30 – it is itself significant; for its symbolic meaning was Marriage.[15]

On a wider view, the framing effects are no less remarkable. On Rose's analysis (113), the play scene has a polyptychal structure: *Address to players / Hamlet and Horatio / Mousetrap / Hamlet and Horatio / Recorder scene*. And in terms of stage action there is yet another effect of framing, in that the *Murder of Gonzago* players are watched by Claudius and his court, Claudius is watched by Hamlet and Horatio, Hamlet and Horatio by the real audience, and they by 'the burning eyes of heaven' (II.ii.513). Finally, the play scene as a whole is symmetrically framed by the rest of the play. As Keith Brown remarks,[16] critics have long regarded the scene as *Hamlet*'s 'zenith', 'crisis', 'centre' within a path of rising and falling action (Bradley); as the 'apex ... centring and emotional stressing of the turn of the action' (Mincoff); or as the 'strategic centre' (Barton). It occupies the physical centre of the play's lines, within the flanking array of symmetrically paired scenes of Acts I–II and IV–V, mentioned earlier.

The elaborately framed playlet is traditional and yet anomalous. For although, as we have seen, Shakespeare repeatedly reinforces and emphasizes the framing, he also blurs it with modifying informalities, in that the Player's speech and *The Murder of Gonzago* are both interrupted by main-play characters. These interruptions serve as alienation devices, to prevent the inserted playlet from becoming the main play for the real audience as it is for the stage one. But they also keep delaying the forward movement, in such a way as to give an impression of arrested action. And they contrast with the formality of the playlet, with the effect of enforcing the 'natural' style Hamlet desiderated in his speech to the players. Unlike other revenge plays of its group, *Hamlet* must be regarded as comparatively naturalistic. Whereas the dumb-show in *The Spanish Tragedy* is explained by Revenge, and that in *Antonio's Revenge* by a ghost (V.i.3–25), in *Hamlet* it is human characters who provide the explanation, in the course of a realistic conversation. Moreover, the dumb-show itself hardly belongs with the 'inexplicable dumb shows' Hamlet scorns, since it is not allegorical; although (like modern ballet) its mime nevertheless calls for clarification.

The naturalism has led critics of *Hamlet* to debate why Claudius took no alarm earlier, during the dumb-show.[17] But without the advantage of stage directions, he would expect the conventional dark allegory, and perhaps feel only diffused guilt and anxiety, until Lucianus's action and Hamlet's comment ('A poisons him i'th' garden') made clear what the actions of the mime had purported.[18] His hermeneutic difficulties are matched by Ophelia's, as reflected in her speculation. She makes no mere formal request for an explanation of the dumb-show, like Andrea, or the King in *The Spanish Tragedy* ('I sound not well the mystery', I.iv.139); but instead offers a theory herself, in a natural way – 'Belike this show imports the argument of the play' (III.ii.136). Claudius's first betrayal of uneasiness – 'Is there no offence in't?' – could be accounted for by his not having been provided with an 'argument', so that to him the murder play is dangerously unpredictable.

The greatest departure of *Hamlet* from *The Spanish Tragedy* is structural: namely, that the *Murder of Gonzago* performance seems to lead to no unmasking, no confrontation, no satisfaction of justice. Claudius is frightened; but apparently only by 'false fire' (III.ii.260).

What dramatic purpose does this departure serve? For Shakespeare surely means us to notice it. The elaborately important framing of *The Murder of Gonzago* must in part be designed to create an expectation of conclusive action. As Dieter Mehl puts it, the 'long drawn-out introduction ... heightens the dramatic tension' and leads the audience to expect 'something decisive'.[19] The repeated delays, occasioned first by the dumb-show, then by the prologue and interruptions, and finally by Lucianus's miming ('Leave thy damnable faces and begin') raise expectation to an extreme height. (The scene is easily acted too fast: it should be held to a sinister, denatured slowness.) This painful expectancy comes to a focus in Hamlet's highly wrought and unstable state of mind, confusedly attempting to combine contradictory actions. The moment is more crucial for him than criticism has generally allowed.[20] For he means 'The Mousetrap' as far more than a test of guilt: he believes that it may move Claudius, as others have been moved by plays and 'proclaim'd their malefactions' (II.ii.588).[21] Immediately before the performance, indeed, he voices the hope that Claudius will 'unkennel' his guilt – confess, and submit to judgement. In the event, this immediate denouement does not eventuate. Claudius is too hardened a sinner to unbosom himself so readily: Hamlet (who was perhaps unrealistic to expect it) seems to have failed to play on his pipes. Nevertheless, the swift action that follows 'Give me some light. Away' – a theatrically effective contrast – by no means discourages the assumption that a conclusion is imminent. The revenge must surely come at once.

This assumption is confirmed by Rosencrantz's talk of how 'the cess of majesty' (III.iii.15) draws all down with it. And Hamlet's opportunity when he comes on Claudius praying continues on the same line. The opportunity offered by 'The Mousetrap' had somehow passed; but here is one still more convenient. It gives a chance of immediate revenge, of open confrontation like that of the elder Hamlet and Fortinbras. Now the play can end.

Hamlet, however, succumbs to a cruel and bloodthirsty passion – the Senecan mood prefigured in the soliloquy of the last scene, 'Now could I drink hot blood....' That had seemed mere posturing;[22] but now we hear Hamlet taking actual decisions in the same moral tone. It is not enough for him to send Claudius to judgement: he must kill him with 'a more horrid hent', catching him in a mortal sin that will damn him. The scene is thus doubly ironic. With exact counterpoise it shows the murderer Claudius trying to pray, the honourable Hamlet lusting to kill as cruelly as possible.[19] It is a characteristically Shakespearian insight – 'Who is the villain here?' For although outwardly 'The Mousetrap' was only partially successful (Hamlet: 'Would not this ... get me a fellowship in a cry of players?' Horatio: 'Half a share'), inwardly it has not left Claudius untouched. Perhaps he felt spiritual as well as physical darkness when he called for light;

certainly the prayer scene shows him in the grip of remorse. And, by a sharper irony still, Claudius's inability to pray (having just decided upon a new murder) has put him in precisely the state of mortal sin desired by Hamlet in his immoderate passion. Revenge at this moment would have executed justice in full measure; but Hamlet in his presumption must usurp God's place and decide for himself on Claudius's damnation. The audience are allowed to know a little more than Hamlet about the state of Claudius's soul, and this different knowledge dissociates them from his cruel fantasy.

By his indulgence in passions and his unrealistic absorption in 'The Mousetrap', Hamlet failed to capitalize on its partial success. His unformulated idea of moving Claudius by a play – to conversion? to exposure? – worked, but was not enough. And now, by not revenging simply, he fails more decisively. He has fallen short of sovereignty, and his fortunes now take a downward turn. For in the following closet scene Hamlet's passion again leads him astray, so that he kills the wrong man – and with an unfair, covert blow. Here, if not before, the audience's feelings must be alienated, since Polonius's foolishness has made him a favourite. And Hamlet's own destruction is now inevitable, by the undeviating conventions of the Elizabethan stage.[23] What may be less obvious is that a new revenge mechanism has been set in motion, with a new revenger, a new intriguer.

Hamlet has usefully been discussed as a revenge play in other respects; so that it may help to look at its structure from the same viewpoint. When one does so, it at once stands out that a *Hamlet* only slightly transformed on the model of *The Spanish Tragedy* could easily end with a variant of the prayer scene. But we also need to see that in the version we have, a revenge play does in fact end at this point. *Hamlet* constitutes one of the clearest instances of the typical Shakespearean two-part structure, to which Emrys Jones has drawn attention.[24] Hamlet's revenge – the play with a high-principled, scrupulous, hesitating revenger – has reached its abortive inconclusion. Now a new, more fatal action begins. In this, Hamlet is no longer free to delay or refrain. It is no longer the play of Hamlet's revenge at all, indeed, but of Laertes'. As Harold Jenkins has rightly emphasized (144 n.), Hamlet becomes now the object of revenge, and so displays the paradoxical duality characteristic of human nature. In literal fact

The plays within the play of *Hamlet* 175

he combines agent and victim, justice and atrocity, as all revengers do in moral effect. With the killing of Polonius, all is changed.

In the first part, Hamlet has to contend with the old-style half-comic intrigues of Polonius; but in the second he must come to grips with a younger, darker world. It is the world of the unscrupulous Laertes; of young Fortinbras; and of the new Machiavellianism of Claudius and his lethal if unwitting instruments Rosencrantz and Guildenstern. *Hamlet* is already tragic in its first part; but in its second it is altogether grimmer and more desperate. Revenge and blood lead to more blood and more revenge. Nevertheless Hamlet himself learns at last not to intrigue but to await in readiness ('the readiness is all', V.ii.218). And in the denouement, Laertes' revenge becomes the providential means whereby justice is executed.

There were several other double revenge tragedies – including Chapman's *Bussy* and *Byron* double plays, and Marston's *Antonio and Mellida* and *Antonio's Revenge*. Indeed, *The Spanish Tragedy* itself had an obscurely related prequel, *The Spanish Comedy*. But the internal double structure of *Hamlet* has nothing to do with the business of following up popular success. Indeed, Shakespeare's structural model need not have been a dramatic one at all. Aristotle had weighed tragedy against epic; so that a writer of Shakespeare's aspirations, pursuing as he was in *Hamlet* the highest nobility, would be likely to have in mind Virgil's epic. And in the Renaissance the *Aeneid* was analysed structurally as a double epic, of which the first half imitated Homer's *Odyssey*, the second his darker *Iliad*.[25]

The double revenge in *Hamlet* also relates, however, to Shakespeare's known preference for two-part structures, possibly although not certainly based on a division of the plays by an interval in performance. On the latter assumption, Emrys Jones – the two-part structure's subtlest analyst – argues for division of *Hamlet* after IV.iv (the passage of Fortinbras's army). I accept that Hamlet's departure makes a natural break in the action, and that there is possible support in a 'structural rhyme' between the appearances of Fortinbras in the last scenes of Jones's Parts One and Two.[26] Nevertheless, several considerations count against this division. First, as Jones concedes, it is so late as to be out of line with Shakespeare's other divisions; and perhaps even too late for a workable interval. Second, it departs from Jones's own account of the two-part structure. Instead of a Part One that ends in an exciting provisional conclusion and a Part Two that begins gradually with a fourth act at low tension, it results in a Part One that peters out in the fourth Act, and a Part Two that is almost all event. Third, the Fortinbras structural rhyme can be explained differently. As we have seen, Fortinbras in V.ii can be thought of as linked with the armed ghost in I.i, as part of Brown's recessed symmetry. Finally, rather more structural rhymes support the earlier division, after the prayer scene (III.iii). An interval without a corresponding break in the action can be effective theatrically, so long as it is planned by the dramatist. In any case, Shakespeare's two-part structure may be internal and not interval-based – may serve, indeed, as a suture to counter any disintegrative effect of the division.

However that may be, the earlier division, after III.iii, is supported by several structural rhymes. These include scene correspondences not accounted for by Keith Brown's recessed symmetries. Thus, the first part begins with an appearance of the Ghost on the rampart; and the second part begins with the appearance in Gertrude's closet. The lost opportunity of the second last scene in Hamlet's revenge, the play scene (III.ii), corresponds to the lost opportunity of the grave scene (V.i) in Laertes' revenge. The division of the play is interesting not so much for its mechanical precision, however, as for its heuristic possibilities. For example, we may be led to see that, just as the denouement of the first part is precipitated by the inserted Mousetrap performance, so the denouement of the second is precipitated by another inserted entertainment, the fencing match. We may see an analogy between the adulterated playet used by Hamlet and the doctored foil used by that other man of honour, Laertes. Or, a connection may be suggested between Hamlet's cruelties to Ophelia in III.ii (preceded by his meditation on death in 'To be or not to be ...' and his rejection of her) and his leaping into her grave in the corresponding scene V.i, in a theatrical bid to out-Laertes Laertes. We have to decide whether the connection movingly underlines Hamlet's countinued love, or shocks by exposing his obliviousness in imagining that he can still use his love for her to make a point of honour.

At the juncture of the two half-plays, the closet scene occupies a pivotal, numerologically central position. It is pivotal because it marks a point of no return, when Hamlet goes beyond acting passion and starts to act passionately. His ill-considered and ignoble killing of Polonius – his first outright act of revenge – is multiply fatal in its multifarious consequences. And it moves him decisively into the purlieus of death.[27] The closet scene is also the numerological centre of *Hamlet*, being the tenth of its nineteen scenes. As such, it invites comparison with the 'strategic centre' of the action, the play scene – and in particular with the elaborately framed inserted playlet. The similarities are striking. Both involve appearances of the elder Hamlet. And just as 'The Mousetrap' is intended 'to catch the conscience of the king' (II.ii.601), so Hamlet in his interview with his mother intends to catch the conscience of the Queen – to 'set you up a glass /Where you may see the inmost part of you' (III.iv.19). Both initiatives are partly successful. Indeed, so successful is Hamlet in shaming his mother that the Ghost tells him to 'step between her and her fighting soul' – presumably to prevent her 'amazement' (bewilderment) from driving her to madness or desperate action. Gertrude may have been passive, lustful, inert; but now she has, in her way, taken a deeper impression of remorse than Claudius. (The location of the scene – specified at III.ii.322 – symbolically accords with this view; for, although doubtless chosen by Polonius merely for privacy, a closet was the usual place for meditation.[28])

The two 'central' scenes of conscience-catching prove to frame equivalent although contrasting 'sentences', which are thus multiply emphasized. In the closet scene, the Ghost's appearance is itself central. His opening words, intensely solicited by Hamlet, occupy the exactly central line of the scene: 'Do not forget.' This brief message, recalling as it does his final words on his last previous appearance – 'Remember me' – places tremendous weight on the keeping of the vow of I.v. In the play scene, similarly, *The Murder of Gonzago* is much concerned with the keeping of faith with the dead. As I have shown, the elaborately prefaced and framed fragment expresses formally the harmonious accord before Gonzago's (the elder Hamlet's) death, and places great structural emphasis on his long 30-line speech. This grave and sombre speech is about the fallibility of human vows. For this theme the audiences have already been prepared by Hamlet's comment on the brief prologue – 'Is this a prologue, or the posy of a ring?': ring posies commonly made vows of eternal faithfulness. The central passage, beginning with the eighth of its fifteen couplets, is as follows:

> This world is not for aye, nor 'tis not strange
> That even our loves should with our fortunes change,
> For 'tis a question left us yet to prove,
> Whether love lead fortune or else fortune love.
> (III.ii.195–8)

But the Player King says nothing about revenge. On the contrary, as Dodsworth has noticed, he speaks for 'an acceptance of human nature in its weaknesses and its fallibility'.[29] But Hamlet in his passion grasps nothing of the Player King's argument against exaggeration of honour. Indeed, Hamlet is as untouched by 'The Mousetrap' as he wrongly believes Claudius to be.

The two centres of *Hamlet* are thus closely related. In the secrecy of their formal emphasis they deliver reminders of two troths, complementary yet opposed: human honour and Christian obligation. These two centres correspond to voices that sound throughout the play. Which will Hamlet listen to?

From this perspective we see him as veering helplessly between the two – and very often choosing mere honour. When the Ghost's second visitation finds him guilty, he imagines his guilt to be worse than that of which he has just accused his mother. She has forgotten her marriage vows; he has forgotten (as he supposes) a vow more sanctified still.

Keith Brown's rationale – that the closet scene's presentation of a 'truly sovereign figure' justifies its numerological centrality[30] – seems persuasive, so far as it goes. The elder Hamlet is certainly contrasted at length by Hamlet with the 'cutpurse of the empire and the rule', the 'king of shreds and patches' – not only in terms of legality but of kingly qualities. A further reason for the scene's centrality, however, lies in the fact that it contains a visitation of the Ghost. The Ghost is truly kinglike; but, more than that, he is an embodiment of honour – of the moral task imposed on Hamlet by his inheritance.

The seriousness of the supernatural for Hamlet is hard to overestimate; but it is also hard to get in focus. In any revenge play, the Ghost is a representative (however perfunctory) of inarguable, supernaturally sanctioned duty. (Sometimes, it

The plays within the play of *Hamlet* 179

appears to symbolize duty in conflict with the prevailing social order – a vocation to reform.) But in *Hamlet*, we have to do with the most numinous and compelling of all Elizabethan ghosts. There are, to be sure, Protestant doubts about his credentials.[31] But Shakespeare does not allow these to occupy our attention. And, as events confirm the Ghost's information, we are tempted to allow these rational doubts to dwindle. For Hamlet, the temptation is much stronger. Emotionally, he is powerfully drawn to credit the Ghost's authenticity – to find a divine imperative, almost, in his commission. This already finds reflection in the ritual oathtaking of I.v, boisterously entered into as it is. Hamlet's evasive lightness of tone, his aristocratic *sprezzatura*, conceals his sense of a terrifying crisis in his life.

The ritual itself is commonly passed over. But it should be noticed that the Ghost says 'swear' no fewer than four times. The number of times Hamlet and his friends take the oath has been disputed; but Harold Jenkins shows conclusively that they swear three times (I.v.163,169,189): 'Threefold oaths had a particularly binding force (sometimes explained by their invocation of the Trinity), and this one will have still further solemnity from seeming to be sworn at the behest not of Hamlet only but of a supernatural agent also' (459). This count, however, omits Hamlet's earlier solitary oath at 1.112: 'I have sworn't.' Altogether, therefore, he swears four times. This fourfold oath has a very specific meaning; for it alludes to the sacred *tetractys* by which Pythagoreans swore their ancient oath. As Renaissance arithmologists explain, the *tetractys* or quaternion symbolizes the foundation of all existence, the *vinculum* of corporeal and incorporeal, the harmony of nature and the fount of virtue. It was often represented by allusions to its various forms – 1 (its fount), 4, and 10 (sum of its aliquot parts).[32] Hamlet's oath, however unChristian it must ultimately be regarded, is thus given the colourable sanctity of metaphysical implications. An audience will easily conclude that he is committing himself to an unquestionable duty. Indeed, the apparent authority of honour mattered enough to Shakespeare for him to repeat the *tetractys* pattern in the locations of the Ghost's appearances. These come in the first, fourth and tenth scenes of the play. They can almost be seen, therefore, as an artistic equivalent of supernatural visitations – of the divine dramatist's 'insert' in the *opus magnum* of nature. (The idea is replicated in microcosm with a human dramatist in *The Murder of Gonzago*, in the speech that Hamlet arranges to 'set down and insert in't', II.ii.536.) But this should by no means be taken as authorial vindication of the Ghost. For the Pythagorean oath, however solemn, however religious, remains pagan.

The structure of *Hamlet*, framed and doubly centred and diptychous though it is, does not merely follow a period style, but expresses distinct emphases. It focuses attention on the difficult duty of keeping faith. And it contrasts two attitudes to offences against personal honour – one of tolerance, the other a grim compulsion to revenge. It is consonant, in fact, with the ordonnance of pairs of contrasted figures to which modern criticism has drawn attention. For these pairs – the elder Hamlet and Claudius, Hamlet and Claudius, Hamlet and Fortinbras, Hamlet and Pyrrhus, Hamlet and Laertes – are not only offenders and revengers, but revengers of different types. Of all the oppositions, that between the revenges of the would-be scrupulous Hamlet and the unprincipled Laertes is the most fully developed.

Underlying more than one of these oppositions is the characteristically Shakespearian contrast of old and new social values. The fashionable Laertes unmistakably embodies an emergent nihilism – outwardly prudential but inwardly capable of ruthless and anarchic passion – that is not unlike the life-style of the Greeks in *Troilus and Cressida*. The divided Hamlet, to be sure, is not without his own moments of hard modernity; but he also feels the ambivalent attractions of his ancestral heritage. Lost in passionate fantasies and confused as to his duties, he is drawn to admire his father's perfect honour. The elder Hamlet's dangerous venerability shows in all we learn of him; not only from his heroic personal combat with the sledded Polacks, but from his very speech. Thus, he uses old-fashioned romance alliteration – 'With witchcraft of his wit ... /O wicked wit' (I.v.43–4) – and an antiquated rhetoric of scheme and Ciceronian amplification: 'the fat weed /That roots itself in ease on Lethe wharf' (32–3). The supernatural insert is an intrusion, it seems, of older values.

Even more questionably antiquated is the work from which Hamlet remembers Pyrrhus's iconic speech in a Marlovian heroic style. This play, of 'honest method, as wholesome as sweet' (II.ii.440–1), may be taken to represent a respected

The plays within the play of *Hamlet* 181

heritage of dramatic tradition. Yet at a darker level – less wholesome and sweet – it stands for the repellent social inheritance of revenge. For Pyrrhus's speech, which by a naturalistic criterion would be disproportionately long, has the function of realizing the horror of remorselessness:

> When she saw Pyrrhus make malicious sport
> In mincing with his sword her husband's limbs.
>
> (II.ii.509–10)

Old or new? The ambivalent type of revenger as pitiless killer was ancient, yet ever available for recrudescence.

Between these ambivalences Hamlet turns in anguish, coming near to self-destructive madness. In this connection, Gordon Braden's analysis of the impasse is penetrating: Hamlet 'immediately censor[s]' any impulse to Senecan rage; 'His reflective nature internalizes the aggression to which he is called; declamatory fury becomes relentless self-laceration.'[33] Nevertheless, reformer as he is, Hamlet also shows some consciousness of the sin of revenge, of his dual role.[34] One can almost glimpse a moment of self-discovery in the rapidity with which he turns from accusation of Gertrude ('A king of shreds and patches') to confession of his own guilt, however misconceived – 'Do you not come your tardy son to chide...?' (II.iv.102,107).

We may say, then, that the double structure of *Hamlet* accords with its complex presentation of duty. For the imperative summons to revenge is partly duty, partly temptation – presumption, even, of a divine mission to reform a world out of joint. It is itself double, involving vows and duties both to man and to God, obligations both to honour's justice and God's love. And Hamlet himself both keeps and breaks vows in his dealings with Ophelia, Gertrude, Claudius, and Polonius. Having failed to satisfy honour through his plot in the first half-play, he finds himself embarked in the second on a course of blood that ends the Hamlet dynasty altogether. Hamlet is now the target of revenge, not the intriguer; yet God's justice nonetheless vindicates itself in the 'fortuitous' events of the fencing match. (As in the fatal masque of *Women Beware Women*, human intrigues subserve divine ends.) It would be simplistic to infer that *Hamlet* has a message such as 'vengeance is mine ... saith the Lord'.[35] But the play's structure cannot but persuade one that if Hamlet had executed revenge 'successfully' (remorselessly) in the manner of Pyrrhus, it would have been a pyrrhic victory. The double centres emphasize human frailty in keeping vows: this is part of the tragedy of man. Yet hesitation to execute justice also seems to be regarded by Shakespeare as human – and human in a nobler sense.

NOTES

1 Marco Mincoff, 'The structural pattern of Shakespeare's Tragedies', *Shakespeare Survey*, 3 (1950), 58–65; Mark Rose, *Shakespearean Design* (Cambridge, Mass., 1972).

2 Rose says: 'Thinking purely in narrative terms, the fight between the kings is not worth the kind of emphasis that we would expect to find reserved for the crucial fact at the heart of the story.' However, 'it is often a conceptual rather than a narrative element that Shakespeare places at the center of his scenes' (pp. 97–8).

3 '"Form and cause conjoin'd": *Hamlet* and Shakespeare's workshop', *Shakespeare Survey*, 26 (1973), 11–20. Throughout, for convenience of reference, I have followed the conventional number of scenes. But in counting the numerological structures I necessarily return to the Folio conflation of modern I.iv and v.

4 ibid., p. 16a.

5 See David Laird, 'The inserted masque in Elizabethan and Jacobean drama', unpublished dissertation, University of Wisconsin, 1955, cited in Sarah P. Sutherland, *Masques in Jacobean Tragedy* (New York, 1983), p. 3.

6 Sutherland, p. 8.

7 Anne Barton, *Ben Jonson, Dramatist* (Cambridge, 1984), p. 269.

8 As Burton Fishman emphasizes: see Sutherland, pp. 6–7.

9 '"These pretty devices": a study of masques in plays', in *A Book of Masques*, ed. T.J.B. Spencer and S.W. Wells (Cambridge, 1967), p. 443.

10 Kyd's continental orientation followed the lead of the Countess of Pembroke, and is reflected also in his translations, such as *Cornelia* with its formally intricate structure of different verse forms.

11 On some occasions this also may have been mimed, with the accompaniment of speech in 'sundry languages'. See *The Spanish Tragedy*, ed. Philip Edwards (London, 1959), pp. xxxiv–xxxvii.

12 See Michael Goldman, *Shakespeare and the Energies of Drama* (Princeton, NJ, 1972), pp. 77–8. For this reference, and for many other suggestions throughout, I wish to thank Arthur Kirsch.

13 The analysis follows Harold Jenkins's modern text. Line counts agree with Q2 except for the rejected line it wrongly retains at III.ii.162a, and with F1, except for the two couplets it is generally agreed to omit.

14 Instances are given in my *Triumphal Forms* (Cambridge, 1970): see, e.g., pp. 159–60.

15 Pierio Valeriano, *Hieroglyphica* (Frankfurt, 1613), XXXVII. xxxvi, p. 463.

16 '"Form and cause ..."', pp. 13–15.

17 See W.W. Robson, *Did the King see the dumb-show?*, inaugural lecture (Edinburgh, 1975).

The plays within the play of *Hamlet* 183

18 Cf., however, Martin Dodsworth, *Hamlet Closely Observed* (London, 1985), pp. 166, 173, arguing that Claudius is apprehensive earlier, but controls his feelings until Lucianus' 'usurps' (III.ii.254) gives him a pretext for taking offence.

19 *The Elizabethan Dumb Show* (Cambridge, Mass., 1966), p. 113; cf. p. 131.

20 A partial exception is Dodsworth, pp. 161–3.

21 See Roland M. Frye, *The Renaissance 'Hamlet'* (Princeton, NJ, 1984), p. 132.

22 See, e.g., Dodsworth, p. 177.

23 Fredson Bowers, 'Hamlet as minister and scourge', *PMLA*, 70 (1955), 741.

24 *Scenic Form in Shakespeare* (Oxford, 1971), pp. 73–4.

25 See R.M. Cummings, cited in Fowler, *Triumphal Forms*, p. 6; James Nohrnberg, *The Analogy of 'The Faerie Queene'* (Princeton, NJ, 1976), pp. 60–5.

26 For the argument for a division between IV.iv and v, see *Scenic Form in Shakespeare*, p. 79; on the structural rhyme see pp. 76, 80. Jones's division is rejected, however, by Dodsworth, p. 225.

27 Cf. the emphasis of C.S. Lewis in 'Hamlet: the Prince or the poem', *Selected Literary Essays*, ed. Walter Hooper (Cambridge, 1969), pp. 98–9.

28 See N.K. Farmer, *Poets and the Visual Arts in Renaissance England* (Austin, Tex., 1984), p. 80; Mark Girouard, *Life in the English Country-House* (New Haven, Conn., 1978), Index, s.v. *Closet*.

29 Dodsworth, pp. 169–71.

30 '"Form and Cause ... "', p. 16a.

31 These are reviewed in Frye, pp. 16–17.

32 See Alastair Fowler, *Spenser and the Numbers of Time* (London, 1964), pp. 276–8, 287; John MacQueen, *Numerology* (Edinburgh, 1985), p. 73; Francesco Giorgio, *De harmonia mundi totius cantica tria* (Paris, 1595), fo. 50v; Pietro Bongo, *Mysticae numerorum significationis liber* (Bergamo, 1585), pt I, p. 136.

33 Gordon Braden, *Renaissance Tragedy and the Senecan Tradition* (New Haven, Conn., 1985), p. 218.

34 On the dual role of revenger and murderer, cf. Jenkins, pp. 478–9, 508.

35 Cf. *The Spanish Tragedy*, III.xiii.1, where the text is actually cited, only to be ignored.

11
Iago's questionable shapes
KENNETH PALMER

In the last scene of *Othello*, Lodovico, returning to the stage, asks

>Where is this rash and most unfortunate man?

to be answered by Othello himself

>That's he that was Othello: here I am.[1]

The reply is significant. It contrasts sharply with those hasty evaluations, the formulae otherwise used to allude to persons present ('Where is that viper?'; 'If that thou be'st a devil'; 'a damned slave'; 'This wretch'; 'that demi-devil'), all of which belong with the hurried trussing-up of a play's action. On the other hand, it sorts well enough with the penultimate line given to Iago:

>Demand me nothing; what you know, you know.
>
>   (V.ii.300)

Iago's words represent one of his most characteristic pieces of syntax; Othello's, the last example of the language which he derived from Iago; and I point to these two lines because they begin to tell us a good deal about the ways in which Iago's language operates throughout the play.

It is Iago's business (when he is not giving instructions, or playing the blunt good fellow) to isolate other characters from what they know. In *Othello*, characters (and I hope that I may be forgiven this innocent usage) show us little by little that they have pasts — pasts which represent, as they must do in a play, the sum of experience and knowledge which we, the audience, must attribute to those characters. But Iago is different. What we believe that we know of his past is much more largely reflected in the attitudes of other characters

Iago's questionable shapes 185

towards him. He is twenty-eight years old, married, well-thought-of, an experienced soldier recently disappointed in hopes of promotion; apart from that, we know his present; and, for most persons of the play that is all. His past has become distilled (as it were) into a convenient formula. Othello fought, and travelled, and spoke of it; even Cassio went to Staff College, and helped in Othello's wooing; but Iago is reduced to the mere essence of what has been known of him: he loves people (according to his own account, e.g. II.iii.126, 282–3, 297; III.iii.118, 196, 215, 218–19, 381, 413), and he is 'honest'. Any other past experience for which he gives us warrant we know to be fiction. More than most men who help to open the action of a play, he is anonymous. It is not until I.i.57–8 that he can be said to identify himself, and then it is in riddling and conditional terms:

> It is as sure as you are Roderigo,
> Were I the Moor, I would not be Iago.

Eight lines later, he produces the first of his paradoxes: 'I am not what I am.' And that formula, paradox in form, is yet more characteristic of him; for, quite apart from its parody of Exodus 3:14, it depends upon that kind of ellipsis which strict reliance on grammar will permit.

To look a little further into that first scene would be to find most of the other devices that Iago uses: his habit of defining and categorizing; his way of imposing his own style and syntax upon another man's speech, even to the point of interruption; his insistence on the present moment; and his way of translating or redefining (usually with a change of register). These devices interact; but I should like first to suggest how it is that Iago can even begin the process of isolating other characters from their knowledge and from their modes of knowing. The process involves control of men's movements, emphasis upon his own terminology, and the use of misleading syntax.

(1) Physical control of others is essential to Iago's purposes. Throughout the play, he separates people, tries to prevent them from meeting lest they should exchange information (even to the point of attempting murder: e.g. setting Roderigo to kill Cassio, in V.i), or at least contrives to manage their movements. He leaves Roderigo to face Brabantio alone (I.i.143f.); manages the brawl (II.iii), and causes the alarm

bell to be rung; forces Othello to allow him to join in the ritual vow (III.iii); keeps Cassio from Othello (IV.i); places Othello to overhear Cassio (IV.i); and even instructs Othello in the best way to kill his wife. Of some twenty examples of the imperative *go* in the play, Iago uses fifteen. It is indeed small wonder that his part is the longest in the play: the length does not derive from his soliloquies, but from the simple fact that he is engaged for much of the time in dialogue merely. Provided that he can, to a sufficient degree, control each conversation, then the isolation of the other character, in terms of space and time, can be developed further by linguistic means.

(2) Whenever Iago is involved with any other character for a short time, he adapts his style of speech with some precision to that character. The form of adaptation varies: sometimes Iago tries to tempt a man to act, or speak, in a given way; sometimes he tries to persuade people to have confidence in himself; and sometimes he encourages a specific attitude or emotional response. He is not always successful. At I.ii.50–1, in talking to Cassio, he uses an obscure metaphor in reference to Desdemona ('a land carrack'), and Cassio apparently affects incomprehension. Again, at II.iii.15–16, 18, 20–1, 23, and 25, he tries to involve Cassio in what seems to be his own view of Desdemona's sexuality, and is discreetly snubbed. On the other hand, the contemptuous phrases which he uses before Roderigo, in disabling both Desdemona and Othello, seem to have their effect (II.i.212–62), and the prose of the passage contrives to be at once knowing and weighty, marked especially by the repeated formula of adjective a adjective a noun; e.g. pregnant and unforced position; salt and most hidden loose affection; slipper and subtle knave; master and main exercise (224, 228, 229, 247 – this formula is by no means peculiar to Iago, but it is one of his linguistic disguises).

(3) There is, however, one linguistic device which Iago uses when with a variety of other speakers, and it serves not to control or to persuade them, as with (1) or (2), but rather to dissociate them from their normal and native responses. It takes two forms.

(i) The most obvious case is found at I.i.76–8, where Roderigo, agreeing to rouse Brabantio, is immediately told how to do it, in a lengthy simile which is pure stage direction:

> Do, with like timorous accent and dire yell,
> As when, by night and negligence, the fire
> Is spied in populous cities.

Iago's questionable shapes

But this is more than simile: it elaborates the details of what is compared; so that what matters is less the mode of utterance, and much more the contextual details – the modifiers. Iago wants to emphasize *timorous*, *dire*, *by night and negligence*, *in populous cities* – all, indeed, that is common to both the real and the postulated context, without need for translation. He goes to work in the same way at II.iii.160–2:

> Friends all but now, even now,
> In quarter and in terms like bride and groom,
> Divesting them for bed;

where the simile refers directly to Othello's own condition.

(ii) The other device occurs whenever Iago uses a syntax lending itself to complex subordination. The number of main clauses is not very important: what matters is the weight which the speaker contrives to give the subordinate clauses and phrases. Consider Iago's first long speech: despite the logical primacy of the main clauses (which, after all, sustain the narrative), those clauses serve chiefly to articulate the phrases which are subordinate to them ('as loving his own pride and purposes, / ... with a bombast circumstance / Horribly stuffed with epithets of war'). Something similar occurs even at I.i.28–30, where there is but one subordinate clause:

> of whom his eyes had seen the proof
> At Rhodes, at Cyprus, and on other grounds
> Christian and heathen,

but its length is considerable; and within the main clauses the word order is so rhetorically disjointed, and the nouns, pronouns and verbs so far modified, or translated into metaphor (lee'd and calmed: debitor and creditor: counter-caster), that it is the modifiers – those devices which affect emphasis and evaluation – which dominate the sentence. The same tendency can be seen in the satirical account of the 'duteous and knee-crooking knave' (I.i.44–8). But the chief use is of course to be found in III.iii.145–52, where the syntax appears almost to have broken down. Iago's preceding speech had offered, in question form, arguments for his silence; now, he begs Othello to ignore his comments, in a syntax and phrasing that exploits to the full the ambiguity of the situation:

> I do beseech you,
> Though I perchance am vicious in my guess –

[Now? Habitually? Is the vice in the guesser, or in the matter of the guess?]

> As I confess it is my nature's plague
> To spy into abuses,

[Real abuses? or matters of suspicion?]

> and oft my jealousy

[= critical enquiry, but the sexual context is already there, to weight the word]

> Shapes faults that are not

[But *faults* is not cancelled by *are not*]

> I entreat you then

[Q reading – anacoluthon]

> From one that so imperfectly conjects,

[*imperfectly* = (a) incompletely (b) faultily (c) viciously; *conjects* (Q only) = (a) conjectures (b) supposes (c) prognosticates (d) (perhaps) devises (but not noted after 1552)]

> Would take no notice, nor build yourself a trouble
> Out of my scattering and unsure observance.

[i.e., Othello may see more clearly than Iago]
The whole effect is to render untrustworthy the very language in which Othello might examine his possible cause of suspicion. Each sentence speaks doubtfully of reason, but persuasively of feelings. In old-fashioned terms, tone and attitude dominate sense. Logic is subordinate to rhetoric.

Iago's definitions and categories take a variety of forms, of which the simplest and most obvious are his 'old fond paradoxes' in II.ii. In them, as in Jaques's Seven Ages of Man, the neatness is misleading, for what in each case looks like a complete statement is in fact only partial: not all 'fair and wise ones', for example, commit foul pranks, nor should charity and humility and chastity be lumped together with 'small beer'. But all of that belongs to the Iago who is known to be blunt and sceptical, and who classifies foreigners by their facility in drinking: more important is what pertains to the Iago who appears to think in the forms of grammatical relationships, or in terms of dramatic function. We have already noticed the former of these two ('I would not be Iago.... I am not what I am'), and another example occurs at IV.i.261–3, where Iago says

> He's that he is; I may not breathe my censure
> What he might be. If what he might he is not,
> I would to heaven he were.

It is a puzzling riddle: it seems at first to shrug off the difficulty of answering Lodovico's 'Are his wits safe?' To say 'He's that he is' is almost to say 'you may see for yourself', yet it is also a kind of tautology – it asserts the obvious in a pleonastic form, which nevertheless may derive more significance from context (as is true also of circumstantial evidence, such as handkerchiefs). To continue

>   I may not breathe my censure
> What he might be

grows more ambiguous: it seems to imply that 'He's that he is' means 'Othello is badly disturbed, though not yet crazed' by saying in its turn 'I hardly dare admit how bad he could become' (if 'What he might be' bears that sense). But, in that case, the speech then turns back on itself, for the remainder of it makes 'What he might be' refer to the sanity and self-command that Othello should show. Any hint that Iago has committed himself here to an opinion is of course withdrawn by his final speech (IV.i.267–72), which compels Lodovico to make his own observations.

The alternative form of definition is a very different matter, and it is found in the first scene of the play. Here, Iago overrides Roderigo's ineffectual formality, to impose his own disrespectful assertiveness: the more insulting of these two speakers in the dark street tells Brabantio that he is

> one of those that will not serve God if the devil bid you. (I.i.109–10)

and five lines later, in reply to an indignant question, answers

> I am one, sir, that comes to tell you your daughter and the Moor are now making the beast with two backs. (I.i.115–16)

The shocked 'Thou art a villain' provokes the pregnant retort 'You are a senator.' At one level, of course, it is broad comedy, and must always have got its laugh; but its real, and lasting, effect is not comic at all. Iago is insisting, by imposing his own linguistic terms upon this encounter in the dark, that the only thing that matters is function, and not identity. To be known, as Roderigo is known, is to have one's testimony ruled out of court; but to have scored one's point – to have put Desdemona's absence in the lewdest form – is to have established uncertainty in Brabantio without making testimony depend upon the probity of the witness. (Roderigo's next speech, we may notice, is heard out, and believed.) Iago has hit upon an essential fact in his own kind of drama: that a known man brings with him his strengths or weaknesses, his truth or falsehood, but the unknown, provided he may have a hearing, can speak from a void – he has no past or origin, but only a function; and his hearer, the more he listens to him, partakes of his condition.

I have laid myself open to the riposte that this is not the method by which Iago really operates, for his manipulation of Othello succeeds precisely because he *is* known and trusted. But the objection is apparent, not real. What Iago does, in the main action of the play, is to translate himself into a function that might have been Othello's: he becomes, that is, the alternative attitude to experience, the other way of thinking, that Othello hardly realized was there to be used. And, lest I be supposed to be rewording the doctrine that Iago 'is' the dark side of Othello, it must be made clear that the danger which Iago manifests does not lie within the heart and mind of Othello; it lies much rather in the nature of language itself – in that other way of articulating experience which belongs to Iago's dialect, and not to that of Othello.

For Iago to offer, as in effect he does, the possibility of a new language is really to dissociate other speakers from what they know most intimately. Our 'world', our experience, is not wholly comprehended by the language that we use, but we feel most nearly in control of it when that language is commensurate with it; and the language must be trusted and trustworthy. At crises, it may prove inadequate: Othello finds it so at IV.i.40–1 (where incoherence leads on to a fit), and almost so at II.i.188–9; but for the most part we know, and we control, by what we say, in the way in which we habitually speak. Another man's speech is not ours: his experience is not congruent with ours. If we speak with his speech, we know inwardly the strangeness of his experience. And if his mode

Iago's questionable shapes 191

of speech should begin to open rifts in language – to discover doubt where we expected none – then we are doubly estranged from what we thought we knew. The ambiguity we derive from another man may cause a flaw in our own metaphysical system.

The most obvious way in which Iago can impose his own mode of speech upon another man is the most blatant and theatrical: it is to take control of tone and tempo by interruption. Iago does it to Roderigo most of all, taking over the assault on Brabantio's house, and insisting upon not only his shocking news but his shocking style, in defiance of time, place, and dignity. With Roderigo, again, he talks his opponent down (I.iii) with a variety of techniques: iteration ('our raging motions, our carnal stings, our unbitted lusts'); repeated command ('Put money in thy purse'); consistent scepticism (love is a sub-division of lust; a woman is a guinea-hen; no marriage lasts); copious and familiar allegory ('Our bodies are our gardens'); paradox (no man can love himself; virtue is irrelevant or non-existent); exotic vocabulary ('acerb as the coloquintida') – as typical of Iago as of Othello, despite the common opinion. But with Roderigo he can afford to be blatant, for the man is a fool, and lacks the wit to retain an argument.

Negation is not, in its most simple form, Iago's favourite weapon, for although he tells the lie direct in both negative and affirmative forms, he seldom uses the negative form in order to suggest what he formally denies. Indeed, while many of his other devices depend upon such indirect allusion, negation is usually a little more devious, and is found with a variety of phrasing; that is, Iago employs the simple formula of *not a* verb, but he also makes play with the related forms *none, never, nothing*, together with the occasional use of the derived form with prefix (*im*perfectly, *un*sure). Whatever method he may choose, the negative is almost always supported by other devices. For example, in II.iii, when called upon to explain the brawl, he begins with two straightforward negatives ('I do *not* know' [160]; 'I *cannot* speak' [165]), defends himself against Montano's imputation with another ('Touch me *not* so near' [201]), uses three different negatives ('*nothing* wrong him' [205]; 'I *ne'er* might say' [217]; 'More ... can I *not* report' [221]), and names Cassio six times (so that very iteration makes the name suspect). The full naming, at II.iii.202–3,

> I had rather have this tongue cut from my mouth
> Than it should do offence to Michael Cassio

does more damage still, for its hypothesis is allowed to work in two ways: it implies that offence might easily be done, while the following lines, turning grudgingly on 'Yet', insist that truth could readily wrong the man:

> Yet, I persuade myself, to speak the truth
> Shall nothing wrong him.

But this is uncomplicated. Much more telling are the two formulae used in III.iii:

> I speak not yet of proof   (198)

> I do not in position
> Distinctly speak of her   (236–7)

each of which uses a term from formal argument, and the former of which is combined with the adverbial *yet* (which contrives at once to suggest more potent testimony to come, while allowing Iago an escape if he should fail to provide it). The most powerful uses are those which operate in set; besides a pair at 164–5 ('You cannot, if my heart were in your hand, /Nor shall not, while 'tis in my custody') there are such sets at 200/201–2/204–6/220–2/224–5:

> *not* jealous, *nor* secure.

> I would *not* have your free and noble nature,
> Out of self-bounty, be abused.

> they do let God see the pranks
> They dare *not* show their husbands. Their best conscience
> Is *not* to leave't *un*done, but keep't *un*known.

> I am to pray you *not* to strain my speech
> To grosser issues *nor* to larger reach
> Than to suspicion.

> My speech should fall into such vile success
> As my thoughts aimed *not* at.

The effect of these is primarily to establish a growing but undefined sense of uncertainty: doubt is cast not only on what

Iago's questionable shapes 193

Othello might know of Venetian customs, but also on the 'right' degree of suspicion that he should show, as well as the firmness of Iago's judgement of his own words. The most subtle group of negatives occurs earlier in the same scene, where 'I like *not* that'; '*Nothing*'; 'I know *not*'; '*No*'; 'I *cannot* think it' follow in rapid succession, and draw attention away from the factual context, so that Othello may focus instead upon liking, thinking and knowing.

Questions achieve an effect akin to that of negation: grammatically, neither forms an assertion, but logically each presupposes what is then left open, or negated. If Keats says: 'I cannot see what flowers are at my feet', we concede the effect of dusk upon human vision, but we concur in believing, with him, that at his feet there are flowers. When Iago says,

> Would you, the supervisor, grossly gape on?
> Behold her topped? (III.iii.396–7)

we know that direct witness would be needed to prove adultery, and that Iago must so express the matter; but his question, asked in order to show the impossibility of providing that witness, nevertheless implies what it says it cannot demonstrate. Of themselves, of course, questions may be innocent or even playful (as with Desdemona's 'What! Michael Cassio, /That came a-wooing with you ...?' [III.iii.70–1]), and one may set aside as merely neutral most questions asked by men in authority. Othello's first question to Iago (I.ii.32) serves only to have confirmed what was offered as a guess, and is promptly withdrawn: 'Is it they?' virtually expects the answer no, and, following as it does an assertion of patience and confidence, it comes perhaps as close to indifference as a question can do. Indeed, it is the assurance that comes from birth and rank that determines the tone of another of Othello's questions: in the brief scene III.ii, his enquiry, 'This fortification, gentlemen, shall we see't?' is at once an invitation ('Perhaps you would care to accompany me?') and a concealed command ('Show me the fortification'). It is a question only in form; and its effect is to reinforce an authority that is so natural as to be almost unconscious. Even during the brawl in II.iii, his questions are modified by the commands which flank them: 'Are we turn'd Turks...?' is meant to reduce, and not stir up, excitement, and stands between 'From whence arises this?' (a typical search for fact and causation) and a series of orders, so that the ensuing 'What is the matter, masters? ... /Speak. Who began this?' grow less urgent, and more judicious, than they might otherwise be. Significantly, when the culprits can be identified in the darkness and addressed directly, Othello's questions set action against reputation, and invite each man to pass judgement upon himself:

> How comes it, Michael, you are thus forgot?
> ...
> Worthy Montano, you were wont be civil:
> The gravity and stillness of your youth
> The world hath noted; and your name is great
> In mouths of wisest censure. What's the matter
> That you unlace your reputation thus,
> And spend your rich opinion for the name
> Of a night-brawler? Give me answer to it.
>   (II.iii.169–77)

The effect overall is to make questions part of a process by which stability is reasserted: they restore the *status quo ante*. Like the commands, they refer to a known system of order, to which other men also subscribe. They do not try to negate that order, or to suggest any other, not yet otherwise defined.

But if Othello's questions attempt, by determining facts, to establish order, Iago's go clean contrary. He opens his temptation scene with a question which appears to have no real motive, and which provokes questions from Othello, serving to produce imperfect utterance in Iago: 'Indeed?'; 'Honest, my lord?'; 'Think, my lord?' (III.iii.100,103,106). This is already a minor victory, for it allows Iago to revert to questioning; but it also moves attention from circumstances to language, and begins to cast doubt on those words and phrases which determine thought and evaluation (*think*: *thought*: *honest*: *know*) so that 'I dare presume, I think that he is honest' follows quite naturally.

Iago's questions, therefore, operate in two ways. With the first kind, questions interrogate while keeping in our minds the form of the assertion from which they derive. With the second kind, which Iago uses in the latter part of the play, the question is highly elliptical, as we find it to be at IV.i.1f.:

> *Iago.* Will you think so?
> *Oth.*   Think so, Iago?

Iago's questionable shapes

Iago.   What,
    To kiss in private?
Oth.   An unauthorised kiss!
Iago. Or to be naked with her friend in bed
    An hour or more, not meaning any harm?
Oth. Naked in bed, Iago, and not mean harm?

It tends to provoke questions in reply (as here, with Othello). It can be linked to the conditional or concessive mood:

    But if I give my wife a handkerchief –   (IV.i.10)

and naturally employs an aposiopesis – as it does again at IV.i.18; indeed, as the interrogative gives way to the conditional, the aposiopesis takes over (IV.i.28,32,34). The two forms, from Iago's point of view, go together: the question or the conditional form opens up the latent possibilities of the sentence, and the aposiopesis then serves a double purpose, saving Iago from the need to complete the syntactical pattern, and forcing Othello to find the answer for himself.

The effect of such questions is twofold. The first is to demonstrate that, despite his apparent reliance on rhetoric, Iago has in fact practised as a logician. For Iago is a Ramist, and it is Ramism that offers us a hint of Iago's method.

To see anything in a predicament is, for Ramus, to argue; and from that follows Iago's habit of shifting the object of discussion from its normal context, and seeing it under a different aspect. (Such a notion explains Iago's willingness to be seen by function [as in I.i] rather than by identity.) But more important is the Ramist alteration of the nature of proof. For Ramus, proofs need not be syllogistic: they need merely to derive from the nature of man's reason, and follow the natural order of the operation of the understanding. This is why Iago's ordering of the affair is so persuasive, and why he can refer so casually (but so confidently) to 'the other proofs', for 'proof' in the Ramist sense is precisely what his evidence has become. There is the further point that Ramist logic deals (as with the enthymeme) with probability, and not with absolute proof: but in the circumstances of Othello's case nothing could be more suitable.[2]

The purpose of Iago's rhetoric is to create a situation in which Othello is to perceive enthymemes, and complete them. Cassio receives every excuse from Iago for his drunken brawl, in *rhetorical* enthymemes (if Cassio drew his sword, he probably had good reason) as well as a *logical* enthymeme ('But men are men; the best sometimes forget'); but it is left to Othello to find the true form of argument: it is criminal to be drunk and quarrelsome on guard; Cassio was drunk and quarrelsome on guard; (suppressed conclusion) therefore Cassio was criminal. A similar pattern arises from Iago's gnomic verses at III.iii.169–72, which leave Othello to deduce the alternative courses of action open to him (jealous misery, or hatred of Desdemona) while tacitly accepting the premise that he is a cuckold.

The second general effect of questions like Iago's is that they do not only divide habitual significance from language but also habitual significance from visual images; hence, Iago is able to make Cassio mime a lie without Cassio knowing it. Indeed, IV.i demonstrates both aurally and visually Iago's disjunctive techniques and their effects. They are, to list them briefly:

(1) disjointed utterance (35f.) in Othello;
(2) Othello's fit (because consciousness cannot bear co-existent contradictions);
(3) a series of aposiopeses from Iago (10, 18, 29, 32);
(4) assertions by Iago, coupled with negations (16, 30–2);
(5) interruptive speech (215, 222, 228);
(6) violence: Othello strikes Desdemona, because language no longer suffices his purposes;
(7) two syntactical patterns simultaneously (248–54).

By contrast, IV.ii shows Othello adopting one of the characteristics of Iago's speech. Unable to make sense of language once more by forcing Desdemona to take an oath, he tries to express the situation, not by stating the case but by *exclaiming*, in an attempt to utter his inward anguish by metaphor, or by comparing the actual with the hypothetical. He expresses, that is, effects alone, and never facts or opinion of facts. This response to a cause never named is something that Desdemona cannot understand at first, and when she begins to see his drift, Othello refuses to give an explicit answer to her question (70–80). He deals only with the consequences of an act which he cannot name, and which nothing natural can bear to hear of. It is not until he breaks out with 'Impudent strumpet!' that his meaning becomes clear to her.

How far Iago succeeds in making Othello adopt some of his ways of speaking may be seen in the use of the conjunction *yet*.

Iago's questionable shapes

Iago is very fond of it at the beginning of the play, using it four times in the first two scenes, and three times again in his satirical rhymes (II.i) as well as twice in describing Cassio's brawl (II.iii). The danger of the word (as Iago uses it) is that it purports to maintain a balance, but in effect makes a concession, and even appears at times to issue a warning. The more judicious and temperate Iago seems to be, the more ominous is the warning tone (cf. Othello's comment on Iago's hesitation at III.iii.119–21). The effect can be observed at III.iii.250 ('Yet if you please to hold him off awhile') and again at IV.i.90 ('But yet keep time in all'), and it persists even when *yet* might be adverb rather than conjunction ('Yet be content', III.iii.451). After IV.ii.203, where he speaks to Roderigo, Iago dispenses with the conjunction; but Othello, who had hitherto used it rarely, and then in speculation ('And yet how nature erring from itself', III.iii.229), now makes it habitual. His usual practice applies it in making judgements on people – as for example on Emilia ('yet she's a simple bawd /That cannot say as much .../And yet she'll kneel and pray', IV.ii.19–22) or in condemning Desdemona before Lodovico ('Sir, she can turn, and turn, and yet go on', IV.i.244), although these may be evidence of his uncertainty about observed fact. More significant is the way he uses it in coming to terms with his divided feelings ('but yet the pity of it, Iago!', IV.i.184), or maintaining his equivocal position in V.ii ('It is the cause. Yet I'll not shed her blood'; 'Yet she must die, else she'll betray more men'; 'I that am cruel am yet merciful').[3]

From IV.i onwards, Othello and Iago do not meet until, in V.ii, Desdemona is dead. During the interim, Iago's language undergoes a change. His tentative consolation of Desdemona appears natural enough, and so does his conversation with Roderigo; but after the attempted assassination of Cassio his manner grows melodramatic, and indeed almost self-parodic. He can risk this before Gratiano and Lodovico because they know him chiefly by repute ('This is Othello's ancient ... a very valiant fellow', V.i.51–2), and because they fear to expose themselves to unknown danger in the darkness ('These may be counterfeits: let's think't unsafe /To come in to the cry', V.i.43–4), so that for *them* his language corresponds to what they believe the situation to be. For the audience, by contrast, Iago's language is exaggerated and false:

> Lend me a light. Know we this face or no?
> Alas, my friend and my dear countryman!
> Roderigo? No – yes, sure – O, heaven, Roderigo!
> (V.i.88–90)

This passage is known for what it is – namely, play-acting, with stage-directions for the benefit of the audience on stage; the effect of black comedy is comparable with that in IV.i, when Othello watches, but cannot overhear, Iago and Cassio.[4] Evidently, Iago feels that he can risk broad effects in the darkness of the scene, as he did in the opening of the play; and his questions and exclamations, although apparently natural enough, serve as a grimly comic commentary on the scene in which he has just played, and acted as prompter and producer.

And this is the last time that Iago can play both actor and dramatist, for in V.ii he is forced once more to rely upon action ('Fie /Your sword upon a woman!', 221–2) in trying to silence hostile witnesses. He answers questions, or tries to stop Emilia from talking; but at no point does he seem to speak to Othello (since 'I bleed, sir, but not killed' must surely be addressed to Lodovico), unless it be to Othello that he speaks his question-begging brag ('what you know, you know') and his final determination upon silence. Both language and action (despite his attempt on Cassio, and his successful killing of Emilia and Roderigo) betray him in the end.

Othello's case is different. He hardly appears in IV.iii. or V.i – like other Shakespearian protagonists, he is 'rested' before the climax[5] – and when he enters at the beginning of V.ii, his language represents something quite unexpected: an attempt to restore an order which he had formerly destroyed. The opening of the scene is a noble failure to find a symbol or ritual which will enable him to speak of Desdemona's death without thinking of himself as a revenger (as he had at III.iii.448, 452, and as he does again at V.ii.64–5, 75–6, 116–17): it is Desdemona's natural reaction of fear toward physical danger which breaks down his precarious control. His difficulty lies in the nature of the balance which he tries to hold. Ever since IV.i, he has been liable to sustain two incompatible attitudes at once ('Ay, let her rot and perish.... She might lie by an emperor's side and command him tasks.' IV.i.172–5); now, he recognizes that the moment of the present before killing Desdemona, and the moment of the present after

Iago's questionable shapes

killing her, will satisfactorily bear up the notion of a sacrificial action. Only the action itself is something that he cannot, in calmness, contemplate; and he is able to refer to it only in metaphor ('Put out the light'; 'If I quench thee, thou flaming minister'; 'When I have plucked the rose'). His purpose here is to maintain the stasis of the moment when the killing is merely potential: Desdemona asleep is as if Desdemona dead; and Othello can contemplate both cases indifferently:

> Be thus when thou art dead, and I will kill thee
> And love thee after.   (V.ii.18–19)

Indeed, his purpose – perhaps unconfessed – is to transform Desdemona to an object: something which he could love because it would not change, and could not betray. It would be an object effectually existing out of time, something belonging to a changeless present. Othello has already been able to see himself in the third person as early as III.iii.358 ('Othello's occupation's gone'), again at IV.ii.88–9 ('that cunning whore of Venice /That married with Othello'), and after at V.ii.268, 269, 281 ('a rush against Othello's breast'; 'Where should Othello go?'; 'That's he that was Othello'); and that is halfway to seeing himself as an object. The first sign that another attitude is possible to him is made clear at V.ii.98: 'My wife, my wife! What wife? I have no wife.' The exchanges with Emilia proceed almost stichomythically:

> *Oth.* You heard her say herself it was not I.
> *Emil.* She said so; I must needs report the truth. (128–9)

> *Oth.* She turned to folly, and she was a whore.
> *Emil.* Thou dost belie her, and thou art a devil.
> *Oth.* She was false as water.
> *Emil.*   Thou art rash as fire (133–5)

as two opposed opinions confront one another. Othello's next concession comes as he asserts that he proceeded justly (139), and is backed by the awful conditional claim that a chaste Desdemona was more precious than a world formed of topaz (142–5) – perhaps another form of his desire to think of her as perfect and unchanging, except that this image is the comparative part of an hyperbole. And then, as Emilia calls for help, Othello becomes silent (save for his single line of confession at 187), until, having cried out wordlessly, he reverts to the calm he showed in I.ii. (The two speeches at 199–202 and 209–16 are surprisingly low-toned and factual, with their reliance upon short, laconic main clauses – 'I scarce did know you'; 'there lies your niece'; 'Cassio confessed it'; 'I saw it in his hand'; 'It was a handkerchief.')

His teasing of Gratiano is important. In one respect his ironic mock is like his behaviour towards Brabantio and his servants (I.ii.59–61, 81–5, 87–91), even to the detail of the sword not used, in each case. In another, it leads on in sustained irony to a recollection of what he has been, and a rejection of all the postures that he might now adopt:

> But, O vain boast!
> Who can control his fate? 'Tis not so now.
> . . .
> Man but a rush against Othello's breast,
> And he retires. Where should Othello go?
> (V.ii.262–3, 268–9)

The two actions which, without ironic mockery, he can now perform, he does: he tries to kill Iago, and he believes and begs pardon of Cassio. But, having done that, and having learned that his authority is taken off, he seems to realize that although he has been stripped of all that belonged to him in the course of the play, he can once more recognize himself. To discover the truth about Iago's lies is to regain his own identity: he is no longer the General, nor the husband of Desdemona, but he *is* once more Othello, who can refer again to himself in the first person ('I have done the state some service and they know't'). The opportunity has at last offered itself, to bring his past and his present together (though the combination is destructive), so that he can, and does, truly unite word and act: 'And smote him thus.' In acting so, he achieves something like what he intended to achieve with the killing of Desdemona (sacrifice, not murder; justice, not revenge), and he contrives to sum up the pattern which, effectually, the play's language has enacted, by dying upon a chiasmus:

> I kissed thee ere I killed thee: no way but this,
> Killing myself, to die upon a kiss.

But Othello, despite the purely formal elaboration of his last words, builds the structure of them from the simple binary pattern which was formerly characteristic of him. Iago, by contrast, produces a form of words ('what you know, you know') which is at once a tautology and an unsolved problem (for who can know what is known, or is yet to be known?); so that to refuse to speak is indeed the only course left to him.

NOTES

1   V.ii.280–1. These and all subsequent quotations from the play are taken from the New Cambridge edition of Norman Sanders (Cambridge, 1984), unless otherwise indicated.

2   The enthymeme is, strictly, an argument of probabilities (an imperfect syllogism) and was so explained by Aristotle, who thought it the most persuasive form of argument; but the word came by misunderstanding to be applied to the abbreviated syllogism, in which one term (usually the conclusion) was omitted.

3   Of the examples of *yet* as a conjunction, Iago speaks 21 and Othello 16; all the other speakers account for 13.

4   Such 'eavesdropping' and spying are usually comic devices (cf. *Much Ado*, II.ii and III.i, though the narration in III.iii has an unhappy consequence). In *Troilus and Cressida*, V.ii, eavesdropping takes a far more complex form. But here, Othello briefly hears the attack on Cassio and is, unfortunately, spurred to action, although the overhearing was not apparently intentional (V.i. 28–36).

5   Consider, for example, Hamlet, from IV.vi to V.i, or *Lear*, from III.vi to IV.vi.

12

On the copy for
Antony and Cleopatra

MARVIN SPEVACK

Since the First Folio (1623) offers the first and only text of *Antony and Cleopatra*, the textual situation should be simple or at least notably simpler than that of plays with both quarto and folio versions. To a certain extent it is. Yet despite the fact that the presence of only one text limits the evidence, it has not restricted the speculations and conclusions. For although all cannot but agree that a manuscript must have been used as copy by the compositor, there is little agreement about the nature of that manuscript. In the absence of direct evidence about it, scholars have had to reconstruct the transmission process on the basis of deductions made from the printed Folio version.

But there is no complete consensus on the evaluation of the printed text either. Many editors up to Furness (ed. 1907, vi–vii) – most notably Hudson (ed. 1855, 8:441) and White (ed. 1861, 12:5) – agree substantially, if not verbatim, with the first to comment explicitly on the text, Knight (ed. 1841, [6]:277): 'The text is, upon the whole, remarkably accurate; although the metrical arrangement is, in a few instances, obviously defective. The positive errors are very few. Some obscure passages present themselves; but, with one or two exceptions, they are not such as to render conjectural emendation desirable.' Yet in his second edition Hudson (ed. 1881, 16:3) – doubtless influenced by Delius (ed. 1856), whose opinion he seems to translate literally – changes his mind strikingly: 'I must add that the original text of this play is not very well printed, even for that time or that volume, and has a number of corruptions [presumably the punctuation and lineation mentioned by Delius (2:1)] that are exceedingly trying to an editor.' Twentieth-century editors tend to a benevolent posi-

On the copy for *Antony and Cleopatra* 203

tion, like Kittredge's (ed. 1941, vii) almost casual 'Misprints are plentiful, but they are usually easy to correct' or Everett's (ed. 1964, 187) 'As a text, it is relatively good: it contains many slips but few real difficulties.' Wilson (ed. 1929, Introduction, n.p.) goes so far as to make a virtue out of the vice of irregularities: 'The very roughness of the text ... is a guarantee of its authenticity.'

It is precisely this paradox – a 'good' text marked or marred by certain aberrations and corruptions – which enables scholars to make deductions about the nature of the copy. For the 'minor' difficulties – like spelling, punctuation, even lineation – are thrown into relief by the otherwise 'good' text. Even well- or overdeveloped areas, like the abundance of stage directions, are more evident because of the surroundings, as in the seeming paradox of Greg's (1955, 403) view that the 'undoubted source of F [is] in *foul* papers', yet (398) 'behind the Folio lies a very *carefully* written copy' [italics are mine]. So too the coincidence of opposites on another level, as in Hudson's (ed. 1881, 16:4) explanation of the underlying situation: 'The style of the play is so superlatively idiomatic, and abounds in such splendid audacities of diction and imagery, that it might well be very puzzling to any transcriber or printer or proof-reader, unless the author's handwriting were much plainer than it appears to have been.'

The evidence which the transmitted text of F provides has led to a number of speculations about the copy, two of which reflect the concern – which the Elizabethans themselves shared – with the interaction of speaking and writing in the evolution of modern English orthography. The first theory, evident in commentary notes by Theobald (ed. 1733), supported in one way or another by Malone (ed. 1790) and Steevens (ed. 1793), and reaching a climax of sorts in Furness (ed. 1907, viii), attributes many orthographic peculiarities to aural misapprehensions, notably the 'practice of reading the copy aloud to the compositor'. Quite apart from the fact that the practice itself has just about been questioned out of existence (see McKerrow [1927, 239f.] and Albright [1927, 325f.]), Furness's (viii–ix) compilation of 'some of these errors of the ear' evaporates under closer scrutiny. 'Mine Nightingale' (2670) for 'My Nightingale' and 'mine Nailes' (3467) for 'my Nailes' may not be too common, but they are not in themselves automatically 'errors' and are most unlikely examples of mishearing, for they create longer units, whereas the euphony underlying such mishearings normally shortens by means of elision, telescoping, and the like. The same would be true in the case of 'should'st stowe' (2086) for 'should'st towe' (Wilson [ed. 1950, 125], incidentally, calls these 'seeming dittographs'). *Thantoniad* (1978) for 'The Antoniad' and 'places' (295) for 'place is' ('place's') are simple, widely practised elisions. 'Whose' (302) for 'Who's' is a common Elizabethan spelling (the opening words of the Q2 of *Hamlet* are 'Whose there?'); 'neere' (Lust-wearied) at 661 is orthographically interchangeable with the homophone 'ne'er', which Furness suggests is 'correct' (although both readings have their supporters); likewise 'in' (3088) and 'e'en' have been shown to be possible spelling variants as early as Dr Johnson (ed. 1765), who retained F's spelling and glossed as 'mere' (although, unlike the others, these two are not normally homophones). In 'vouchsafe to' (437) for 'vouchsafed to' there is less a particular compositor's hearing error (still less, as held by Walker [1860, 2:61–2], a compositorial confusion resulting from the 'old method of writing' final *e*/*d*) than the common linguistic phenomenon of assimilation, found often in Shakespeare.

The few examples cited by Furness which fulfil the formal requirements for aural misapprehension are not convincing as such for the simple fact that *both* readings have their advocates: 'greet together' (662) for 'gree together', 'your proofe' (819) for 'your reproof', 'wayes a Mars' (1171) for 'way he's a Mars', and to an extent even 'your so branchlesse' (1710) for 'yours so branchless', and 'Vnarme *Eros*' (2867) for 'Unarm me Eros.' In 'toward Cittadell' (2828) for 'tower'd Citadel' there is just as likely a compositorial misreading of the minuscule *e* or even a spelling variant (the *OED* gives 'towerde' as a spelling variant of 'toward') as a mishearing. These last groups, it must be clear, are also typical visual slips, as is 'You reconciler' (1717) for 'Your reconciler'. Further, 'hither' (1764) and 'he there' are unconvincing aural alternatives because of the difference in stress; a compositorial blunder seems a more reasonable explanation.

Orthographic evidence, cited to support the claim of aural misapprehension – the oldest theory of transmission – is equally prominent in the most recent theory. For the concentration on special orthographic features has served bibliographers not merely in compositor identification but in author identification. The collaborative effort of Alfred W. Pollard, W. W. Greg, E. Maunde Thompson, J. Dover Wilson, and R. W. Chambers, *Shakespeare's Hand in The Play of 'Sir Thomas More'* (1923), one of the seminal works of the New Bibliography, attempts to establish, among other criteria, the connection between spellings in the *More* fragments held to be in Shakespeare's hand and parallels in the quartos. Certain spellings, deemed 'abnormal', were declared to be Shakespeare's. And although the evidence was at first limited to 'good' (albeit 'badly' printed) quartos, it was extended, on the presence of even a few spellings, to the entire corpus, to multiple-text as well as Folio-only plays. Wilson's (Pollard, 1923, 114–15) delineation of 'abnormal spellings' and his widely accepted reconstruction of the work-habits of compositors is well worth quoting, for it speaks for itself as an impressionistic view of English orthography, not to mention overworked or tired compositors.

> By 'abnormal spellings' is meant such spellings as a reputable compositor of Shakespeare's day is not likely to have wittingly introduced into the text himself. Many spellings which to us seem archaic were of course quite 'normal' at that period. Yet the spelling of sixteenth and seventeenth century compositors was on the whole far more modern than that of the average author with whose manuscript they had to cope; and withal far more consistent, since at that time spelling differed not only from author to author, but often from page to page, or even from line to line, in the same manuscript. It was, indeed, this chaos of usage which forced the compositors to be more or less systematic; for, to set up a manuscript in type letter by letter would have been not only tedious but costly. Time was money, even in those days; and speed was an important element in the compositor's skill. Further, speed meant carrying a number of words at one time in the head, and the head-carrying process meant altering the spelling. Why, then, is it that abnormal spellings frequently crop up in the quartos? The answer is that they come, most of them, from the manuscript; they are words which have caught the compositor's eye. An unskilful compositor, i.e. one not able to carry many words in his head at a time, will naturally cling close to his 'copy', and so introduce a number of his author's spellings into print. But even an accomplished craftsman

will at times let copy-spellings through – when he is tired, or when a difficult passage confronts him which has to be spelt out. Thus, by making a collection of such abnormal spellings, it is possible to learn a good deal about an author's orthographic habits.

There are obvious weaknesses in this description. For one, consistency in spelling is the one feature that is conspicuously absent from all Shakespearian texts. For another, it is difficult to overlook such inherent contradictions as the compositor, under pressure, both altering spelling and yet clinging to his copy – i.e. both modernizing spelling and yet retaining archaic forms in a manuscript such as that of *Antony and Cleopatra*, for example, almost twenty years old – and also inserting 'unintelligent' punctuation which in turn, as mentioned above, is interpreted as contributing a 'roughness of the text [which] is a guarantee of its authenticity'. Most damaging, however, an examination of the application of the theory to *Antony and Cleopatra* reveals that the evidence for the strongly held and widely accepted position is limited and circumstantial, even illogical, at any rate not nearly as conclusive as its proponents would like to have it. The staunchest advocate of Shakespeare's own manuscript of *Antony and Cleopatra* as being the copy for F is Wilson (ed. 1950, 124f.), who, applying the methodology of the *Hamlet* investigation and expanding somewhat the view he had proposed in the Introduction to his facsimile of the F text of *Antony and Cleopatra* (1929), finds three interrelated groups of words directly associated with Shakespeare: forms attributable to odd spelling, to odd penmanship, and to a combination of both spelling and penmanship.

The first (124) consists of 'a number of spellings of an unusual or, by 1623, of an archaic character, such as are either found in "good" quarto and other F. texts, or are of similar type to those found therein'. Although his net is very widely cast, Wilson (124–5) can come up with only very few:

> Here are a handful: one (on) [50]; how (ho!) [204]; to (too) [1035]; too (to) [3175] etc.; reciding (residing) [425], [726]; hard (heard) [937]; arrant (errand) [2279]; in (e'en) [3088]; triumpherate (triumvirate) [1781]. The last two look like misprints. Yet 'in' (e'en) occurs again in *Merch.* (Q1) 3.5.20, *Rom.* (Q2) 5.1.24, *Err.* (F.) 2.2.101, and *All's Well* (F.) 3.2.18; and so can hardly be anything but a Shakespearian spelling.

As for the remarkable 'triumpherate', *L.L.L.* (Q1) which like *Antony and Cleopatra* was almost certainly printed from a Shakespearian MS. lends its support in 'triumpherie' for 'triumviry'. Equally noteworthy is the spelling or perversion of the classical names. Working presumably with North under his eye, Shakespeare was nevertheless restrained by no habits of 'correctness' or consistency so long as the names sounded all right on the stage. Thus he spells 'Sicyon' 'Scicion' ([204], etc.), 'Taurus' 'Towrus' ([1954], etc.), 'Actium' 'Actiom', which is not unnaturally printed 'Action' ([1920]). 'Medena' for 'Modena' ([493]) and 'Brandusium' for 'Brundusium' ([1884]) are probably simply misreadings, while misreading and inconsistency will account for variations like 'Camidius', 'Camidias' and 'Camindius' for 'Canidius' and the occurrence twice of 'Ventigius' for 'Ventidius', a name which assumes even stranger forms in *Timon*. Sometimes a variation is, I think, deliberate. 'Anthonio', for example, an acceptable spelling of the period as the quotation in note 1.1.10 [14] shows, seems to suggest familiarity or intimacy on the part of the speaker at [686] and [1056]. And a form in which I think we are bound to follow Shakespeare is 'Thidias', the name he gives to Caesar's emissary who gets a good thrashing, possibly because the 'Thyreus' he found in North was so difficult for an actor to speak. For 'Thyreus', though all editors read it, has no authority, since the name in Plutarch is 'Thyrsus'.

Wilson's thesis is 'that the copy for F. ... was Shakespeare's own manuscript'. His main evidence is orthographic and phonetic; his supporting evidence is distributional: 'F. certainly contains a number of spellings of an unusual or, by 1623, of an archaic character, such as are either found in "good" quarto and other F. texts, or are of similar type to those found therein.' The first part of the statement implies orthographic norms: else, how is 'archaic' to be defined? The statement is obviously based on observation and intuition. It is an educated guess, of course, which must be respected: good editors work this way, and Wilson was extremely well read and experienced. But since the method of enquiry is being scrutinized as well as the conclusions, it remains a guess nevertheless. For there is very little substantial empirical evidence for any changes, any unusualness, in the first quarter of the seventeenth century. This is not to say that there was no change; this is just to emphasize that there is little precise detail about what did change and how and when. On the contrary, Wilson's collaborator, Pollard ('Elizabethan spelling', 1923, 5), had in the same year as the *More* study pronounced a more accurate view: 'The tragedy of Tudor spelling is not that it had no system, but that it had a bewildering number of rival systems.' Still less convincing is the condescending attribution by Pollard (8), and implicitly by Wilson, of 'old-fashioned spellings' to a 'man educated in a country grammar school'.

Linguistically, the evidence cited is likewise insufficient. Wilson offers a vague 'handful' of spellings. A 'handful', however, is not nearly as accurate a measure as a foot or even a span. Against a total of some 900,000 word-tokens in the Shakespeare corpus – a total compounded, as Wilson says elsewhere (Pollard, 1923, 115), by a transmission process involving (in the case of the fifteen good quarto texts) 'some nine or ten different printing-houses over a space of twenty-nine years' – it is hardly a measurement at all. But the shortcomings are not merely statistical. The examples are indeed a 'handful' in that they lack differentiation. True, the pairs may all represent possible phonetic interchangeables (with the exception perhaps of *in/e'en*). Yet there is a world of difference between, say, *to/too* and *triumpherate/triumvirate*. This first – *to* for *too* – is hardly 'unusual' or 'archaic', and is too frequent to be an error, or a sign of carelessness, or an idiosyncratic sign of a particular writer or author. The second – *triumpherate* for *triumvirate* – is indeed remarkable: it is an ignorant spelling. Wilson (ed. 1929, Introduction, n.p.) may find it 'amusing', and the *OED* 'erron[eous] ... (by confusion with *triumph*)'. But it is most unlikely that Shakespeare – even with small Latin (which incidentally was really quite good, as Binns [1982, 119–28] has shown) – could have so misunderstood the etymology, especially when writing plays featuring the three men. (Franz [1939, 583] regards *triumpherate* as a blending of *triumvirate* and *triumph*, also a questionable surmise because Shakespeare seldom practises this kind of invention and, when so, usually in comic situations.) The same might be said of *reciding* for *residing*: phonetically, English interchangeables perhaps, but not to one who had ever read or heard elementary Latin. The *one* for *on* example is likewise interesting but for different reasons: for one thing, it is evidence that the two were possibly homophonic; for another, there is at least a slight chance

On the copy for *Antony and Cleopatra* 209

of a genuine misunderstanding of the sense of the passage since both forms are to a point grammatically acceptable.

Wilson's assertions about the 'spelling or perversion' of classical names are similarly a 'handful': statistically inadequate, qualitatively obtuse. Their premise – 'Shakespeare was ... restrained by no habits of "correctness"' in the spelling of names – is at odds with the generally accepted view that a consistent spelling of names is only a relatively modern development (not to mention Spielmann's [1947, 94–102] attempt to justify rhetorically the 'extraordinary copiousness of presentation of one and the same word'). A few examples should make the point. If *Towrus* for *Taurus* 'sounded all right on the stage', then why attribute 'misreading and inconsistency' to a pair which are as phonetically alike, *Ventidius/Ventigius*? There is, further, no evidence that Shakespeare wrote *Actiom* for *Actium*; even if he did, there is no compelling reason why there should be still another change, 'not unnaturally' or otherwise, to *Action* (which, incidentally, is the Greek form). Why must *Medena* for *Modena* be a misreading and not a phonetic rendition? Surely Wilson's opinion on variation (or, as some would call it, register) – '"Anthonio" ... seems to suggest familiarity or intimacy' – is linguistically and statistically hard to prove, if not untenable. Cleopatra uses it this once (1056) to the Messenger; she uses *Anthony* (32 times) or *Antony* (3 times) to everyone else, including Antony. Enobarbus uses *Anthonio* this once (686) to Lepidus; he uses *Anthony* (22 times) to everyone else, including Antony. That is, they do not use *Anthonio* directly as an indicator of intimacy: Cleopatra, dying, calls 'O *Anthony*!' (3566); Enobarbus's dying words are 'Oh *Anthony*, Oh *Anthony*!' (2720). A metrical consideration – the extra syllable in *Anthonio* – achieved through a morphological variation, seems not unlikely. And just as surely, Wilson is unconvincing not merely in saying that Plutarch has *Thyrsus* – all contemporary editions of North's translation have *Thyreus* – but, more important, in asserting that *Thyreus* was somehow 'so difficult for an actor to speak' (as unconvincing as is Ridley [ed. 1954, 3.13.31n.], who feels 'it was the other way round'), when a slightly flapped *r* (Elizabethan or modern) will make it sound all but indistinguishable from *Thidias*.

In addition to the supposedly typical Shakespearian spellings, Wilson also finds Shakespeare's handwriting behind still other orthographic forms in *Antony*. In fact, he ascribes (125–6) 'most of the F. misprints' to Shakespeare's script and conveniently classifies 'this two dozen' (actually 23) under the same 'minim errors' groupings he 'found convenient in dealing with the misreadings in *Hamlet*.' Closer examination of them, however, reveals a different picture and certainly a different conclusion. The examples reflect Wilson's preferred readings and not the historical situation. Wilson deems as 'errors' the following F readings although there is editorial support, at times considerable, for all of them: *windes* (200), *gloue* (916), *Vassailes* (492); *suites* (3325); *away* (3572), *change* (83), *there* (1418), *would* (1738); *now* (59), *Lessons* (2124); *dumbe* (580), *vouchsafe* (437), *fine* (1039), *embrace* (2218); *smile* (2345), *look't* (1693). Of the remaining seven 'errors', five concern proper nouns. *Camidias* (1881) and *Camindius* (2594) are both corrected by Rowe to *Canidius*, following Plutarch. Since the *m* is at issue, it is most likely that Shakespeare's script was not at fault, for all the ten speech-prefixes have the *m*; what is more probable is that Shakespeare, as elsewhere and for whatever reason, simply regarded the character as Camidius, Roman-sounding enough. Or, as Greg (1955, 402) says, 'We must allow Shakespeare to name his characters as he will.' *Sidnis* (897) and *Cidnus* [*Cidrus*] (3474) must be dealt with separately, as Wilson does in grouping them under different headings. If the first is an example of a minim error for *Cydnus* involving *u* and/or *i*, then the compositor had to make not one but two changes; *S* for *C* and *i* for *u* to 'mistake' *Sidnis* for *Cidnus*. Homophony, often present in the rendering of foreign proper nouns, seems a less intricate explanation and perhaps a more convincing one. *Cidrus* (3474) and *Mandragoru* (526) are without doubt errors involving accidentals, but there is no more proof that they were due to Shakespeare's handwriting than to the compositor's inattention: Compositor B might be excused for producing a non-word for the exotic *Mandragora* (though the unaccented *u* and *a* may be well-nigh indistinguishable), which was altered immediately (to *Mandragoras*) by F2, but hardly for misconceiving *Cydnus*, surely a simple visual lapse whose typicality is demonstrated by the fact that it escaped the scrutiny of F2–F4. Remaining are *Saue* (159) and *wan'd* (665), both of which were noted and altered by F2 (*Saw*, *warr'd*) and accepted by all subsequent editions. Misreading of a difficult script is a possible explanation, to be sure, even, if

On the copy for *Antony and Cleopatra* 211

probability is stretched, in the first instance, for the *u/w* 'error' to apply as well to *ue/w*, and, in the second, for the not necessarily common *n/r* 'error' to apply to *n/rr*. Other explanations might well be adduced. But more important is the fact that these two instances are the only ones which might be used as evidence. And the consequence is that for *Antony* at least these two alone can hardly be support enough for Wilson's hypothesis (Pollard, 1923, 115) that 'it is safe to attribute them [peculiarities of spelling] to the one constant factor behind them all – the pen of William Shakespeare'.

A small final group (126) – 'involving both spelling and handwriting' – is worth examining because it exemplifies another typical flaw in Wilson's argumentation. Like the artful magician, he focuses the reader's attention on one phenomenon while at the same time performing other operations. For example, he says that the 'error "foretell" for "fertile" [116] seems to be an *e:o* misreading of the spelling "fertill" which occurs in *Ham.* (Q2) 5.2.87'. He fails to mention, however, that of the fourteen instances of *fertile* in Shakespeare *fertill* is also the copy-text spelling in *The Tempest* I.ii.338, II.ii.148, and *Twelfth Night*, I.v.255, and that the dominant copy-text spelling is *fertile*, which occurs ten times, including plays possibly from the author's manuscript, like *1 Henry IV*. Most important, however, is that Wilson fails to mention the fact that the *e* after the *r* has not been accounted for. *Foretell* in Shakespeare always has a copy-text *e* after the *r*; *fertile* never has one. And he fails to mention that this 'error' would also involve an *e:i* 'misreading' in the second syllable. In other words, Wilson's conclusion involves *three* changes, his discussion but one. Similarly, 'One' (432) for 'Our', which Wilson regards as 'simply of course the contraction "o^r" misread "on", which ... is a Shakespearian spelling for "one"', involves at least five assumptions: the existence of a contraction (although no other instance has been found in the Shakespeare corpus; even the two in the *More* fragment III are unconvincing because the raised *r* follows a lower-case *o*, not a capital as Wilson's supposition would require); the misreading of the contraction (although the raised *r* is 'usually only a kind of modified *z*, instead of the formal *r*' [Tannenbaum, 1930, 135]); the extremely doubtful suggestion that a compositor would employ a raised *n*, an abbreviation which does not exist; the at least questionable assumption (Wilson's 'simply of course' is too blithe) that the very rare spelling *On* for *One* is necessarily employed here; and the assumption that *Our* is the only possible reading (although it was first conjectured rather late, toward the mid-eighteenth century by Styan Thirlby, first adopted in Singer [ed. 1826], and generally accepted only since Collier [ed. 1853]).

Wilson's (126) inclusion of 'Theobald's palmary emendation of "autumn" for "Anthony" at [3305], a misprint which is seen to be the common spelling "autome" taken for "antonie"; two words which might be virtually identical in script' employs the same diversionary gambit. *Autumn* is never written with an *o* in Shakespearian texts; it is never used with an indefinite article. With only two exceptions (one of which is due to line justification), it is written with an *mn* in all quartos and F: in this Shakespearian spelling there are too many strokes in *mn* for it to be necessarily mistaken for *ni*. And *Anthony* is spelled with an *h* 169 times in text and stage directions in the play; only in one line (3013) without, and that is certainly because of line justification. Finally, it is often overlooked that the following 'it was' was of metrical necessity also emended by Theobald to *'twas*; but in all the possible copy-texts of the Shakespeare corpus only one verse line ends in *'twas* (in Q1 of *Titus Andronicus*, V.i.95, which the following quartos and F place at the beginning of the next line, reading 'And 'twas').

Wilson himself diminishes the value of his next two examples by presenting half-hearted qualifiers ('probably', 'may') instead of evidence or even interesting hypotheses: 'The "loue" for "leaue" at [279] is probably a misreading of "leue", while "leaue" for "live" at [3179] *may* [italics are Wilson's] be a misreading of the same spelling for *live*, though I have not found this elsewhere in Shakespeare.' There is little purpose in reconstructing the numerous steps involved in these strained examples. Suffice it to say that, as is the case with the other examples, neither of the forms proposed enjoys total acceptance among editors. Wilson's final sentence (127) – 'lastly may be noted as characteristic of Shakespearian copy the frequent occurrence of colloquial abbreviations such as a'th', i'th', to th', etc.' – relies on too common a practice of authors and compositors of the time (Compositor B, for example) to be of any conclusive interest.

To be sure, there are further explanations, which can only

On the copy for *Antony and Cleopatra* 213

be mentioned here. One is advocated by Greg (1942, 148), who does not accept Pollard's (1920, 67–8) view that the F text was derived from a prompt-copy (ultimately deriving from the author's autograph): 'I can see only a very carefully written copy, elaborately prepared by the author for the stage with directions respecting the manner of production. There is no sign of its having been used as a prompt-book, and the directions are not of a kind that would be convenient in actual performance. In fact it is a producer's copy not a prompter's.' Greg's view is based, among other things, on the observation that the 'directions are unusually full and afford beautiful examples of what the author writes' (147). Since Chambers (1930, 1:477), however, observes that the 'stage-directions are not markedly full, but there are occasional notes for action or for the grouping and attitude of personages', to which Greg (1955, 398) concedes, 'A few directions are detailed, but on the whole their elaboration may sometimes have been overstressed', it is obvious that a basic contradiction will have to be resolved if an acceptable conclusion is to be reached. Another explanation, widely accepted of late though not yet substantiated, is offered by Bowers (1955, 31), who questions Greg's distrust of 'any intermediate manuscript, whether authorial or scribal, filling the gap between foul papers and the preparation of prompt copy', and goes on to say (114, n.9): 'Dr. [Philip] Williams is now able to conjecture on bibliographical evidence that *Coriolanus* is definitely from a scribal copy, and though his investigation of *Antony and Cleopatra* is not yet concluded at the moment of my writing, he informs me that the evidence here is also tending towards scribal copy and away from autograph. I may suggest that if, as seems likely, his full investigations materially reduce the number of Folio plays which can be thought of as set from autograph, more weight in the future will need to be given to the question of the intermediate transcript.'

In sum, so the carousel of theories: the copy for *Antony and Cleopatra* was Shakespeare's foul papers, or his fair papers, or a prompt copy, or a producer's copy – in Shakespeare's autograph or in a scribal hand, as the case may be. Conclusive proof is still missing in all instances. And in all likelihood it will never exist. At least not until such time as new documents emerge from libraries and record offices, if not attics and cellars, for it is hard for scholars to accept that everything has been lost. Until then, as is the case with all Shakespearian studies, the discussion continues.

NOTE

References to the play are by the Through Line Numbering of *The Norton Facsimile: The First Folio of Shakespeare*, ed. Charlton Hinman (New York, 1968).

REFERENCES

Albright, Evelyn May, *Dramatic Publication in England, 1580–1640*, MLA Monograph Series, 2 (New York, 1927).
Binns, J.W., 'Shakespeare's Latin citations: the editorial problem', *Shakespeare Survey*, 35 (1982), 119–28.
Bowers, Fredson, *On Editing Shakespeare and the Elizabethan Dramatists* (Philadelphia, 1955).
Chambers, E.K., *William Shakespeare: A Study of Facts and Problems*, 2 vols (Oxford, 1930).
Collier, John Payne, ed., *Plays* (London, 1853).
Delius, Nicolaus, ed., *Werke*, 7 vols (Elberfeld, 1854–[61]).
Everett, Barbara, ed., *Antony and Cleopatra*, The Signet Classic Shakespeare (New York, 1964).
Franz, Wilhelm, *Die Sprache Shakespeares*, 4th edn (Halle, 1939).
Furness, Horace Howard, ed., *Antony and Cleopatra*, New Variorum Edition (Philadelphia, 1907).
Greg, W.W., *The Editorial Problem in Shakespeare: A Survey of the Foundations of the Text* (Oxford, 1942; 3rd edn 1954).
Greg, W.W., *The Shakespeare First Folio: Its Bibliographical and Textual History* (Oxford, 1955).
Hudson, Henry N., ed., *Works*, 11 vols (Boston and Cambridge, Mass., 1851–6).
Hudson, Henry N., ed., *Works*, Harvard Edition, 20 vols (Boston, 1880–1).
Johnson, Samuel, ed., *Plays*, 8 vols (London, 1765).
Kittredge, George Lyman, ed., *Antony and Cleopatra* (Boston, 1941).
Knight, Charles, ed., *Comedies, Histories, Tragedies, and Poems*, 8 vols (London, [1838–43]).
Malone, Edmond, ed., *Plays and Poems*, 10 vols (London, 1790).
McKerrow, Ronald B., *An Introduction to Bibliography for Literary Students* (Oxford, 1927).
Pollard, Alfred W., *Shakespeare's Fight with the Pirates and the Problems of the Transmission of His Text*, 2nd edn (Cambridge, 1920; repr. 1967).
Pollard, Alfred W., 'Elizabethan spelling as a literary and bibliographical clue', *The Library*, 4 (1923), 1–8.

Pollard, Alfred W., et al., *Shakespeare's Hand in the Play of 'Sir Thomas More'* (Cambridge, 1923; repr. 1967).
Ridley, M.R., ed., *Antony and Cleopatra*, The Arden Shakespeare (London, 1954).
Rowe, Nicholas, ed., *Works*, 6 vols (London, 1709).
Singer, Samuel W., ed., *Dramatic Works*, 10 vols (Chiswick, 1826).
Spielmann, M.H., 'Sixteenth and seventeenth century spelling: a suggested reason for its variability', in *Essays by Divers Hands*, ed. Harold Nicolson, Transactions of the Royal Society of Literature, NS 23 (London, 1947), 94–102.
Steevens, George, and Isaac Reed, eds, *Plays*, 15 vols (London, 1793).
Tannenbaum, Samuel A., *The Handwriting of the Renaissance* (New York, 1930).
Theobald, Lewis, ed., *Works*, 7 vols (London, 1733).
Walker, William Sidney, *A Critical Examination of the Text of Shakespeare*, ed. W. Nanson Lettsom, 3 vols (London, 1860).
White, Richard Grant, ed., *Works*, 12 vols (London, 1857–66).
Wilson, J[ohn] Dover, 'Bibliographical links between the three pages and the good Quartos', in Alfred W. Pollard et al., *Shakespeare's Hand in the Play of 'Sir Thomas More'* (Cambridge, 1923; repr. 1967), 113–31.
Wilson, J[ohn] Dover, ed., *Antony and Cleopatra* (London, [1929]).
Wilson, J[ohn] Dover, ed., *Antony and Cleopatra*, New Shakespeare (Cambridge, 1950).

13

A world of figures: enargeiac speech in Shakespeare

S. K. HENINGER, Jr

In the early scenes of *1 Henry IV* the plot is propelled by Hotspur's anger at the King, who demands the Scottish prisoners captured at the Battle of Holmedon. Despite Henry's imperious ultimatum, Hotspur vehemently vows to defy the order unless Mortimer is ransomed from capture in Wales. In this state of high dudgeon, the young Percy is easily manipulated by his father and uncle, readily rallied to their rebellious cause. Worcester, especially, repeatedly exhibiting the sang-froid and trickery of a master politician, exploits the opportunity of playing upon Hotspur's strong sense of honour. In a carefully crafted exchange practising the rhetorician's art of *enargeia* (or vividness), this elder Percy depicts 'a world of figures' which leads to Hotspur's most impassioned and reckless outburst. To understand the full degree of Worcester's cunning, and the rhetorical theory by which he achieves it, we must reconstruct with some care the powers that Shakespeare assigned to the imagination, the faculty of the soul concerned with images and consequently with enargeiac speech. It is a device that Shakespeare often employed.

Discussion of Shakespeare's concept of the imagination usually takes its cue from Theseus's familiar speech in the last act of *A Midsummer Night's Dream* about 'antique fables' and 'fairy toys' (V.i.3), the subject matter of Spenser's recently published *Faerie Queene*. Theseus is wary of the imagination and sceptical of its value, and perhaps Shakespeare is speaking through him to poke fun at the old-fashioned feats and fay fictions that Spenser and his partisans had so pretentiously foisted upon the public. In any case, Theseus denigrates the imagination, particularly the poetic imagination, and equates it with that notably unreliable faculty, the fancy. 'Lovers and madmen', he warns, 'have such seething brains, /Such shaping fantasies, that apprehend /More than cool reason ever comprehends'. Theseus pointedly sets up an opposition between reason and fancy, between *com*prehending and *ap*prehending. Echoing a well-known passage from Plato's *Phaedrus* (244A–245C), he lumps together 'The lunatic, the lover, and the poet' as fantastical apprehenders, deficient in truth and understanding because they 'Are of imagination all compact'.

Concentrating finally upon the poet, Theseus with obvious scorn offers his version of how the poetic imagination works:

> The poet's eye, in a fine frenzy rolling,
> Doth glance from heaven to earth, from earth to heaven;
> And as imagination bodies forth
> The forms of things unknown, the poet's pen
> Turns them to shapes, and gives to airy nothing
> A local habitation and a name.

To compose his poem, claims Theseus, the poet submits to the *furore divino* so rapturously extolled by the Florentine Platonists,[1] and he exercises his imagination to produce palpable images of what he pretends to have witnessed in an ecstatic trance. Through the use of language, the medium of poetry, he purports to express the otherwise ineffable truths of the Platonic world of essences, so that he gives to airy nothing a seemingly material identity, a local habitation and a name. His imagination bodies forth the otherwise unknowable (because immaterial) heavenly beauty.

But while Theseus paraphrases the oft-quoted passage from the *Phaedrus* and invokes the much-revered authority of Plato, he remains sceptical. 'Such tricks hath strong imagination', he concludes, 'That, if it would but apprehend some joy, /It comprehends some bringer of that joy.' Theseus's purpose is to cast doubt upon the account of the midsummer night's adventures reported by the four young lovers; he is a practical man with the responsibility of governance. Hippolyta, however, rightly responds to his scepticism by noting that the young lovers mutually confirm one another, and therefore 'all their minds transfigur'd so together, /More witnesseth than fancy's images.' In refutation of Theseus, she concludes that their 'story of the night' could well be true, and that it 'grows to something of great constancy', some eternal verity, albeit imagined.

This fretful exchange between the Duke of Athens and the Queen of Amazonia reflects a continuing dispute over the nature of the imagination, which in turn reflects a radical shift that at the time was taking place in the prevailing worldview. At the beginning of the Renaissance, as it emerged from the Middle Ages, the ultimate constituents of reality resided among the essences in a Platonic world of being, or, the theological equivalent, among the heavenly host centred upon the throne of God in a Christian heaven. This ontology dictated a corresponding epistemology. The celestial beauty – and, therefore, reality, the unchanging – could be known only by ascent of the soul to the heaven beyond the heavens. In consequence, the task of the poet consisted of effecting such an ascent, perhaps with the aid of the Muse or by meditation; then returning from this ecstasy to the mortal sphere, where he resumed his human powers; and finally encoding his privileged vision in a verbal system that would render it comprehensible to fellow mortals.

But as the Renaissance proceeded – and, indeed, the Renaissance may be defined in these terms – an increasing number of those oriented toward this world relocated the ultimate constituents of reality so that now they resided among the sense-perceptible phenomena of an objective nature. A materialist ontology replaced the idealist assumptions of the Christian Platonists, and an empiricist epistemology ensued. Reality was now known by the observation of physical nature. And the imagination now formed its images not by deducing ideas from above, but rather by gathering data from nature and accurately describing them. The imagination might extrapolate from known data and hypothesize. By an inductive logic, it might abstract and generalize, so that its final images might result in part from a mental process. But for the empiricists it started with observable facts, not immaterial ideas. Indeed, an imagination that purports to body forth the forms of things unknown, as Theseus insinuates, is highly suspect. His wedding of Hippolyta is anything but the marriage of true minds. This disagreement over the nature of the imagination is a serious impediment to marital harmony.

Certainly, their colloquy about it comes to no conclusion. Rather, it is interrupted by the entrance of the young lovers, 'full of joy and mirth', so the argument over the validity of the imagination is abruptly terminated. The question of who is right – Theseus or Hippolyta? – remains unsettled. But it continues to hover in the air and provides a pregnant context for the interlude of Pyramus and Thisbe presented by the Athenian artisans that immediately follows. Like the very logistics of a play within a play, it invites us to view the performance of the interlude from several perspectives at once. With Hippolyta (as well as Bottom and his companions), we view it sympathetically and seriously, responding to the sad story of Pyramus and Thisbe as though it were a poignant tragedy. With Theseus (as well as Demetrius and Lysander), however, we view it with detachment and disbelief, responding to the performance, if not to the story itself, as though it were a farce. Thereby the play fulfills its advance billing as not only both 'Tedious and brief', but also both 'Merry and tragical' (V.i.58).

So by incorporating the Renaissance debate about the imagination, Shakespeare demonstrates the polysemous nature of poetry. The same text, he shows, may have more than one meaning, dependent upon the attitude assumed by the interpreter toward the text – empathetic insider, or caustic outsider. Even further, Shakespeare has demonstrated the paradoxical nature of literature, since the same text is both comical and tragical. And in the perfectly ambiguous circumstance of the paradox, when opposites both appear to be equally valid, the interpreter, in order to determine which of the two possibilities is likely to be preferable, must turn to the question of how such a choice can be made. He must specify the conditions which allow either choice to be true, which permit both choices to express verifiable meaning. By setting up such a paradoxical circumstance, therefore, the poet eventually forces the audience to analyze his medium.

As others have noted, therefore, in the final scene of *A Midsummer Night's Dream* Shakespeare contrives a means of calling attention to his own craft, and he daringly invites the audience to assess the illusory nature of a play. He risks such a tactic again when Cleopatra (played by an adolescent boy) proclaims her fear that in Rome some 'squeaking' actor will 'boy my greatness /I' the posture of a whore' (*Antony and Cleopatra*, V.ii.219–20), and when Prospero announces that 'Our revels now are ended' and 'These our actors, / ... were all spirits' (*The Tempest*, IV.i.148–9). Many have read Prospero with his magic wand controlling the scenario and directing the other characters as a metonym for Shakespeare the playwright, and they have probable cause for such a judgement. Shakespeare was a most self-conscious artist, and he often dares his audience to regain their willingly suspended disbelief.

In this prolonged debate about the imagination by Theseus and Hippolyta, then, the exact nature of the imagination and its reliability remain uncertain. And the fact that the two disputants change their positions later in the scene – Hippolyta petulantly declares, 'This is the silliest stuff that ever I heard', to which Theseus apologetically replies, 'The best in this kind are but shadows; and the worst are no worse, if imagination amend them' (V.i.207–9) – merely confirms the impossibility of settling the issue. There is no firm ground to stand upon. Products of the imagination must be taken on faith, and the sceptic will no doubt reject them.

We must not, however, limit ourselves to this passage in *A Midsummer Night's Dream* when discussing Shakespeare's concept of the imagination. Rather, we must recognize that Shakespeare so clearly recalls the *Phaedrus* in order to raise questions about the Platonist assumption that in a divine frenzy the poet is privileged to view essential truth, beauty, goodness, which he then reports upon in his poem. Even, perhaps, as I have insouciantly suggested at the first, Shakespeare is taking this occasion to poke gentle fun at the author of *The Faerie Queene*, who repeatedly professes to practice such a poetics. We must also recognize the motive of self-critique, which Shakespeare so skilfully achieves by drawing attention to the shifting, even illusory, nature of a play. In this passage Shakespeare has ulterior aims that complicate the issue, since he wishes to tease his audience with the artificiality and arbitrariness of the theatre. Elsewhere, though, he is much less problematical.

Actually, for the most part Shakespeare, like others of his day, derived his concept of the imagination from Aristotle, not Plato. In two related treatises, *De anima* and *De sensu*, Aristotle had presented in detail the make-up of the soul (in Greek, *psyche*), and he had set forth a carefully articulated scheme by which it processes data received from the phenomenal world. This theory, known as faculty psychology because Aristotle specified a number of 'faculties' inherent in the psyche, prevailed without radical revision until the end of the seventeenth century. It was pretty much an unexamined premise in Shakespeare's circle.

According to this theory, the soul comprises five distinct faculties: common sense, imagination, fancy, reason, and memory; and these faculties interrelate according to a simple scheme.[2] Quite briefly, the common sense, the lowest of the soul's faculties, receives data directly from the five external senses and reduces these disparate phenomena to a common state that permits further intellection. The imagination accepts these homogenized data and by filling out omissions forms a composite image, which accurately reflects the external reality. The imagination – so called because it produces images – can then refer the image to the fancy, which is a distributive faculty that can decompose the image and uninhibitedly transpose its elements into arbitrary new images; or the imagination can refer the image to the reason, which is a judgemental faculty that evaluates the truthfulness of the image, approving or rejecting it; or the imagination can refer the image to the memory, a faculty for storage, from which the image can be later retrieved when needed. For our present purposes, the important point is that the imagination is the faculty charged with producing images to correspond with actuality.

Several passages in Shakespeare's plays indicate that he subscribed to this concept of the imagination and the images that it conceives. After the exit of Bertram in the first scene of *All's Well That Ends Well*, Helena confides in soliloquy: 'my imagination /Carries no favour in't but Bertram's', and she recalls 'His arched brows, his hawking eye, his curls' (I.i.80–1, 92). Similarly, in *The Tempest* Miranda disingenuously confesses to Ferdinand that she has seen no man other than himself and her father, and therefore she has no measure for judging a man's handsomeness. Nonetheless, she cannot imagine a male more attractive than he:

> I would not wish
> Any companion in the world but you;
> Nor can imagination form a shape,
> Besides yourself, to like of.   (III.i.54–7)

Here the imagination is still dependent upon the common sense for its immediate data, but it assumes a certain degree of creativity, an ability to abstract and generalize. Even more so is this true when, after Hamlet sees the Ghost, Horatio observes: 'He waxes desperate with imagination' (I.iv.87) – that is, with constructing the possibilities stemming from the Ghost's charges against Claudius. Elsewhere in *The Tempest* the imagination acquires the power of projecting an image into a hoped-for future: when Sebastian and Antonio plot against Alonso, Antonio urges Sebastian to overthrow his brother and claims, 'My strong imagination sees a crown / Dropping upon thy head' (II.i.203–4). Sometimes the word 'imagination' is used for the image itself. In *The Merry Wives of Windsor*, for example, Master Page chastises Master Ford when he comes home and suspiciously begins to look for Falstaff: 'Fie, fie, Master Ford, are you not ashamed? What spirit, what devil suggests this imagination?' (III.iii.198–9). Again, while Hamlet schemes to catch the conscience of Claudius in 'The Mousetrap', he expresses a concern that the Ghost might be sent to damn him, in which case 'my imaginations are as foul /As Vulcan's stithy' (III.ii.83–4).

As we can see in these examples, the imaginaton formed its images from the precise data supplied by the common sense. But in the absence of complete data, it could fill in details, producing by autogenesis what the common sense failed to supply. And eventually, by extension of this license, it gained the authority to create an unprecedented image, to 'fantasize' in the modern sense. When old Gaunt attempts to reconcile his son to exile in the first act of *Richard II*, Bolingbroke bitterly rejoins: 'O, who can ... / ... cloy the hungry edge of appetite /By bare imagination of a feast?' (I.iii.294–7).

In *The defence of poesie* published in 1595, it is precisely this ability to go beyond actuality that Sidney cites in order to extoll poetry above all other learned disciplines. 'Only the poet', he says, 'lifted up with the vigour of his own invention, doth grow in effect another nature, in making things either better than nature bringeth forth, or, quite anew, forms such as never were in nature, as the Heroes, Demigods, Cyclops, Chimeras, Furies, and such like'.[3] The poet not only has the license to improve upon nature, and even to project supernatural forms, but he has the mandate to present, in Aristotle's vocabulary, what might be or should be according to probability or necessity (*Poetics* 1451a 36–8). The image produced by the imagination is no longer a simple compilation of sense data transmitted through the common sense. Now the imagination is charged to produce an image that represents the universal, an abstraction that exists nowhere except in the mind of the poet. And this, of course, is where Theseus finds his grounds for disbelief.

Sidney was sensitive to the likes of Theseus, however, so he tried to forestall such a subversion of the imagination by adding that the poet must stay within the bounds of what is likely, or at least possible. He may form his fantastic creatures and fabricate his astonishing events, but only 'so as he goeth hand in hand with nature'. Sidney further backs and fills, however, not satisified to circumscribe the poet's imagination, and equally unwilling to release it from all constraint. So he concludes this crucial passage by equivocating: the poet is 'not enclosed within the narrow warrants of her [nature's] gifts, but freely rang[es] only within the zodiac of his own wit'. In effect, the poet may create any image within the bounds of reason. The only firm rule is that he must not shock his audience into automatic incredulity.

Early in our cultural history the ability of the imagination to produce images was appropriated by the rhetoricians, the most purposeful of our wordsmiths.[4] In fact, a number of figures were devised specifically to effect this means of swaying an audience – for example, *hypotyposis*, *effictio*, *similitudo*, *prosopopoeia*, and even *metaphora*. Aristotle had characterized such figures by a quality that he called *energeia*, or 'forcefulness'. Quintilian adopted this technique, but he complicated it by conflating *energeia* with a similar term, *enargeia*, or 'vividness'. By the exercise of *enargeia*, according to Quintilian, a rhetor can describe something so graphically that the audience responds as though it were actually appearing before their eyes. The auditors are transformed into spectators, and act accordingly. After Cicero, it became common to designate a quasi-sense faculty to receive the enargeiac images projected by the rhetor, what in English came to be called 'the mind's eye'. Just as the rhetor exercises his imagination to produce images, the audience activates the *oculi mentis* to receive them. It was easy, of course, for poets to appropriate this mechanism for producing, transmitting, and receiving images. As Sidney argues, 'Poetry is an art of imitation' – more particularly, a 'figuring forth to speak metaphorically'.[5]

Again, it can be readily demonstrated that Shakeseare was familiar with this notion of a mind's eye. Horatio uses the phrase (I.i.115), and Hamlet, even before sighting the Ghost, claims to have seen his father 'In my mind's eye' (I.ii.185). A more extended instance occurs in the deteriorating action of Act IV in *Much Ado About Nothing*, when Friar Francis reassures Leonato by predicting Claudio's response when he learns of Hero's reputed death:

> When he shall hear she died upon his words,
> Th'idea of her life shall sweetly creep
> Into his study of imagination,
> And every lovely organ of her life
> Shall come apparell'd in more precious habit,
> More moving-delicate and full of life,
> Into the eye and prospect of his soul
> Than when she liv'd indeed.   (IV.i.223–30)

In 'the eye of his soul' Claudio will reconstruct a portrait of Hero replete with vivid detail. The mind's eye, the equivalent of the imagination, is an active and effective faculty, full of images.

Just how full it can be populated with figures is well illustrated by a major scene in *Richard II* that Shakespeare purposefully added to his sources. In the last act of his play, Richard undergoes separation from his wife, isolation in prison, and assassination. But rather than defeat, there is exaltation because the former king for the first time understands what it means to be wholly human. He gains this understanding by active deployment of his imagination. Like Gloucester, though he fails to see while a participating member of society, he finally discerns truth by means of an inner eye.

In his last scene, Richard languishes in prison, a broken man removed from the busy world that formerly he ruled. So to fill the void of solitude, he creates an imagined world with his thoughts. He opens his soliloquy by confiding that he has been attempting to construct a *similitudo*: 'I have been studying how I may compare /This prison where I live unto the world' (V.v.1–2). He encounters difficulty, however, 'because the world is populous /And here is not a creature but myself.' At first, he falters: 'I cannot do it.' But by dint of determination, he resumes: 'Yet I'll hammer it out.' And he delineates precisely how he will go about it:

> My brain I'll prove the female to my soul,
> My soul the father, and these two beget

A generation of still-breeding thoughts,
And these same thoughts people this little world,
In humours like the people of this world.

As he creates his world of figures, Richard details the method whereby the imagination conceives an image. Drawing upon Platonist assumptions, he thinks of the soul as a form, and therefore masculine. In contrast, the brain, being filled with the matter of experience, is feminine. The male soul then imprints its form within the female brain, impregnating it, producing a new entity. This act is thought of in sexual terms; it is a 'conception', a conceit.[6] By this method of generation, Richard then projects an imaginary society to mirror the one he formerly knew.

After creating his air-drawn universe populated by thoughts as diverse as the people who make up the real world, Richard remains fragmentedly undecided about his own identity. He oscillates wildly between being a beggar and being a king:

> Thus play I in one person many people,
> And none contented. Sometimes am I king,
> Then treasons make me wish myself a beggar,
> And so I am. Then crushing penury
> Persuades me I was better when a king;
> Then am I king'd again, and by and by
> Think that I am unking'd by Bolingbroke,
> And straight am nothing.   (V.v.31–8)

This puzzlement, this inability to decide his true essence, brings Richard to the brink of despair:

> But whate'er I be,
> Nor I, nor any man that but man is,
> With nothing shall be pleas'd, till he be eas'd
> With being nothing.

This embracing of nothingness, this existential nihilism, is comparable to the despair of Macbeth when he defines life as a tale of sound and fury signifying nothing.

It is at this very moment, however – providentially? – that a stable-boy arrives, the groom who formerly looked after Richard's horse, the lowest of the low in Richard's household. Suddenly, unexpectedly, Richard hears music played by this groom of the royal stable. Richard first resents this intrusion, because the sweetness of the music seems so out of keeping with his desolation. But then he recognizes the music for what it is, a gesture of sympathy, and he relents, still soliloquizing:

> Yet blessing on his heart that gives it me,
> For 'tis a sign of love.　　　　　　　　(V.v.64–5)

The stable-boy then enters, addressing Richard by his proper title: 'Hail, royal prince'; and Richard replies, 'Thanks, noble peer', acknowledging their comradeship in misery, realizing that wretchedness, like death, is a great leveller. But now ameliorating that pessimism – indeed, dispelling it – is the realization also that this wretchedness of the human condition can be alleviated by freely-given love. It is at this point that Richard, too late, achieves an identity, bestowed upon him by the stable-boy. And quite appropriately Richard's acceptance into the brotherhood of suffering is signalled by the musical metaphor of universal harmony – that still, sad music of humanity. Richard's understanding may not match the cosmic grandeur of Lear's; but his *similitudo* of a busy world, first expressed in enargeiac soliloquy, closes full in man.

In another play, *Antony and Cleopatra*, Shakespeare once more calls upon enargeiac speech to bestow identity upon a fallen creature. Antony, like Richard, is overthrown by his errors. But to counter any slander that lingers to malign his memory, Cleopatra exercises her ingenuity to create a lasting image of undiminished perfection. She claims to have 'dreamed' such an Antony, and she recounts that vision in a compelling *effictio*.

Bereft of Antony in the final scene of her tragedy – in preparation for a suicide that she stages also with an eye toward making legend out of history – Cleopatra suddenly announces to Dolabella and her attentive retinue: 'I dreamt there was an Emperor Antony' (V.ii.76). And like Helena and Miranda, her younger counterparts, she racks her mind to keep alive the image of the man she loves: 'O such another sleep, that I might see /But such another man!' When Dolabella interrupts to carry on Caesar's business, Cleopatra ignores him and begins her ecstatic description of Antony:

> His face was as the heavens, and therein stuck
> A sun and moon, which kept their course, and lighted
> The little O, the earth.

Transcending the realistic features of a mere mortal, Cleopatra depicts Antony in cosmic terms. His face was as spacious and

Enargeiac speech in Shakespeare

serene as the very heavens, and his eyes were like the greater and the lesser lights. Since the sun and moon clock the succession of day and night, they mark the perpetual round of time itself and guarantee the orderly progression of human affairs. Here enargeiac speech exceeds the vividness of accurate description and ventures into the compelling realm of emblematics. Cleopatra makes of Antony an ideogram of eternity, of divinity.

Dolabella again tries to interrupt: 'Most sovereign creature. ...' But Cleopatra once again ignores him and continues her enargeiac apotheosis of Antony:

> His legs bestrid the ocean, his rear'd arm
> Crested the world: his voice was propertied
> As all the tuned spheres.

When Dolabella can no longer tolerate the political threat of this eulogy – 'realms and islands were /As plates dropp'd from his pocket', claims the serpent of the Nile – Caesar's emissary rudely interrupts: 'Cleopatra!' To her plaintive question, 'Think you there was, or might be such a man /As this I dreamt of?' Dolabella answers no. But Cleopatra rounds upon him: 'You lie up to the hearing of the gods.' And she concludes this virtuoso performance of creating an Antony before our eyes by asserting that her image of him carries more authority than actuality does, and therefore whether he actually existed is an indifferent question:

> But if there be, or ever were one such,
> It's past the size of dreaming: nature wants stuff
> To vie strange forms with fancy, yet to imagine
> An Antony were nature's piece, 'gainst fancy,
> Condemning shadows quite.   (V.ii.96–100)

Her description of Antony, even if a product of the fancy, has become more real than reality itself. She has erased the pages of history, rewriting the events as she wishes them to be remembered. In our mind's eye, Cleopatra's imagined Antony replaces the 'strumpet's fool' that Philo had commanded us to 'behold and see' in the opening speech of the play (I.i.13).

In these several plays Shakespeare manifests his respect for the enargeiac power of language. We have seen his skill in adapting theories of the imagination for a variety of dramatic purposes. So we are now in a position to appreciate the full implications of Worcester's use of enargeiac speech to sway Hotspur by stimulating his mind's eye.

Early in *1 Henry IV* after the King exits with the threat, 'Send us your prisoners, or you will hear of it' (I.iii.122), Hotspur rants: 'And if the devil come and roar for them /I will not send them.' Worcester enters at this moment. After listening to Hotspur rave against the King and gauging his mood, Worcester begins cagily to review the history of the situation. By a sort of political catechism, Worcester leads Hotspur to the realization that Mortimer has the strongest claim to the throne, thereby fuelling his nephew's anger and ambition. To terminate a long, hysterical speech by Hotspur and divert him to a more practical pursuit, Worcester interrupts: 'Peace, cousin, say no more' (I.iii.185). And Worcester offers to 'unclasp a secret book' that will answer Hotspur's discontented questions. 'I'll read you matter deep and dangerous', Worcester promises, with a strong hint of worse scandal yet to come; and now he resorts to a *similitudo* to express the hazard of the suggested enterprise:

> As full of peril and adventurous spirit
> As to o'er-walk a current roaring loud
> On the unsteadfast footing of a spear.

Worcester speaks in terms of communicating through verbal discourse: he will 'read' Hotspur 'matter' from a 'book'. And Hotspur responds by vividly visualizing Worcester's *similitudo*. In his mind's eye he imagines the scene fraught with danger that Worcester describes: a man attempting to transverse a raging torrent with no safer footing than his spear placed unsteadily over it for a crossway. But the great odds against the survival of this daredevil merely exacerbate the rash courage of Hotspur, and he views accepting such a challenge as an act required by honour. While Hotspur excitedly imagines the scene that Worcester has described, he exclaims:

> If he fall in, good night, or sink, or swim!
> Send danger from the east unto the west,
> So honour cross it from the north to south,
> And let them grapple.

Northumberland, watching his son in agitated reverie, is moved to observe: 'Imagination of some great exploit /Drives him beyond the bounds of patience' – where 'patience', of course, from *patior*, means 'submissiveness'.

Worcester has achieved his purpose of arousing his nephew, and the scene proceeds immediately to Hotspur's most outrageous speech:

> By heaven, methinks it were an easy leap
> To pluck bright honour from the pale-fac'd moon,
> Or dive into the bottom of the deep,
> Where fathom-line could never touch the ground,
> And pluck up drowned honour by the locks,
> So he that doth redeem her thence might wear
> Without corrival all her dignities.

To this bombastic outburst, the canny Worcester wryly replies: 'He apprehends a world of figures here, /But not the form of what he should attend.' Worcester complains that Hotspur, like Richard II, has filled his head with a world of figures, but doesn't discern the appropriate course of action. Only by threatening to leave the scene and only after Northumberland's intervention does Worcester bring Hotspur back from his imagined world of dangerous adventure and focus the conspirators upon the practical business of fomenting rebellion.

Repeatedly, Shakespeare points to the importance of the imagination in human affairs, and several times he demonstrates the enargeiac power of language to activate it. This is, indeed, the basis for his art, as Puck invites us to contemplate when at the end of *A Midsummer Night's Dream* he steps forward to conclude the antique fables and fairy toys which comprise that play:

> If we shadows have offended,
> Think but this, and all is mended,
> That you have but slumber'd here
> While these visions did appear.   (V.i.409–12)

In other plays, Shakespeare makes an even bolder and balder pitch for our acquiescence in his patently contrived world of figures. *Henry V* begins with an extraneous speaker who brazenly questions the propriety of theatre:

> can this cockpit hold
> The vasty fields of France? or may we cram
> Within this wooden O the very casques
> That did affright the air at Agincourt?   (Prol. 11–14)

Yet he begs for our complicity in the deception of answering yes: 'let us, ciphers to this great accompt, /On your imaginary forces work.' This brash mediator between us and the literary text operates in much the same fashion throughout the play, and in the prologue before the final act he makes great demands upon our mind's eye to follow the frenetic movements of the triumphant King: 'So swift a pace hath thought that even now /You may imagine him upon Blackheath' (15–16). Similarly, in *Pericles* Gower serves as a chorus to hold together the far-flung adventures of that romance. Before the storm that opens Act III, for example, Gower sets the scene:

> In your imagination hold
> This stage the ship, upon whose deck
> The sea-tost Pericles appears to speak.   (58–60)

This exchange between the theatre and our lives that the imagination allows, this interplay between illusion and reality, is perhaps Shakespeare's greatest achievement. He more than any other artist has convinced us that all the world's a stage, and vice versa.

NOTES

1   For example, by Cristoforo Landino, *Scritti critici e teorici*, ed. Roberto Cardini, 2 vols (Rome: Bulzoni, 1974), vol. 1, 143–5.

2   For a concise discussion of faculty psychology by an authority congenial to the Elizabethans, see Pierre de la Primaudaye, *The second part of the French academie*, trans. Thomas Bowes (London, 1594), pp. 144–7.

3   *Miscellaneous Prose of Sir Philip Sidney*, ed. Katherine Duncan-Jones and Jan van Dorsten (Oxford: Oxford University Press, 1973), p. 78.

4   For development and documentation of the argument condensed in this paragraph, see my '"Metaphor" and Sidney's *Defense of Poesy*', *John Donne Journal*, 1 (1982), 135–46.

5   *Defence*, pp. 79–80. In the phrase 'to figure forth' it is likely that Sidney implies a pun: to use human figures as in a narrative, but also perhaps to use rhetorical figures of speech.

6   See Robert J. Bauer, 'A phenomenon of epistemology in the Renaissance', *Journal of the History of Ideas*, 31 (1970), 281–8.

14

"For now we sit to chat as well as eat": conviviality and conflict in Shakespeare's meals

JOHN W. MAHON

> Feasts are regularly important throughout Shakespeare, but are so obvious that one accepts them without thought. It is the mark of greatest literature to play on such fundamentals of human existence.... Eating and drinking are continually given dramatic emphasis, with various ethical implications.... (G. Wilson Knight)[1]

Shakespeare uses the most ordinary and common human rituals, those of eating and drinking, as focal points for themes of conviviality and conflict, but he stages these rituals rarely. If, indeed, one accepts feasts as 'obvious', it may be a shock to discover how few are actually mounted. Since meals are such powerful expressions of human community, Shakespeare presents them only when he wishes to emphasize in a special way the 'ethical implications' of community, successful or not.

Eating and drinking are often discussed, and imagery associated with meals appears everywhere in the plays; Cleopatra, for example, characterizes herself as 'a morsel for a monarch' in those 'salad days, /When I was green in judgement' (I.v.31, 73-4). But while it is true that Romeo and Juliet meet during the dance after Capulet's feast and that Antipholus of Syracuse in *The Comedy of Errors* enjoys offstage a dinner prepared for his twin, Shakespeare rarely stages full-fledged meals. The tavern scenes in the *Henry IV* plays and the bacchanal in *Antony and Cleopatra* cannot be considered meals, nor can the moment in the penultimate scene of *Richard II*, when the deposed Richard refuses to take the meat he is offered because his jailer will not 'taste of it first' (V.v.99).

There are, in fact, only nine Shakespearean scenes in which tables are set and people actually sit down, or attempt to sit down, to a meal, and not all of these are elaborate feasts by any means.[2] These scenes are found in *Titus Andronicus, The Taming of the Shrew, As You Like It, Macbeth, Timon of Athens,* and *The Tempest.*

Practical difficulties obviously militate against mounting such scenes in any theatre, Elizabethan or contemporary. There is the problem of providing fresh supplies of food for stage consumption, and a spectacle like the royal feast in *Macbeth* also demands a number of actors to serve food and drink as well as to occupy the many places at table. The opening lines of Act I, scene v, in *Romeo and Juliet* suggest the difficulty of clearing the stage and setting it again: the Servingmen must 'Be brisk awhile' as they clear the 'great chamber' (I.v.15,13) after Capulet's feast in order to prepare the room for dancing.

But the rarity of meals in the plays cannot be attributed solely to practical difficulties. Elizabethans, even more than moderns, attached symbolic significance to meals; Shakespeare, therefore, presents this powerful symbol most sparingly, only when it can have maximum impact as a focus for theme and character. After a review of the context in which Shakespeare worked, an examination of the meal scenes, especially the important examples in *As You Like It* and *Macbeth,* will demonstrate their function as visual metaphors for conviviality and conflict.

Many details about meals in sixteenth-century England can be found in accounts like William Harrison's *Description of England* (1577, 1587). We know that bread was the staple of every diet – Harrison discusses the various kinds of bread at length. Certain foods were associated with certain feasts and celebrations: pancakes for Shrove Tuesday, hot cross buns for Lent, goose for Michaelmas.[3] Dinner, the main meal, was eaten in the middle of the day, as the wonderful confusion in *The Comedy of Errors* demonstrates.

The rituals surrounding mealtime are also known in detail. Meals ranged from state banquets to quotidian repasts. At the more formal end of the spectrum,

> The guests, often retaining their hats on their heads, sat long hours on their joint-stools while [being served]. Talk there was in plenty, but not clamour; more than one observer noted the 'gravity' and sober demeanour during meals.[4]

Conviviality and conflict in Shakespeare's meals

Guests often 'retained their hats' while eating, but since inferiors, like Launcelot Gobbo, usually uncovered in the presence of superiors, like Lorenzo, Gobbo puns on the multiple meanings of *cover*:

> *Lor.* ... Bid them prepare dinner!
> *Laun.* That is done too sir, only "cover" is the word.
> *Lor.* Will you cover then sir?
> *Laun.* Not so sir neither, I know my duty.
> *Lor.* ... I pray thee understand a plain man in his plain meaning: go to thy fellows, bid them cover the table, serve in the meat, and we will come in to dinner.
> *Laun.* For the table sir, it shall be serv'd in, – for the meat sir, it shall be cover'd.... (III.v.45–56)

Moments later, as Lorenzo urges Jessica to accompany him to dinner, she replies, 'Nay, let me praise you while I have a stomach.' But Lorenzo suggests that such praise can

> serve for table talk,
> Then, howsome'er thou speak'st, 'mong other things
> I shall digest it. (III.v.81–4)

One of the best sixteenth-century sources for a knowledge of meals is Claudius Hollyband's primer for Englishmen learning French, *The Elizabethan Home Discovered in Two Dialogues*. Here formality is greatly relaxed, as the editor suggests: 'When Hollyband's good citizen entertains his guests to dinner it is no mere formal banquet ... but a homely affair.'[5]

It was customary for the children in the family to say Grace both before and after the meal. But not always – in *Love's Labour's Lost*, Holofernes tells Nathaniel,

> I do dine to-day at the father's of a certain pupil of mine; where, if (before repast) it shall please you to gratify the table with grace, I will ... undertake your *ben venuto*. ...
> (IV.ii.147–51)

In the Hollyband dialogue called 'The Citizen at Home', the wife suggests that one child 'reade a chapter or two of the New Testament' while he waits for his meal to be served. The father tells his son to continue reading in 'the seconde of S. John'. After the reading, father comments: 'There is a fayre chapter truly: god geve us grace to doo the contence thereof....'[6] There is a succession of courses, boiled meat followed by roasted; there is much talk of wines, and at one point the father toasts all of his guests. Fruits are served for dessert.

Clearly, Elizabethans, like human beings before and since, approached their meals with a variety of rituals; Shakespeare's characters demonstrate their easy familiarity with these gestures, especially in their references to Grace, a ritual that introduces an explicitly religious dimension into meals. In *Titus Andronicus*, the Clown anachronistically puns on this ritual:

Tit. Tell me, can you deliver an oration to the emperor with a grace?
Clo. Nay, truly, sir, I could never say grace in all my life.
(IV.iii.96–9)

In *Measure for Measure*, the matter-of-fact reference to Grace before meals leads Lucio to consider grace as a theological concept:

1 Gent. ... There's not a soldier of us all that, in the thanksgiving before meat, do relish the petition well that prays for peace.
2 Gent. I never heard any soldier dislike it.
Lucio I believe thee; for I think thou never wast where grace was said. . . . Grace is grace, despite of all controversy; as for example, thou thyself art a wicked villain, despite of all grace. (I.ii.14–26)

In explaining the first gentleman's remark, J.W. Lever quotes a typical formula for Grace: 'God save our Queen and Realm, and send us peace in Christ' (Arden edn, pp. 9–10). In *Coriolanus*, the familiar ritual, again in an anachronistic context, contributes to an elaborate metaphor describing the popularity of Coriolanus among the Volscians:

> Your soldiers use him as the grace 'fore meat,
> Their talk at table and their thanks at end. (IV.vii.3–4)

A modern audience, watching the enactment of meals on stage, is aware of all that meals imply about fellowship, sharing, hospitality, common ritual. The Elizabethan theatregoer would have felt these same things, but he would also have thought of the many scriptural allusions to meals and of the symbolism of the Holy Communion in which the Lord's Supper with his disciples is commemorated. Both Old and New Testaments make abundant use of the imagery of meals; in Psalm 23, for example, 'thou doest prepare a table before me in the sight of mine adversaries' (v. 5), or Luke: 'Then shall come manie from the East, and from the West, and from the North, and from the South, and shall sit at table in the kingdome of God' (13:29). These passages from the Geneva translation of 1560 emphasize the heavenly aspect of meals; the scene of the Last Supper in the Gospels is, for Christians, the culmination of such references.

Reformation theology suggests that Elizabethans would readily associate meals with liturgy, with 'ritual for public worship'. The Protestant Reformers rejected the Roman Mass and its doctrines of transubstantiation and sacrifice as superstitions unsupported by Scripture. They pointed to the Gospel narratives to support their claim that the Last Supper was a meal, not a sacrifice at an altar. Further, they argued that eucharistic liturgies were memorial reconstructions of the Passover meal Jesus shared with his disciples. Since Holy Communion was a meal, it was celebrated at a table; the celebrant faced the congregation; he used the vernacular. Holy Communion, the Reformers argued, was not the private act of the celebrant; they objected to Masses in which only the priest communicated; if there was no congregation, there should be no celebration.

The rubrics and formulas of the Book of Common Prayer, and the exhortations of the Homilies, reinforce this Reformation understanding of Communion. One rubric specifies that 'there shalbe no celebracion of the lordes Supper, except there be a good nombre to communicate with the Priest according to his discretion'.[7] This rubric is part of the 1552 version of the Prayer Book, the basis of the Elizabethan Prayer Book of 1559. The order for Holy Communion stresses the need for worthiness in communicants; in the words of one rubric, the public sinner should not 'presume to the Lordes Table, untyll he have openly declared himself to have truely repented, and amended his former naughtye lyfe' (377). The service begins with a review of the Ten Commandments; various exhortations are provided for the curate if he 'shal see the people negligent to come to the holy Communion' (382); and a general confession precedes the Preface: the celebrant, 'in the name of al those that are mynded to receive the holy

Communion', acknowledges 'oure manyfolde synnes and wyckednes' and begs for mercy (386).

The 1552 Prayer Book consistently refers to the *altar* of the 1549 Book as a *table*, and a significant change is made in the words of administration. The 1549 Book merely translates the Latin of the Roman formula: 'The body of our Lorde Jesus Christe which was geven for thee, preserve thy bodye and soule unto everlasting lyfe' (225). This suggestion of the eucharistic Real Presence is removed in 1552; the words now recited are: 'Take and eate this, in remembraunce that Christ dyed for thee, and feede on him in thy heart by faythe, with thankesgiving' (389). The Prayer Book of 1559, seeking the *via media*, runs the two formulas together. Despite this compromise between Roman and Calvinist theology, it is clear that in the Anglican Communion service reception of Communion is the heart of the rite – the 'meal' is paramount (the Roman Mass, in contrast, placed the consecration of the bread and wine at the centre). The Homily 'Of the worthy Receiving of the Sacrament of the Body and Blood of Christ' reinforces this emphasis of the Prayer Book.

Although Shakespeare's plays reflect his awareness of Reformation controversies (for example, Lucio's comment, quoted earlier, that 'Grace is grace, despite of all controversy'; or the comments of the Porter in *Macbeth* about equivocation), he does not deal directly with the eucharistic controversy. In appropriate contexts, Shakespeare shows familiarity with Roman practice; thus in *Richard II*, York describes the conspiracy against Bolingbroke:

> A dozen of them here have ta'en the sacrament,
> And interchangeably set down their hands
> To kill the king at Oxford.   (V.ii.97–9)

The Ghost in *Hamlet* judges it 'O horrible! O horrible! Most horrible' that he has died 'Unhousel'd, disappointed, unanel'd' (I.v.79,77). Since every Englishman was required by law to worship every Sunday, Shakespeare was also familiar with the Prayer Book and the Homilies, and his plays reflect this knowledge. The marriage service and the homily 'Of the State of Matrimony', for example, are echoed in the plays, as in Katherina's speech on the appropriate behaviour for a wife. As a member of a transitional generation, Shakespeare knew both the old faith and the new; he uses doctrines from both to suit his dramatic purposes.

Religious controversy and religious practices were as much a part of everyday life as meals were, and audiences would see biblical and liturgical dimensions in enactments of meals on stage. Meals affirm human community; when they are abortive, they fail because community has failed. Indeed, Shakespeare uses meals more often than not to dramatize the *absence* of good fellowship and a sense of community. He seems deliberately to manipulate audience expectations of happy meals in order to emphasize the disorder and hostility in a given situation. This contrast between expectation and reality is particularly heightened when Shakespeare echoes religious ritual, in language or in gesture. Of the nine meals, only two succeed completely: the second meal in *The Taming of the Shrew* and the meal in *As You Like It*. Most of the meals are interrupted. A pattern, then, emerges, in which Shakespeare uses meals to dramatize conflict rather than conviviality.[8]

Only in *The Taming of the Shrew* does he provide examples of both conflict and conviviality. There are three meals in the play, but the wedding feast for Katherina and Petruchio is not staged because the groom whisks his bride away before she can dine. In IV.i, a 'supper' is served, but the wily Petruchio throws the meal at the servants as part of his scheme to subdue Katherina ("Tis burnt, and so is all the meat', IV.i.148). In order, then, to underscore the distance between Katherina and Petruchio, Shakespeare arranges for that most ordinary of human activities, a meal, to be frustrated.

Alone among the comedies, *The Taming of the Shrew* concludes with a meal on stage; the meal (actually a 'banquet', for Elizabethans the dessert course of a larger feast, although modern productions usually stage a complete feast) follows directly upon a brief conversation between Katherina and Petruchio in which, as the Arden editor suggests, 'for the first time, there seems to be affection between the two, and the kiss seems a genuine expression of love' (286). Reconciled to each other, they can join the community in a meal, and are invited to do so by their host:

> Brother Petruchio, Sister Katherina, ...
> Feast with the best, and welcome to my house.
> My banquet is to close our stomachs up
> After our great good cheer. Pray you, sit down,
> For now we sit to chat as well as eat.   (V.ii.5–11)

It is during this meal that Petruchio tests Katherina for the last time, and her famous statement of the 'duty' wives 'owe their lords and husbands' (V.ii.132) proves that she has taken to heart his instruction.

At both ends of his career, Shakespeare introduces meals into tragedy, predictably in order to emphasize conflict and the failure of community. In the case of *Titus Andronicus*, the 'Banket' of III.ii presents a perverse community of revenge: Marcus strikes his dish with his knife to kill 'a black ill-favour'd fly /Like to the empress' Moor' (III.ii.66–7) in anticipation of the revenge to come. The meal of Act V focuses wonderfully all the horrors of the play and prompts a final round of slaughter, as guests and host fall before each other's knives:

> *Trumpets sounding, enter* Titus, *like a cook, placing the dishes, and* Lavinia ...
> *Tit.* . . . welcome, all: although the cheer be poor,
>   'Twill fill your stomachs; please you eat of it.
>   (V.iii.28–9)

After killing Lavinia, Titus identifies Chiron and Demetrius as her ravishers. When the Emperor orders them to appear, Titus says:

> Why, there they are, both baked in this pie;
> Whereof their mother daintily hath fed,
> Eating the flesh that she herself hath bred. (V.iii.60–2)

Thus Shakespeare provides a final horror, an act of cannibalism that defiles the parent–child relationship, as a climax to the lesser horrors in earlier scenes. Having defiled the basic human ceremony of unity and made a mockery of the laws of hospitality, Titus kills Tamora, Saturninus kills Titus, and Lucius kills Saturninus. In Prayer Book terms, none of these characters is worthy of sharing a community meal. A feast, which should promote harmony and community, becomes a bloodbath. The staged meal is an effective device for the denouement and seems to reflect an effort by Shake-

Conviviality and conflict in Shakespeare's meals 239

speare to focus the conclusion more concisely than his source does.[9]

In *Timon of Athens*, two meals are staged to support the structure of a play that breaks neatly into two halves, the first a portrait of a prodigal, the second a manifestation of a misanthrope. As H.J. Oliver notes, 'There is no reason to think that the play was ever acted in Shakespeare's lifetime' (Arden edn, xl); practical difficulties, then, were never addressed. Shakespeare's stage directions suggest the great superficial difference between the two meals. For I.ii, we read, '*Hautboys playing loud music. A great banquet serv'd in. ...*' For the second meal, in III.vi, we get merely, '*The banquet brought in.*' Yet in both instances, the Grace before meals makes quite apparent just how hollow the occasion is.

The play contains pointed scriptural allusions. During the first meal, Apemantus comments: 'What a number of men eats Timon, and he sees 'em not! It grieves me to see so many dip their meat in one man's blood' (I.ii.39–41). Later in the same speech, 'the fellow that sits next him, now parts bread with him, pledges the breath of him in a divided draught, is the readiest man to kill him' (I.ii.46–9). These remarks suggest a comparison between Judas's betrayal of Jesus and the hypocrisy of Timon's friends. As Frank Kermode comments, 'Wilson Knight was obviously justified in staging the banquet scenes so that they resembled the Last Supper of the painters.'[10]

The first feast begins in leisurely fashion, with Timon offering a toast, 'My lord, in heart; and let the health go round' (I.ii.53). The misanthropist Apemantus provides the ironic commentary; his Grace defies convention:

> Grant I may never prove so fond
> To trust man on his oath or bond. ...
> Amen. So fall to't:
> Rich men sin, and I eat root. (I.ii.64–5, 70–1)

Although this meal is surrounded with festive appearances, the audience has already recognized both the false good cheer of Timon's 'friends' and Timon's own blindness to reality: the meal focuses the theme of prodigality.

In the meal in Act III, after the worthlessness of his friends has been amply demonstrated, Timon does not pause for a toast; he invites his guests to hurry to their places in language that conveys his contempt:

> Each man to his stool, with that spur as he would to the lip of his mistress. . . . Make not a City feast of it, to let the meat cool ere we can agree upon the first place. Sit, sit.   (III.vi.64–7)

He then offers Grace: 'Make the meat be belov'd more than the man that gives it. . . . For these my present friends, as they are to me nothing, so in nothing bless them, and to nothing are they welcome.' He turns to his guests: 'Uncover, dogs, and lap' (III.vi.74–82). What the guests find is lukewarm water, thrown into their faces as Timon calls them a 'knot of mouth-friends' (III.vi.85). An Elizabethan audience would recognize a reference to Revelation 3:16: 'Therefore, because thou art luke warme, and nether cold nor hote, it will come to passe, that I shall spewe thee out of my mouth' (Geneva). This second meal introduces Timon as misanthrope, a role he develops with relish in the rest of the play.

The Tempest also presents a frustrated meal, 'Shakespeare's most elaborate experiment in stage spectacle' (Arden edn, 155). The playwright evidently considered this scene important *despite* the practical difficulties it entailed, whether staged at Blackfriars or at the Globe. Act III, scene iii, opens as the shipwrecked courtiers, exhausted, pause to rest. Antonio and Sebastian, aside, rejoice that the King abandons hope of finding Ferdinand, and they eagerly anticipate an early opportunity to carry out their plot to assassinate the King and Gonzalo.

In this context come stage directions in which, as 'solemn and strange music' plays and Prospero watches, invisible to the others,

> *Enter several strange Shapes, bringing in a banquet; and dance about it with gentle actions of salutations; and inviting the King, etc., to eat, they depart.*

The strange shapes startle the group, and King Alonso hesitates to eat this meal. Sebastian persuades them to proceed. But when the courtiers attempt to eat, Ariel appears as a Harpy, '*claps his wings upon the table; and, with a quaint device, the banquet vanishes*'. Ariel then denounces Alonso, Sebastian, and Antonio and explains that they have suffered shipwreck be-

Conviviality and conflict in Shakespeare's meals 241

cause of their treachery (III.iii.53–82). These men have destroyed community in their usurpation of Prospero's throne and in their attempt to murder him and Miranda. Clearly, these men are unworthy to partake of the meal set before them. The scene is crucial to the structure of the play since the courtiers first learn here why they are on the island. Predictably, Alonso expresses remorse for his misdeed. Antonio and Sebastian are concerned only to fight off the 'fiends'.

The phenomenon of the interrupted meal reaches its ultimate expression in *The Tempest*, where the food vanishes before it can be approached. The meal in *As You Like It* is also interrupted, but only temporarily. Like *The Tempest*, *As You Like It* presents a picture of the human capacity for love and loyalty as well as for ingratitude, and in the Forest of Arden the play develops a series of remarkable transformations that suggest man's ability to reform and begin anew. Events in the forest transform the treachery of the opening scenes into the fraternal and sexual union of the close. The harmony of the conclusion, which includes all of the characters except Jaques, is anticipated in the convivial forest meal of Act II.

The meal occurs in the last scene of the Act. Three Acts remain, but the threats to the well-being of the good characters have been virtually eliminated by the end of Act II; despite the threatening tone of III.i, earlier moments of the play suggest that the Forest of Arden provides safe refuge for Rosalind and Orlando, as it has earlier for Duke Senior.

The meal of II.vii has been developed from a description of Gerismond's (Duke Senior's) birthday party in the source of the play, Thomas Lodge's *Rosalynde* (1590):

> that day in honour of his birth [Gerismond] made a feast to all his bold yeomen, and frolicked it with store of wine and venison, sitting all at a long table under the shadow of limon trees. (Arden edn, 132)

In Lodge's story, the incident passes quickly, and it is only one of many forest meals. Shakespeare chooses to focus on one meal and to linger over it. Shakespeare also prepares for the meal carefully. In II.v, Amiens tells his fellow courtiers to 'cover the while: the Duke will drink under this tree' (28–9). At the end of the scene he leaves to 'seek the Duke; his banquet is prepared' (59). In scene vi, Shakespeare presents vivid evidence of the suffering that can result from lack of food; the desperate hunger of Orlando and Adam contrasts with the convivial meal already laid in scene v and under way in scene vii. Orlando promises to satisfy Adam's need for food: 'If this uncouth forest yield any thing savage, I will either be food for it, or bring it for food to thee' (II.vi.6–7). Even before we witness the distress of Orlando and Adam, we are reassured that they will be fed. These last three scenes of Act II reflect the action of the larger play – dangers and perils there are, but we never really doubt the final outcome.

The meal is a perfect visual metaphor for what Helen Gardner calls 'the Christian ideal of loving-kindness, gentleness, pity, and humility' that is invoked often in the play. The characters must still pass through the comic crucible of the encounters in Arden, where they will learn that folly can be wisdom and vice-versa. But the audience has already witnessed a tableau that prepares it for the closing, especially for Hymen's first words, which 'with their New Testament echo are more than conventional',[11]

> Then is there mirth in heaven,
> When earthly things made even
>   Atone together. (V.iv.107–9)

Duke Senior, in the opening speech of Act II, prefers the hardships imposed by nature to those which people impose on each other. In their desire to escape such treachery, both Rosalind and Orlando risk the perils of the forest. The meal verifies Duke Senior's point: it is easier to provide Orlando and Adam with food than to secure Orlando's birthright from a treacherous brother. The song that Amiens sings during the meal underlines the message:

> Blow, blow, thou winter wind,
> Thou are not so unkind
>   As man's ingratitude.
> Thy tooth is not so keen,
> Because thou are not seen,
>   Although thy breath be rude.
> Heigh-ho, sing heigh-ho, unto the green holly
> Most friendship is feigning, most loving mere folly.
>   (II.vii.174–81)

Conviviality and conflict in Shakespeare's meals

Man's ingratitude is not completely overcome until the end of the play, but the circumstances surrounding the meal foreshadow the conclusion, in which friendship is not feigning and love is not folly. While Amiens sings bitterly and Jaques expounds cynically, the action in the scene is an icon of communion and brotherhood. Driven to violence, Orlando demands food with drawn sword, but he finds force unnecessary. Instead he discovers men willing to share their meal, willing also to wait for Adam before they begin to eat. No sooner has Jaques pictured 'second childishness' (II.vii.165) in a recitation that ignores human warmth and kindness than Orlando enters with Adam on his back and the Duke says: 'Welcome. Set down your venerable burden, /And let him feed' (II.vii.167–8). Helen Gardner observes: 'What Jaques has left out of his picture of man's strange eventful pilgrimage is love and companionship, sweet society, the banquet under the boughs to which Duke Senior welcomes Orlando and Adam.'[12]

This meal presents a picture of unity at table (always excepting Jaques, who nevertheless does eat) that adumbrates the unity in marriage of the conclusion. In the Anglican Communion service, confession of sins precedes reception of Communion; in *As You Like It*, a variety of confusions and evils must be overcome before the festivities of the conclusion. But the pattern is already present in II.vii; when Duke Senior responds kindly to Orlando's menacing demand for food, Orlando acknowledges his error and is then admitted to the meal:

> Speak you so gently? Pardon me, I pray you.
> I thought that all things had been savage here. . . .
>   (II.vii.106–7)

If words like *icon* and *tableau* describe the meal in *As You Like It*, they are even more relevant to a discussion of the feast in *Macbeth*. In the opening paragraph of his study of *Scenic Form in Shakespeare*, Emrys Jones writes:

> It can be an illuminating experience to see Shakespeare acted in a completely unfamiliar language. A few years ago appeared a Japanese film version of *Macbeth*. The adaptation was very free. . . . [But] the banquet scene . . . came across as a dramatic invention of the highest power; even without Shakespeare's words, the scene made a strong effect.

The same can be said of the banquet scene as it occurs, sung in Italian, in Verdi's opera of *Macbeth*: although translated to a different artistic medium, it preserves a good deal of its force. When the scene is acted in English or read in its full poetic context in the play as Shakespeare wrote it, so much significance of a verbal and poetic nature claims attention that it is possible, perhaps even natural, to overlook or not to notice its basic structural shaping: that formal idea which gives the scene its dramatic unity and which was made to stand out in the film and opera. What Shakespeare has invented is something – a structure, an *occasion* – which may be said to be (however dangerous the phrase) independent of the words which are usually thought to give the scene its realization.

In his analysis of the play, Jones writes that 'the scene of the feast ... gathers together all the themes of this act [Act III] and magnificently transcends expectation. For all its comparative brevity it is undoubtedly one of Shakespeare's greatest scenic inventions.'[13] Unlike the unique example of *As You Like It*, where the interrupted meal ultimately continues, the royal feast in *Macbeth* follows the Shakespearian pattern: the interrupted meal symbolizes the radical disruption in the community that partakes of it.

There are other meals in the play; but one takes place offstage and the other is not human. The stage direction for I.vii is: '*Hautboys and torches. Enter, and pass over the stage, a Sewer, and divers Servants with dishes and service. Then enter* Macbeth.' While Duncan and the other guests feast, Macbeth absents himself from the hall in order to meditate upon his future course. His absence from the meal is a visual reinforcement of his murderous thoughts; his bloody plans separate him from a joyous human ritual.

Guilty of two murders and planning still more, Macbeth visits the witches in IV.i, a scene in which they prepare a hellish brew in what the stage-direction calls 'a boiling cauldron'. But this cauldron provides riddling apparitions and false encouragement instead of nourishment and good company. Macbeth's 'feast' at the cauldron, and his readiness to accept its ambivalent 'messages', indicate just how far he has fallen.

But the centrepiece of the play, literally, is Act III, scene iv, the feast haunted by Banquo's ghost. As in *As You Like It*, Shakespeare develops a critical scene from the merest sugges-

Conviviality and conflict in Shakespeare's meals   245

tion in the source: 'He [Macbeth] willed therefore the same Banquho with his sonne named Fleance, to come to a supper that he had prepared for them' (Arden edn, 180). In Holinshed, it is *after* the supper, as Banquo and Fleance ride home, that Macbeth's assassins strike. Again as in *As You Like It*, Shakespeare carefully prepares for this feast; each of the earlier scenes in Act III anticipates it. In III.i, for example, both Macbeth and Lady Macbeth urge Banquo to attend; he is the 'chief guest' for a 'solemn supper': 'Fail not our feast' (11,14,27). Hearing the word *guest*, the audience might remember, from Duncan's experience, how dangerous it is to be Macbeth's guest.

The scene of the feast is highly ritualistic, with its formal welcomes and its attempts at toasts. We must envision tables set, probably end-to-end across the stage with enough places to accommodate the whole court, which would arrange itself in order of rank. Macbeth and his Queen process to their thrones, placed above and behind the tables. After inviting everyone to sit down, Macbeth emphasizes his desire to be one with his court:

> Ourself will mingle with society,
> And play the humble host.   (III.iv.3–4)

His attempt to 'mingle with society' will fail.

Like Timon, Macbeth suggests beginning with a toast, but before the group can 'drink a measure /The table round' (III.iv.11–12), the first murderer appears at the door, his face smeared with Banquo's blood. The order and ritual of the occasion is undercut; as the Queen reminds him, 'the sauce to meat is ceremony; /Meeting were bare without it' (III.iv.35–6). The King offers a hopeful toast: 'Now, good digestion wait on appetite, /And health on both!' (III.iv.37–8).

But the ritual of this state occasion, the *only* formal state occasion of Macbeth's reign that we witness in the play, breaks down several times over. First, Macbeth absents himself to confer with the murderer (at the earlier feast with Duncan, Macbeth had also absented himself; then, as now, Lady Macbeth questions his absence). Second, Banquo's ghost appears to Macbeth as Macbeth tries to sit down to the feast (the ghost sits, as the stage direction specifies, 'in Macbeth's place', significantly, given Banquo's prophesied role as progenitor of kings), and Macbeth loses control despite his

Queen's efforts to cover for him and to shame him into normality. Third, Banquo's ghost reappears when Macbeth tries to renew his toast:

> Come, love and health to all;
> Then I'll sit down. – Give me some wine: fill full: –
> I drink to th' general joy o' th' whole table,
> And to our dear friend Banquo, whom we miss;
> Would he were here!
>   *Re-enter Ghost.*
>   To all, and him, we thirst,
> And all to all.
> Lords.   Our duties, and the pledge.
> Macb.   Avaunt! and quit my sight! let the earth hide thee!
>   (III.iv.86–92)

As Macbeth again addresses Banquo's ghost, his guests stare in wonder. When the ghost vanishes, Macbeth tries to regain his composure:

> Why, so; – being gone,
> I am a man again. – Pray you, sit still.
> Lady M. You have displac'd the mirth, broke the good meeting
>   With most admired disorder.   (III.iv.106–9)

When Lady Macbeth realizes that Macbeth remains haunted by his experience, she dismisses the guests with significant words, 'Stand not upon the order of your going' (118). The two are left alone in the empty hall, the feast destroyed, like sleep, by their sins. In murdering Duncan, his guest, Macbeth violates hospitality, and now his attempt to offer hospitality fails following the murder of another guest.

The language of earlier scenes in the play freely uses religious imagery to portray Macbeth's predicament. He speaks of the murder of Duncan as a 'poison'd chalice' (I.vii.11) even while Duncan feasts as his guest. Planning Banquo's murder, Macbeth says that the murder of Duncan has 'Put rancors in the vessel of my peace' (III.i.66). When he recounts the murder of Duncan to his wife, Macbeth says he could not pronounce 'Amen' because the word 'Stuck in my throat' (II.ii.32).

When we examine the factors that ruin the feast, we see how liturgy could have influenced the audience's reaction.

Conviviality and conflict in Shakespeare's meals 247

The physical set-up itself could remind viewers of the Last Supper. But all is topsy-turvy here. While Jesus brings life, Macbeth brings death. While Judas leaves the table and the room to betray his master and friend, Macbeth merely moves to the door of the room to confirm the murder of Banquo. Or, in an alternative staging of the scene just as powerfully metaphorical, the murderer, disguised as a servant but with bloodied face, approaches the table with Macbeth's cup of wine. Macbeth cannot sit at the table and share the meal because he is unworthy of human company. Macbeth's community is that of the 'weird sisters'.

There are other passages in the play which feed into the central feast. As Mark Rose expresses it,

> Feasting is this play's metaphor for social harmony, and in the centre, the banquet scene, the image of life's feast is concretely realized. In murdering Banquo – possibly a pun is intended in his name – Macbeth has excluded himself from the banquet of life. He is barred from the table by the image of his own tyranny, the gory figure of the man he has slain.[14]

The feast Macbeth cannot share becomes a meal in which the blood of murder, clearly visible on the ghost's face, supplants the wine of celebration and communion. At the interrupted feast, there is no opportunity to offer Grace before meals. Lady Macbeth sends their guests home, but it is she and her usurper husband who are excommunicated.

The communion, then, the at-one-ment, that Shakespeare celebrates in *As You Like It* becomes excommunication and alienation in *Macbeth*. The meal in *As You Like It* expresses harmony and conviviality; the feast in *Macbeth* dramatizes anarchy and conflict.

A study of these meal scenes suggests that eating, the most commonplace of human activities, can become an important focus of theme and characterization for a play. Of the nine meals Shakespeare presents on stage, only two successfully express community. All the other meals focus attention on elements of disunity and on characters who fail, in one way or another, to find communion, atonement, with their fellows; as Shylock says to Bassanio, 'I will not eat with you, drink with you, nor pray with you' (I.iii.32–3). More often than not,

"Fanned and Winnowed Opinions"

Shakespeare's meals are interrupted, in some cases even before they can begin; only in *As You Like It* is the interruption absorbed by an organic human community. In this context, the religious significance of meals would occur naturally to an Elizabethan audience, and awareness of this dimension reinforces the negative atmosphere, most notably in *Macbeth* and in *Timon of Athens*, where meals echo the Anglican Communion service.

To conclude, a pattern emerges in which Shakespeare stages meals rarely and uses them to defeat the expectations of the audience, to dramatize disunity by presenting it in a context associated with unity. In every instance, the meals play an important structural role.

NOTES

1   *The Crown of Life* (London: Methuen, 1948), pp. 215–16.
2   It could be argued that a scene like that in Shallow's orchard in *2 Henry IV* (V.iii) qualifies as a part of a meal, since apples are served, but there is much more emphasis on drinking than on eating. However this scene is categorized, it does not contradict the pattern I identify.
3   In *The Elizabethan Renaissance: The Life of the Society* (New York: Scribner's, 1971), A.L. Rowse discusses many of these customs, pp. 233–9.
4   Allardyce Nicoll, *The Elizabethans* (Cambridge: Cambridge University Press, 1957), p. 100.
5   Ed. M. St Clare Bryne (London: Cobden–Sanderson, 1930), p. xi.
6   ibid., pp. 36–7.
7   *The First and Second Prayer Books of Edward VI* (London: Dent, 1910), p. 392. Subsequent references to this volume will be made in the text.
8   The pattern persists in three scenes I will not consider because many editors, including the Arden ones, regard them as non-Shakespearian. In *Pericles*, the hero meets his future wife Thaisa at a festive banquet (II.iii). In *King Henry VIII*, Cardinal Wolsey hosts a feast at York Place (I.iv); Anne Bullen makes her first appearance in this scene, and here too she and Henry meet for the first time – a festive meal, but an ominous one. In *The Two Noble Kinsmen*, Arcite brings meat and wine to Palamon, but their meal degenerates into the old quarrel over Emily (III.iii). Of these three meals, then, only that in *Pericles* is truly convivial.
9   See the Arden editor's summary of the source-story, pp. xxviii–xxix.
10   In his Introduction to the play in *The Riverside Shakespeare*, ed. G. Blakemore Evans (Boston: Houghton Mifflin, 1974), p. 1443.
11   '*As You Like It*', reprinted in *Shakespeare: The Comedies*, ed. Kenneth Muir (Englewood Cliffs, NJ: Prentice-Hall, 1965), pp. 70–1.
12   ibid., p. 67.
13   (Oxford: Clarendon, 1971), pp. 3, 215.
14   *Shakespearean Design* (Cambridge, Mass.: Harvard University Press, 1972), p. 160. In 'The structural function of the banquet scene in *Macbeth*', *Shakespeare Quarterly*, 14 (1963), 370–8, J.P. Dyson provides an exhaustive analysis of the scene, and he emphasizes his perception that it represents the turning point in the action and the structure of the play.

15

"Wives may be merry and yet honest too": women and wit in *The Merry Wives of Windsor* and some other plays

SANDRA CLARK

I should like to examine the treatment in a few plays, mainly by Shakespeare, of a kind of alternative wit in women. Wit in drama, at least of the late sixteenth and seventeenth centuries, tends to be thought of in terms of qualities exhibited in dialogue, like quickness of speech, eloquence, skill in the arts of rhetoric; such qualities, though found in women, are more commonly the prerogative of men, especially if combined with powers of argument and strength of intellect. But there is another sort of wit, which expresses itself characteristically in cleverness of action rather than of speech; it incorporates resourcefulness, craftiness, cunning, and guile, and is demonstrated in an ability to turn situations to one's own advantage. This other wit, though found in men, has its distinctively female forms. The women who possess it often exercise it in collaboration with other women, and as a way of getting back at a world dominated by men. It is associated particularly with two traditional female stereotypes, the wanton wife and the shrew. My discussion of this kind of wit will move towards a focus on *The Merry Wives of Windsor* by way of a preliminary consideration of the literary tradition of women's wit; a brief study of Shakespeare's verbally witty heroines such as Beatrice or Rosalind will show how readily their skills in speech may become assimilated to the notions of the shrew or the wanton. The more bourgeois female protagonists of the turn-of-the-century city comedies, while often vindicating themselves from charges of wantonness, work to redeem the image of the shrew in women's favour. In conclusion, I hope to clarify some of the implications of this alternative wit, normally a comic subject, by comparing *The Merry Wives of Windsor* with *Othello*.

Leo Salingar, in examining some possible sources for *The Merry Wives of Windsor*, traces a 'joint narrative and stage tradition' of tales of women outwitting their husbands or lovers going back to Boccaccio.[1] The *Decameron* contains many such stories as that of Monna Tessa, 'not a little knowing and keen-witted' (II, 97), who deceives her superstitious husband Giovanni by pretending that the knocking of her lover at the door is the sound of an evil spirit which must be exorcised;[2] of Peronella, who not only hides her lover in a tub when her husband returns unexpectedly, but also contrives that her husband shall clean out the tub for the lover, and deliver it to his house; and of Beatrice, who sends her husband out on a fool's errand, disguised as herself, while she lies with her lover. Scores of similar stories illustrating this sort of quick and unscrupulous thinking by women can be found in collections such as Ser Giovanni Fiorentino's *Il Pecorone* or in Cinthio's *Hecatommithi* or Bandello's *Novelle*, which were used time and again as source material by Shakespeare and his contemporaries. In this literary tradition all of the characters are stereotypes, the men no less than the women; the roles of wanton wife, amorous widow, and shrew are matched by those of foolish cuckold, gallant, and henpecked husband. Adultery is taken for granted; the husband is always the dupe, and if, as sometimes happens, he is discovered by his wife in an adulterous liaison, she invariably gets her own back. In the *Decameron* the women's skill in trickery is praised and admired; such comments as 'all ... commended the lady, for that she had done well and treated her caitiff husband as he had deserved' (II, 112) or 'rare indeed was deemed by common consent the subtlety shown by Madonna Beatrice in the beguilement of her husband' (II, 127) are frequent.

Although in the English tradition the attitude expressed towards a woman's successful deception of her husband is less wholeheartedly admiring than in Boccaccio, there is still a good-humoured acceptance of women's astuteness and invention in trickery. 'The wiser, the waywarder' (*As You Like It*, IV.i.152–3). But at the same time, there is a strong satiric tradition of misogyny, in which the masculine perspective is dominant, the feminine totally suppressed, and any manifestation of wit or spirit in a woman likely to be condemned as forwardness, indecorous self-assertion. From this viewpoint, the connection between wit and lasciviousness, celebrated by Boccaccio, is to be reviled: woman's cunning which brings about her husband's downfall derives from Eve, the mother of lies. The Wife of Bath is made to assert that women possess peculiar powers of verbal deception, which form an intrinsic aspect of the female nature:

> For half so boldely kan ther no man
> Swere and lye as a womman kan.
> ...
> For al swich witte is yeven us in our byrthe, –
> Deceite, wepyng, spynnyng, God hath yive
> To wommen kyndely whil they may lyve.
> (Prologue to the Wife of Bath's Tale, 227–8, 400–2)

The threat to men posed by women's wit is realized in the figure of the shrew or scold, in whom a quick mind and ready tongue are indicators of a lascivious disposition. Lisa Jardine shows how Renaissance writers conflate the two metonymic uses of the female tongue, as women's weapon against men and as sexual instrument, to form a convenient link between scolding and uncontrolled sexuality.³ Conversely, the meek, obedient, and silent woman is elevated into an ideal. 'To be slow in words is a woman's only virtue', says Launce in *Two Gentlemen of Verona*. The host of traditional proverbs and sayings on the theme of woman's restless tongue substantiates the point.

Many of the women in Shakespeare's comedies are witty in the conventional sense of possessing a gift for apt and sparkling utterance which goes beyond mere verbal dexterity. This skill in the arts of speech, though it appears to be more conspicuous in his women than in his men, is not essentially a gender-related quality, as is evident in plays where witty women are matched with witty men, such as *Love's Labour's Lost*, or *Much Ado About Nothing*. Nonetheless, the women's use of this wit is related to alternative wit in two ways: in an element of sexual challenge and competitiveness, and in its associations with the conception of shrewishness. These comic heroines, for instance the Princess of France and Rosaline, Portia, Beatrice, and Rosalind, are all educated women of good birth, such as might appropriately be allowed the power to express themselves well and the confidence to do so, but their wit is always finally limited or curtailed in its operation. They may, like Portia and Rosalind, be at their wittiest in male disguise, or they may, like Beatrice, and Katharine from *The Taming of the Shrew*, have a licence to express themselves as wittily as men while they are still unmarried, but must give up their right with their change of status. 'Peace! I will stop your mouth', says Benedick to Beatrice, and silences her for the rest of the play. An older, married woman, such as Paulina in *The Winter's Tale*, can speak out boldly, but she may be reviled for doing so.

The court ladies of *Love's Labour's Lost* are among the wittiest characters in a play to which an exploration of wit and its meanings is central, and there is perhaps a difference from other plays in Shakespeare's treatment of wit in men and women here in that the constraints placed on wit apply to both sexes, and are in fact levelled by the women against the men, rather than the other way round. The difference between the men and the women is that the latter know that wit is play and must sometimes give place to what is serious. Berowne tries to follow their lead by discarding 'Taffeta phrases, silken terms precise' in favour of 'russet yeas and honest kersey noes' when it comes to something important like wooing, but old habits die hard. 'Sans "sans", I pray you', Rosaline requests gravely, her own wit employed to mock her lover's inept attempt at earnestness. When the King tries to console the Princess for her father's death, he cannot find the 'honest, plain words' that 'pierce the heart of grief', and the Princess's brief reply to his self-consciously eloquent speech demonstrates the gulf that lies between the women's notion of linguistic fitness and the men's. That the women are capable both of using their wit, and, where proper, restraining it, rather than, as the men do, submitting themselves wholly to its domination, shows that it is they who possess the greater understanding of its nature.

In *As You Like It*, the disguised Rosalind dominates Orlando because she has a wider range of wit at her command, but also because he is partially *hors de combat*, as a romantic lover to whom the sharp edge of wit is inappropriate. Rosalind is never allowed to exceed the limits of what is womanly, and although in her persona as Ganymede she can present a

Women and wit in *The Merry Wives of Windsor* 253

perspective on woman as the traditional shrew and wanton wife, she is distanced from this image by her disguise. Her scenes alone with Celia give the opportunity for wit-displays rather like those of the ladies in *Love's Labour's Lost*, but they are noticeably more intimate and less competitive. The two women together take a pleasure in devising word games and 'sports' such as mocking fortune, but they do not vie with one another in cleverness; rather they combine together in creating a joint edifice of wit, each building on what the other contributes. It is in her role as Ganymede that Rosalind not only exercises her wit competitively but also adopts a perspective on women's wit that would be inappropriate spoken in her own person. Playing at being a man she attempts to deflate Orlando's romantic vision of love and marriage by a bathetically down-to-earth account of the married state, based heavily on the commonplaces and proverbs of masculine tradition:

> Maids are May when they are maids, but the sky changes when they are wives. I will be more jealous of thee than a Barbary cock-pigeon over his hen, more clamorous than a parrot against rain, more new-fangled than an ape, more giddy in my desires than a monkey. I will weep for nothing, like Diana in the fountain, and I will do that when you are disposed to be merry. I will laugh like a hyen, and that when thou art inclined to sleep. (IV.i.140–8)

Ganymede develops this conception of the married woman's wayward disposition in a passage which identifies this behaviour as 'wit', of the sort of mental agility that allows a wife to dominate her husband. When Orlando cannot believe that his Rosalind is capable of such capricious behaviour, Ganymede assures him that all women are alike:

Orl. O but she is wise.
Ros. Or else she could not have the wit to do this. The wiser, the waywarder. Make the doors upon a woman's wit, and it will out at the casement; shut that, and 'twill out at the keyhole; stop that, 'twill fly with the smoke out at the chimney.
Orl. A man that had a wife with such a wit, he might say, 'Wit, whither wilt?'
Ros. Nay, you might keep that check for it, till you met your wife's wit going to your neighbour's bed.
Orl. And what wit could wit have to excuse that?

Ros. Marry, to say she came to seek you there. You shall never take her without her answer, unless you take her without her tongue. (IV.i.151–64)

The wife who uses her wit both to get herself into the neighbour's bed, and then to excuse herself to her husband once discovered, is a typical character from Boccaccio or the fabliaux; her answer is that of the shrew, whose readiness with words is her weapon against men. This version of womanhood is not realized in the behaviour of any female character in the play, but Rosalind offers it as a possibility to be entertained. After all, it is her skill in speaking that enables her to get the better of Jaques as well as Orlando.

In *Much Ado About Nothing*, the wit of Beatrice has a dangerous affinity with shrewishness, in the judgement of male and female characters alike. Her uncles, Leonato and Antonio, think it will ruin her marriage prospects, and her shy cousin Hero finds it intimidating: 'O, she would laugh me /Out of myself, press me to death with wit!' (III.i.75–6). Hero also criticizes Beatrice's wit as a kind of self-esteem improper for a woman:

> Disdain and scorn ride sparkling in her eyes,
> Misprising what they look on, and her wit
> Values itself so highly that to her
> All matter else seems weak. She cannot love,
> Nor take no shape nor project of affection,
> She is so self-endeared. (III.i.51–6)

Benedick's wit, of course, is never subjected to such criticism; in him it is becoming and appropriate, admired by his friends Claudio and Don Pedro, and part of his repertoire of charms. In the final exchanges Beatrice lives up to her image of the witty woman as long as she can, but the last words are given to Benedick, who silences his lover with a kiss. Beatrice is allowed no riposte to Benedick's ironic advice to the Prince: 'Prince, thou art sad; get thee a wife, get thee a wife! There is no staff more reverend than one tipped with horn' (V.iv.120–2).

In the comedies of London life which took the stage at the end of the century, adultery is not as in Shakespeare's comedies, just a possibility, but a staple situation, and one which regularly results from a contriving woman's wit. The ingredients consist of the worthy citizen, his wife, and her gentleman-lover. The motives of the wife combine a desire

Women and wit in *The Merry Wives of Windsor* 255

for excitement with the satisfaction of upward social mobility, those of the lover lust and greed. Both enjoy the pleasure of deceiving the husband but it is usually the wife who carries out the necessary plotting and contriving. In some comedies, however, women's wit is used to different effect when the authors subvert their audience's expectations of adultery between wives and gallants by having the wives deceive the gallants and remain chaste after all. The women are still the same shrewd, and shrewish, plotters, but with the difference that in the end their plots are turned against their lovers rather than their husbands. In *Westward Ho* by Dekker and Webster, for instance, the image of city wives created at the beginning of the play seems to confirm what Alexander Leggatt calls 'the joking acceptance of immorality'.[4] Mistress Birdlime, the bawd, praises Mistress Justiniano, the merchant's wife, for her 'good City wit' and continues:

> Your Lady or Iustice-a-peace Madam, carries high wit from the Citty, namely, to receive all and pay all: to awe their Husbands, to check their Husbands, to controule their Husbands. (I.i.30–2)[5]

Chastity in city wives represents not virtue but deficiency: as Birdlime says, 'Many are honest, either because they have not wit, or because they have not opportunity to be dishonest' (I.i.92). The three wives of the play's second plot, Mistress Tenterhook, Mistress Honeysuckle, and Mistress Wafer, have each a gallant, and agree to go to Brainford to spend the night with their lovers. While the wives are off to Brainford, their husbands are in Mistress Birdlime's brothel with the prostitute Luce; when they discover what their wives are up to they hurry away to catch them in the act, but the sympathies of Birdlime and Luce are with the wives, whom Birdlime decides to help. In these city plays female solidarity is often a force to be reckoned with; the women collude together in order to pit their wits against a world where men nearly always get dealt the best hand. The wives get to Brainford and enjoy an evening's drinking and merriment, but no more; they lock their bedroom doors and thwart their gallants' expectations:

> They shall know that Citizens wives have wit enough to outstrip twenty such guls; tho we are merry, let us not be mad: be as wanton as new married wiues, as fantisticke

and light headed to the eye, as fether-makers, but as pure about the heart, as if we dwelt amongst em in Black Fryers.
(V.i.159–63)

Though the values of marriage are – just – preserved, the husbands as well as the gallants look foolish; it is the game of female trickery which is at the heart of the play, the ability of women, especially when acting in concert, to catch men out at their own games. This, rather than any upholding of ideals of marital fidelity, is the play's real concern.

In *The Roaring Girl* by Middleton and Dekker, the authors again preserve the chastity of their city wives contrary to expectations raised in the opening scenes. Mistress Gallipot's gallant, Laxton, says of her that she 'has wit enough to rob her husband' (II.i.81) and that she 'puts out a candle with the best tricks of any drugster's wife in England' (II.i.117). He also compliments her on her wit by comparing it with Satan's:

> that wile
> By which the serpent did the first woman beguile
> And ever since all women's bosoms fill;
> Y'are apple-eaters all, deceivers still.   (III.ii.253–6)[6]

The rich, absurdly doting Master Gallipot, whom his wife dismissively describes as an 'apron' husband and a 'cotquean', seems ideally cut out to be cuckolded by such a scheming wife. But it soon becomes clear that neither Mistress Gallipot nor her companion Mistress Openwork will actually get seduced. For Laxton's remarks about Mistress Gallipot's wit illustrate not his admiration but his fear of it; he is in fact a reluctant wooer, simulating lust only for fashion's sake in the hopes of getting his hands on Master Gallipot's money by means of his wife. His sexual interests lie elsewhere. Mistress Openwork has her suitor too, the predatory gallant Goshawk, who tells her that her husband is keeping a whore in the suburbs so that she will sleep with him for revenge. But she is disgusted when she discovers his stories are lies, and the two women decide together to reject their gallants: 'Happy is the woman can be rid of 'em all: 'las, what are your whisking gallants to our husbands, weigh 'em rightly, man for man?' asks Mistress Openwork (IV.ii.40–2). But this is not a case of women using their wit to turn tables on their suitors, as in *Westward Ho*. The wives stay honest because their gallants are so untrustworthy that it is not worth all the plotting to keep the liaisons in operation.

Women and wit in *The Merry Wives of Windsor* 257

But if the wit of the citizens' wives doesn't amount to much in this play, the central character of Moll, the roaring girl, vindicates both women's wit and chastity in a flourishing style, and stands entirely outside the conventional stereotypes. She is far from being a courtly figure, and her underworld connections as well as her unconventional dress horrify Sir Alexander Wengrave when he thinks his son is planning to marry her. She is not witty in the manner of Beatrice or Rosalind, but she is witty in the other way, resourceful in contriving plots to help the oppressed or unfortunate, and intelligent in constructing for herself an ideal way of life as a free woman. Her bisexual appearance is a witty image for her independence of traditional gender distinctions; it symbolizes her refusal to submit either to the cynical male vanity of someone like Laxton who thinks every woman that looks at him is in love with him, or to the conventional acceptance of woman's physical and financial dependence on a man.

Moll defines wit in terms of female self-sufficiency:

> She that has wit and spirit
> May scorn
> To live beholding to her body for meat,
> Or for apparel, like your common dame
> That makes shame to get her clothes to cover shame.
> Base is that mind that kneels unto her body.
> (III.i.132–7)

The usual association of female boldness with prostitution is made by Moll's enemies, particularly Sir Alexander Wengrave and Laxton, but her strength and spirit make nonsense of this sexual stereotyping:

> I scorn to prostitute myself to a man,
> I that can prostitute a man to me.   (III.i.109–10)

The heroine's male attire may have different connotations in a dramatic world modelled on Jacobean London from those of Rosalind's Arden or Portia's Venice, but it serves the same functions, to license the expression of her wit, and to allow her to triumph over men not just in woman's conventional qualities of wiliness and cunning, but also in championing the cause of the underdog and winning out through the exercise of intelligence.

The women of Shakespeare's *The Merry Wives of Windsor*

seem at first glance more akin to Mistresses Gallipot and Openwork than to Moll, though they operate as she does to destroy certain stereotyped conceptions of women. 'Hath mirth no kindred in the world but lust?' asks Moll indignantly, and Mistress Page asserts in the same spirit that 'Wives may be merry, and yet honest too.' The play is a comedy in the early mode of *The Taming of the Shrew* and *The Comedy of Errors*, urban and bourgeois in setting, concerned with marital relations rather than romantic love. Its title seems to promise citizen comedy in the vein of Middleton featuring adulterous liaisons; 'merry' was then an epithet with less innocent connotations, and 'merry tales' often included a strong element of bawdy. A capacity for mirth in women, like wit, tended not to go with chastity. Mistress Page, however, supports her assertion that wives can combine mirth and chastity with a proverb:

> We do not act that often jest and laugh;
> 'Tis old, but true: 'Still swine eats all the draff'.
>
> (IV.ii.97–8)

'Act' here carries a sexual sense; she implies that it is those quiet women, the 'still swine', who do not 'jest and laugh', who get up to all the mischief. As in *Westward Ho* and *The Roaring Girl*, the citizens' wives preserve their chastity, but in a positive and deliberate way, making their intentions clear from the start. They are witty wives in the accepted style, quick of mind and tongue, always ready with an answer, not nice or delicate in conversation between themselves. They are conscious of themselves as women in a society where women's and men's values, particularly in matters of sexual priorities, tend to be different, and they operate together, as a women's league against men; but at the same time they also share fully in the men's attitudes towards property and self-preservation, and in no way do they represent the subversive element in womanhood which some critics have identified as a major aspect of the function of women in the comedies. They do not, for instance, embody the 'outlaw feminine principle' of Marilyn French[7] nor could it be said that their feminine nature 'challenges the status quo either overtly or through its command of socially subversive forces like sexuality, romantic passion, household revels'.[8] But there is a tension between the implications of their activities together as women, tricking Falstaff and deflating Ford's jealousy, and their involvement

Women and wit in *The Merry Wives of Windsor* 259

in the dominant value-system of Windsor society upheld by almost all the other characters in the play; nothing much comes of this tension, and the overriding principle of self-interest may be seen to account for both aspects of the wives' behaviour, yet the conception of women's value (to which the kind of wit I have been discussing is central) is distinctive, especially if it is seen in relation to Shakespeare's later treatment of marriage and the threats posed to its stability from within and without in *Othello*.

In some ways, Windsor seems very much a society which revolves around women's activity. Mistress Quickly, who knows, or thinks she knows, everybody's business, remarks on the excellence of Mistress Page's domestic arrangements:

> Truly, Master Page is an honest man. Never a wife in Windsor leads a better life than she does; do what she will, say what she will, take all, pay all, go to bed when she list, rise when she list, all is as she will. (II.ii.110–14)

She also tells Falstaff how Mistress Ford has been the centre of admiring attention when the court was in residence at Windsor: 'Yet there has been knights, and lords, and gentlemen, with their coaches – I warrant you, coach after coach, letter after letter, gift after gift' (II.ii.60–2). Mistress Ford dominates her husband's thoughts too, for he is totally preoccupied with the matter of her fidelity, and the activities of the two wives occupy much of the play; for the rest of it, sweet Anne Page, though she has little more than 30 lines to speak, commands the attention of three suitors and several other interested parties besides.

The wives are vigorous, realistic, down-to-earth women, not closely distinguished from each other in speech or manner but all the more forceful in presenting a united front. Mistress Page's reaction to Falstaff's letter is characteristic; she knows that the 'holiday time' of her beauty is past and she is not flattered by his approach. She feels at once that her own behaviour must have been open to misinterpretation but also that Falstaff's readiness to spy an invitation where none was intended is typical of men in general: 'O wicked, wicked world. ... Why, I'll exhibit a bill in the parliament for the putting down of men' (II.i.20–1, 28–9). She determines immediately on taking an independent revenge for the insult which she perceives as directed not against her marriage but against her womanhood. When the two wives realize that they have both been treated in the same way, and the insult is at least doubled, they feel their reputations at stake and are ready to do almost anything to redeem them, with one proviso: Mistress Ford is keenly conscious of her husband's jealousy: 'I will consent to act any villainy against him that may not sully the chariness of our honesty' (II.i.95–6). Though Shakespeare does not develop the point, he allows the wives the momentary awareness that they are in that situation peculiar to women, where the very attempt to defend their reputation may sully it the more, unless they use means which their male judges will deem appropriate. As Moll points out to Laxton in *The Roaring Girl*, from the usual, that is male, viewpoint a man's advances to a woman are more likely to cast aspersions on her moral character than on his; it is incumbent on the woman to be twice as careful of herself as a man need be:

> Th'art one of those
> That thinks each woman thy fond flexible whore:
> If she but cast a liberal eye upon thee,
> Turn back her head, she's thine: or, amongst company,
> By chance drink first to thee, then she's quite gone,
> There's no means to help her. . . .
> How many of our sex, by such as thou
> Have their good thoughts paid with a blasted name
> That never deserved loosely or did trip
> In path of whoredom beyond cup and lip.
>
> (III.i.70–5, 79–82)

Naturally, then, the Windor wives do not seek the help of their husbands against Falstaff, but go instead to Mistress Quickly, who plays her part as go-between with gusto, cunningly inflaming Falstaff's hope of success with Mistress Ford on account of the 'ill life ... a very frampold life' she is thought to lead with her jealous husband. The wives are skilful planners, staging the first trick on Falstaff with a careful regard to details like timing and the briefing of minor players in their roles. John and Robert are ready at hand with the buck-basket, and Falstaff's page, Robin, is co-opted into the scheme with a promise of a new doublet and hose in return for his assistance. In pleasurable collaboration, they set the scene for their playlet:

Women and wit in *The Merry Wives of Windsor*

Mrs Page. ... I'll go hide me.
Mrs Ford. Do so. – Go tell thy master I am alone. [*Exit Robin.*]
   Mistress Page, remember you your cue.
Mrs Page. I warrant thee; if I do not act it, hiss me.
(III.iii.31–4)

Despite these preparations, however, all does not quite go according to plan; their intent to get rid of Falstaff by pretending that Master Ford is on his way is overtaken by events, for Ford, along with Page, Caius, and Evans, actually appears. But the wives are in no way put out by this unexpected turn and, like resourceful schemers, are able to absorb it into their own purposes, and even to capitalize on it. Far from being outfaced they are actually delighted:

Mrs Page. Is there not a double excellency in this?
Mrs Ford. I know not which pleases me better, that my husband is deceived, or Sir John. (III.iii.163–5)

It is Mistress Page's next idea to improve on the first trick by combining a new trick on Falstaff with a device to expose the grossness of Ford's jealousy. This is not simply trickery for its own sake, since Mistress Page is soon proved right in her belief that one humiliation is not enough to deter Falstaff: 'his dissolute disease will scarce obey this medicine' (III.iii.177–8). Ford's jealousy is a masculine vice as threatening to women's autonomy as is Falstaff's lust, and the women use their wit against it in the same way. In both cases the male principle is defeated by the women acting as a united force against it. Ford is not wide of the mark in his fear of the women's league. Meeting Mistress Page on her way to visit her friend, he remarks sarcastically, 'I think, if your husbands were dead, you two would marry.' Mistress Page quips back at once, 'Be sure of that – two other husbands' (III.ii.12–14). He is intuitively right, too, in his mistrust of women's cunning, which he regards as a vice inherent in the sex:

> I will rather trust a Fleming with my butter, Parson Hugh the Welshman with my cheese, an Irishman with my aquavitae bottle, or a thief to walk my ambling gelding, than my wife with herself. Then she plots, then she ruminates, then she devises. (II.ii.290–5)

Next time, then, when Falstaff, duly advised by Quickly, turns up at the appointed hour, Mistress Page is forewarned that Ford and his band of supporters are on their way; the audience has not been let in on the details of the wives' plan, as they were with the buck-basket trick, so that their device of disguising Falstaff as the old woman of Brainford, whom Ford is known to detest, is given the air of happy on-the-spot resourcefulness.

Not only is Ford twice tricked, by being exposed to ridicule as he tosses the contents of the basket all over the room to the amazement of his friends and the secret delight of the wives, and then lets Falstaff once more escape under his very nose in his female disguise, but Falstaff himself is again humiliated and physically abused, when Ford mounts a violent attack on what he believes to be 'A witch, a quean, an old cozening quean!' (IV.ii.158). There are added dimensions of significance in that the choice of disguise as a wise woman has particular irony for Falstaff, whose behaviour towards the wives implies such a low opinion of woman's wisdom, and in that Ford's irrational hatred of the 'old woman', which causes him to give 'her' such a drubbing, is suggestive of sexual insecurity. The wives are properly overjoyed with the success of their contrivances, and decide not to pursue Falstaff with any further revenge; they agree that, if they let their husbands in on the joke, their second purpose of curing Ford's jealousy will also be served. Even so, they are not yet quite done with Falstaff, for Mistress Ford feels 'there would be no period to the jest should he not be publicly shamed' (IV.ii.208–9).

The men's reactions to the women's revelation of their plot confirm its complete success. Parson Evans praises their wit: ''Tis one of the best discretions of a 'oman as ever I did look upon' (IV.iv.1–2), and Ford is so totally humbled by the evidence of his wife's loyalty and his own folly that he achieves a moment of poetic eloquence:

> Pardon me, wife. Henceforth do what thou wilt:
> I rather will suspect the sun with cold
> Than thee with wantonness; now doth thy honour stand,
> In him that was of late an heretic,
> As firm as faith. (IV.iv.6–10)

Though the final stage of the plot against Falstaff is undertaken as a joint enterprise by the men and the women together,

Women and wit in *The Merry Wives of Windsor* 263

the women remain in control, and arrive between themselves at the 'device' whereby Falstaff will be lured to Herne's Oak, and pinched and mocked. The nature of the trickery, however, has changed. This is to be 'public sport' for the whole community, and no longer a private act of revenge by women acting together against a man who has insulted them. Falstaff's disruptive lust is to be exorcised from Windsor society; as Mistress Page promises,

> We'll all present ourselves, dis-horn the spirit,
> And mock him home to Windsor.   (IV.iv.63–4)

Falstaff is not ejected but only 'dis-horned' and rendered harmless; he can be safely invited back to the Pages' house to 'eat a posset' and share in the communal mirth.

In *The Merry Wives of Windsor*, the wives' wit operates as a means of obtaining revenge for women against the insults offered to their honesty by the male vices of lust and jealousy, and also as a way of restoring to the community the values of order and domestic stability which have temporarily been misplaced by Falstaff and Ford. They participate in the same code of bourgeois social values as their menfolk, and share the attachment of the men to property and wealth. Falstaff's motives in wooing the wives are compounded of lust and greed; he also believes that the wives will be tempted by his title. In this, he underestimates both their intelligence and their loyalty to the ethic of the middle-class. 'What? ... Sir Alice Ford?' laughs Mistress Page, who, like her husband, rejects the gentlemanly Fenton as a suitor for Anne, and prefers Caius because he is 'well-moneyed'. Her first idea of revenge on Falstaff is to hit him where it most hurts, in his purse.

The money-oriented values of Windsor society are more fully displayed in the Anne Page plot where the 'possibilities', in Parson Evans's words, of Anne's 'pretty virginity' are much enhanced by her £700 a year, and Slender's sole qualifications as Anne's husband are his land and his £300. Anne gets Fenton in the end but not because she exercises her wit to do so. In conspicuous contrast with the other women in the play, Anne is quiet, self-effacing, apparently the passive recipient of what others choose to do and give to her. Perhaps it is that women's wit and romantic love are not reconcilable. Fenton is shown taking charge of the plotting which will ensure that true love wins out. The only time that Mistress Page is outwitted is when she plots against the wishes of her husband and her daughter in contriving for Caius to run off with Anne during the Herne's Oak scene. The active pleasure she takes in the contemplation of her husband's discomfiture is not compatible with the play's final re-establishment of social order, so that, in this one instance, a woman's wit must misfire.

The Merry Wives of Windsor may at first seem a far cry from *Othello*, but the connection between the two portrayals of marital jealousy reflects interestingly on both plays. Ford seems like a comic early version of Othello, although, as Brian Vickers observes, his 'ludicrous conclusions about opportunities for infidelity' ('this 'tis to have linen and buck-baskets!') are remarkably similar to the morals drawn from *Othello* by Thomas Rymer.[9] Marilyn French contrasts the attitudes of the two husbands, suggesting that the presentation of Ford's emotions is determined by the play's overall stress on property and cosenage. Ford, unlike Othello, is not concerned with the loss of his wife's affection or her relation to him, and he does not fear public shame or exposure; rather he drags the whole community into his house to witness his degradation, because 'his fear of cuckoldry is a fear of theft'.[10] For Carol Thomas Neely, *Othello* is 'a terrifying completion of the comedies' when men's propensities for 'folly, cuckoldry, promiscuity, and cruelty' are laughed to scorn by the women in a process of re-educating them into fit husbands.[11] Thus *The Merry Wives of Windsor* has aspects of a comic obverse of *Othello*, not only in the outcome of the jealousy plot, but in the larger treatment of relations between men and women. But Shakespeare's source is a tragic novella not a comic fabliau, and in his version it seems to be Iago and not any woman who appears as the exponent of wit: 'Thou knowest we work by wit, and not by witchcraft', he tells the dull Roderigo, who trusts implicitly in the skills of his contriving friend. Unlike Shakespeare's witty women Iago works entirely alone; his ends are neither the curing of vice nor the achievement of harmless laughter, and the complete self-absorption of his wit is a quality foreign to women.

Yet the women are not without their wit though it seems at first weak against Iago's cunning. In the scene at the harbour on Cyprus, Desdemona and Emilia indulge in badinage with Iago while passing the time until Othello's arrival. The topic of their exchanges is the wiles of women, which arises quite naturally out of Iago's bad-tempered remark to Cassio about Emilia's shrewishness:

> Sir, would she give you so much of her lips
> As of her tongue she has bestow'd on me,
> You'ld have enough.　　　　　　　　　(II.i.100–2)

The theme of the tiresomeness of woman's incessant talk is so much a masculine commonplace that Iago can use it to insult his wife publicly without seeming to say anything obtrusive or odd. Desdemona intervenes on behalf of Emilia, who tries herself to contradict her husband, but Iago takes no notice, and sweeps on with offensive jocularity:

> Come on, come on, you are pictures out o' doors;
> Bells in your parlours; wild-cats in your kitchens;
> Saints in your injuries; devils being offended;
> Players in your housewifery; and housewives in
>   your beds.　　　　　　　　　　　　(II.i.109–12)

Desdemona then engages Iago in a passage of what has been labelled by a modern editor 'backchat',[12] which several critics have found offensive because it makes her seem too forward and knowing for an innocent girl; this culminates in Iago's conventionally misogynistic couplets on the witty woman, whose best office in life is 'to suckle fools, and chronicle small beer'. Though Desdemona cries out against this 'lame and impotent conclusion', she gets no support from the other listeners, and indeed Cassio remarks complacently, 'He speaks home, madam.' There are several points here: that it is Iago who is made the mouthpiece of traditional misogynistic commonplaces, as his means, perhaps, of counteracting the florid courtliness of Cassio's greetings to Desdemona and Emilia; that the image of woman as wanton wife and shrew is both directly presented in Iago's attitude to Emilia and indirectly implied in the manner of Desdemona's engagement in this dialogue.

For all Desdemona's later submissiveness and Brabantio's attempts to type-cast her as an ideally silent and obedient daughter, she is still in different ways a witty wife; she puts forward the idea that it was her choice and her decision to marry Othello, and defends her actions with spirit, and she is not reticent about coming to Cassio's defence. In his depiction of this latter situation Shakespeare allows the shadow of the shrew to be seen behind in Desdemona's behaviour. 'Our general's wife is now the general', says Iago insinuatingly to Cassio when he is suggesting that Cassio solicit Desdemona to be his advocate, and Cassio himself has called her, more innocently, 'our great captain's captain'; when Desdemona plans her campaign on Cassio's behalf, she determines to use what she sees as a wife's privileges to get her own way with Othello:

> my lord shall never rest,
> I'll watch him tame, and talk him out of patience;
> His bed shall seem a school, his board a shrift,
> I'll intermingle every thing he does
> With Cassio's suit.   (III.iii.22–6)

But where she dares to be bold in someone else's cause she is unable to muster the same spirit for herself. When Othello strikes and insults her she can bring no wit to her own defence, and it is now Emilia's turn to take the woman's part. In IV.iii, the one scene when the two women are alone together, their warm intimacy and mutual trust, so strongly contrasted by implication with the facade of friendship between Othello and Iago, is not diminished by the difference in their social status. Now that Desdemona must be the virtuous and suffering woman, the patient Griselda, Emilia steps forward as the witty wife, shrewd or shrewish, in her vindication of the steps women take in self-preservation from masculine transgression and disloyalty:

> I do think it is their husbands' faults
> If wives do fall: say, that they slack their duties,
> And pour our treasures into foreign laps;
> Or else break out in peevish jealousies,
> Throwing restraint upon us: or say they strike us,
> Or scant our former having in despite,
> Why, we have galls: and though we have some grace,
> Yet have we some revenge. Let husbands know,
> Their wives have sense like them.   (IV.iii.86–94)

But her tone is not simply bitter; before this serious speech, she contrives a witty justification of adultery on the ground of marital affection: 'who would not make her husband a cuckold, to make him a monarch? I should venture purgatory for it.' At the play's conclusion Desdemona dies because she has surrendered wit to the wisdom of wifely obedience; Emilia, however, plays out the role of shrew and outspoken woman to the bitter end. When Iago tries to quell her outburst of truthtelling he treats her as the disobedient and babbling wife: 'go to, charm your tongue', 'What, are you mad? I charge you get you home', resorting to sexual insult when she refuses to heed him, with 'Villainous whore!' and 'Filth'. But Emilia, hitherto suppressed and resentful in the face of her husband's provocation, stands up for herself and for Desdemona, fully accepting, even relishing, the risks she is running:

> Good gentlemen, let me have leave to speak,
> 'Tis proper I obey him, but not now:
> ...
> 'Twill out, it will: I hold my peace sir, no,
> I'll be in speaking, liberal as the air,
> Let heaven, and men, and devils, let 'em all,
> All, all cry shame against me, yet I'll speak.
>   (V.ii.196–7, 220–3)

Though in this play women's wit has not the corrective power it has in the comedies, especially in *The Merry Wives of Windsor*, to tame and re-channel men's destructive impulses, the strength of the women's bond is startlingly vindicated.

NOTES

1 *Shakespeare and the Traditions of Comedy* (Cambridge, 1974), p. 232.
2 Quotations from the *Decameron* are from the translation by E. Hutton, Everyman's Library, 2 vols (London and New York, 1931).
3 *Still Harping on Daughters: Women and Drama in the Age of Shakespeare* (Brighton, 1983), pp. 121–2.
4 *Citizen Comedy in the Age of Shakespeare* (Toronto, 1973), p. 130.
5 All quotations from *Westward Ho* are taken from *The Dramatic Works of Thomas Dekker*, ed. Fredson Bowers, vol. 2 (Cambridge, 1955).
6 All quotations from *The Roaring Girl* are taken from the edition by A. Gomme, New Mermaid Plays (London, 1976).
7 *Shakespeare's Division of Experience* (London, 1981), p. 23.
8 Linda Bamber, *Comic Women, Tragic Men: A Study of Gender and Genre in Shakespeare* (Stanford, 1982), p. 29.
9 *The Artistry of Shakespeare's Prose* (London, 1968), p. 155.
10 French, p. 108.
11 'Women and men in *Othello*: "What should such a fool /Do with so good a woman?"' in *The Woman's Part: Feminist Criticism of Shakespeare* (Chicago, 1980), p. 212.
12 M. R. Ridley, Arden edn of *Othello*, note to II.i.109–66.

16

Shakespeare and Massinger: resemblances and contrasts

KENNETH MUIR

In considering the relationship between Philip Massinger and William Shakespeare in this essay, I have tried to do three things: to reconsider Massinger's debt to Shakespeare, to examine the weakness of Massinger's imagery compared to Shakespeare's, and to consider why Massinger persisted in writing his plays in verse although, as critics agree, he had little poetic talent.

The extent of Massinger's debt to Shakespeare has exercised many critics during the present century. Although Fletcher was the most popular dramatist during the years when Massinger was collaborating with him and writing his own best-known plays, Shakespeare's were still in the repertory and it would have been surprising if Massinger, a notoriously imitative writer, had not been influenced by the greater dramatist. David L. Frost, who regards Massinger as a spurious legatee of Shakespeare[1] and casts doubt on many suggested borrowings, allows that one episode in *The Bondman* (II.ii) owes something to Iago's story of his sleepless night with Cassio:

> Some times
> I lie with my Ladie, as the last night I did,
> Shee could not say her prayers for thinking of you,
> Nay, she talked of you in her sleepe, and sigh'd out,
> O sweet *Asotus*, sure thou art so backward,
> That I must rauish thee, and in that feruor
> She tooke me in her arms, threw me vpon her,
> Kis'd me, and hug'd me, and then wak'd, and wept,
> Because 'twas but a dreame.[2]

Frost allows that the parallels between the *Duke of Milan* and *Othello* are extensive, and that the quarrel between

Marcelia and Mariana (II.i) clearly echoes that between Helena and Hermia in *A Midsummer Night's Dream*. But he points out that many supposed echoes, such as the Olympus/ molehill comparison, may well be proverbial. A. H. Cruickshank listed numerous parallels with Shakespeare, but A. K. McIlwraith expressed doubt of many of these,[3] and I confess that I am sceptical of some which he accepted. But there is not much doubt that 'euerie word's a Poynard' (*The Duke of Milan*, I.249) is an echo of Benedick's complaint of Beatrice, that 'she speaks poniards and every word stabs' (II.i.231–2). The detailed comparison by T.A. Dunn of the remarks of the two dramatists on the effect of the performance of a tragedy on a murderer in the audience, though derived perhaps from Plutarch, shows that Massinger had *Hamlet* in mind:

> I have heard
> That guilty creatures sitting at a play
> Have, by the very cunning of the scene,
> Been struck so to the soul that presently
> They have proclaim'd their malefactions. (II.ii.584–8)

> I once obseru'd
> In a Tragedie of ours, in which a murther
> Was acted to the life, a guiltie hearer
> Forc'd by the terror of a wounded conscience
> To make discouerie of that which torture
> Could not wring from him. (*The Roman Actor*, III.39)

There is nothing in Massinger's speech to correspond with Hamlet's additional remark:

> For murder, though it have no tongue, will speak
> With most miraculous organ. (589–90)

Although it is clear that Massinger was steeped in Shakespeare, some of the pitfalls of such comparisons may be illustrated by the work of H. Dugdale Sykes, who was a great believer in the use of parallels as a proof of authorship.[4] He proved to his own satisfaction that Massinger, rather than Shakespeare, was Fletcher's collaborator in *The Two Noble Kinsmen* and *Henry VIII*. There are, it is true, numerous valid parallels between the non-Fletcherian scenes of both plays and the plays of Massinger. (Many now believe that Shakespeare himself was responsible for the whole of *Henry VIII*, and one critic has claimed for him the sole authorship of *The Two Noble Kinsmen*.) Sykes points out, for example, that Katherine begins her appeal to the King with the words 'Alas, Sir', and that there are examples of the same initial words in six of Massinger's plays, written some years afterwards. As Massinger may well have been impressed by an impressive scene, this can tell us nothing about the authorship of that play. In the same way, Massinger's frequent use of the idea that a character has not enough blood to make a blush[6] does not prove that he collaborated in *The Two Noble Kinsmen* where the same idea occurs:

Allow'st no more blood than will make a blush.[7]

The idea lodged in his memory, just as did Beatrice's words to her father in *The Changeling*,

O come not near me, sir, I shall defile you –

in Massinger's line:

O come not neere me sir, I am infectious.[8]

Professor Dunn, who provided us with the most comprehensive analysis of Massinger's style, complained that he did not vary his syntax to suit the character speaking,[9] and that, compared with Shakespeare, he was 'a much more conscious, deliberate and parsimonious user of metaphor'.[10] Caroline Spurgeon, similarly contrasting Massinger with Shakespeare, confessed that there was 'little that is individual to note' about Massinger's imagery.[11] Spurgeon's method of classification does not in itself distinguish between original and derivative images, but there is an obvious difference between the use of imagery by the two dramatists. This is not so much in the fields from which their images are drawn, different as they are, but in the contrast between the organic nature of Shakespeare's imagery and the merely rhetorical and illustrative nature of Massinger's metaphors and similes. Shakespeare's images evolve from one another in a continual succession; and, taken as a whole, they provide a key to the interpretation of the plays in which they appear. Massinger does not attempt to use iterative imagery, or even seem to be aware of its existence, though at least two of his contemporaries – Webster and Ford – had penetrated the secret of Shakespeare's Figure in the Carpet.

Shakespeare and Massinger

If one takes a typical speech from one of Shakespeare's major plays – Hamlet's first soliloquy, Othello's lines before the murder of Desdemona, Cleopatra's speech on the death of Antony, Brutus's resolution to murder Caesar, Macbeth's soliloquies before the murder of Duncan – all are crowded with images; and some speeches are emptied of everything except images. In Ulysses' discourse to Achilles on time, there are some twenty images in 45 lines, and each image is born out of its predecessor. Moreover, the theme of the speech, placed as it is between the union and the separation of Troilus and Cressida, illuminates their vows of eternal fidelity just before, and Troilus's later curse of 'Injurious Time' (IV.iv.41). Love is one of the values which, Ulysses claims, is subject to envious and calumniating Time:

> Time hath, my lord, a wallet at his back,
> Wherein he puts alms for oblivion,
> A great-siz'd monster of ingratitudes.
> Those scraps are good deeds past, which are devour'd
> As fast as they are made, forgot as soon
> As done. Perseverance, dear my lord,
> Keeps honour bright: to have done is to hang
> Quite out of fashion, like a rusty mail
> In monumental mockery. Take the instant way;
> For honour travels in a strait so narrow
> Where one but goes abreast. Keep then the path;
> For emulation hath a thousand sons
> That one by one pursue; if you give way,
> Or hedge aside from the direct forthright,
> Like to an enter'd tide they all rush by
> And leave you hindmost:
> Or, like a gallant horse fall'n in first rank,
> Lie there for pavement for the abject rear,
> O'er-run and trampled on. Then what they do in present,
> Though less than yours in past, must o'er-top yours;
> For Time is like a fashionable host
> That slightly shakes his parting guest by th' hand,
> And, with his arms out-stretch'd, as he would fly,
> Grasps in the comer. Welcome ever smiles,
> And farewell goes out sighing. O let not virtue seek
> Remuneration for the thing it was;
> For beauty, wit,
> High birth, vigour of bone, desert in service,

> Love, friendship, charity, are subjects all
> To envious and calumniating Time.
> One touch of nature makes the whole world kin –
> That all with one consent praise new-born gauds,
> Though they are made and moulded of things past,
> And give to dust that is a little gilt
> More laud than gilt o'er-dusted.
> The present eye praises the present object:
> Then marvel not, thou great and complete man,
> That all the Greeks begin to worship Ajax,
> Since things in motion sooner catch the eye
> Than what stirs not. The cry went once on thee,
> And still it might, and yet it may again
> If thou wouldst not entomb thyself alive
> And case they reputation in thy tent,
> Whose glorious deeds but in these fields of late
> Made emulous missions 'mongst the gods themselves,
> And drave great Mars to faction. (III.iii.145–89)

The imagery and the meaning are one. Omit the imagery and nothing is left except the trite advice that inactivity leads to the loss of reputation.

Massinger, on the other hand, has no speeches of this kind. When he puts forward a substantial argument, as for example, the defence of the stage in *The Roman Actor* (I.iii.42f.), it proceeds logically and prosaically, and what imagery he uses is so well-worn that the reader may remain unconscious of it: 'sold to his lusts', the 'snares of bauds', to take 'faire Vertue for our guide', 'lawful pledges of a former bed' – such images are still-born. If one does come across vivid imagery, one can be fairly certain that Massinger was not responsible for it. One example will illustrate this. Sykes argued that the scene in *The Two Noble Kinsmen* in which Palamon, Arcite, and Emilia pray to their respective deities was by Massinger. The improbability of this attribution can be seen from Arcite's invocation of Mars, in which the diction, as well as the imagery, are quite beyond Massinger's range:

> whose havoc in vast field
> Unearthed skulls proclaim, whose breath blows down
> The teeming Ceres' foison, who dost pluck
> With hand armipotent from forth blue clouds
> The mason'd turrets, that both mak'st and break'st
> The stony girths of cities. (V.i.51–6)

Shakespeare and Massinger 273

It need hardly be said that the fact that Shakespeare does not elsewhere use *unearthed* and *mason'd* does not tell against his authorship, since every one of his plays contains words found only once in his works.

Occasionally, however, Massinger learned from Shakespeare without being guilty of slavish imitation. The lines

> she transcendes, and makes
> Credulitie her debtor

show that Massinger could, like his master, fuse the abstract and the concrete; but his plays as a whole are a mortuary of dead metaphors.[12] We read of pouring oil on fire, of swimming against the current, of swimming through seas of blood, of a sea of tears, of lancing festering sores, of lancing a seared up conscience, of hearts made of flint, of the false glass of flattery, of a lion pinched with hunger, of a serpent swollen with poison, of a river of love, of mountains of sins, of the anchor of hopes, of the firm base of mercy, of the ocean of a woman's virtue, of the impossibility of washing an Aethiop white, of covering pills with sweetness, of putting off from the shore of innocence, of sowing seeds in the barren sands, of being driven upon a desperate strait, of torches quenched, of fortune's wheel, of the dew of forgiveness, of falling like a meteor, of a tedious pilgrimage. Massinger frequently refers to classical mythology – Venus, Diana, Thetis, Jupiter, Neptune, Saturn, Juno, Cupid, Atropos, Pandora, Pygmalion – but always without an individualizing touch. He twice refers, for example, to the poisoned shirt of Nessus. When Shakespeare's Antony, proud of his descent from Hercules, does so, it is because he feels he has been betrayed by the woman he loves, as his ancestor had felt too:

> The shirt of Nessus is upon me, teach me,
> Alcides, thou mine ancestor, thy rage.
> Let me lodge Lichas on the horns o' th' moon.
>
> (IV.xii.42–5)

We are reminded of the whole story, and of what Seneca made of it. In Massinger's play, *The Picture*, the jealous Sophia merely says that 'the spoiles and salaries of lust' cleave to her 'like *Nessus* poyson'd shirt' (III.254). This lacks completely the appropriateness and resonance of Antony's words. The other reference to Nessus, in *The Unnatural Combat* (II.244), is equally feeble:

my sonnes bloud,
(That like the poyson'd shirt of *Hercules*
Growes to each part about me).

This is not to pretend that Shakespeare's images are always original. But where they are borrowed from literature or iconography, like the image of Time with a wallet, there is nearly always some distinguishing touch which makes them come alive.

Although Professor Dunn, following Aristotle, argued that metaphor is the first essential of poetic drama,[13] Massinger should not be condemned on this ground alone. After all, Christopher Fry, once overpraised, and now unduly neglected, used more imagery, more *original* imagery, than T. S. Eliot did in his plays. There are seventeen images in the first four pages of *The Lady's Not for Burning*, and none at all in the first four pages of *The Confidential Clerk*. *The Elder Statesman* is even barer. One original simile, comparing a lover's struggle to express himself to 'the asthmatic struggling for breath' – the only surviving image in the revised version of the last scene of the play[14] – is striking, but inappropriate; and some of Eliot's later images are as stale as anything in Massinger. Only one or two seem both new and effective.[15] But in all Eliot's plays, including *Sweeney Agonistes*, it is the overall poetic conception, rather than the imagistic detail, which is important. There are, however, many unsophisticated readers of Eliot's later plays, who feel that the lines, apparently so prosaic, should be printed as prose. They are wrong, of course; the verse, which skims the surface of prose, demands to be spoken as verse. The very form reminds us that the plays are nearer to Aeschylus or Sophocles than to the drawing-room comedies some of them superficially resemble.

With this in mind, we may recall Coleridge's view of Massinger as a better model for modern writers – the poets of the early nineteenth century – than Shakespeare, because the verse 'is much more easily constructed and may be more successfully adopted'. Coleridge thought that Massinger provided the 'nearest approach to the language of real life at all compatible with a fixed metre'.[16] Is he right? Several modern critics have demurred, arguing that Massinger's style is rhetorical rather than colloquial, that he was never really a poet, that he was forced by the existing theatrical conventions to write in verse, a medium totally unsuited to his talents. It is true that all tragedies were written in verse, but many comedies were not; and even verse comedies usually had scenes in prose. Yet Massinger chose to write his comedies in verse; he did not even mingle verse and prose as Shakespeare had done, and as Fletcher did. It is therefore proper to enquire why a dramatist with minimal poetic talents chose nevertheless to write only in verse.

John Middleton Murry argued in *The Problem of Style* that if a passage of Massinger's verse were printed as continuous prose, its effectiveness would thereby be enhanced.[17] Although, as I believe, there are many passages, and even whole scenes, where such an experiment would fail, it is easy to cite passages where it appears to succeed:

> Sir, he is no lesse, and that there may be nothing wanting that may render him compleat, the sweetnesse of his disposition so winnes on all appointed to attend him, that they are rivales ev'n in the coursest office, who shall get præcedencie to doe him service: which they esteeme a greater happinesse then if they had beene fashion'd and built up to hold command o're others. (*The Great Duke of Florence*, I.i)

> Since *Arcadius* death, our late great Master, the protection of the Prince his Sonne, the second *Theodosius*, by a generall vote and suffrage of the people, was to her charge assigned, with the disposure of his so many Kingdomes. For his person, shee hath so train'd him vp in all those arts that are both great and good, and to be wished in an Imperiall Monarch, that the Mother of the *Gracchi*, graue *Cornelia* (Rome still boasts of) the wise *Pulcheria* but nam'd, must be no more remembered. (*The Emperor of the East*, I.i)

It should be mentioned, however, that both these passages come from the first scenes of plays, where the audience have to be put in possession of certain facts, facts which are inevitably prosaic. Moreover there are a number of lines in both passages which are perfectly regular pentameters.

It may also be remarked that there are many speeches in Shakespeare's later plays to which Murry's experiment might be applied, especially as the shattering of the formal blank verse pattern in some of the plays goes much further than anything in Massinger. Murry himself wholeheartedly approved of this in Shakespearian passages in *Pericles* and *The*

Two Noble Kinsmen, and he would doubtless have approved of Imogen's speech, here printed as prose:

> I would have broke mine eye-strings, crack'd them, but to look upon him, till the diminution of space had pointed him sharp as my needle: nay, followed him, till he had melted from the smallness of a gnat, to air: and then have turn'd mine eye, and wept. (*Cymbeline*, I.iv.17–22)

It would be more difficult to mark the line-endings in this passage than in either of the Massinger ones. It could, indeed, be argued that what is wrong with the Massinger passages is not so much that they are prose chopped up into lengths, as that the verse is far too regular. In any case, the fact that his verse can be printed as prose, if not with positive gain, as Murry thought, at least with no great loss, does not in itself prove that Massinger was essentially a prosaic writer, condemned by the conventions of the age to write in verse, for, as we have pointed out, he could have followed Jonson's example and written his comedies in prose, or, like Shakespeare and Fletcher, mingled verse and prose.

If one reconsiders the idea, now almost accepted as orthodoxy, that Massinger's verse ought to be recognized as good prose, one begins to have doubts, especially when one finds Murry declaring, before quoting a passage from *The Roman Actor*, that

> It must have been delivered quite conversationally, for to impose a blank verse rhythm upon it would be monstrous. ... Obviously, Massinger would have been much happier, had he been freed from the obligation of cutting his prose up into lines.[18]

The passage in question (II.i.95–107) is concerned with the didactic effect of drama, and it follows one quoted earlier and compared with Hamlet's words about guilty creatures sitting at a play. But Murry's comments seem highly questionable.

>   Nor can it appeare
> Like an impossibilitie, but that
> Your Father looking on a covetous man
> Presented on the Stage as in a mirror
> May see his owne deformity, and loath it.
> Nor could you but perswade the Emperour

> To see a Comedie we have that's stilde
> *The Cure of Avarice*, and to commaund
> Your Father to be a Spectator of it,
> He shall be so Anatomiz'd in the Scæne,
> And see himselfe so personated; the baseness
> Of a self torturing miserable wretch
> Truely describ'd, that I much hope the obiect
> Will worke compunction in him.[19]

Printed so, in verse, the passage does present the actor with one difficult enjambement between the second and third lines (that/Your); but all the later plays of Shakespeare pose similar problems. These drive some directors to instruct their actors to ignore the line-endings. One foolish director of *Antony and Cleopatra*, in which the difficulties are fewer than in *Cymbeline*, solved them at a stroke by having the whole text retyped as prose. I cannot see that anything is gained by printing the above Massinger speech, or any speech in his plays, as prose. No doubt, as Murry says, the lines should be delivered conversationally — more conversationally, at least, than the soliloquies of Tamburlaine or Macbeth — and it would be counter-productive to torture the lines into entirely regular pentameters. Nevertheless, it would be even more disastrous to ignore the line-endings, as any competent actor could demonstrate.

Yet Murry and the other critics who have a low opinion of Massinger's poetic abilities are essentially right. If he had been born fifty years later he would probably have confined himself to prose, although he might well have tried his hand at heroic drama. But although his poetical talents cannot compare with those of Webster, Middleton, and Ford, and are even inferior to those of Dekker, Marston, and Fletcher, he used verse not merely because it was expected of him, but because he must have realized that the themes of his tragedies and the violent passions displayed in them would have been absurd in the cooler medium of prose. His rhetorical verse was generally adequate to his purposes; but since he wrote after the citizen comedies of Middleton, after the prose of Falstaff, Rosalind, and Hamlet, after the mingling of prose and verse in the plays of his collaborator, Fletcher, the use of verse in *A New Way to Pay Old Debts* and *The City Madam* (except for Stargaze's prophecies) must have been a deliberate choice.

We can only guess at the reason; but it seems possible that Massinger was aware that he did not possess the gift of creating characters with an individual manner of speech, and that this weakness was more damaging in prose than in verse, which does not pretend to be colloquial, and more damaging in comedy than in tragedy. One does not need speech-prefixes in *The Way of the World* because Congreve gives each of his characters an individual style. We know at once whether Millamant or Mrs Fainall is speaking, whether it is Witwoud or his brother, whether it is Marwood or Lady Wishfort. Even Mincing and Foible are distinguished by their speech-patterns. In verse drama such linguistic individualization is both rarer and less necessary. In *A New Way to Pay Old Debts*, the characters are differentiated by what they do and say, and by what others say of them, rather than by their manner of speech.

Some dramatists are able to transcend the restrictions of verse by varying it to suit some at least of their characters. Ferdinand and the Duchess of Malfi, Beatrice-Joanna and DeFlores, Giovanni and Annabella are easily distinguished by their voices; more significantly, Ferdinand and the Cardinal, Livia and Bianca, where identity of sex makes it more difficult, can all be distinguished by their style. In this respect Shakespeare's gradual mastery contrasts with Massinger's continued lack. In his early plays, Shakespeare's verse acted as a stylistic solvent. All the noblemen in *1 Henry VI* talk alike, however different they are in character. The break-through came with Gloucester's soliloquy in *3 Henry VI*. Then, in *Romeo and Juliet*, Shakespeare shattered the uniformity that the verse tended to impose in the Nurse's brilliant garrulity, in the Queen Mab speech, and in the contrast between Romeo's speeches before and after his meeting with Juliet. Yet, as everyone notices, many of Shakespeare's most vital characters in the plays of his middle period speak mainly in prose: Shylock, Beatrice, Benedick, Rosalind, and Falstaff. In the last five years of the sixteenth century, he appears to have felt the desirability of a greater naturalism than verse could provide, influenced no doubt by the increasing naturalism in the acting of his company.

Then in *Hamlet* the utter naturalness of the hero's speeches, whether in prose or verse, is built partly on the contrast between them and the rhymed couplets of 'The Mousetrap' and the rhetorical excess of the Dido speeches. Coming after the long prose dialogue in II.ii, Aeneas's tale to Dido is as magnificently artificial as a *tirade* by Phèdre or Athalie; and the soliloquy which follows seems in its context to be the natural outpourings of a human being, rather than a set piece in which a great actor could display his ability to tear a passion to tatters. In the later tragedies prose is kept to a minimum, and used for specific purposes – for Iago's manipulation of Roderigo and Cassio, for Othello's fit, for Lady Macbeth's somnambulism, for the assorted madnesses in *King Lear*, for the orgy on Pompey's galley, for the clown who brings figs and freedom to Cleopatra, for the Plebs and servants in *Coriolanus*. In the verse scenes the characters are all perfectly differentiated by the verse they speak. Compare, for example, Lady Macbeth's idiom with that of her husband, both in dialogue and soliloquy. In the plays of the last period, as we have seen, the verse has become so flexible that all peculiarities of character are revealed; and we are barely conscious of the medium except in such outstanding poetic passages as Iachimo's description of the sleeping Imogen, Perdita's distribution of the flowers, or Prospero's farewell to his art.[20]

Shakespeare's development as a dramatic poet, so crudely outlined here, can therefore be seen as a search for a kind of verse which would not interfere with the expression of character in all its variety and individuality, and thus serve as a perfect dramatic medium for Burbage and his fellow actors. Massinger's problem was quite different. Although he was uninspired as a poet, he could in all his extant plays turn out competent verse, a satisfactory vehicle for his actors. But he lacked, or thought he lacked, the ability possessed by many of his contemporaries to vary his style to suit the character. This did not greatly matter in the plays then in vogue, in which the excitement of individual scenes always outweighed consistency of characterization. But it did matter with prose. However talented the actor, he could not quite camouflage the fact that the style did not vary to suit the character, that he, and not the dramatist, was creating the character.

We do not know whether Massinger tried and failed in prose, and was recommended to stick to verse, or whether he was self-critical enough to realize that he had a bad ear for catching varieties of tone. As soon as Tharsalio speaks in Chapman's *The Widow's Tears* we know him for what he is;

when Crispinella discourses in Marston's *The Dutch Courtezan* on the disadvantages of kissing, she steps out of the frame; and when Zeal-of-the-Land Busy compromises with his conscience in permitting a visit to Jonson's Bartholomew Fair, the idiom he uses is both individual and universal.[21] Massinger who lacked this gift of ventriloquism was wise to stick to verse.

NOTES

1 *The School of Shakespeare* (1968), ch. 3.
2 *Massinger – Plays and Poems*, ed. Philip Edwards and Colin Gibson (Oxford, 1976). All subsequent quotations from Massinger's plays come from this edition.
3 McIlwraith's annotated copy of Cruickshank's *Philip Massinger* (1920) is in the library of Liverpool University.
4 *Sidelights on Shakespeare* (1919); *Sidelights on Elizabethan Drama* (1924).
5 *The Guardian*, I.i; *The Bondman*, IV.iii; *Believe as You List*, I.i.
6 *The Duke of Milan*, IV.iii, and presumed Massinger scenes in *The Spanish Curate* and *The Little French Lawyer*.
7 V.i.141. In *The Riverside Shakespeare*, ed. G. Blakemore Evans (Boston, 1974).
8 *The Changeling*, V.iii.149, and *The Unnatural Combat*, V.ii.198. Noted by Edwards and Gibson.
9 *Philip Massinger* (1957), p. 218.
10 ibid., p. 251.
11 *Shakespeare's Imagery and What It Tells Us* (1935), p. 41.
12 References to the last quotation and to those which follow are to the volumes and pages of the edition of Edwards and Gibson, except for *The Virgin Martyr*, for which references are to the pages of the Fredson Bowers edition of Thomas Dekker, 4 vols (Cambridge, 1953–61). *The Emperor of the East*, III. 409; *The Virgin Martyr*, 380; *The Roman Actor*, III.25; *The Duke of Milan*, I.250; *The Virgin Martyr*, 422; *The Bondman*, I.350; ibid., 326; *The Unnatural Combat*, II.213; ibid., 218; ibid., 242; ibid., 211; ibid., 242; *The Emperor of the East*, III.417; *The Duke of Milan*, I.235; *The Bondman*, I.391; *The Duke of Milan*, I.240; ibid., 246; *The Grand Duke of Florence*, III.108; ibid., 137; *The Emperor of the East*, III.411; *The Virgin Martyr*, 388; ibid., 422; ibid., 460; *The Picture*, III.255.
13 Dunn, pp. 250f.
14 The prompt-book reveals the many changes made during rehearsals and after the opening night at the Edinburgh Festival. See also E. Martin Browne, *The Making of T. S. Eliot's Plays* (1969), pp. 329–37.
15 See, e.g., *Collected Plays*, p.302:
It's just like sitting in an empty waiting room
In a railway station on a branch line
After the last train, after all the other passengers
Have left, and the booking office is closed
And the porters have gone.
16 S. T. Coleridge, *Lectures and Notes on Shakespeare* (1893), pp. 403–4, 534.
17 (1922), p. 56.

18 ibid.
19 It is difficult to believe that the Volpones and Overreaches would be reformed by watching a play.
20 After Shakespeare's retirement, the loosening of blank verse had been carried so far that Milton regarded his immediate contemporaries as bad models. For *Comus* he reverted to the kind of verse prevalent a generation earlier.
21 *The Widow's Tears*, I.i, II.i; *The Dutch Courtezan*, III.i; *Bartholomew Fair*, I.vi.

HAROLD JENKINS:

LIST OF PUBLICATIONS

BOOKS AND ARTICLES

The Life and Work of Henry Chettle (London: Sidgwick and Jackson, 1934), viii + 276 pp.

'On the authenticity of *Greene's Groatsworth of Wit* and *The Repentance of Robert Greene*', *Review of English Studies*, 11 (1935), pp. 28–41.

'Towards a biography of Edward Benlowes', *Review of English Studies*, 12 (1936), pp. 273–84.

'A poet in Chancery: Edward Benlowes', *Modern Language Review*, 32 (1937), pp. 382–93.

'Peele's *Old Wive's Tale*', *Modern Language Review*, 34 (1939), pp. 177–85. Repr. in Max Bluestone and Norman Rabkin (eds), *Shakespeare's Contemporaries* (Englewood Cliffs, NJ: Prentice-Hall, 1961), pp. 22–30.

'Cyril Tourneur', *Review of English Studies*, 17 (1941), pp. 21–36.

(Letter) 'Chettle and Dekker', *The Times Literary Supplement*, 25 October 1941, p. 531.

'Where shall John go? IX. South Africa', *Horizon*, 13 (June 1946), pp. 418–29. Repr. in *British Thought 1947* (New York: Gresham Press, 1947), pp. 200–12.

'Benlowes and Milton', *Modern Language Review*, 43 (1948), pp. 186–95.

'Readings in the manuscript of *Sir Thomas More*', Modern Language Review, 43 (1948), pp. 512–14.

(Edited) *The Tragedy of Hoffman* (Oxford: Malone Society, 1951), xxvi + [80] pp.

'The 1631 Quarto of *The Tragedy of Hossman*', *The Library*, 5th ser., 6 (September 1951), pp. 88–99.

(With Gladys Jenkins) 'Thomas Winter's Confession', *The Month*, n.s., 7 (1952), pp. 83–8.

(With Gladys Jenkins) 'Thomas Winter's Confession: a rejoinder', *The Month*, n.s., 7 (1952), pp. 290–5.

Edward Benlowes (1602–1676): Biography of a Minor Poet (Cambridge, Mass., and London: Harvard University Press and Athlone, 1952), xii + 372pp.

'Shakespeare's history plays: 1900–1951', *Shakespeare Survey*, 6 (1953) pp. 1–15.

'The year's contributions to Shakespearian study. 2. Shakespeare's life, times and stage', *Shakespeare Survey*, 7 (1954), pp. 138–46.
'William Shakespeare: a biographical essay', in C. J. Sisson (ed.), William Shakespeare, *The Complete works* (London: Odhams, 1954), pp. ix–xvii.
(Edited) *Sir Thomas More*, in C. J. Sisson (ed.), William Shakespeare, *The Complete Works* (London: Odhams, 1954), pp. 1235–66.
'The relation between the Second Quarto and the Folio text of *Hamlet*', *Studies in Bibliography*, 7 (1955), pp. 69–83.
'*As You Like It*', *Shakespeare Survey*, 8 (1955), pp. 40–51. Repr. in Leonard F. Dean (ed.), *Shakespeare: Modern Essays in Criticism* (New York: Oxford University Press, 1957), pp. 108–27; rev. edn (1967), pp. 114–33; Eleanor Terry Lincoln (ed.), *Pastoral and Romance: Modern Essays in Criticism* (Englewood Cliffs, NJ: Prentice-Hall, 1969), pp. 102–18.
The Structural Problem in Shakespeare's Henry the Fourth, Inaugural Lecture, Westfield College, London, 19 May 1955 (London: Methuen, 1956), iv + 28 pp. Repr. in R. J. Dorius (ed.), *Discussions of Shakespeare's Histories* (Boston: D. C. Heath, 1964), pp. 41–55; Norman N. Holland (ed.), *Henry IV, Part Two*, Signet Classic Shakespeare (New York, 1965), pp. 212–33; G. K. Hunter (ed.), *Shakespeare: Henry IV Parts I and II*, Macmillan Casebook (London: Macmillan, 1970), pp. 155–73; William A. Armstrong (ed.), *Shakespeare's Histories: An Anthology of Modern Criticism* (Harmondsworth: Penguin, 1972), pp. 202–21.
'How many grave-diggers has *Hamlet*?', *Modern Language Review*, 51 (1956), pp. 562–5.
'Shakespeare's *Twelfth Night*', *Rice Institute Pamphlet*, 45 (1959), pp. 19–42. Repr. in Kenneth Muir (ed.), *Shakespeare: The Comedies* (Englewood Cliffs, NJ: Prentice-Hall, 1965), pp. 72–87.
'Two readings in *Hamlet*', *Modern Language Review*, 54 (1959), pp. 391–5.
(With S. Brigid Younghughes, edited) *The Fatal Marriage* (Oxford: Malone Society, 1959), xii + 102 pp.
'Playhouse interpolations in the Folio text of *Hamlet*', *Studies in Bibliography*, 13 (1960), pp. 31–47.
'The Tragedy of Revenge in Shakespeare and Webster', *Shakespeare Survey*, 14 (1961), pp. 45–55. Extract repr. in G.K. and S.K. Hunter (eds), *John Webster* (Harmondsworth: Penguin, 1969), pp. 263–6.
'Supplement to the Introduction', in *Sir Thomas More* (Oxford: Malone Society, repr. 1961), pp. xxxiii–xlvi; also in Malone Society *Collections*, 6 (1962), pp. 177–92.
Hamlet and Ophelia, British Academy Shakespeare Lecture, 3 April 1963, *Proceedings of the British Academy*, 49 (1963), pp. 135–51. Repr. in *Interpretations of Shakespeare: British Academy Shakespeare*

Lectures, selected by Kenneth Muir (Oxford: Oxford University Press, 1985), pp. 142–60.
'*Hamlet* then till now', *Shakespeare Survey*, 18 (1965), pp. 34–45. Repr. in Kenneth Muir and Stanley Wells (eds), *Aspects of 'Hamlet'* (Cambridge: Cambridge University Press, 1979), pp. 16–27.
'Edward Benlowes' and 'Henry Chettle', in *Encyclopedia Britannica* (1967), vol. 3, p. 479, and vol. 5, p. 475.
The Catastrophe in Shakespearean Tragedy, Inaugural Lecture, University of Edinburgh, 3 November 1967 (Edinburgh: Edinburgh University Press, 1969), 22 pp.
(Letter) 'T.S. Eliot and Keith Douglas', *The Times Literary Supplement*, 16 July 1970, p. 775.
'Fortinbras and Laertes and the composition of *Hamlet*', *Rice University Studies*, 60 (1974), pp. 95–108.
'John Dover Wilson 1881–1969', *Proceedings of the British Academy*, 59 (1973), pp. 383–418.
'Hamlet and the Fishmonger', *Jahrbuch* of the Deutsche Shakespeare-Gesellschaft West (1975), pp. 109–20.
'John Dover Wilson (1881–1969)', in *The Dictionary of National Biography 1961–1970* (Oxford: Oxford University Press, 1981), pp. 1093–4.
(Letter) '*Henry V*', *The Times Literary Supplement*, 11 April 1980, p. 415.
'Hamlet's voyage', *Notes and Queries*, 226 (n.s., 28) (April 1981), pp. 135–6.
(Edited) *Hamlet*, The Arden Shakespeare (London: Methuen, 1982), xviii + 574 pp.
'Kent and Alcibiades and the dating of *Timon of Athens*', in *KM 80*, A birthday album for Kenneth Muir, 5 May 1987 (Liverpool: Liverpool University Press, 1987), pp. 78–9.
'The ball scene in *Much Ado About Nothing*', in *Shakespeare: Text, Language, Criticism*, in honour of Marvin Spevack, eds Bernhard Fabian and Kurt Tetzeli von Rosador (Hildesheim: Olms, 1987), forthcoming.

REVIEWS

A. Bosker, *Literary Criticism in the Age of Johnson* (Groningen, 1930), *Modern Language Review*, 26 (1931), pp. 357–8.
John Wilson, *The Cheats*, ed. M. C. Nahm (Oxford, 1935), *Modern Language Review*, 31 (1936), pp. 215–16.
Joseph Opatoshu, *In Polish Woods*, trans. Isaac Goldberg (Philadelphia, 1938), *Common Sense* (Johannesburg), 1 (1939), p. 15.
Barbara A. Mackenzie, *Shakespeare's Sonnets: Their Relation to His Life* (Capetown, 1946), *Modern Language Review*, 42 (1947), pp. 261–2.

Sir William Cornwallis, the Younger, *Essayes*, ed. Don Cameron Allen (Baltimore, 1946), *Modern Language Review*, 43 (1948), pp. 106–8.
Woodstock: A Moral History, ed. A.P. Rossiter (London, 1946), *Review of English Studies*, 24 (1948), pp. 66–8.
John Fletcher, etc., *Rollo Duke of Normandy or The Bloody Brother*, ed. J. D. Jump (Liverpool, 1948), *Modern Language Review*, 44 (1949), pp. 563–4.
Samuel Daniel, *The Tragedy of Philotas*, ed. Laurence Michel (New Haven, Conn., 1949), *Modern Language Review*, 45 (1950), pp. 243–4.
Alan Reynolds Thompson, *The Dry Mock: A Study of Irony in Drama* (Berkeley and Los Angeles, 1948), *Modern Language Review*, 45 (1950), pp. 255–6.
Marlowe's 'Doctor Faustus' 1604–1616: Parallel Texts, ed. W. W. Greg (Oxford, 1950); Christopher Marlowe, *The Tragical History of the Life and Death of Doctor Faustus*, A conjectural reconstruction by W. W. Greg (Oxford, 1950), *Modern Language Review*, 46 (1951), pp. 82–6.
The Three Parnassus Plays, ed. J.B. Leishman (London, 1949), *Review of English Studies*, n.s. 2 (1951), pp. 164–6.
The Plays of Nathan Field, ed. William Peery (Austin, Tex., 1950), *Modern Language Review*, 46 (1951), pp. 484–6.
Thomas Philipott, *Poems (1646)*, ed. L. C. Martin (Liverpool, 1950), *Modern Language Review*, 47 (1952), pp. 221–2.
John Day, *Law Tricks*, ed. John Crow (Oxford, 1949), *Review of English Studies*, n.s. 3 (1952), pp. 389–90.
W. W. Greg, *Jonson's 'Masque of Gipsies' in the Burley, Belvoir and Windsor Versions: An Attempt at Reconstruction* (London, 1952), *Modern Language Review*, 48 (1953), pp. 70–3.
Jean Jacquot, *George Chapman (1559–1634): sa vie, sa poésie, son théâtre, sa pensée* (Paris, 1951), *Review of English Studies*, n.s. 4 (1953), pp. 169–71.
Louis Cazamian, *The Development of English Humor* (Durham, NC, 1952), *Modern Language Notes*, 68 (1953), pp. 492–5.
Nathaniel Woodes, *The Conflict of Conscience*, ed. Herbert Davis and F. P. Wilson (Oxford, 1952); Samuel Rowley, *When You See Me, You Know Me*, ed. F. P. Wilson (Oxford, 1952), *Modern Language Review*, 49 (1954), pp. 64–6.
Mary Lascelles, *Shakespeare's 'Measure for Measure'* (London, 1953), *Review of English Studies*, n.s. 5 (1954), pp. 409–11.
Theatre Miscellany: Six Pieces Connected with the Seventeenth-Century Stage (Oxford, 1953), *Review of English Studies*, n.s. 6 (1955), pp. 86–8.
E. B. Everitt, *The Young Shakespeare: Studies in Documentary Evidence* (Copenhagen, 1954), *Modern Language Review*, 51 (1956), p. 96.

Shakespeare, *The Merchant of Venice*, ed. John Russell Brown (London, 1955), *Modern Language Review*, 51 (1956), pp. 584–7.
Ennis Rees, *The Tragedies of George Chapman: Renaissance Ethics in Action* (Cambridge, Mass., 1954), *Review of English Studies*, n.s. 8 (1957), pp. 67–8.
Samuel Schoenbaum, *Middleton's Tragedies: A Critical Study* (New York, 1955), *Modern Language Notes*, 72 (1957), pp. 214–17.
W. K. Wimsatt (ed.), *English Stage Comedy* (New York, 1955), *Modern Language Review*, 52 (1957), pp. 588–90.
Gerald Eades Bentley, *The Jacobean and Caroline Stage*, vols 3–5: *Plays and Playwrights* (Oxford, 1956), *Review of English Studies*, n.s. 9 (1958), pp. 196–202.
Thomas Dekker, *Dramatic Works*, ed. Fredson Bowers, vol. 3, (Cambridge, 1958), *Modern Language Review*, 54 (1959), pp. 417–18.
Thomas Middleton and William Rowley, *The Changeling*, ed. N. W. Bawcutt (London, 1958), *Review of English Studies*, n.s. 11 (1960), pp. 82–4.
Fredson Bowers, *Textual and Literary Criticism* (Cambridge, 1959), *Modern Language Review*, 55 (1960), pp. 258–9.
Richard Hindry Barker, *Thomas Middleton* (New York, 1958), *Review of English Studies*, n.s. 11 (1960), pp. 326–7.
Edwin Haviland Miller, *The Professional Writer in Elizabethan England: A Study of Nondramatic Literature* (Cambridge, Mass., 1959), *Modern Language Notes*, 76 (1961), pp. 53–5.
Harry Levin, *The Question of Hamlet* (New York, 1959), *Modern Language Review*, 56 (1961), pp. 101–2.
W. W. Greg, *A Bibliography of the English Printed Drama to the Restoration*, vols 3–4 (London, 1957–9), *Review of English Studies*, n.s. 12 (1961), pp. 201–4.
John Webster, *The White Devil*, ed. John Russell Brown (London, 1960), *Review of English Studies*, n.s. 12 (1961), pp. 292–4.
L. C. Knights, *An Approach to 'Hamlet'* (London, 1960), *Modern Language Review*, 56 (1961), p. 583.
G. K. Hunter, *John Lyly: The Humanist as Courtier* (London, 1962), *Modern Language Review*, 59 (1964), pp. 104–6.
William Shakespeare, *Hamlet: The First Quarto, 1603*, ed. Albert B. Weiner (Great Neck, NY, 1962), *Notes and Queries*, 209 (n.s.11) (April 1964), pp. 155–7.
John Russell Brown and Bernard Harris (eds), *Hamlet* (London, 1963); Kenneth Muir, *Shakespeare: 'Hamlet'* (London, 1963), *Modern Language Review*, 59 (1964), pp. 631–2.
Martin Holmes, *The Guns of Elsinore* (London, 1964), *Notes and Queries*, 210 (n.s.12) (March 1965), pp. 117–18.
Morris Weitz, *'Hamlet' and the Philosophy of Literary Criticism* (London, 1965), *Modern Language Review*, 61 (1966), pp. 492–4.

Robert Grams Hunter, *Shakespeare and the Comedy of Forgiveness* (New York, 1965), *Studia Neophilologica*, 39 (1967), pp. 180–2.
Gerald Eades Bentley, *The Jacobean and Caroline Stage*, vols 6–7 (Oxford, 1968), *Review of English Studies*, n.s. 20 (1969), pp. 222–4.
Maurice Charney, *Style in 'Hamlet'* (Princeton, NJ, 1969), *Yearbook of English Studies*, 3 (1973), pp. 277–8.
Harold Fisch, *Hamlet and the Word: The Covenant Pattern in Shakespeare* (New York, 1971), *Yearbook of English Studies*, 4 (1974), pp. 273–6.
Cay Dollerup, *Denmark, 'Hamlet' and Shakespeare*, 2 vols (Salzburg, 1975), *Yearbook of English Studies*, 7 (1977), pp. 233–5.
Kenneth Muir (ed.), *Shakespeare Survey*, 32 (Cambridge, 1979), *Theatre Notebook*, 35 (1981), pp. 140–1.
Andrew Gurr, *'Hamlet' and the Distracted Globe* (Edinburgh, 1978), *Shakespeare Quarterly*, 34 (1983), pp. 247–8.
Roland Mushat Frye, *The Renaissance 'Hamlet': Issues and Responses in 1600* (Princeton, NJ, 1984), *Shakespeare Quarterly*, 37 (1986), pp. 258–60.
Kenneth Muir, *Shakespeare: Contrasts and Controversies* (Brighton and Norman, Okla., 1985), *Shakespeare Quarterly*, 37 (1986), pp. 539–41.

Notes on Contributors

Harold F. Brooks, Emeritus Professor of English at the University of London, served as General Editor of the Arden Shakespeare for thirty years, from 1952 to 1982, and Harold Jenkins was his co-editor for twenty-four of those years. Professor Brooks himself edited *A Midsummer Night's Dream* for the series. His most recent book is *T. S. Eliot as Literary Critic*.

Sandra Clark studied under Harold Jenkins at Westfield College, University of London, and now teaches at the University's Birkbeck College. Her publications include a study of *The Elizabethan Pamphleteers*, and she has completed studies of *The Tempest* and Webster's tragedies.

Alastair Fowler succeeded Harold Jenkins in the Regius Chair of Rhetoric and English Literature at the University of Edinburgh, which he occupied from 1972 to 1984; he now divides his time between the Universities of Edinburgh and Virginia. He has published an edition of *Paradise Lost* and several volumes of poetry; his most recent book is a short history of English Literature.

Brian Gibbons edited *Romeo and Juliet* for the Arden Shakespeare. Professor of English Literature at the University of Zurich, he serves as General Editor of The New Mermaid Series and of The New Cambridge Shakespeare, for which he is editing *Measure for Measure*.

Antony Hammond, editor of *Richard III* for the Arden Shakespeare, is Professor of English at McMaster University in Hamilton, Ontario. He co-edited and contributed to *Poetry and Drama 1570–1700*, a Festschrift for Harold F. Brooks. He and two other scholars are preparing the new edition of Webster for Cambridge University Press.

Notes on contributors

S. K. Heninger, Jr is University Distinguished Professor of English at the University of North Carolina, Chapel Hill. He has published many books, including *The Cosmographical Glass: Renaissance Diagrams of the Universe*, and he recently completed a major study, *Sidney and Spenser: The Poet as Maker*.

E. A. J. Honigmann is Joseph Cowen Professor of English at the University of Newcastle-upon-Tyne and joint General Editor of The Revels Plays. His work includes *The Stability of Shakespeare's Text*, *Shakespeare: The 'Lost Years'*, and, most recently, *John Weever*.

Arthur R. Humphreys, Emeritus Professor of English at the University of Leicester, edited both parts of *Henry IV* and *Much Ado About Nothing* for the Arden Shakespeare. He has also edited the New Penguin *Henry V* and *Henry VIII*, and *Julius Caesar* for the Oxford Shakespeare.

John W. Mahon teaches British and Comparative Literatures of the Renaissance and the twentieth century at Iona College in New Rochelle, New York. He has published in the *Evelyn Waugh Newsletter*, *Notes and Queries*, and *Hamlet Studies*.

Kenneth Muir, Emeritus Professor of English Literature at the University of Liverpool, has edited five of Shakespeare's plays, including *Macbeth* and *King Lear* for the Arden series. The author of many books on Shakespeare and the editor of *Shakespeare Survey* for many years, he currently serves as Vice President of the International Shakespeare Association.

Ruth Nevo studied under Harold Jenkins at the University of the Witwatersrand, South Africa. A member of the Israel Academy and Professor of English at the Hebrew University in Jerusalem, her books include *Tragic Form in Shakespeare*, *Comic Transformations in Shakespeare*, and *Shakespeare's Other Language*.

Kenneth Palmer studied under Harold Jenkins in London after service in the RAF during World War II. Lecturer in English at University College, London, he has edited *Troilus and Cressida* for the Arden Shakespeare.

Thomas A. Pendleton is Professor of English at Iona College, New Rochelle, New York. He has published in *Hamlet Studies*, *Mid-Hudson Language Studies*, and the *Shakespeare on Film Newsletter*, and has recently done a study of the so-called Shakespearean lyric, 'Shall I Die? Shall I Fly?'

Richard Proudfoot, Professor of English at King's College, University of London, has served as General Editor of the Arden Shakespeare since 1982, and served as General Editor of the Malone Society from 1971 to 1985. He is engaged in editing the Shakespeare *Apocrypha* and writing a book on *Measure for Measure*.

Marvin Spevack is Director of the Englisches Seminar and also of the Institutum Erasmianum at the University of Münster. Creator of the monumental Shakespeare Concordance, he is preparing *Antony and Cleopatra* in the New Variorum edition.

George Walton Williams is Professor of English at Duke University. He has edited *Romeo and Juliet* and Crashaw's poetry. His most recent book is *The Craft of Printing and the Publication of Shakespeare's Works*.

Index

absurd, vision of world as 13–14, 22
Alexander of Pherae 160–2
alienation 146, 148; *see also* illusion; realism
allegory 71, 172
All's Well That Ends Well: family relationships 32–6, 38–41; 'impropriety' 27–8; 'loose ends' 28–9, 30; Oedipus complex 39; sexuality 42–4, 45–7; unpopularity of characters 26–7; youth v. age 30–3, 41–2
ambiguity: in effect of *Henry V* 134–5, 138–44; Iago's creation of 190–1, 192–4
ambition, in *Henry VI* plays 101, 103–7
anachronisms 234
Antonio's Revenge (John Marston): inserted masque 90, 168–9, 172; revenge and social criticism 83; sequel 175
Antony and Cleopatra: epic sense 113; food imagery 231; imagination 226–7; orthography and textual scholarship 202–4, 206–7, 208–13; as prose 277
archetypes: Cain and Abel 69, 135; pastoral 69
Aristotle: 'energeia' (forcefulness) 223; faculty psychology 220–1; metaphor and drama 274; *Poetics* 222–3
Arthos, John, on *Henry VI* plays 102, 104–5, 107

As You Like It: interest in form 53–4, 59; meal showing true community 241–3, 244, 247–8; parodies romance conventions 66, 73–4; self-consciousness 52, 54–5, 70–2, 74; sources 52, 55, 57–8; transformation through love 69, 74, 76; use of pastoral 53, 54, 55, 71–2, 77; wit 70, 74–6, 250; *see also* Lodge, Thomas: *Rosalynde*; Sidney, Sir Philip: *Arcadia*
audience: analysis of paradoxes 219; degree of knowledge 162, 174; Elizabethan 17–18, 134, 151–2; expectations challenged 9, 54–5, 135–8, 142, 144–6, 237, 248; and 'mind's eye' 223; modern 134–5; response to *Troilus* 23–4; sense of wonder 67, 77; unconscious feelings 29; *see also* illusion; imagination
aural misapprehension, and textual errors 203–4

Bald, R. C.: on Middleton 83–4
Barber, C.L.: on history plays 99
blank verse 275–6, 278–9, 281n.20
Boccaccio, Giovanni 79; *Decameron* 250, 251
Braden, Gordon: on Hamlet's sense of guilt 181
Brecht, Bertolt 146, 147
Brockbank, Philip: kingship and morality 108
Brooks, Peter: reading between the lines 29

Brown, Keith: 'recessed symmetry' in *Hamlet* 166–7, 171, 176, 178
Bullough, Geoffrey: on *Henry IV* plays 122–3; *Henry VI* plays 107; *King John* 110; *Measure* 80; use of Sir John Oldcastle 121; Shakespeare's reading 119
Burbage, Richard 85, 94–5

Cecil, Sir Robert 120
Chambers, E. K. 84, 123, 205, 213
Chambers, R. W.: 'The Elizabethan and Jacobean Shakespeare' 100
Changeling, The (Middleton and Rowley) 168, 270
Chapman, George 175, 279
chastity: in *All's Well* 37, 40; and wit 249, 250, 253–4, 258; in *Measure* 79; *see also* sexuality
Chekhov, Anton: *The Cherry Orchard* 67, 68
chivalry: in *All's Well* 37, 41, 45; in *Troilus* 7, 10–11, 12, 23, 25n.10
Chorus, dramatic use of: in *Henry V* 133, 135–7, 142, 143, 146; in *Romeo and Juliet* 137; in *Pericles* 133, 149n.1, 230
Cinthio, Giraldi: *Epitia* 79; *Hecatommithi* 250
city comedies 249–50, 254–8; *see also* Middleton
Cobham, Lord (Sir John Oldcastle) *see* Oldcastle, Sir John
Cobham, Henry, Lord (Henry Brooke) 120, 121–2, 124
Cobham, William, Lord (William Brooke) 119–20, 121, 122, 128–31
Coghill, Nevill 110
Coleridge, Samuel Taylor 26, 159n.1; admiration for Massinger 274; 'suspension of disbelief' 148, 220
comedies, festive 27, 28; *see also under As You Like It*
comedy, 'black': in *Othello* 198, 264; *Troilus* as 21–3, 24; *see also* problem plays

Comedy of Errors, The 231, 232, 258
community, depicted in meals 231, 241–3, 244, 247–8; and disruption 243–8
conflict: depicted in meals 237–41, 245–8; in *Hamlet* 180–2; theme of history plays 101–5, 107; in *Troilus* 7, 9–10, 12
conscience 22, 246; in *Hamlet* 155, 160–5, 177, 181; *see also* repentance
Coriolanus 23, 105, 234
Croce, Benedetto: *Shakespeare, Ariosto and Corneille* 100
Cymbeline 50, 68, 276, 277

degree, in society 17–18, 23
despair 13–14, 22, 225–6
Devereux, Robert, 2nd Earl of Essex, *see* Essex, Earl of
'dialectical text', as opposed to 'rhetorical text' (Stanley Fish) 144–5
disguise 18, 262; 'disguised duke' convention 81–2, 86–9, 90–1, 96; and romantic love 26, 28, 46, 76
Dryden, John 148; *Fables* 111
dumb-shows 171–2; *see also* masques
Dunn, T. A. 269, 274
duty, and structure of *Hamlet* 180, 181

Eccles, Mark 80
Eliot, T.S.: use of imagery 274
ellipsis: in *All's Well* 37, 38; in *As You Like It* 67; in *Othello* 185
Ellis-Fermor, Una: *The Frontiers of Drama* 113
enargeia (vividness) 216, 223–7; *see also* imagination
England, as theme in history plays 99, 109–15, 116
enthymemes (arguments of probabilities) 195–6, 201n.2
epic: achieved in history plays 99, 109–15, 116; and structure of

Index

Hamlet 175; reduced in *Troilus* 21–2
Essex, Robert Devereux, 2nd Earl of 120–5, 127–8, 131; and *Henry V* 145
Ewbank, Inga-Stina: 'ritual' of revenge 169

fables 69
faculty psychology (Aristotle) 220–1, 230n.2
Falstaff, Sir John 111, 112, 115, 278; *see also under* Oldcastle, Sir John
Famous Victories of Henry V, The 118–19
feasts *see* meals
Fish, Stanley: 'dialectical text' 144–5
Fletcher, John 268
Foakes, R.A.: on symmetries 166
folly, exposure of 47–9, 260–2
'fools': in *All's Well* 33; in *As You Like It* 53–4, 71, 75; in *Troilus* 8, 16, 18–21, 22
Fowler, Alastair: *Triumphal Forms* 166
framing, in Jacobean drama: plays within the play 167–70, 172, 177; structure 166, 171, 172–3, 174–8, 180–2; symmetries 166–7, 170–1, 176, 179
French, Marilyn 264; 'outlaw feminine principle' 258
Freud, Sigmund: family quadrangles 35
Friar Francis (author unknown) 164–5
Frost, David L.: on Massinger 268–9
Fry, Christopher 274
Furness, Horace Howard: on text of *Antony* 202, 203–4

Gardner, Helen: on *As You Like It* as ideal 242, 243
Grace, as ritual and metaphor 233–4
Greg, W. W.: on text of *Antony* 203, 213

Hall, Sir Peter 100–1
Hamlet 6, 12, 35, 136; accession of Claudius 151, 152, 159n.3; and classical epic 175; Gertrude's role 160, 165, 177, 181; and imagination 221–2, 223–4; 'The Mousetrap' 152, 160–5, 171–3; New Arden edition 1, 2–4; plays within the play 167–70, 171–2, 177; reference to religion 236; as a revenge play 172, 174–82; role of Polonius 156–7, 158; structure 166–7, 171–3, 174–8, 180–2; supernatural elements 177, 178–80; symmetries 166–7, 170–1, 176, 179; theme of duty 181–2
Harrison, William: *Description of England* 232
Hazlitt, William: on *Henry V* 135
Henry IV plays: date 122–4; epic quality 99, 111; as historical reality 100; language 111–12; meals in, 231, 248n.2; as portrait of England 113–15; persuasion of Hotspur 216, 228–30; role of Sir John Oldcastle *see under* Oldcastle, Sir John
Henry V: inherent contradictions 134–5, 138–44; morality of Henry 139–40, 143–4; play as illusion 229–30; as portrait of England 115; role of Chorus 115, 133, 135–7, 142–3, 146, 148–9
Henry VI plays 278; ambition 105–7; divine dimension 108; energy and conflict 101–6; success 109
Henry VIII 110, 248n.8, 269–70
Heywood, Thomas: *Apology for Actors* 163–4
Holinshed, Raphael 119, 141, 143, 245
Holland, Philemon: translation of Plutarch's *Lives* 161
Hollyband, Claudius: *The Elizabethan*

Home Discovered in Two Dialogues 233–4
homosexuality 15, 21, 42–3, 47
honour: in *Hamlet* 178, 180, 181; in *I Henry IV* 216, 228–9; in *Troilus* 9–11, 18, 23–4, 180; *see also* chivalry
Hotson, Leslie: *Shakespeare's Motley* 19
Hudson, Henry N.: on text of *Antony* 202, 203
Hymen, epiphany of 68, 76–7, 242; in *The Spanish Tragedy* 169

identity, crises of 181, 199–200, 224–6
illusion, drama as 54–5, 219, 220, 229–30; Shakespeare's emphasis on stage 100
imagery 31–2, 271–4; *see also* metaphor; rhetoric
imagination 224–6, 228–9; Aristotle's definition 220–1, 222–3; audience to use 135, 148–9, 223–4; criticized 216–17; and inferior art 136; influence of imagination 229–30; theories of 218–19, 221–2
irony 136–7, 149, 173–4

James I and VI, King of England and Scotland 82, 83; *Basilicon Doron* 83
James, Richard 118, 123–4
Jardine, Lisa: Renaissance writing on women 251
jealousy: in *Merry Wives* 259, 261–2, 264
Jenkins, Gladys 1
Jenkins, Harold: on *Hamlet* 151, 152, 155, 174–5, 179
Johnson, Samuel: on Chorus in *Henry V* 115
Jones, Emrys: on two-part structure 174, 175–6; *Scenic Form in Shakespeare* 243–4

Jonson, Ben 148, 276; *Bartholomew Fair* 82; *Every Man Out of His Humour* 53
Julius Caesar: world as a stage 100
justice 9–10, 23, 108, 181–2; *see also* honour; revenge

Kermode, Frank: on *Timon* 239
King John 109–10
King Lear 106, 279
Kittredge, George Lyman: on text of *Antony* 203
Knight, Charles: on *Antony* 202
Kott, Jan: early history plays 116
Kyd, Thomas: *The Spanish Tragedy* 169, 172, 174, 175

language 155–6, 217, 243–4; *see also* imagery; metaphor; poetry; rhetoric
Last Supper, the 234–5, 239, 247
Lawrence, W. W.: on *Measure* 81
Lever, J. W. 83, 95, 234; disguised duke convention 81; sources of *Measure* 80, 87, 92, 94
Lodge, Thomas: *Rosalynde* adaptation of 69, 73, 76, 77n.5, 241; as imitation of pastoral 57; rhetorical style 64–6; as source of *As You Like It* 52, 55, 241
Love's Labour's Lost 136, 167, 233; wit displays 251–3
love, romantic: corrective power 49, 69, 76, 243; and idealism 12–15, 256; and war 6–8; and wit 252–4, 263; *see also* sexuality
Lyly, John 52, 65

Macbeth 108; religious imagery 246–7, 248; symbolism of meals 243–8; verse flexibility 279; violence 107
McKeen, D. M.: on Sir John Oldcastle 121, 128–9
Maid's Tragedy, The (Beaumont and Fletcher) 168
Malcontent, The (John Marston): date

84–6; disguised duke convention 83, 86; source for *Measure* 80, 81, 89–94
Mansfield, Katherine 26
Marston, John: *The Fawn* 82, 83, 84; *Certain Satires* 94; *see also Antonio's Revenge*; *Malcontent, The*
Mary of Nimmegen (Dutch play) 162–3
Massinger, Philip: choice of verse as medium 277–80; 'dead' metaphors 273–4; debt to Shakespeare 268; *Duke of Milan* 268–9; *A New Way to Pay Old Debts* 278; *The Roman Actor* 269, 272; verse like prose 274–7
masques 167; in *Hamlet* 170–1, 172–3; in revenge drama 168–9; *see also* framing; Hymen
materialist values, in *Merry Wives* 258–9, 263, 264
'maturation' comedies 41, 50; *see also under All's Well*; *As You Like It*
meals: difficulty in staging 232; infrequency 231–2; religious symbolism 231, 232, 234–7; showing true community 231, 241–3, 244, 247–8; stressing conflict 237–41, 245–8; and structure 248n.14
Measure for Measure 26, 49; date 83–4; development from sources 79–81; discussion of Grace 234; disguised duke structure 81–2; limited success 94, 95–7; similarities with *The Malcontent* 89–94; similarities with *The Phoenix* 86–9
Mehl, Dieter: on *Hamlet* 172
Merchant of Venice, The 233, 247; Portia's wit 251–2
Merry Wives of Windsor, The: concept of imagination 222; female wit 249, 258, 261–3; honesty and wit 258, 260, 263; 'shuffling' 153; and Sir John Oldcastle 128, 129, 131;

sources 250; women collaborating 259
metaphor: in Iago's rhetoric 187; Massinger's 'dead' metaphors 273–4; used by Othello 199; and poetic drama 274
Midsummer Night's Dream, A: and Massinger's *Duke of Milan* 269; mechanicals' play ('Pyramus and Thisbe') 135–6, 146–7; nature of imagination 216–19, 220; Peter Brook's staging of 148; and play as an illusion 219, 229
Miles, Rosalind 81, 82, 97 n.12
Milton, John: *Comus* 281 n.20; *Paradise Lost* 107–8
Mincoff, Marco: organic structure in Hamlet 166, 171
'mind's eye' and imagination of audience 223–4; in *Antony* 226–7; in *1 Henry IV* 228–30; in *Richard II* 224–6; *see also* enargeia
misogyny 250–1, 261, 265; *see also* women
modesty, in women 40–1, 251, 263, 265; *see also* chastity; wit
'monstrous ransom' story 79–80; *see also under Measure for Measure*
morality *see* conscience; honour
Morgann, Maurice 116
'Mousetrap, The', 152, 160–5, 171–3; *see also* framing; *Hamlet*
Much Ado About Nothing 27, 224; wit 74, 251–2, 254
Muir, Kenneth 16, 25n.11, 80
Murder of Gonzago, The see Hamlet
Murry, John Middleton: *The Problem of Style* 275–7
music: in *As You Like It* 59, 76, 242; in *Richard II* 226
'myth of concern' (Northrop Frye) 145–6, 149

naturalism: in *As You Like It* 67–8; in *Hamlet* 172; in Shakespeare's use of prose for his actors 278

Neely, Carol Thomas: on *Othello* and the comedies 264
North, Thomas: translation of Plutarch's *Lives* 161
Oedipus complex 39–40, 50n.4
Oldcastle, Sir John (Lord Cobham): life 125–6; Shakespeare's use of in *Henry IV* 118–19, 120, 124–5, 127–8; in *Merry Wives* 129–31; offence to his family *see under* Cobham
Oldcastle, Sir John (play) 124
Oliver, H. J.: on *Timon of Athens* 239
Olivier, Laurence, film of *Henry V* 134, 140
order, social, and restraint of wit 252, 258, 263–4
Ornstein, Robert: on Chorus in *Henry V* 136, 138, 146
orthographic evidence: and author identification 204–6; and text of *Antony* 206–11
Othello 193, 199–200; Iago's use of rhetoric *see under* rhetoric; and *Merry Wives* 264; women's wit 264–7; parallels with Massinger's *Duke of Milan* 268
Ovid, and interpretation of pastoral 64

paradox: in *Othello* 185, 188–9; and response of audience 219
pastoral 241–3; ambiguity 75–6; improbability inherent 72; self-consciousness 70; Shakespeare's choice of 52–4, 57; *see also under* Sidney, Sir Philip
patriotism: in portrait of England 99, 109–15, 116; more equivocal in *Henry V* 134–5, 138–44
Pericles: meal 248n.8; use of Chorus 133, 149n.1, 230; verse like prose 275
peripeteia (temporary frustration of expectation) 137–8; *see also* irony
Plato: *Phaedrus* 217, 220

play within the play *see under* framing
Plutarch: *Lives* 161
'poetic personality' (distinct from narrator) 146
poetry: purpose 218, 222; variety of meanings 219; *see also* imagination; *see also under* Sidney, Sir Philip
Phoenix, The (Thomas Middleton): date 83–5; and *Measure* 80, 81, 82, 86–9, 97n.12
Pollard, Alfred W.: 'Elizabethan spelling' 208; on text of *Antony* 213
prayer: Claudius at prayer 152–3; Elizabethan prayer books 235, 236; several meanings of grace 233, 234–5
problem plays 6, 26; *see also All's Well*; *Hamlet*; *Measure*; *Troilus*
prose 278–80; juxtaposed to verse 53–4, 59
'Pyramus and Thisbe' 135–6, 146–7, 219–20; *see also Midsummer Night's Dream, A*

Quintilian, and concept of enargeia 223

Ramism, and Iago's 'proof' 195
Rape of Lucrece, The 120
realism: in *As You Like It* 75–6, 168; *see also* illusion; imagination; pastoral
reality: changing definitions 218–19; and imagination 221, 227; and nature of drama *see* illusion
Reformation, the 235–7
religion: and medieval world view 218; symbolized in meals 231, 232, 234–7, 242, 248
Renaissance, the, and changing world view 218
repentance 235–6, 243
revenge: double revenge in *Hamlet* 174–82; in *Titus Andronicus* 238;

Index

tradition 168, 172; through wit 256, 263
Revenger's Tragedy, The (Cyril Tourneur) 169
rhetoric: in romance conventions 66
rhetoric, Iago's use of 198; adaptation to others 186, 197; to control others 185–6, 191, 196–7; dissociating others 186–91; ellipsis and paradox 184–5; exaggeration of style 197–8; final failure 199, 201; Ramist concept of proof 195; repetition 191; terms of formal debate 192; use of negatives 191, 193; use of questions 193–5, 196
'rhetorical text', as opposed to 'dialectical text' (Stanley Fish) 144–5
Richard II 99, 108, 109, 231; date 123; ideal of good kingship 110, 111; importance of personality 116; power of imagination 222, 224–6; and religion 236
Richard III 108, 109; power of characterization of Richard 115–16; waiting for battle 140, 141
Riche, Barnabe: *Brusanus* 80, 87
Roaring Girl, The (Middleton and Dekker) 256–8, 260
romance convention 50, 53
romances, Shakespeare's 168, 219–22, 276, 277; *see also Cymbeline*; *Pericles*; *The Tempest*; *The Winter's Tale*
Romeo and Juliet 137, 231, 232
Rose, Mark: *Shakespearean Design and organic structure in Hamlet* 166, 171, 182n.2; on *Macbeth* 247
Royal Shakespeare Company 100, 103–4, 147

Salingar, Leo: sources for *Merry Wives* 250
satire: in *King John* 109; and literary form 216, 220; savage in *Troilus* 16; *see also under* Oldcastle, Sir John
Senecan tragedy 102; *see also* revenge tradition
sexuality: and ageing 31–2; development of 42, 45–6, 49, 59–64; perverted attitudes to 20–1; fear of 43–4, 262; and unfaithfulness 8, 12–15; virginity 37, 40, 79; *see also* chastity; love, romantic
Shakespeare, William: attitude to war 134–5; development as dramatic poet 148–9; on kingship 108; extent of reading 119; as satirist 116, 120, *see also under* Oldcastle, Sir John; self-conscious dramatist 219–20; sense of humour 118; spelling 206–12; view of society 17–18; *see also under* individual plays
shrewishness: in *Othello* 265–7; and sexuality 251, 253–4; stereotype 249; *see also* wit; women
Sidney, Philip: *An Apologie for Poetrie, or, The Defence of Poesie* 75, 160, 222–3, 230n.5; *Arcadia* 52, 59–64, 71, 74; emphasizes artifice 55–6; influence on Shakespeare 57–8; self-discovery in love 60–1, 63, 74; use of theatrical metaphor 61, 64
Sharpham, Edward: *The Fleire* 82, 83
Smith, Richard 130
society, Shakespeare's view of 17–18
Sonnets, The, and *All's Well* 44–5
sources: for *As You Like It* 52, 55, 57–8; for *Hamlet* 160–5 *see also* revenge tradition; for *Measure* 79–81
Southampton, Earl of (Henry Wriothesley) 120, 121–2, 124–5
Spenser, Edmund: *The Faerie Queene* 216, 220
Spurgeon, Caroline: Massinger's imagery 270
structure 133; meals as structural

device 237–48; two-part in *Hamlet* 166, 171, 172–3, 174–8, 180–2; *see also* framing
Styan, J. L.: *The Dramatic Experience* 113
supernatural elements: ghost in *Hamlet* symbolizing Christian duty 180, 181; ghost in *Macbeth* 244–7
Sutherland, Sarah: on significance of play within a play 168
Sykes, H. Dugdale: on Massinger 269–70

tableaux: in *Arcadia* 59–64; in *As You Like It* 59, 241–3; *see also* Last Supper; masques
Taming of the Shrew, The 236, 258; limiting of female wit 252; meals 237–8; *see also* shrewishness
Taylor, Gary 134; on Chorus of *Henry V* 136, 137–8, 141–2, 147
Tempest, The 68, 168; concept of imagination 221, 222; frustrated meal 240–1; play as an illusion 168, 219–20
tetractys (four-part) pattern of oath-taking in *Hamlet* 179–80
theatre and reality *see* audience; illusion; realism
theatres, closing of (1603–4) 83, 84
Thynne, Francis: *History of the House of Cobham* 119, 130
Tillyard, E. M. W.: history plays as epics 99, 107, 111
Timon of Athens 239–40
Titus Andronicus: reference to Grace 234; meal and revenge combined 238–9
Todorov, Tzvetan: the 'poetic personality' 146
tragedy: compared to epic 99; and insight of hero 18, 25n.7; in *Troilus* 18, 22–4; *see also Hamlet*; *Macbeth*; *Othello*; revenge tradition

tragicomedy 53, 82; *Troilus* as 22–4; *see also* comedy, black
Trewin, J. C.: statesmen in *Henry VI* plays 101
Triumphal Forms (Alastair Fowler) 166
Troilus and Cressida: as 'black' comedy 21–3, 24; fools in the play 16, 19–21; justice and order defined 9–11; play as illusion 100; themes of love and war 6–9, 107; themes of romance and realism 11–16, 17–18; as tragedy 18, 22–4; Ulysses' speech on time 271–2; use of Prologue 138
Twelfth Night 33, 53, 74; and use of 'shuffling' 153–4
Two Gentlemen of Verona, The: the ideal woman defined 251
Two Noble Kinsmen, The 248n.8, 269–70, 272–3, 275–6

unified characters 144

Vickers, Brian: on *Merry Wives* 264
violence: and ambition in *Henry VI* plays 100, 101–2, 105–7; in *As You Like It* 69–70, 73; in *Hamlet* 173, 175; in *Macbeth* 107; in revenge tragedy 102, 169; in *Titus* 238; in *Troilus* 18, 23; *see also* conflict
virginity 37, 40, 79; *see also* chastity; sexuality

Walter, J. H.: on *Henry V* 134, 137
'wanton wife', stereotype of 249, 250, 253–4
Warning for Fair Women, A (anon) 163, 164
Way of the World, The (Congreve) 278
Webster, John: induction for Marston's *The Malcontent* 85, 94
Weever, John: *The Mirror of Martyrs* 124; *see also under* Oldcastle, Sir John

Index

Westward Ho (Dekker and Webster) 255–6, 258
Wheeler, Richard: on *All's Well* 44, 47
Whetstone, George: *Promos and Cassandra* 79
Wife of Bath's Prologue (Chaucer) 251
Wilders, John: Chorus in *Henry V* 143, 146
Wilson, J. Dover: on *Henry V* 134; text of *Antony* 203, 205–6, 207–12
Wilson Knight, G.: dramatic implications of meals 231, 239
Winny, James: energy in early history plays 107
Winter's Tale, The 167, 252
wit: in comic heroines 251–2; corrective power 75, 257, 262–3, 267; displays 253; Iago's use of 264–5 *see also* rhetoric, Iago's use of; limitations on 242; and romantic love 253, 263; and female self-sufficiency 257; and unfaithfulness 250–1; women collaborating in 249, 253, 255; women's control of 252
women: disparagement of 7, 250–1, 261, 265; female solidarity 249, 255, 258; friendship between 253, 266–7; frustration of 102–3; heroines balancing male and female sides of their natures 46; and honesty 258; outwitting men 256, 263; self-sufficiency and wit in women 257; as subversive element in comedies 258; and unfaithfulness 12–15, 250–1
Women Beware Women (Middleton) 169, 181

Yeats, W. B.: 'Emotion of Multitude' 113

For Product Safety Concerns and Information please contact our EU
representative GPSR@taylorandfrancis.com
Taylor & Francis Verlag GmbH, Kaufingerstraße 24, 80331 München, Germany

www.ingramcontent.com/pod-product-compliance
Lightning Source LLC
Chambersburg PA
CBHW070301010526
44108CB00039B/1441